Seeing Jesus in the
Eyes of the Oppressed

Previous Volumes in United States Franciscan History Project

Seeing Jesus in the Eyes of the Oppressed:
A History of Franciscans Working for Peace and Justice

Paul T. Murray

The Academy of American Franciscan History
Oceanside, California
2021

Library of Congress Cataloging-in-Publication Data

Names: Murray, Paul T., author.
Title: Seeing Jesus in the eyes of the oppressed : a history of Franciscans
    working for peace and justice / Paul T. Murray.
Description: Oceanside, California : Academy of American Franciscan
    History, [2021] | Includes bibliographical references and index. |
    Summary: "Since World War II, Franciscans in the United States have
    worked to establish peace and justice in the United States. This volume
    provides mini-biographies of eight Franciscans working to promote racial
    justice, economic justice, and peace and non-violence: Nathaniel
    Machesky, Antona Ebo, Booker Ashe, Thea Bowman, Alan McCoy, Patricia
    Drydyk, Joseph Nangle, and Louie Vitale"—Provided by publisher.
Identifiers: LCCN 2021032209 | ISBN 9780883822715 (hardback)
Subjects: LCSH: Franciscans—United States—Biography. |
    Franciscans—United States—History—20th century. | Christianity and
    justice—United States—History—20th century. | Peace—Religious
    aspects—Christianity—History—20th century.
Classification: LCC BX3608 .M87 2021 | DDC 271/.302—dc23
LC record available at https://lccn.loc.gov/2021032209

Table of Contents

Cover photo: Father Louie Vitale being arrested in San Francisco, September 6, 2004. Photo by Paul Chinn, *San Francisco Chronicle*, Polaris.

Preface

Franciscans have long been part of the American experience arriving with the earliest explorers of the so-called New World in the late fifteenth century. They played an integral role in the development of colonial Latin America, and much has been written about their efforts; less has been written about Franciscans in the nineteenth and twentieth centuries in the United States. Our new series, the *United States Franciscan History Project*, seeks to address this lacuna. The Franciscan family is a diverse one including but not limited to Friars Minor, Capuchins, Conventuals, Third Order Regular, Poor Clares, Franciscan orders of women religious, and Secular Franciscans. Each group has played a role in the unfolding story of the Franciscans in the United States.

Our third volume, by Paul T. Murray, *Seeing Jesus in the Eyes of the Oppressed: A History of Franciscans Working for Peace and Justice* examines the role Franciscans played in attempting to create a more just and equitable society in the United States following the Second World War. Taking a biographical approach, Murray examines the contributions of eight Franciscan men and women in the areas of racial, economic, worker, and international justice. Though Franciscans have long been involved in serving the poor and disadvantaged, following the war Franciscans combined their charitable and educational endeavors with the struggle for social justice, especially emphasizing nonviolent protest and solidarity with the poor. Dorothy Day once lamented, "Where were the saints to try to change the social order, not just to minister to the slaves but to do away with slavery?" Murray provides eight model Franciscans who took up Day's challenge.

Our series will explore other elements of Franciscan life in the United States as well: Franciscan media, U.S. Franciscan missions to China and Latin America, Franciscan education, and Franciscan arts. Our hope is to make this little-known history accessible to scholars and students and to integrate the history of Franciscans in the United States into the larger narrative of U.S. history.

Jeffrey M. Burns
Director
Academy of American Franciscan History
Oceanside, California

Introduction:
Seeing Jesus in the Oppressed

During the early 1960s most workers who planted, cultivated, and harvested California's abundant fruit and vegetable crops were Mexican and Mexican American Catholics, complemented by a significant number of Filipino Catholics. The majority of agricultural employers also were Catholic. When farm workers led by Cesar Chavez began organizing a union to secure better wages and improved living conditions, and to uphold the dignity of the workers, they met with determined resistance from growers who refused to recognize the nascent union. California's Catholic bishops initially were silent on this conflict. Despite the official teaching of Pope Leo XIII, in his encyclical *Rerum Novarum* (1891), that working people have the right to organize unions, the bishops did not defend the farm workers' unionization effort. Their inaction gave tacit backing to the growers, who had powerful allies in government and law enforcement.

For Franciscans this situation began to change in 1967. That year, friars of the St. Barbara Franciscan Province elected Father Alan McCoy, OFM, as their provincial minister. He sent young Franciscan priests who were sympathetic to the United Farm Workers (UFW) union to staff Our Lady of Guadalupe parish in Delano, California. They did more than say Mass and hear confessions for their farm worker parishioners; they actively supported the unionization drive by reopening the parish hall for union meetings, patrolling picket lines to keep peace between strikers and their opponents, and taking the Eucharist to Chavez during his public fasts. The St. Barbara Franciscan Province aided the farm workers' movement in other ways as well, including making a substantial interest-free loan to the UFW strike fund and offering refuge for Chavez on Franciscan properties.

The title of this work, *Seeing Jesus in the Eyes of the Oppressed,* is taken from an address given by Father Alan at the Cathedral of St. John the Divine at an event celebrating the 800th anniversary of the Birth of St. Francis of Assisi. His advice to see Jesus in the eyes of the oppressed could easily have come from any of the Franciscans profiled in this volume.

Throughout the United States, Franciscan priests, brothers, sisters, and lay members of the Third Order, have fought for peace and social justice. For twenty years, Sister Patricia Ann Drydyk, OSF, worked tirelessly to advance the farm workers' cause. In Greenwood, Mississippi, Father Nathaniel

1

Machesky, OFM, assumed leadership of a nonviolent movement that won the first significant concessions for the city's African American citizens. Brother Booker Ashe, OFM Cap, preached racial reconciliation to White Catholics and created the House of Peace to aid the residents of a riot-torn Milwaukee, Wisconsin, neighborhood. Sister Thea Bowman, FSPA, taught her African American students in Canton, Mississippi, to take pride in their cultural heritage and aspire to positions of influence in a desegregated society. Father Louie Vitale, OFM, inspired thousands of pilgrims to protest nuclear testing in the Nevada desert. Sister Antona Ebo, FSM, traveled to Selma, Alabama, to join the drive for African American voting rights. Father Joseph Nangle, OFM, returned from fifteen years of mission work in Latin America to encourage Catholics in the United States to stand with the poor of the world against oppression and economic inequality.[1]

*   *   *   *   *

The Franciscan family has many branches—men and women, Capuchin, Conventual, and others, religious and lay. Despite their varied circumstances, all Franciscans embrace a way of life governed by rules that St. Francis established and share a dedication to spreading his message in the world. The following chapters profile eight American Franciscans of the post–World War II era who distinguished themselves in their pursuit of peace and social justice. None of them worked alone, so this book also discusses their colleagues and the congregations that sustained them as they followed in the footsteps of St. Francis.

Franciscan values have shaped my own life course. When I reached the age of seven, my mother enrolled me at St. James School in Wausau, Wisconsin, where Franciscan Sisters of Perpetual Adoration (FSPA) taught me. I learned about the founder of the Franciscan order in fourth grade when I was selected to portray St. Francis in a school pageant. Dressed in a miniature brown robe, I paced on stage, listening to the voice of God resounding from an off-stage speaker say, "Francis, go and rebuild my church." Two years later, on a field trip to St. Anthony's Friary in Marathon, Wisconsin, I first encountered male Franciscans—bearded members of the Capuchin order. In the summer of 1966, as a civil rights volunteer in rural Madison County, Mississippi, I briefly met Sister Thea at the Holy Child Jesus Mission. When I applied to be a conscientious objector, I cited the rule laid down by St. Francis

---

1. Those profiled in this book will be addressed in their respective chapters, the introduction, and the conclusion by their honorific and their first name (e.g., Sister Thea), as will religious sisters and brothers, following the use of those who know them well. All others, including priests, will be identified by their honorifics and surnames on subsequent reference.

forbidding members of the Third Order from bearing arms. From 1979 until my retirement in 2016, I taught at Siena College, founded and administered by friars of the Holy Name Province. Father Dan Dwyer, OFM, a professor in Siena's history department, approached me about writing a book about Franciscans working for peace and social justice in the United States. After he assured me that I could write about Franciscan sisters as well as friars, I readily accepted his offer.

Beginning in elementary school, and continuing through my professional career, I have absorbed inspirational stories drawn from the life of St. Francis. Over the centuries, these legends have guided his followers along the path of peace and justice. Perhaps best known is Francis's encounter with the leper, a powerful example of Christ-like willingness to embrace "the other." During the Middle Ages, lepers were reviled and segregated from the rest of society. People shunned them because they believed their disease was highly contagious. Many also believed that lepers were being punished by God. Young Francis shared this revulsion. In his testament, dictated on his deathbed, Francis recalled, "While I was in sin, it seemed very bitter to me to see lepers."[2] In Francis's time, religiously motivated individuals cared for those suffering with leprosy in hospices outside of cities and towns. One day, as Francis was passing near a leprosarium not far from Assisi, he unexpectedly encountered a leper. Initially, he was disgusted by the sight and smell of the leper's wounds, but he overcame this abhorrence, placed alms in the leper's hand, and kissed him. After the two parted, Francis declared, "That which seemed bitter to me was changed into sweetness of soul and body."[3] Just as Jesus embraced those who were despised by society, so too did Francis open his arms to sinners, social outcasts, the wretched of the Earth. This incident turned Francis's world upside down. He realized that his meeting with the leper was really an encounter with Jesus. According to Marie Dennis, Father Joe Nangle, Cynthia Moe-Lobeda, and Stuart Taylor, "Once he [Francis] was able to transcend that dreaded barrier [between himself and the leper], he seemed to be able to move beyond and allow himself to be open to 'the other' whom he had previously imagined to be so awful."[4]

St. Francis also was an advocate for peace. His most notable instance of peacemaking involved his encounter in Egypt with Sultan Malik al-Kamil. In the summer of 1219, Francis sailed from Italy to Egypt with the forces of the Fifth Crusade. He did not travel as part of the military effort; rather, he hoped

---

2. Francis of Assisi, *Testament of St. Francis*, https://ofm.org/wp-content/uploads/2016/11/Testament.pdf.

3. Francis of Assisi, *Testament*.

4. Marie Dennis, Joseph Nangle, Cynthia Moe-Lobeda, and Stuart Taylor, *St. Francis and the Foolishness of God*, rev. ed. (Maryknoll, NY: Orbis Books, 2015), 5.

he could bring an end to the fighting. The Crusaders were camped on the west bank of the Nile. On the opposite bank lay the fortified city of Damietta. The Muslim army had recently repulsed a Christian attempt to conquer the city. The armies of both sides were recuperating from their wounds and preparing for another battle. Francis and his companion, Brother Illuminato, slipped away from the Crusader camp and crossed the Nile, where they were captured by Muslim sentries. Francis called out, "Sultan, Sultan," indicating he wanted to meet with their commander. The two Franciscans were taken to the sultan's headquarters, where they were interrogated by al-Kamil himself. He may have suspected that they were Christian spies or perhaps that they were bearing an offer to negotiate a peace. Instead, Francis began with the greeting he used everywhere—"May the Lord grant you peace." He told the Muslim ruler that he wished to talk about religion. The sultan was receptive to Francis's offer. He hoped that Francis might provide a bridge to peace, something they both desired. For several days, the two men discussed the beliefs of their respective faiths. Rather than being imprisoned as enemy spies, Francis and Illuminato were welcomed as honored guests. Although the two men were unable to end the warfare, each came away from their conversations with a deep respect for each other and for the other's religion. Although Francis did not succeed in ending the warfare between Christians and Muslims, this encounter exemplified an approach to problem solving based on respect for one's enemy, a method Franciscans have continued to employ over the centuries.[5]

For eight hundred years, Franciscans have emulated their founder by seeking Jesus in their encounters with the poor and marginalized. For many, this search has involved acts of charity—providing food, shelter, clothing, and health care for those in need. Capuchins, for example, are famous for serving nutritious meals to homeless individuals from their soup kitchens in big cities. Increasingly, however, Franciscans and other social activists have come to realize that, in addition to charity, justice is needed to remediate the problems of modern societies. Whereas charity addresses the symptoms of social ills, justice seeks to address the underlying causes of poverty, oppression, and discrimination. Justice asks, Why do these people suffer? What causes their suffering? How can we change the social structures that contribute to their misery?

During the second half of the twentieth century, Franciscans in the United States increasingly focused their efforts on striving for social justice. The years following the end of World War II was a time of growing national prosperity. The nation had recovered from the economic woes of the Great

---

5. Information in this paragraph is based largely on chapter 13 of Paul Moses's excellent study, *The Saint and the Sultan: The Crusades, Islam, and Francis of Assisi's Mission of Peace* (New York: Doubleday Religion, 2009), 126–47.

Depression and escaped the widespread devastation that affected nations of Europe and Asia. American Catholics were moving into the middle class in large numbers. Catholic congregations, once largely populated by immigrants, now consisted of second- and third-generation Americans. The 1960 election of John F. Kennedy as the United States's first Catholic president signaled the arrival of his coreligionists in the corridors of power. The religious orders that built the parishes, schools, and hospitals that served immigrant communities began focusing on other people in need. For some this refocusing meant reaching out to African Americans and joining their long crusade against institutionalized discrimination. For others, it involved helping Mexican American farm laborers win collective bargaining rights for their unions. Building movements to promote world peace, stop the international arms race, and halt nuclear testing absorbed the energies of other followers of St. Francis.

In 1950, Franciscan friars from the Assumption Province established St. Francis Mission in Greenwood, Mississippi. In this racially polarized environment, they ministered to the African American population. The friars recognized that African American youngsters needed a better education than that provided by Mississippi's underfunded and overcrowded segregated public schools. The friars established the St. Francis School and recruited the Sisters of St. Joseph of the Third Order of St. Francis to teach in it. Kate Foote Jordan, a native Mississippian and Catholic convert, opened the St. Francis Information Center, which offered a variety of services and programs for local youths and adults. Jordan and other pious women who staffed the center formed the Pax Christi Franciscans, a secular religious institute. When White political leaders refused to grant legitimate Black demands for improved city services, better employment opportunities, and courteous treatment, Father Nathaniel organized a boycott of local businesses that finally gained many of the objectives they sought.

Motivated by a similar desire to educate African American youth, the FSPA came to Canton, Mississippi, where they operated Holy Child Jesus School. Making the most of limited resources in an inhospitable environment, the sisters offered a welcoming alternative to the woeful public schools. Bertha Bowman, one of their first students, was so impressed by their kindness and dedication that she joined the same Franciscan order, taking the name Sister Thea. After training in Wisconsin, Sister Thea returned to Holy Child Jesus School, where she taught for seven years before embarking on a career as a celebrated scholar, speaker, and nationally known advocate for multicultural understanding within the Catholic Church.

Sister Antona, a member of the Franciscan Sisters of Mary, spent only a short time in the Deep South, but she made a lasting contribution to the struggle for African American voting rights. A medical records librarian from St. Louis, Missouri, she boarded a chartered plane bound for Selma, Alabama, as part of an ecumenical delegation organized by Cardinal Joseph Ritter. As one of two African American sisters in the Selma protest, Sister Antona was sought out by reporters. She told them, "I am a Negro and very proud of it. . . . I feel every citizen, every Negro citizen, as well as the whites, have a right to vote and should be given that right."[6] For the next half-century, Sister Antona was a spokesperson for civil rights and interracial justice.

Brother Booker was the first African American member of the Capuchin order. As the civil rights movement gained national momentum in the 1960s, he emerged as a leading Catholic voice for racial justice. In 1968, he came to riot-torn Milwaukee, where he was the first director of a Capuchin mission located in the city's inner core. The House of Peace, as this project was named, promoted Black pride and cultural awareness. It also provided food, clothing, and children's toys at Christmastime, summer academic enrichment for school kids, and trips to sites of national significance. Brother Booker shared his love of theater with young people by producing and directing popular theatrical performances. In addition, he was a leader of African American Catholic clergy and religious who were seeking recognition in the American Catholic Church.

Father Alan, a friar of the St. Barbara Franciscan Province, devoted much of his seventy-year career as a Franciscan to struggles for social justice. As pastor of St. Mary's Parish in Stockton, California, he aided migrant farm workers by creating programs to provide food, shelter, clothing, and medical care. He was a vocal opponent of the US government's *bracero* program, which enabled growers to undercut agricultural laborers' attempts to organize for better wages and working conditions. He also helped prepare a generation of newly ordained Franciscans to minister to needy populations. After being elected provincial minister in 1967, he guided the province in taking bold stands on social justice issues. Foremost of these was encouraging the UFW organizing campaigns, headed by Chavez. Later, as president of the Conference of Major Superiors of Men (CMSM), Father Alan continued seeking justice, this time on an international scale. He traveled to Central America many times, investigating human rights abuses and collaborating with leaders of other denominations to persuade political leaders in the United States to end military assistance to repressive political regimes.

Franciscan sisters also fought for the rights of farm workers. Sister Pat, of the Sisters of St. Francis of Assisi, began her career teaching English and journalism to high school students. In 1971, she moved to Los Angeles, where she produced educational materials for the Franciscan Communications Center. For a filmstrip on farm workers, she interviewed Chavez, who

---

6. Mike Bush, "A Celebration of Sister Antona Ebo," NCB NewsChannel5, YouTube video, 5:41, https://www.youtube.com/watch?v=kDfMqo1kC_8.

convinced her to use her talents in the farm worker movement. Sister Pat met with congregations of sisters across the United States, encouraging them to bear witness to the farm workers' cause and recruiting sisters to participate directly in the movement. In 1976, she joined the staff of the National Farm Worker Ministry (NFWM), rising to become its executive director ten years later. She was responsible for organizing consumer boycotts of grapes and lettuce in solidarity with striking members of the UFW. During the 1980s, she worked closely with farm laborers in Ohio and Michigan. When their union called for a boycott of Campbell Soup products in support of a strike by tomato and cucumber pickers, Sister Pat toiled tirelessly to ensure its success.

During the 1980s, thousands of Americans protested the testing of nuclear weapons at a remote location in the Nevada desert sixty miles north of Las Vegas. Each year during Lent, they marched to the gates of the test site and offered prayers. Many then crossed onto US government property and nonviolently submitted to arrest. The inspiration for this antinuclear movement was Father Louie, a friar of the St. Barbara Province. The son of a prosperous Southern California family and an Air Force veteran, Father Louie was drawn to movements for social change while he was a graduate student at UCLA. Assigned to ministry in Las Vegas in 1968, he aided African American mothers on welfare who were demanding increased benefits for their children. When he discovered that the US government was conducting underground tests of nuclear weapons in the Nevada desert, he and fellow activists created the Nevada Desert Experience (NDE) to mount antinuclear demonstrations. Marches and mass arrests continued through the 1980s until the United States ceased testing. Father Louie and his colleagues can rightly claim part of the credit for the Comprehensive Test Ban Treaty signed by world leaders in 1996.

Father Joe, a priest of the Holy Name Province, spent fifteen years as a missionary in Bolivia and Peru. He returned to the United States in 1975 on fire with the teachings of liberation theology. He chose to settle in Washington, DC, where he could be most effective in reshaping the policies of the US government and the American Catholic Church. He was employed by the National Conference of Catholic Bishops (now the United States Conference of Catholic Bishops, or USCCB), where he dealt with international issues such as US arms sales to developing nations. In 1982, he was hired by Father Alan as a special assistant for social justice issues at CMSM. Much of his efforts in these years focused on ending human rights abuses in Central America and aiding refugees from oppression who were seeking asylum in the United States. Father Joe has continued advocating for social justice with other organizations while serving in a pastoral role for Catholic immigrants from Latin America.

The following profiles of these eight dedicated individuals illustrate the diverse ways in which Franciscans have endorsed and led campaigns for peace and social justice in the United States and the world. Their examples remind us that the divine calling to minister to the poorest of the poor continues to motivate the men and women who follow St. Francis of Assisi 800 years after his death.[7]

---

7. I originally intended to include a ninth Franciscan on this list, Father Christopher Schneider, OFM, a friar of the St. John the Baptist Province. However, his heroic efforts to integrate the parish school at Our Lady of Good Harbor in Buras, Louisiana, have been ably chronicled by Father David Endres in another volume in this series. See David J. Endres, *Many Tongues, One Faith: A History of Franciscan Parish Life in the United States* (Oceanside, CA: Academy of American Franciscan History, 2018), 91–105.

Chapter 1

Father Nathaniel Machesky: Civil Rights Leader

Cities across the United States teetered on the brink of racial warfare on April 5, 1968. African Americans seethed with anger following the assassination of Martin Luther King Jr. As inner-city ghettoes exploded in flames, many Blacks argued that King's nonviolent philosophy was a failure. Whites, fearing assaults on their privileges and property, armed themselves against imagined invasion. Troops mobilized to put down rebellious Blacks with lethal force.

For a time, Greenwood, Mississippi, appeared likely to join the list of riot-stricken cities. The morning after King's murder, African American students poured out of Threadgill High School, roaming the streets and calling for revenge. A White Franciscan priest, Father Nathaniel Machesky, OFM, together with Black ministers, averted disaster by persuading the youths that confrontation with heavily armed police and sheriff's deputies would be suicidal. Father Nathaniel proposed a peaceful demonstration, instead of rioting, to commemorate their slain hero. "Let's not show them we are dumb," he told them. "We can organize. So if you all go home peacefully we will have a march this afternoon at 2:00 PM."[1]

Father Nathaniel and Reverend Aaron Johnson, pastor of the First Christian Church, hurried downtown to meet with Greenwood's mayor, Charles E. Sampson. The mayor, fearing what might happen if an unorganized march were launched, gave his permission for the demonstration, a first for him.[2] That afternoon, between one thousand and fifteen hundred mourners streamed through the streets of Greenwood under the watchful eyes of hastily mobilized National Guard troops. At the Leflore County courthouse, they held a memorial service for the martyred civil rights leader. The *Greenwood*

Parts of this chapter previously appeared in the *Journal of Mississippi History* and the *National Catholic Reporter*. Reprinted with permission.

1. Nathaniel Machesky, interview by Joe Sinsheimer, 29 November 1998, 14, Joseph A. Sinsheimer Papers, 1962–1987, Duke University Libraries.

2. Charles M. Payne, *I've Got the Light of Freedom: The Organizing Tradition and the Mississippi Freedom Struggle* (Berkeley: University of California Press, 1995), 326.

Commonwealth stated, "Police reported no trouble from the large crowd. The march was termed as very peaceful."[3] A yellowed newspaper photograph from that day shows twenty solemn leaders standing on the courthouse steps, their heads bowed in prayer. All but one are African American. The sole white face belongs to Father Nathaniel.

During the late 1960s, Father Nathaniel emerged as the unlikely leader of the Greenwood Movement, a grassroots organization seeking racial justice. Working closely with African American clergy and veteran civil rights activists, he forged a coalition that mounted a highly effective boycott of White-owned businesses. After more than eighteen months of picketing, strife, mass meetings, and legal challenges, city officials and merchants made the first significant concessions to longstanding Black demands. Movement supporters celebrated a hard-won victory.

At a time when the Black Power ideology was growing in popularity nationwide and many African American organizers told sympathetic Whites they were no longer welcome in Black communities, how did this middle-aged, White, Catholic priest become a leader of a militant Black protest organization? What did this dynamic friar and his Franciscan colleagues contribute to the success of the movement and to the welfare of Greenwood's African American citizens?

Franciscans Come to Mississippi

After the end of World War II, Bishop Richard O. Gerow, prelate of the Diocese of Natchez, Mississippi, had a desperate need for more priests. Home-grown clergy were rare in this overwhelmingly Protestant state. The number of priests who were recruited from Ireland—15 percent to 20 percent of the diocesan clergy—plus those who came from other states were barely enough to minimally staff existing parishes.[4] To expand the Catholic presence in the state, the bishop needed additional priests, brothers, and sisters. Bishop Gerow did what any modern executive would do: he advertised.

In 1947, the Natchez diocese mailed a glossy, three-color, eight-page brochure to leaders of religious orders across the United States. *The Cross Casts a Weak Shadow over Mississippi* asserted the title on the cover of the bishop's brochure. Inside, he outlined a dire situation: thirty-three of Mississippi's eighty-two counties had no Catholic church; fifty-three counties had no resident priest; sixty-seven counties, covering "an area greater than the whole of Ireland," had no Catholic school. The situation for Black Catholics

---

3. "Police Docket," *Greenwood Commonwealth*, April 6, 1968.
4. Michael V. Namorato, *The Catholic Church in Mississippi, 1911–1984: A History* (Westport, CT: Greenwood Press, 1988), 165.

was even more desperate: parishes and schools serving people of color were lacking in seventy-one Mississippi counties. Only one out of every two hundred Black Mississippians was Catholic. Bishop Gerow concluded with an urgent appeal to the heads of religious communities, beseeching them to dispatch priests and sisters to cultivate Mississippi's "back yard mission field."[5]

One recipient moved by this plea was Father Theophane Kalinowski, OFM, provincial minister of the Assumption of the Blessed Virgin Mary Province, a mostly Polish congregation of Franciscan priests and brothers headquartered in Pulaski, Wisconsin. Responding by letter to Bishop Gerow's missive, he confided that in past years the numbers in his own province had been "rather small." Caring for the religious needs of Polish American immigrants and their children had been all that the provincial personnel could handle. But more recently, religious vocations were surging. He now counted "120 priests and about 100 brothers" in the ranks of his province. Father Kalinowski offered to send "about five of our Priests" to undertake mission work among Mississippi's African American population.[6]

Nine weeks later, having received no response from Bishop Gerow, Father Kalinowski fired off a second letter, inquiring if, "perchance, [his letter had] been lost in transit."[7] This time the bishop responded by telegram, apologizing for his delay and requesting that the provincial minister withhold his offer "till next year when we will be prepared to make definite assignments."[8]

In April 1948, Father Kalinowski informed the bishop, "We could assign two to four members of our province [to work in the Natchez diocese] this Summer."[9] The first two Franciscans, Fathers Bonaventure Bolda, OFM, and Chrysostom Okon, OFM, arrived in the Magnolia State behind the wheel of a Pontiac Streamliner station wagon on July 29, 1948. Because the friars did not yet have a home friary, they were assigned to assist at established "White" parishes. In theory, all Catholic churches were open to any worshipper regardless of race, but segregation was the rule in Mississippi and throughout the South. Most Black Catholics worshipped at separate parishes. If they attended predominantly White churches, they were required to sit apart from the rest of the faithful and to receive Holy Communion only after White parishioners did, a situation that Blacks found very demeaning.

---

5. *The Cross Casts a Weak Shadow over Mississippi*, 1947, Archives of Assumption of the Blessed Virgin Mary Province, hereafter cited as Assumption Archives. Michael V. Namorato credits Father Joseph Brunini (later bishop) with developing the brochure. *Catholic Church in Mississippi*, 77.

6. Theophane Kalinowski to Richard O. Gerow, 10 March 1947, Saint Francis Mission, Assumption Archives. At the same time, Kalinowski was preparing to send the province's first overseas missionaries to the Philippines.

7. Kalinowski to Gerow, 17 May 1947, Assumption Archives.

8. Gerow to Kalinowski, 5 July 1947, Assumption Archives.

9. Kalinowski to Gerow, 7 April 1948, Assumption Archives.

Father Bolda first went to Brookhaven, Mississippi, but soon was reassigned to assist the elderly pastor at Immaculate Heart of Mary parish in Greenwood. Father Okon was placed in Sulphur Springs in Madison County and then went to a parish in Leland. In whatever time the friars could spare from their parish duties, they scouted for a location suitable for a Franciscan mission to African Americans. Their search dragged on for more than two years. Some properties for sale were not large enough to accommodate the friars' ambitious plans. In other instances, owners were not willing to sell to Catholics. In March 1950, Father Bolda observed that the friars were doing "grand work among whites but still the work among Negroes has not been done."[10]

In February 1950, Father Okon was recalled to Wisconsin, and one month later Father Nathaniel was sent as his replacement. The new Assumption provincial, Father Isidore Cwiklinski, OFM, introduced Father Nathaniel as "a most capable young priest, [who has] expressed his zeal toward the Negro missions repeatedly."[11] Born in 1919, the son of a Polish American auto worker in Detroit, Father Nathaniel had spent three years following his ordination teaching English at St. Bonaventure High School in Sturtevant, Wisconsin. This work was not why he became a Franciscan. Writing about himself in the third person, Father Nathaniel said, "As a student for the priesthood, he knelt many times in the seminary chapel begging heaven through the Blessed Mother that he would be allowed to go to the poorest of the poor," as St. Francis had done.[12] This new assignment was an answer to his prayers.

Father Nathaniel spent his first months in Oxford, Mississippi, assisting the local pastor and working with students at the nearby University of Mississippi. In his free time, he familiarized himself with Southern culture and inspected properties for sale. He wrote back to Wisconsin that he "tried to get acquainted with 'our people' by daily walks into their sections."[13] In June, he joined Father Bolda in Greenwood, where both friars assisted Monsignor John F. Clerico at Immaculate Heart of Mary parish. In addition, Father Bolda and Father Nathaniel broadcast weekly programs explaining the Catholic faith on radio stations WGRM and WABG.[14]

---

10. "Chronicle of Father Bonaventure Bolda," March 1950, Assumption Archives.

11. Isidore Cwiklinski to Gerow, 13 February 1950, Assumption Archives.

12. Nathaniel Machesky, "No Winter Now" (unpublished manuscript), n.d., Assumption Archives.

13. "Chronicle of Father Nathaniel Machesky," March 1950, Assumption Archives.

14. "Chronicle of Father Bonaventure," July 1950, Assumption Archives. Monsignor John F. Clerico had been pastor of Immaculate Heart of Mary Church since 1912. In addition, he ministered to Catholic congregations in Lexington and Indianola, Mississippi. Father Bonaventure described him as "worn out by past mission endeavors." "Chronicle of Father Bonaventure," June 1950, Assumption Archives.

Nathaniel Machesky as a seminarian in Burlington, Wisconsin, 1943. Photo courtesy of the Assumption BVM Franciscan Province archives.

Greenwood was a promising location for the Franciscan mission. It was the second largest city in the Mississippi Delta, a region famous for its fertile soil, extensive cotton plantations, and "the birthplace of the blues." The city's population of eighteen thousand was evenly divided between Blacks and Whites. Racial segregation was strictly enforced. Nearly all African Americans held menial jobs—the only exceptions were schoolteachers, ministers, and a few professionals. Streets in Black neighborhoods were unpaved; Black homes were not connected to sewer lines. Biased enforcement of Mississippi laws made it nearly impossible for Black citizens to become registered voters. For decades, African Americans had toiled as sharecroppers and tenant farmers in Mississippi cotton fields, but Southern agriculture was changing. African American farm workers, displaced by tractors and mechanical cotton pickers, moved to cities like Greenwood, although they found only limited employment opportunities. Many others left for the North.

Father Bolda and Father Nathaniel continued seeking potential properties for their mission. After a lengthy search, they discovered a 12.6-acre parcel on Highway 82 on the eastern outskirts of Greenwood. The property included a small house and a larger structure that once was home to an African American nightclub, the Blue Moon Café. The friars obtained an option on the property and concluded the purchase for $22,000 on November 17, 1950.[15] Father Nathaniel went back to Wisconsin to claim a used bus and drove back in the vehicle jammed with "many articles that will be used for the . . . mission" to people of color.[16] According to Father Nathaniel, the years spent searching for a suitable property were not wasted. During this time, "he learned the cruelty of enforced segregation and social ostracism. He came to know the perpetual hurt in the hearts of Colored people."[17]

The friars set to work cleaning, painting, and renovating the newly acquired buildings. The provincial chronicles reported, "The local white people [from Immaculate Heart parish] were most generous in donating financial help, time and labor to the work of remodeling the buildings, clearing and beautifying the lands."[18] The former nightclub served as a combined chapel and priests' residence, with two rooms set aside as classrooms for a projected school. The small house was prepared as a convent in anticipation of sisters who would teach at the school. The friars celebrated the first Mass at their new St. Francis of Assisi Mission on December 15, 1950.[19] Because the Franciscan parish was not yet approved by the Vatican, they could not offer a public Mass.

Bishop Gerow petitioned Rome for permission to establish a Black parish in Greenwood. He assured Father Cwiklinski, the provincial minister, that "in every case in the past in which I have asked permission from the Holy See to establish a separate parish for the colored they have readily granted the permission."[20] On this occasion, however, his petition was denied. On March 7, 1951, Bishop Gerow informed Father Cwiklinski, "We are not going to be able to establish a separate parish" for Blacks in Greenwood.[21] Vatican policy had changed: "national parishes"—those intended for members of a specific ethnic group—were no longer acceptable. However, Bishop Gerow was not dissuaded. Acting on advice from the apostolic delegate, Archbishop Amleto Cicognini, the bishop submitted an ingenious but misleading revised plan. He proposed that a parish for the Franciscan fathers be created consisting of Carroll County, to the east of Greenwood, and a narrow slice of Leflore County extending westward to Greenwood's eastern city limits.[22] This arrangement did not trespass on Immaculate Heart's territorial boundaries, but it gave the Franciscans access to proselytize among Greenwood's large African American population. In effect, Bishop Gerow's scheme created sep-

---

15. "Chronicle of Father Bonaventure," November 1950, Assumption Archives.
16. "Chronicle of Father Bonaventure," October 1950, Assumption Archives.
17. Machesky, "No Winter Now," Assumption Archives.
18. *Chronicle of Assumption BVM Province* 20, no. 3 (July 1966): 152.
19. *Chronicle of Assumption BVM Province* 20, no. 3 (July 1966): 152.
20. Gerow to Cwiklinski, 2 October 1950, Assumption Archives.
21. Gerow to Cwiklinski, 7 March 1951, Assumption Archives.
22. "Chronicle of St. Francis of Assisi Mission," August 1951, 22, Assumption Archives.

arate White and Black congregations without appearing to violate the Vatican's ban on racially segregated parishes. Given the social reality of Mississippi's deep racial divisions, establishing an all-Black mission seemed to be the most practical means to win African American converts to Catholicism.

On February 15, 1951, a third Franciscan arrived at the Greenwood mission. Brother Adrian Kolanczyk, OFM, a Chicago native, quickly made himself indispensable by cooking for his fellow friars, assisting in the renovation of buildings, playing the organ at Mass, driving the bus that Father Nathaniel had brought from Wisconsin, and performing a multitude of other tasks. Brother Adrian was a key member of the Greenwood Franciscan team for more than four decades.

On August 15, 1951, the bishop informed the Franciscans that the Vatican had accepted his revised proposal for a new parish. Eleven days later, they celebrated the first public Mass at the mission. The friars now had an officially approved parish, but they remained connected to Immaculate Heart parish. Father Bolda was to serve as "assistant to Msgr. Clerico for the 'general work' of the Monsignor's parish," and Father Nathaniel was designated an "assistant to the Monsignor for the purpose of reaching the . . . [Blacks] of that parish." Father Nathaniel was thereby given the right to instruct and baptize the African Americans of the adjacent parish. "Quite a situation!" he remarked.[23] Although these additional duties increased the friars' workload, their involvement with Immaculate Heart parish brought significant benefits. One benefit was the "extraordinary goodwill" the mission enjoyed "on the part of the white Catholics in town." Father Nathaniel wrote to his superior, "If we were to cut ourselves off completely from the other parish . . . the people in the white parish would resent our abandoning them and their aged pastor."[24]

St. Francis School

From their earliest days in Greenwood, the Franciscans planned to open a school for African American children. Catholic missions among African Americans in the South almost always started with a school. As Father Bolda noted, "Mission work will be most effective wherever there is a school."[25] White missionaries found that offering education was one of the best ways to gain acceptance in African American communities and eventually to make converts. Many African American parents, especially those with higher aspirations for their children, recognized that a Catholic education was superior to the instruction provided in segregated and underfunded public schools. They sacrificed to pay

---

23. "Chronicle of Father Nathaniel," August 1951, Assumption Archives.

24. Machesky to Kalinowski, August 22, 1951, Assumption Archives.

25. "Chronicle of St. Francis of Assisi Friary," January 1951, Assumption Archives.

the modest monthly three-dollar tuition, and they exposed their children to instruction in the Catholic faith in exchange for a superior educational experience. Interested parents who were unable to make tuition payments were never turned away.[26] Georgette Griffin started first grade in 1951 and was among the first ten students to graduate from eighth grade. Her mother was Baptist, but "she wanted [us] to have the best. She wanted us to have what she didn't have," Griffin recalled in an interview.[27] Wilburn "Bill" Williams attended St. Francis School from kindergarten through eleventh grade. His mother, an English teacher at Broad Street High School (later renamed Threadgill High School), was an enthusiastic supporter of the new school. He observed in an interview, "Some of the more forward-thinking, more ambitious [African American] parents realized that going to St. Francis [School] offered opportunities that were different from those in the public school system."[28]

Even before the first teachers were in place, Father Nathaniel, dressed in his distinctive Franciscan brown robe and sandals, walked the streets of Greenwood's Black section spreading news about the school the friars planned to open. Space for two classrooms had been set aside, but as the start of the 1951–52 school year neared, no order of sisters had yet committed teachers for the new school. In June, Father Bolda reported, "We have no assurance of sisters yet but hope that some will be forthcoming."[29] On August 4, he wrote to tell Father Kalinowski that he had contacted "about 65 groups of Sisters," inviting them to send teachers for St. Francis School, "but none had thus far given a positive response."[30] In a typical letter he wrote, "A small chapel and residence for the Fathers, a convent for the future Sisters and a temporary school are all in readiness. We hope to open the school in September with the first two primary grades."[31] Then, just when the situation looked most bleak, a ray of hope appeared. Mother Josaphat of the Sisters of St. Joseph of the Third Order of St. Francis, a mostly Polish congregation, agreed to visit the mission. She arrived on August 13, and when she departed the next day, she "left the wonderful news that their congregation would supply Sisters for the mission school."[32]

26. The tuition charge was justified by the belief that parents would place greater value on the education their children received and would be more willing to cooperate with the teachers if they paid for it. "Chronicle of Father Nathaniel," September 1951, Assumption Archives.

27. Georgette Griffin, in an interview with the author, August 8, 2010.

28. Bill Williams, in an interview with the author, March 14, 2019.

29. "Chronicle of Father Bonaventure," June 1951, Assumption Archives.

30. Bolda to Kalinowski, 4 August 1951, Assumption Archives.

31. Bonaventure Bolda to Reverend Mother Provincial, Sisters of St. Joseph, 1 May 1951, Archives of Sisters of St. Joseph of the Third Order of St. Francis.

32. "Chronicle of Father Nathaniel," August 1951, Assumption Archives.

Six weeks after that visit, word arrived in Greenwood that the Vatican approved the boundaries of the new parish. These two long-awaited developments caused much rejoicing among the Franciscans in Greenwood. The anonymous author of the "Chronicle of St. Francis Mission" (probably Father Nathaniel) wrote, "It is difficult to describe the joy and sheer exultation of knowing that the sisters would soon arrive and that Rome had given us definite parochial status to begin our work."[33] The formal recognition of the Franciscans' Greenwood parish and the opening of St. Francis School closed the first chapter of their Mississippi mission. These were challenging but rewarding years. Later, in 1953, Father Nathaniel wrote, "The human side to this Mission . . . involves three trying years of patient waiting on the part of the first friars in Mississippi. It involves the manifold difficulties that go with a strange people, a strange section of the country and the tools at hand to eliminate this strangeness. In the beginning there was aloofness, suspicion, doubt and wonderment in the people. In time, however, the people came to know the friars, watched them work and felt their love. A change occurred that was both conclusive and dramatic."[34]

On August 27, 1951, three Sisters of St. Joseph arrived in Greenwood: Sisters Ulrica (Mary) Morenc, SSJ, and Lucianna Wantuch, SSJ, both teachers, plus Irma Kronkowski, SSJ, their cook and housekeeper. School registration took place on August 30 and 31. Classes commenced on September 4 with twenty-six pupils: thirteen in kindergarten and thirteen in a combined first- and second-grade class.[35] By the end of the month, enrollment increased to sixty. Fifteen potential students had to be turned away due to lack of space.[36] Because St. Francis School was a mile and a half from the center of Greenwood's African American community, the students were picked up in the city and driven to the mission. Father Nathaniel drove the bus for the first weeks, but Brother Adrian soon took over this chore. During the first month, Dr. George Nasser, a Catholic physician, gave health exams to all of the students. On October 4, the feast of St. Francis, Bishop Gerow and eight visiting Franciscans—joined by "a goodly number of guests," both Whites and Blacks—participated in the blessing and dedication of the mission.[37] By December,

---

33. "Chronicle of St. Francis of Assisi Mission," August 1951, 26, Assumption Archives.

34. Nathaniel Machesky, quoted in Jerry Tokarz, *The Pulaski Franciscans: The History of the Assumption Province of the BVM Province, 1887–2011* (Franklin, WI: Franciscan Friars of Assumption BVM Province, 2013), 238.

35. Reneta Webb, "The School, Mississippi Ministry, 1945–1996," *Peace and All Good*, February 2016, 30. Original plans called for first and second grades, but when early enrollment lagged, the sisters combined grades one and two and added a kindergarten.

36. "Chronicle (and Diary) of St. Francis of Assisi Mission," September 1951, 25, Assumption Archives.

37. "Chronicle (and Diary) of St. Francis of Assisi Mission," October 1951, 26, Assumption Archives.

Leola Williams (mother of Bill Williams) organized a parent-teacher association that began to raise money for a Christmas party for the students.[38]

With so many parents applying to admit their children to the school, provincial observers questioned the criteria used to decide which applicants to accept, especially those whose parents were not legally married. Father Nathaniel expressed his position on that issue with a note of sarcasm: "We here found the 'screening' a bit difficult in practise. One does not simply ask the parent if the child is legitimate. Then too, chances are that even illegitimate children have souls and we are just Franciscan enough to think of that too. Nor does one ask the parent about taking instructions in the Faith in order to accept the child for school. We here hope to do good which will be our best argument for conversion."[39]

The 1950s were a time of growth and building at St. Francis of Assisi Mission. Early in 1952, the friars began drawing up plans for a new school building—the classrooms in the old Blue Moon Café were already overcrowded and never had been considered a permanent arrangement. The school was scheduled to expand by one grade each year until it reached eight grades. Before construction could begin, however, the friars had to raise $40,000 to cover building costs. In late May, they sent a direct mail solicitation to hundreds of potential donors across the United States. The first returns arrived in early June. Before long, a steady stream of checks was coming in, so many that the friars "were forced to forget all other work but to keep the typewriters ticking out our replies."[40] Their appeal raised more than $7,000; however, most of that amount was spent on extensive remodeling and modernization of the Blue Moon building to provide larger and more suitable living quarters for the sisters. The friars then moved into the former sisters' residence.

The need for a permanent building became more urgent in September 1952 when 106 students registered for kindergarten and three primary grades. "Every available inch in the two classrooms" was taken.[41] Ground for the new school was broken on September 7. Pupils and teachers moved into the completed half of the new building on February 23, 1953. Construction on the second half began two years later and was finished in time for the 165 students who registered for grades K–5 in September 1965.[42]

---

38. "Chronicle (and Diary) of St. Francis of Assisi Mission," December 1951, 28, Assumption Archives.

39. "Chronicle of Father Nathaniel," October 1951, Assumption Archives.

40. "Chronicle (and Diary) of St. Francis of Assisi Mission," June 1952, 40, Assumption Archives.

41. "Chronicle (and Diary) of St. Francis of Assisi Mission," September 1952, 44, Assumption Archives.

42. "Chronicle (and Diary) of St. Francis of Assisi Mission," September 1965, 81, Assumption Archives.

St. Francis of Assisi School, Greenwood, Mississippi, 1953. Sister Ulrica Morenc with 1st and 2nd grade students. Photo courtesy of Sisters of St. Joseph of the Third Order of St. Francis archives.

Enrollment in the elementary grades steadily rose to a peak of 297 for the 1967–68 school year.

Everyone pitched in to help raise funds for St. Francis School. Students staged operettas at the Elks Hall in town. An annual fall festival was held in October around the feast of St. Francis. "You had different types of games that you could play," Griffin remembered. "They would throw and hit a ball. Prizes were donated. We would sell tickets to raffle off a bicycle." Every Fourth of July a barbeque took place on the St. Francis School grounds. Plates of delicious food were sold for five dollars apiece.[43] Brother Adrian baked and sold the Polish doughnuts known as paczki. Bill Williams described his treasured memories of these sweet treats, which were "about the size of a baseball, filled with jelly and coated with sugar. Absolutely delicious! Everybody loved them."[44] Brother Adrian also took orders to make cakes for weddings and

---

43. Griffin, interview.
44. Williams, interview.

other special occasions. In an interview, Jeanne Williams Jones recounted her experience penning individualized letters to distant donors who had helped subsidize the school: "If you were supported on a scholarship, you knew you would be writing a personal letter of thanks to someone in Pennsylvania who happened to make a major contribution. Reminding a person of their contribution and [saying] 'We need your ongoing support.'"[45]

The Smallest High School in Mississippi

St. Francis School continued adding a grade every year. In June 1959, seven boys and three girls comprised the school's first graduating class. That fall, the three girls became the first students at St. Francis High School. (The male graduates chose to attend the public Broad Street High School, where they could participate in sports.) That first year, St. Francis High School students were taught in the elementary school library. "Instead of the students changing classes, the teachers rotated," wrote Griffin in a later account.[46] The high school operated until June 1965, when it closed due to low enrollment. With a peak enrollment of 44 students, St. Francis certainly was one of the smallest high schools in the state, if not the smallest. This meant the students received individualized attention from a dedicated teaching staff. Bill Williams, who eventually earned a PhD from Yale University, fondly remembered his years at St. Francis. "It was a marvelous, marvelous school!" he raved.[47] His younger sister, Jeanne Williams Jones, shared his assessment: "It was just a great education. I give [credit for] that to the Franciscans [friars] and the nuns who were there who insisted that we learn; who took the extra time to tutor; who allowed brighter students . . . to tutor others in language and math and science. It gave me a love for learning."[48]

The environment was highly competitive. St. Francis pupils engaged in oratorical contests and spelling bees, not just among themselves, but with students from other schools. Confirmation of their excellence came in 1963 when Jackson State College, Mississippi's leading state-sponsored higher education institution for African Americans, offered a summer institute for academically gifted students. Admission was based on applicants' standardized test scores. Six St. Francis students took the test. They placed first, second, third, fourth, sixth, and tenth out of more than five hundred students tested.[49] "Because of this fine and unusual showing by our students, two colleges have

---

45. Jeanne Williams Jones, in an interview with the author, March 19, 2019.
46. Handwritten account by Georgette Griffin, 2009, Assumption Archives.
47. Williams, interview.
48. Jones, interview.
49. *Chronicle of the Assumption BVM Province* 17, no. 4 (October 1963): 298, Assumption Archives.

offered full scholarships to our graduates," the friars boasted in their annual Christmas letter that year.[50]

However, instruction was not uniformly outstanding. Bill Williams recalled weak math teaching. When he left Greenwood for his final high school year at New Hampshire's Phillips Exeter Academy, he was placed in a lower-level math course. "My math education was horrible," he declared. The same was true for science teaching. The school had no lab for physics, chemistry, or biology classes. The priests and nuns who taught these classes struggled to stay ahead of their bright students.[51]

The benefits of an education at St. Francis School extended beyond mastery of academic subjects. Bill Williams insisted that the friars, sisters, and Pax Christi women [see below] kept him from developing his own prejudice against White people amid the oppressive Jim Crow system. Speaking of the Franciscans who shaped his adult outlook, Williams claimed, "I was spared having to rid myself of the hatred of White people because I had such wonderful living examples of humanity before me who happened to be White."[52]

Brother Adrian believed that the school children would benefit from learning instrumental music, so he organized a student drum and bugle corps. To be able to instruct the band members, he taught himself to play each instrument. Then he raised money to purchase the needed instruments and uniforms. The musicians and majorettes performed at competitions around the state. Bill Williams remembered one such contest against bands from all over the state on the nearby campus of Mississippi Valley State College in Itta Bena: "We all had to perform on the football field—marching maneuvers and things like that. Then we had to perform in concert formation. We had to perform a few numbers in concert so they could judge us purely on our music. Here we are, this tiny little band. We had middle school students in our band because we didn't have enough high school students for the band. . . . Here we were, this ragtag outfit trained by a self-taught band director. We won. It was amazing."[53]

Bill Williams's sister (Jeanne Williams Jones) played bugle; their brother Jonathan was the drum major. Jones remembers practicing with the band: "We had to learn how to read music. We did not just play something by ear. Being able to march and play at the same time. You remember those practice drills in the schoolyard, marching after school in the heat and the dust."[54]

50. St. Francis of Assisi Mission, "Dear Confreres," Christmas 1963, Assumption Archives.
51. St. Francis of Assisi Mission, "Dear Confreres," Assumption Archives.
52. Williams, interview.
53. Williams, interview.
54. Jones, interview.

Pax Christi Franciscans

Father Nathaniel was an eloquent preacher who frequently traveled out-side Greenwood to lead retreats and days of recollection. Not long after he arrived in Greenwood, Kate Foote Jordan, a thirty-eight-year-old Episcopalian divorcée from a prominent Greenville family, came to Father Nathaniel.[55] She "expressed an interest in the Church and requested instructions." In his teaching he "told her a good deal more than the usual dogmatic teachings of the Church. He dwelt long on the Beatitudes as a way of life."[56] On March 24, 1951, Jordan was received into the Catholic Church. According to Father Nathaniel, she had "a blazing passion to share the treasure of the faith with others."[57] Known by all as "Miss Kate," she took the teachings of Jesus seriously, especially his admonition to the rich young man who wanted to gain eternal life—"Sell what you have and give to the poor" (Matt. 19:21, NABRE). A year after her conversion, she approached Father Nathaniel and told him she would like to assist in his good work. "I would like to save at least one soul," she told him. "My own to begin with, and others if God wills it." Father Nathaniel advised her to pray about her offer and to return in one week if she was serious.[58]

Seven days later, she showed up at the mission asking, "Where do I begin?" "Go to the people," he advised. "Go where there is hunger and sickness or loneliness or pain."[59]

Jordan abandoned the privileged lifestyle she had known and dedicated the rest of her years to serving the poor. Over the next three decades, she and Father Nathaniel forged a dynamic partnership to improve the spiritual and physical welfare of Greenwood's African American citizens.

Jordan's first charitable work was visiting patients at Greenwood's dilapidated twenty-three-bed hospital for Blacks. Accompanied by her young friend, Marguerite Kelly, who worked in her father's Greenwood department store, and Sister Lucianna, one of the teachers at St. Francis School, they distributed magazines, fruit, candy bars, and cigarettes to patients who "could not believe that white ladies were sincerely interested in their welfare."[60] The women returned the next Sunday and the Sunday after that. Soon four other

---

55. Two of Kate Foote Jordan's great-grandfathers were Mississippi governors. A cousin, Walter Sillers, was the longtime speaker of the Mississippi House of Representatives. Another cousin, Shelby Foote, was a well-known novelist and Civil War historian. Her father and half-brother, both named Charles Clark, were federal judges.

56. Machesky, "No Winter Now," Assumption Archives.

57. Nathaniel Machesky, "Rich Little Poor Girl," *Information*, August 1957, 47.

58. Nathaniel Machesky, draft manuscript for "Rich Little Poor Girl," 3, Assumption Archives.

59. Machesky, draft of "Rich Little Poor Girl," 4, Assumption Archives.

60. Machesky, draft of "Rich Little Poor Girl," 5, Assumption Archives.

Pax Christi Franciscans outside St. Francis Information Center, 1952, Greenwood, Mississippi. Back row from left Annie Coleman, Kate Foote Jordan, Gloria Ola, unknown woman. The young men in the first row are unknown. (Photo courtesy of Catholic Diocese of Jackson.)

women joined their group. During the week, after their regular work hours, Jordan and Kelly visited the patients' homes, "bringing food and clothing, cleaning the house, washing the clothes or cooking meals for the children" left behind because their mothers were hospitalized. They discovered that home conditions often were worse than the "filthy, miserable surroundings" at the hospital.[61] These Sunday afternoon visits continued for three years until the hospital was closed. The sight of genteel White women doing menial domestic chores for poverty-stricken African American families must have amazed and confounded all who witnessed these charitable acts.

In March 1952, Father Nathaniel and Jordan called on Bishop Gerow in Jackson. She asked for the bishop's permission to open a Catholic library in Greenwood's African American community; Bishop Gerow gave the project his blessing. Jordan rented a small building at 709½ Walthall Street for forty dollars a month. A café serving Blacks was on one side; "a barber shop [was] on the other." Friends pitched in to clean and paint the office. Brother Adrian built bookshelves and a pamphlet rack. Catholic publishers sent books and magazine subscriptions. "Even before the Center opened officially, children came to play and read while the work was going on. Some of their parents offered to help." Jordan christened the refurbished building the St. Francis

61. Machesky, "Rich Little Poor Girl," *Information*, 48.

Information Center. She stated that the center's purpose was bringing "Christ into the hearts of our colored friends simply through making them feel that we love them for themselves as creatures of God."[62]

From the beginning, religious instruction classes for children and adults taught by Jordan were an integral part of the center's agenda. On Tuesday and Thursday evenings, the Center Ladies, as they were known, continued making home visits to discharged hospital patients and to the homes of children who came to the center. By July, activities increased to such an extent that Jordan rented an adjoining building to provide storage space for donated clothing and a separate recreation room for youngsters. In February 1953, a generous donation from the Virden family of Greenville enabled Jordan to purchase the hospital for Blacks, located on Avenue I, which had been vacated after the construction of the new Greenwood Leflore Hospital. The center's expanded quarters contained private rooms to provide a residence for dedicated staff members and allowed for a substantial increase of programming. Two months later, Jordan quit her bookkeeping job so she could devote "all of her days and most of her nights to errands of mercy" at the center.[63] In 1955, a six-bedroom home was built behind the center to provide additional living quarters.

Jordan was "aware of the explosive implications of a White woman working among" Blacks. Her residence at the center unleashed a storm of criticism.[64] According to Father Nathaniel, "former friends snubbed her rudely in public." She received "anonymous letters designed to break her spirit." Malicious gossip "soon became a concerted effort to 'stop that fanatic from degrading southern womanhood by fooling with niggers.'"[65] These rebukes intensified when Betsy Cole, the twenty-three-year-old daughter "from a very prominent family," joined the center's staff. A delegation of irate White Catholics from Greenwood met with Bishop Gerow and "agitated to have her sent away simply because she was white and working among" people of color. To his credit, the bishop politely told them that she was doing good work, "that she was no child and [that] she had his blessing to do the work."[66]

Father Nathaniel praised Jordan's dedication in the face of hateful criticism: "She never hesitated in her resolve. Kate Foote was forever too busy to seek an answer to this public antipathy, too calm to be disturbed, too sure of her mission to waver or doubt. 'They hated Christ,' she would say; 'what can I expect?'" He paid her the highest possible compliment by comparing her

---

62. Alma Taylor, "Pax Christi: The First Ten Years," 3, Assumption Archives.
63. Taylor, "Pax Christi," 3–5, Assumption Archives.
64. Machesky, "Rich Little Poor Girl," *Information*, 47.
65. Machesky, "Rich Little Poor Girl," *Information*, 48.
66. "Chronicle (and Diary) of St. Francis of Assisi Mission," May 1954, 64. Assumption Archives.

to St. Francis of Assisi: "Kate Foote Jordan, who spent her childhood at magnificent Foote Plantation overlooking Lake Washington, who was one of the brightest debutantes of Washington County society, is now penniless but richer than she ever was—a rich little poor girl who in her own way is doing what St. Francis did centuries ago."[67]

September 1953 brought an unexpected opportunity to extend the center's work to reach teenage boys in trouble with local authorities. Henry A. Cummings donated a 240-acre farm outside Greenwood to the mission. Jordan and Father Nathaniel immediately seized on the idea of converting the site into a replica of Father Edward J. Flanagan's famous Boys Town. From its first days, the center had been a magnet for neighborhood boys lacking a stable home life. Jordan and Father Nathaniel presented an ambitious proposal to Bishop Gerow, but the prelate was not won over. One problem was the poor condition of the property. It was "badly rundown having been abandoned for three years." The road into the farm was eroded, and parts of the land were prone to flooding. A more serious objection was the bishop's justifiable concern that the pair would be initiating another large project without securing adequate financial backing. When the Franciscan provincial, Father Kalinowski, sided with the bishop, the plan was scuttled. "There is a farm but there is no permission for anything about it," Father Nathaniel lamented. The bishop's veto "left us limp and thoroughly discouraged." However, the bishop did agree that the farm could be used to provide a summer camp for city kids.[68]

As word about Jordan's initiatives spread, other pious workers joined the center's staff and helped to expand the center's programs. Catherine Doyle, a seventy-seven-year-old widow, came from Illinois. Alice Stafford came from Georgia. Greenwood residents Dot and Bill Kaiser volunteered. The Center Ladies working with Jordan adopted a pale blue uniform to help identify them when they went into the community. Genevieve Feyen, in an interview, pointed out two important purposes served by wearing uniforms: "It told the police who patrolled in that Black area that we were from the center and don't bother us, and it told the Black people to let us into the houses and talk with us."[69] The implication is clear: Whites present in Black neighborhoods could expect to be harassed by White police. Similarly, Blacks in White neighborhoods could expect to be harassed, if not worse.

With more women volunteering to live and work full-time at the center, Father Nathaniel and Jordan began exploring organizational structures for

---

67. Machesky, "Rich Little Poor Girl," *Information*, 49.
68. "Chronicle (and Diary) of St. Francis of Assisi Mission," September 1953 and November 1953, Assumption Archives.
69. Genevieve Feyen, in an interview with the author, August 12, 2010.

the group. For a time, they considered establishing a community of religious sisters, but their numbers were not large enough to justify becoming a sisterhood. Eventually, they settled on forming a secular institute. This was a new type of consecrated religious life—recognized by the Vatican only a decade before, in 1947—for women or men who dedicated their lives to serving God but lived "in the world" rather than in religious communities. The secular institute structure seemed to better "fit the purposes and desires of the group."[70] On February 1, 1956, the first four members made vows of poverty, chastity, and obedience. Unlike the vows made by religious sisters, their vows were renewable each year. They chose the name Pax Christi Franciscans because they sought to achieve the peace of Christ by serving the people of Mississippi while following the rule of St. Francis. At its peak, the Pax Christi Franciscans institute consisted of seven consecrated members and many associate members who shared in the work of the center but did not live at the center or make the same vows. This organization was unique in Mississippi, over the years it included two African American consecrated members and twenty African American associate members. As their numbers increased, Pax Christi branched out, establishing satellite centers in Clarksdale (1956) and Meridian (1960) in Mississippi. In 1969, three members moved to Jackson, where they opened LaVerna House the next year. At this writing, more than fifty years later, five elderly ladies keep the Pax Christi movement alive there.

In 1957, a second gift from the Virden family made possible the construction of a major addition to the center. The enlarged building included room for a medical clinic, a kitchen, office space, clubrooms, classrooms, and a combined auditorium/gymnasium that was used for community meetings, stage productions, and recreational programs. Additional personnel and facility expansion allowed the center to offer more services. From the beginning, religious instruction was a top priority. Jordan and Father Nathaniel taught catechism and inquiry classes for children and adults. Each year Jordan proudly reported the number of new converts. One early convert was Carolyn Williams, a precocious schoolgirl who had become intrigued with the Catholic faith. Eventually, her mother and siblings followed her into the Church.[71] Distribution of secondhand clothing sent by northern benefactors was another important service. "People really needed these things," said Genevieve Feyen's sister, Kathleen, in an interview. "The stores downtown were too expensive."[72] The clothing was sold for small amounts, rather than being given away, based on the belief that the recipients placed greater value on items they had purchased

---

70. Leola Williams, "Pax Christi History: 1951 through 1980," n.d., Assumption Archives.

71. Carolyn Williams Harris, in an interview with the author, July 20, 2010.

72. Kathleen Feyen, in an interview with the author, August 12, 2010.

themselves. The center's original function as a community library was soon eclipsed by the multitude of recreation and education programs it offered for children who had few other outlets. Young people enjoyed ping-pong, basketball, checkers, and other games. Friday night movies and Saturday night teen dances drew large numbers. Adults attended basic literacy classes. In 1957, the center began offering kindergarten classes for preschool-age children.

Pax Christi members and center volunteers with special skills offered classes in many areas. Bill Kaiser supervised the Boy Scout troop and coached the boys' basketball team. Alma Taylor gave piano and typing lessons. Betsy Cole helped Taylor organize a Girl Scout troop and taught folk- and square-dancing. The center sponsored Little League and Pony League baseball teams. Florence Biggers, a nurse from Greenwood, set up a small dispensary to treat minor ailments. She also made home visits and taught a home nursing class. Genevieve Feyen, a registered nurse who came from New Holstein, Wisconsin, in 1955, also delivered basic health care. Later she became a certified nurse-midwife and often was called in the middle of the night to assist with difficult childbirths. Leola Williams organized a drama club during the summer months when she had time off from her teaching duties at Broad Street High School. Brother Adrian provided art instruction. Mable Craft taught cooking classes. A vacation Bible school was held for three weeks during the summer. Young people who had not completed high school could take GED classes. Older adults learned how to read and write. For Holy Week, teenagers acted in a living Way of the Cross. Jeanne Williams Jones and friends formed a singing group called the Chanticleers, which performed popular hits at center events.[73] Roller-skating was a favorite teen activity. As the young people became more proficient skaters, Genevieve Feyen organized a traveling show called Centerama to display their talents. Members of the troupe performed in Holly Springs, Canton, Greenville, and other Mississippi towns. Audiences were delighted to watch James Markham and Doris Dixon, dressed as Prince Charming and Snow White, waltzing on roller skates.[74]

Bessie Wilburn, a talented local teen, first came to the center for piano lessons. Before long, she was instructing some of the young beginners. She also learned to play the organ for church services. After graduating from college, she returned to Greenwood and became a consecrated member of Pax Christi. Known as "Miss Bessie," Wilburn stayed on the center staff for more than fifty years.

One of the most unique services provided by the center was the *Center Light*, a weekly newspaper reporting on events of interest to the African American community. Except for crime reports, the *Greenwood Commonwealth*, the

---

73. Jones, interview.
74. Taylor, "Pax Christi," 23.

city's daily paper, carried no news about the Black community—not even obituaries or birth announcements. Every Saturday, young boys hawked a thousand or more copies of the *Center Light* paper on city streets for three cents apiece. Beginning in 1960, copies were run off on a multilith offset press donated by the Assumption Province. Father Nathaniel penned the editorials. Center Ladies and volunteers did much of the reporting and production. Jeanne Williams Jones valued the skills she developed putting out the paper during her college vacations. Among the abilities she acquired were "copy layout, placement, editing, writing." She learned to ask critical questions before printing an article: "Is it clear? Does it meet the standards?"[75] It should be noted that the center's many activities were conducted in an environment of unrelenting racism. When racist opponents publicized the names of stores that advertised in the *Center Light* and urged Greenwood Whites to boycott these businesses, the paper lost an important revenue source—but it continued publishing.

Jordan and Father Nathaniel recruited students from the North to spend their summer vacations as volunteers at the center and the mission. In 1965, thirty female high school and college students, fourteen seminarians, and seven nuns came from eighteen states.[76] The women slept on bunk beds in St. Francis School classrooms; the men lived in the rectory with the friars. Michelle Arrell Jerison, a recent graduate of St. Catherine's College in St. Paul, Minnesota, rode twelve hundred miles on a Greyhound bus from her home in Fargo, North Dakota. She spent her summer teaching vacation Bible school at the center and making home visits with the Center Ladies. The extreme poverty she encountered left a lasting impression. She saw how the children suffered, how their homes had no plumbing. She remembered families heating water in large black kettles hanging over open hearths. Many little girls had welts on their arms where they had been burned while carrying boiling water. Jerison taught a group of boys, ages nine through eleven, whose intelligence and creativity impressed her. On the final day of vacation Bible school, the students acted out skits based on Bible stories. Her group enacted the wedding feast at Cana, where Jesus turned water into wine. One boy had a pitcher full of water; another little boy had a package of powdered grape drink mix. He turned his back to the audience and emptied the powder into the water. When he turned back, he showed how the water had miraculously changed into wine. "I was amazed at what they did," Jerison said in an interview more than fifty years later. She also experienced the racism her students endured. Once, while she walked down a dirt street holding hands with one of the boys in her class, a White man deliberately tried to run them down with

---

75. Taylor, "Pax Christi," 23.

76. *Chronicle of Assumption BVM Province* 19, no. 4 (October 1965), Assumption Archives.

his car. Another time, a boy said to her, "I wish you could go swimming with us." But because the Greenwood swimming pools were segregated, none of the White volunteers went swimming that summer.[77]

An important center program was Systematic Training and Redevelopment (STAR), a federal War on Poverty program sponsored by the Catholic Diocese of Jackson begun in 1966. STAR offered basic education classes and job training for low-income adults. Father Nathaniel was an enthusiastic STAR proponent who served on its statewide board of directors. Funded by an initial $7 million grant from the Office of Economic Opportunity and the US Department of Labor, plus $500,000 from the Jackson diocese, the St. Francis Center was one of sixteen program sites across the state. Mississippi segregationists opposed STAR because it operated with a biracial staff and trained Blacks and Whites together. Kathleen Feyen recalled, "No White people from our county [Leflore] came to that program, but out of the hills in Carroll County they came. . . . That probably was the first program that was totally integrated. They were about half Black and half White."[78] In addition, STAR operated independently and was not controlled by local White politicians. The program was terminated by the federal government in 1973 after Washington administrators concluded that "STAR was an expensive program that fell short of its targets,"[79] an assertion that remains debatable.

One issue the Center Ladies did not tackle in their first decade was the unequal relationship between Greenwood's Black and White residents. "We do not believe that forums and discussions on the topic of non-segregation would do any good whatsoever," one of the women wrote in 1953. They feared that any effort in this direction "would incite many and cause much hatred and sorrow that could be avoided."[80] Given the fierce commitment to segregation on the part of Greenwood's White population, this assessment was probably correct. But the center's apparent willingness to accept the racial status quo would change in the next decade.

Economic Self-Sufficiency

Father Nathaniel's vision for the mission extended beyond providing religious instruction and the sacraments, a Catholic education, and social services. In the tradition of Booker T. Washington, he believed that African Americans needed to be self-sufficient in order to gain self-respect and free themselves from economic dependence on White people. When he discovered wild palms grow-

---

77. Michelle Arell Jerison, in an interview with the author, March 19, 2019.
78. Kathleen Feyen, interview.
79. Mark Newman, "The Catholic Church in Mississippi and Desegregation, 1963–1973," *Journal of Mississippi History* 67, no. 4 (Winter 2005): 146.
80. "Pax Christi Chronicles," November 29, 1953, quoted in Taylor, "Pax Christi," 8.

ing outside Greenwood, he hatched a plan to harvest the fronds and market them to northern congregations for distribution on Palm Sunday. Bill Williams remembered being given a day off from his middle-school classes to help with the harvest: "We put on our boots and took our machetes and hopped in trucks and we went out to the fields and chopped these palms. We'd bring them back to the center, and local women would be hired, paid to process these things, and palm fronds would be sent to churches all over."[81] In 1960, the mission shipped eleven orders.[82] Father Nathaniel expanded this enterprise in the following years; in 1963, he reported a profit of $1,100 from the sale of palm fronds.[83]

Because Black residents of Greenwood had difficulty obtaining loans from White-controlled banks, in 1961 Father Nathaniel established a credit union, which made loans to African Americans who could not secure them through established financial channels. In 1961, the St. Francis Federal Credit Union had 250 members.[84] In 1985, Father Nathaniel reported it had assets in excess of $1.5 million.[85]

Another self-help project was the Greenwood Cooperative Club, organized in 1966 "to help combat high prices being charged Blacks in small White- and Chinese-owned stores in the Black neighborhoods."[86] Community members purchased shares, which entitled them to shop in the co-op's Food Fair grocery store located on Carrollton Street in Greenwood's main business district. By the end of 1969, it boasted 454 members. "The store made us independent," said Dorothy Brock, manager of the co-op. "We've been able to show our neighbors we can stand on our own two feet."[87] Volunteers did much of the initial work, but by 1970 the store employed a staff of twelve full-time and part-time workers. "When we began this we had grandiose ideas of starting producers' cooperatives to grow vegetables and market them," Father Nathaniel told a reporter. "Then Rev. Albert J. McKnight, who has done such a great job of organizing cooperatives in Louisiana and other parts of the south, visited us and warned us to make smaller plans to begin with."[88] Members of the Green-

---

81. Williams, interview.
82. *Chronicle of Assumption BVM Province* 14, no. 2 (April 1960), Assumption Archives.
83. Machesky to Remigius Steczkowski, 29 November 1963, Assumption Archives.
84. *Chronicle of Assumption BVM Province* 15, no. 4 (October 1961), Assumption Archives.
85. Machesky, interview by Sinsheimer, 11, Sinsheimer Papers.
86. Art Grimm, "Start Something Then Pretty Soon It Catches On and Snowballs," *Co-op Report*, May/June 1970, 12.
87. "Co-op Means Better Life in Mississippi," *The Anchor* (Fall River, MA), January 15, 1970.
88. Grimm, "Start Something," 12. Father Albert J. McKnight, an African American member of the Congregation of the Holy Spirit, was a pioneer in organizing rural cooperatives throughout the South in the 1970s and 1980s. See "A Warrior for Justice," *In a Word* 34, no. 4 (April 2016), http://www.inaword.com/assets/04_2016.pdf.

First Communion, Easter 1955, Saint Francis Mission, Greenwood, Mississippi. Pictured from left are Jonathan G. Williams, Kenneth Rolling, Jerome Rolling, Nathaniel Machesky, Wilson Granger, Jeanne Patricia Williams, and James Alexander. Photo courtesy of Andrew Brophy.

wood Cooperative Club also played an important role in civic projects. They encouraged voter registration and petitioned city officials to pave streets, install sidewalks, and improve sanitation in African American neighborhoods.

Civil Rights Movement

Father Nathaniel would one day be hailed as a hero of the civil rights movement, but his involvement developed only gradually and with considerable reluctance. During his first decade in Mississippi, building the St. Francis Mission and School and establishing the St. Francis Information Center in partnership with Jordan consumed all his abundant energies. As the number of Black Catholics at the St. Francis Mission grew, the old Blue Moon was no longer an adequate worship space. Indeed, it never had been considered suitable as a permanent home for the congregation. In November 1961, ground was broken for St. Francis of Assisi Church. On the feast of St. Francis in 1962, Bishop Gerow blessed the new building with seating for three hundred worshippers and with altars designed by Brother Adrian.

If these ventures were going to succeed, Father Nathaniel needed the cooperation of Greenwood's White citizens. White priests, sisters, and Center Ladies living in the African American community and ministering to the spiritual and temporal needs of its residents were seen as violating the Jim Crow code requiring facilities for Blacks to be separate from those intended for Whites. This usually meant they were inadequate and unequal. Father Nathaniel believed that the only way he could justify these efforts to the White segregationists who ran Greenwood was by appealing to their paternalistic concern for the welfare of the "poor colored people." Advocating racial equality may have led to the rapid demise of his projects.

The Franciscan friars and sisters saw how quickly the goodwill of White Catholics evaporated following the Supreme Court's 1954 *Brown v. Board of Education* ruling declaring school segregation unconstitutional. Within days of the decision, Father Nathaniel noted, "There has been considerable unrest in town. Many of the members of the white parish have turned quite violently against the Mission. . . . Folks up in town feel that we are against segregation and as loyal Southerners this means they must be against us."[89] Almost immediately, Mississippi segregationists began organizing chapters of the Citizens' Council, a White supremacist movement. Supported by powerful politicians and business leaders, the Citizen's Council was strongest in majority Black counties like Leflore; for several years, its headquarters were in Greenwood. "The aim of the Councils," Father Nathaniel explained, "is to preserve segregation at all levels, particularly in the schools. They plan to accomplish this aim through 'economic pressure.' . . . [White] Citizens are told to 'join up or else' whatever that means."[90] In the mission's chronicle of March 1955 he noted, "New bitterness rankles among the whites. The Citizens Councils are making a lot of loud speeches intended to frighten the wits out of our Colored people. And a lot of our people are indeed frightened. . . . Our people fear for their jobs, their homes and even their physical safety."[91]

In this atmosphere of heightened racial tension, Emmett Till, a fourteen-year-old Black young man from Chicago, was brutally murdered in 1955 by two White men in Money, Mississippi, just eleven miles from Greenwood. Till's alleged offense was whistling at or making a suggestive remark to a White woman. Roy Bryant and J. W. Milam were tried for his kidnapping and murder, and both were acquitted by an all-male, all-White jury after deliberating for less than one hour. Following their trial, they admitted to killing Till but expressed no remorse. "What else could we do?" Milam remarked in a

---

89. "Chronicle of St. Francis of Assisi Mission," May 1954, 64, Assumption Archives.
90. "Chronicle of St. Francis of Assisi Mission," August 1954, 68, Assumption Archives. See Neal McMillen, *The Citizens' Council: Organized Resistance to the Second Reconstruction, 1954–64* (Urbana: University of Illinois Press, 1971). The 1950 US Census reported Leflore County's population as 68 percent Negro.
91. "Chronicle of St. Francis of Assisi Mission," March 1955, 75, Assumption Archives.

Look magazine interview. "As long as I live and can do anything about it, niggers are going to stay in their place."[92]

The modern civil rights movement began with the Montgomery bus boycott only three months after Emmett Till's lynching. However, the most active phase of the civil rights movement did not reach Mississippi until 1961. A year earlier, lunch counter sit-in demonstrations swept much of the South when four African American college students refused to leave after seeking service at a segregated Woolworth's store in Greensboro, North Carolina. Sit-ins quickly spread to many other cities, especially those where historically Black colleges were located. Not until March 27, 1961, when nine Tougaloo College students attempted to use the Whites-only main branch of the Jackson Public Library, did sit-in protests surface in the Magnolia State. That spring and summer, hundreds of Black and White Freedom Riders protesting segregated transportation facilities tried to integrate Jackson's bus and train stations. Most of them wound up serving time in Mississippi's notorious Parchman penitentiary.[93] Elsewhere in Mississippi, Robert Moses, an African American math teacher from New York City and organizer for the Student Nonviolent Coordinating Committee (SNCC), began forming a voter registration campaign in the largely rural southwestern region of the state. His initial efforts met with intimidation, harassment, and violence. Shaken by the death of Herbert Lee, an African American farmer and father of nine children who was murdered by a state legislator in the ironically named town of Liberty, Moses shifted his base of operations to the heavily Black counties of the Mississippi Delta. There he continued working to encourage Black voter registration.[94]

The civil rights movement came to Greenwood in June 1962 in the person of twenty-three-year-old Sam Block from nearby Cleveland, Mississippi. Block began canvassing Black neighborhoods and talking with residents about voter registration. He persuaded a few African American citizens to try registering at the county courthouse, despite the registrar's repeated rejection of their applications.[95] Three more young activists, all of them native Mississippians sent by the Student Nonviolent Coordinating Committee, soon

---

92. J. W. Milam, quoted in Timothy B. Tyson, *The Blood of Emmett Till* (New York: Simon & Schuster, 2017), 197. Having been acquitted, Roy Bryan and Milam could not be retried. Some observers considered the fact that two White men were arrested and put on trial for Emmett Till's murder a sign of progress.

93. See Raymond Arsenault, *Freedom Riders: 1961 and the Struggle for Racial Justice* (New York: Oxford University Press, 2006).

94. See John Dittmer, *Local People: The Struggle for Civil Rights in Mississippi* (Urbana: University of Illinois Press, 1994), 90–115.

95. Mississippi law contained numerous provisions adopted to limit Black voter registration. In addition to the poll tax and literacy requirement, one law said that applicants must interpret a section of the state constitution to the satisfaction of the registrar, and another mandated publication of applicants' names in the local newspaper.

joined Block. Intensified voter registration efforts in 1963 were met with violence and arrests. The SNCC office was burned, and Jimmy Travis, a voter registration worker, was shot. African American residents were shocked and angered when Reverend D. L. Tucker, a respected local pastor, was bitten by a police dog while leading a group to the courthouse. Eventually, the US Justice Department intervened to temporarily suppress the violence.[96]

When an assassin using a high-powered rifle murdered Mississippi NAACP leader Medgar Evers outside his Jackson home in June 1963, civil rights supporters, including the Greenwood Franciscans, were shocked and traumatized. Byron De La Beckwith, the man arrested for (and ultimately convicted of) the murder, was a Greenwood resident. He was defended in court by Hardy Lott, the city's leading attorney. In their Christmas letter that year, the friars of St. Francis Mission wrote, "The racial storm did not harm us of the Mission. . . . Now there is a tense, uneasy calm here but we expect a violent change in the coming year."[97]

Father Nathaniel remained on the sidelines during the early voter registration drives. He excused his absence by saying, "In those days I did a lot of preaching during the summer, conducting sisters' retreats. Very often I was away."[98] Although he was sympathetic to African American aspirations and was a voter registration advocate, Father Nathaniel did not join the civil rights demonstrations. He described his involvement as "very, very low profile. We preached it [racial equality] but we didn't feel that we could demonstrate."[99] He believed that aggressive protest and public confrontation were incompatible with the peaceful Franciscan way. Rather than marching, sitting-in, or going to jail, he saw his role as preaching the Gospel of Christian love and forgiveness in hopes of softening the hearts of Greenwood's Whites.[100] "I was just trying to be a Catholic priest doing what I had to do," he told interviewer Joe Sinsheimer. "I just kind of preached goodness and love until I realized that justice was at stake."[101] Not surprisingly, the sisters teaching at St. Francis School adopted a similar stance. Sister Helen Skok, SSJ, who arrived in Greenwood in 1963 to teach first grade, observed that the sisters generally supported the goals of the civil rights movement, but they "kept a low profile so as not to compromise the success of the school."[102] The idea of priests or nuns participating in civil

96. See Payne, *Light of Freedom*, 132–79.
97. St. Francis of Assisi Mission, "Dear Confreres," Assumption Archives.
98. Machesky, interview by Sinsheimer, 4, Sinsheimer Papers.
99. Machesky, interview by Mark Conway, January 1980, tape recording in author's possession.
100. Mark Conway, "'The Mills of God Grind Slowly': The Civil Rights Movement in Greenwood, Mississippi, During the Sixties" (senior thesis, Middlebury College, 1981), 60.
101. Machesky, interview by Sinsheimer, 2, Sinsheimer Papers.
102. Helen Skok, personal communication to author, July 19, 2019.

rights demonstrations, a phenomenon that became common a few years later, was seen as inappropriate by most American Catholics in the early 1960s.

The summer of 1964 brought an "invasion" of nearly one thousand civil rights volunteers to Mississippi as part of the Freedom Summer project. Most were White college students from the North who worked on voter registration, taught in "freedom schools," and recruited members for the Mississippi Freedom Democratic Party. Greenwood experienced a larger influx than most places because SNCC shifted its national headquarters there for the summer. Mississippi segregationists denounced the summer volunteers as "outside agitators" and communists, but Father Nathaniel did not share this opinion. Many years later, he confessed, "I admired their zeal. They would tramp through the fields and tell people what the score [was] and get them (to attempt) to register to vote." He praised SNCC workers as "the first ones, really, to wake people up and inspire them to not be afraid."[103] In his remarks at the time, however, he was much more critical. "Sponsors of the demonstrations were usually beatnik types whose manners and dress repulsed the local people," he wrote in the provincial *Chronicle* in 1965. "Encouraging little children to take part in the marches was also frowned upon locally."[104] Despite their bravery, he disagreed with their methods, "so we were really not that involved."[105]

Jordan similarly advised the Center Ladies stay away from civil rights workers. "So for the most part, we just kept right on at our business and were careful where we went. . . . We really didn't get very involved in all the freedom stuff," said Genevieve Feyen.[106] One reason Jordan urged others to shun the summer volunteers was her objection to what she considered the permissive lifestyle of some of the youthful workers, especially the White women. "There were a lot of girls I didn't approve of—of the way they dressed, of the way they conducted themselves," Jordan told college student Mark Conway.[107]

Father Nathaniel's and Jordan's rather conservative outlooks mirrored the cautious approach of the elderly prelate of Mississippi's Roman Catholic diocese. Bishop Gerow promoted evangelism and charitable work among African Americans and defended their right to worship beside White Catholics—but like most White Mississippians, he took a dim view of civil rights "agitators." Historian Mark Newman documented how Bishop Gerow told University of Notre Dame seminarians to stay out of Mississippi during Freedom Summer. When he learned that six priests of the Oklahoma City diocese had come to the state that summer without obtaining his permission,

---

103. Machesky, quoted in Conway, "Mills of God," 53.
104. *Chronicle of Assumption BVM Province* 19, no. 3 (July 1965), 278, Assumption Archives.
105. Machesky, interview by Sinsheimer, 7, Sinsheimer Papers.
106. Genevieve Feyen, interview.
107. Jordan, interview by Conway, notes.

he promptly ordered them to leave.[108] The bishop's vigilance extended to censoring speakers he considered controversial. In 1963, when Father Nathaniel asked the bishop's permission to invite Henry Cabirac, a well-known Louisiana Catholic advocate of interracial justice, to speak at St. Francis Church, Bishop Gerow refused, calling Cabirac "a troublemaker" and telling Machesky, "Get someone else."[109]

Nevertheless, Father Nathaniel found other, less public ways to support the movement. In October 1962, the Leflore County Board of Supervisors suspended distribution of federal surplus food commodities such as meal, rice, flour, and sugar, on which many poor Black families depended to tide them over during the lean winter months. This move was widely seen as a reprisal against Black voter registration efforts. Comedian Dick Gregory, with the assistance of northern friends of the movement, collected tons of food and clothing, which he shipped to Greenwood. Fearing the wrath of powerful Whites in retribution, Greenwood's Black ministers refused to let their churches be used for distributing relief supplies. Historian John Dittmer reported, "At first only Father Nathaniel at the Catholic Center made his facility available."[110] In a 1985 interview, Father Nathaniel downplayed his role: "Dick Gregory sent some turkeys and other people sent some stuff in. We helped distribute that at the center. It was strictly a private thing."[111] At the same time, Father Nathaniel let it be known that he disagreed with the methods used by SNCC activists. He insisted that demonstrating was not the best way to achieve civil rights and social justice. "We felt the answer was in education and intelligent preparation," he said. "We felt that these demonstrations would achieve little but animosity. We suspected too that when the storm of the demonstrations was over, our people would suffer serious reprisals." He also criticized the national civil rights organizations for failing to develop leadership among Greenwood's African American population. He accused SNCC organizers of being "more concerned with national publicity than the true interests of our people."[112] Father Nathaniel's judgment was not entirely fair to SNCC workers who sacrificed greatly and suffered much to advance the cause. Nor was it fair to leaders such as Robert Moses who did develop local leaders and who shunned the limelight. Father Nathaniel was still caught in the moderate approach that trusted reason and good intentions would prevail. Often they did not. By 1968, Father Nathaniel's vision had changed.

108. Newman, "Catholic Church in Mississippi," 335.
109. Gerow to Machesky, 4 December 1963, "Summary of Correspondence," Archives of the Catholic Diocese of Jackson, Mississippi.
110. Dittmer, *Local People*, 146.
111. Machesky, interview by Sinsheimer, 4, Sinsheimer Papers.
112. *Chronicle of Assumption BVM Province* 17, no. 4 (October 1963), 297, Assumption Archives.

On at least one occasion, however, Father Nathaniel did openly challenge Mississippi's Jim Crow laws. He was driving a group of St. Francis School students to a spelling bee in Greenville. As they passed through the town of Indianola, Georgette Griffin, one of the students, spied a restaurant and suggested, "Let's stop here and see if they'll serve us." Father Nathaniel stopped the car and entered the eatery with the students. "We went in and they told him, 'We'll serve you, but we won't serve them,'" Griffin related. "We said, 'Well, we'll pray for you,' and walked out."[113] Though hardly an act of civil disobedience, the incident does show the friar's support for the students' desire for full civil rights.

Passage of the 1964 Civil Rights Act triggered another round of confrontations between civil rights workers and segregationists. In Greenwood, homegrown African American activist Jake McGhee, along with his brothers Silas and Clarence, repeatedly tested compliance with the public accommodations provision of the act by trying to integrate restaurants and movie theaters. A crowd of angry Whites beat the brothers outside the Leflore Theatre, police harassed them, and the family home was shot up and firebombed by so-called night riders.[114] When Jake McGhee was fired from his job because of his civil rights agitation and could find no other employment, he approached Father Nathaniel about a job. Kathleen Feyen explained how Jake McGhee most likely found work at the center: "I suppose he came to Father [Nathaniel], and Father told Miss Kate [Jordan] to hire him. So he was our janitor for years."[115] With secure employment, McGhee was able to support his family and continue his civil rights activism.

After the 1964 presidential election, the Mississippi Freedom Democratic Party (MFDP) challenged the seating of the state's five members of the US House of Representatives. The MFDP argued that their election was invalid because African Americans in Mississippi had been systematically denied the right to vote. Lawyers for the MFDP needed to find a neutral location where they could take sworn affidavits from people who had been prevented from voting. The lawyers approached Father Nathaniel, who agreed to let them use classrooms in St. Francis School to take these depositions when school was not in session.[116]

Ratification of the Twenty-Fourth Amendment in 1964 ended the poll tax for federal elections. Passage of the 1965 Voting Rights Act invalidated literacy requirements and allowed potential Black voters to bypass local registrars by signing up with federal officials. These events motivated Mississippi

---

113. Griffin, interview.
114. Payne, *Light of Freedom*, 208–17.
115. Kathleen Feyen, interview.
116. "FDP Depositions," Archives of St. Francis Mission.

civil rights forces to concentrate on registering the largest possible number of African American voters. In many communities, Black voters could hold the balance of power if all eligible citizens were registered. In some districts, like Leflore County, they might constitute a majority of the electorate. In June 1966, James Meredith, the first African American to attend the University of Mississippi, announced his intention to walk from Memphis, Tennessee, to the Mississippi state capital in Jackson. The purpose of this trek, which he dubbed the March Against Fear, was to stimulate Black voter registration, and to show that a Black man could walk through the South without fear. On the second day of his journey, Meredith was shot in an ambush outside the small town of Hernando, Mississippi. Fortunately, his wounds were not life-threatening.

National civil rights leaders, including Martin Luther King and SNCC leader Stokely Carmichael, flew to Meredith's Memphis hospital bedside and pledged to continue his march. What had begun as a quixotic solo crusade quickly became a national media event. Reporters focused on contrasting messages delivered by the fiery Carmichael and the more moderate King. When the marchers neared Greenwood on June 16, an advance party tried to erect their tents at the Stone Street School, but police officers arrested Carmichael and forced the others off the property. Father Nathaniel offered the grounds of St. Francis Mission as an alternative site, but the march leaders insisted on a location on public property in town. Remarkably, they succeeded in pitching their tents at the Broad Street Park. Concerned about rising tensions and the possibility of violence, Father Nathaniel bailed Carmichael out of jail. Bill Virden, whose parents had been major supporters of the mission and the center, claimed that Father Nathaniel's action was motivated by a desire to avert a riot. Specifically, the friar feared that with their leader in jail, irresponsible individuals would seize control of the march, and a riot would ensue. Following his release, the SNCC leader delivered a historic speech urging his followers to demand Black Power.[117] According to Virden, Greenwood Whites never forgave Father Nathaniel for getting Carmichael out of jail.

Increasing the number of African American voters was one of the civil rights movement's great success stories. In Leflore County, 7,161 Blacks became registered voters by September 1966, a drastic improvement over the 281 who were registered just two years earlier.[118]

---

117. See Aram Goudsouzian, *Down to the Crossroads: Civil Rights, Black Power, and the Meredith March Against Fear* (New York: Farrar, Straus and Giroux, 2014), 133–44; William Virden, in an interview with the author, January 20, 2011.

118. Data cited in Conway, "Mills of God," 56. See also Pat Watters and Reese Cleghorn, *Climbing Jacob's Ladder* (New York: Harcourt, Brace, and World, 1967), 246.

Sister Chantal Slyvick, Brother Adrian, and SER-Arts

Unlike some other sisters who avoided identifying with the activists campaigning to dismantle the Jim Crow system, Sister Chantal Slyvick, SSJ, petitioned the leadership of her order to be sent to Mississippi so she could join the fight. Placed in an orphanage as an infant and raised in a series of foster homes, she had "developed a deep sensitivity for those who suffer rejections and are ill-treated."[119] While teaching at a Catholic elementary school in Milwaukee, she became acutely aware of problems of racial inequality and discrimination. Beginning in August 1967, Father James Groppi led members of the NAACP Youth Council in two hundred days and nights of marches to demand that the city council pass an open housing ordinance.[120] "He became my hero," said Sister Chantal, who met the activist priest following a rally. Reading *Black Like Me* by John Howard Griffin, a White Catholic who darkened his skin and traveled through the South disguised as a Black man, convinced her to "get involved helping my Black sisters and brothers."[121] Sister Chantal's first encounter with Mississippi racism happened as soon as she stepped off the train in Grenada: "I was walking down the train steps when suddenly a man came running toward me shaking his hand and pointing his finger in my face shouting. 'You're one of those damn Yankee nigger lovers! We don't want you.'"[122]

Not long after she arrived at the mission, Father Nathaniel invited her for a talk in the rectory. She later wrote, "I found him open and candid. He was easy to like because he made you feel liked by him. One could sense he felt for people and wasn't one to be indifferent to pain or injustice. We discovered a common interest in the arts—a love for music, literature and writing."[123] In an interview she explained further: "I knew he was different from most of the clergy. I say this because, along with his intelligence, he had an unusual openness at a time when many of the church people (especially priests) were very contained." Among his other gifts, she observed, "He had a way of building self-worth in people, and he also encouraged talent. . . . If there were people lacking in confidence, he would build them up and this would enable them to do things which were not known by others."[124]

---

119. Chantal Slyvick Batten, "Sister Chantal's Narrative," manuscript in author's possession. Sister Chantal later left the order, married, and took the surname Batten. The text refers to her as Sister Chantal, the name by which she was known during this time in Mississippi.

120. For more on Father Groppi see Patrick D. Jones, *The Selma of the North: Civil Rights Insurgency in Milwaukee* (Cambridge, MA: Harvard University Press, 2010).

121. Batten, "Sister Chantal's Narrative."

122. Batten, "Sister Chantal's Narrative."

123. Batten, "Sister Chantal's Narrative."

124. Chantal Batten, in an interview with the author, December 15, 2010.

A talented artist, Sister Chantal soon formed a partnership with Brother Adrian. They became acquainted when he wandered into her classroom to inspect the artwork she had hung there. He recognized they shared a common interest. Brother Adrian asked her to collaborate with him in making banners to hang in St. Francis Church. Next they started printing inspirational posters. That partnership evolved into a business they named SER-Arts after St. Francis, the seraphic saint. They approached Father Nathaniel and explained that they wanted to create spiritual greeting cards. "By all means," Father Nathaniel said, "I'm going to release brother [Adrian] from his duties in the kitchen," Sister Chantal later recalled. They set up a studio in the old Blue Moon building and taught themselves how to silkscreen. "We bought some books and learned the basics," Sister Chantal remembered. She created the designs while Brother Adrian handled the silkscreening. In the afternoons, after her students went home, she would go to the studio and work with Brother Adrian when he returned from his bus route. "On Saturdays we would go in the morning and work longer," she recalled. Their first big order for their greeting cards came from the famed St. Benet's Catholic bookstore in Chicago. Sales boomed when they started producing Christmas cards. During their busy summer season, they employed several young people to help them process the orders.[125]

The Greenwood Movement Begins

By 1967, it seemed that the Greenwood civil rights movement had run out of steam. Most SNCC organizers had moved on to more promising venues or had dropped out of the movement. A number of local activists took jobs with antipoverty agencies like STAR and Head Start; as federal employees they could not participate in political activities. Support for the MFDP dwindled as moderate NAACP leaders formed an alliance with liberal, White Young Democrats to wrest control of the Mississippi Democratic Party from the all-White "regulars." Although more African American residents were registered to vote, hardline segregationists still held a monopoly on political power. Little had changed in Greenwood.

In this dispiriting environment, Father Nathaniel moved from the background to the forefront of the local civil rights movement. In the fall of 1967, he met with Mayor Charles Sampson, urging him to take a few small steps toward racial reconciliation. Sampson had been elected ten years earlier with the backing of "a white clique of rich powerful men" who ran the city and county.[126] During the tumultuous years of the early 1960s, the mayor had

---

125. Batten, interview.
126. Machesky, interview by Sinsheimer, 4, Sinsheimer Papers.

presided over city government without yielding to Black demands, and he was not about to begin to accommodate them now. A Catholic writer from the North interviewed Sampson in 1964 about race relations in Greenwood. The mayor said, "We think things are pretty good here and would be a whole lot better if we were just left alone." At the conclusion of the interview, the mayor put his hand on a large Bible and declared, "God made men different, and He meant for them to stay that way." The same writer interviewed Hardy Lott, who was the city attorney, a leader of the Citizens' Council, and one of the mayor's key advisors. When asked why the different factions in the city could not sit down and discuss their problems, Lott responded, "What is there to talk about? I know what they want and I disagree absolutely. There's nothing we can talk about."[127] Neither Sampson nor Lott had changed their views when Father Nathaniel met with the mayor three years later.

Father Nathaniel was furious over Sampson's intransigence. He returned to the rectory and wrote an impassioned editorial for *Center Light*. Invoking sentiments that could well have come from a Black Power advocate like Carmichael, he argued that if Blacks were ever going to accomplish anything they would need power, and that power would come through organization.[128] In the editorial's most controversial passage, Father Nathaniel concluded, "Perhaps the only route to sanity is revolution. We do not like the term, but unless there's a serious change of heart soon, there's no other course."[129]

In addition to the mayor's obstinacy, another decision contributed to the discontent of the African American population in Greenwood. The city's annual Christmas parade was a huge community celebration. Danny Collum, then an eighth-grade student, fondly remembered the parade: "We got the day off of school. Bands came from all over. It went on for hours."[130] In 1967, parade organizers refused to invite the celebrated marching band from historically Black Mississippi Valley State College. The band was good enough to march in the 1965 Tournament of Roses Parade in Pasadena, California, but Greenwood city fathers wanted to keep their Christmas parade an all-White event. Black residents were incensed by the gratuitous insult.

By this point, Father Nathaniel had lived in Greenwood for seventeen years. He had preached and administered the sacraments to White Catholics at Immaculate Heart parish. He was familiar with their racial attitudes. Even Whites who acknowledged the injustice of the Jim Crow system feared to

---

127. Charles R. Sampson and Hardy Lott, respectively, quoted in Michael Real, "Search for Understanding," *Community* 24, no. 6 (February 1965): 8.

128. Conway, "Mills of God," 61.

129. Nathanial Machesky, editorial, *Center Light*, quoted in "Greenwood Mayor Discounts Story," *Jackson Clarion-Ledger*, May 1, 1968. See also Mark Conway, "Mills of God," 61.

130. Danny Collum, in an interview with the author, January 13, 2011.

openly challenge it. He also witnessed the repeated slights and humiliations experienced by the African American parishioners of St. Francis Mission, who wanted nothing more than the opportunity to earn a decent income and provide a better future for their children. He had watched from the sidelines for five years as courageous young civil rights workers suffered arrests, beatings, shootings, and terrorist attacks but had little to show for their heroic efforts.

After his meeting with the mayor, something inside Father Nathaniel snapped. He embraced the militant tactics he previously had rejected. In a 1985 interview, he described his conversion as "falling over the edge."[131] By this he meant making a personal commitment to take whatever steps were needed to gain social and economic justice for African American citizens of Greenwood. He meant being willing to assume a public leadership role. He meant being prepared to accept the insults, threats, harassment, and dangers that he knew would result from this decision. He meant accepting the possibility of being killed, just as Jesus Christ had accepted death on the Cross to win salvation for humankind.

His concerns were not exaggerated. Father Nathaniel's decision to take a leadership role in the movement resulted in many personal consequences, nearly all of them negative. Since coming to Greenwood, he had enjoyed the hospitality of White Catholics from Immaculate Heart parish. He often shared drinks and dinner in their homes; he golfed with them at the country club and played bridge with them in the evenings. He knew these pleasant social contacts would evaporate once he took a prominent part in the boycott. Catholic store owners, many of them descendants of Lebanese immigrants, had supported the St. Francis Mission with cash donations and merchandise gifts. These contributions would cease if he called for a boycott of their businesses. He also faced the very real threat to the institutions he had built over seventeen years, and to the friars, sisters, and lay people who worked with him. The Ku Klux Klan was active in the county. Beckwith, the unconvicted assassin of Evers, a hero in the eyes of some Greenwood residents, roamed free in the city.[132] The St. Francis Church and School faced a busy highway, and they were vulnerable to attacks by night riders. Bullets fired by an unseen assailant could have easily ended Father Nathaniel's life. Terrorists had firebombed and shot into the McGhee home, not far from the mission.

Greenwood businessman Alex Malouf Jr. understood Father Nathaniel's dilemma, as he explained in an interview: "He had a decision to make, whether

---

131. Machesky, interview by Sinsheimer, 8, Sinsheimer Papers.

132. Beckwith was tried twice in 1964 for the murder of Medgar Evers, but both trials ended in hung juries. He was finally convicted after a third trial in 1994 and was sentenced to life in prison. See Maryanne Vollers, *Ghosts of Mississippi: The Murder of Medgar Evers, the Trials of Byron de la Beckwith, and the Haunting of the New South* (Boston: Little, Brown, 1995).

he was going to support the Blacks or the Whites. It wasn't really a choice for him. There was no choice."[133] Father Nathaniel's conscience would not let him shirk his duty to his parishioners. He knew their demands were just. The things they wanted were no more than the rights guaranteed to all US citizens by the Constitution. Whatever path he chose, he faced serious consequences. Yet he did not flinch. He cast his lot with Greenwood's long-suffering African American people. He published his angry editorial in the *Center Light*; he accepted a leadership position in the Greenwood Movement; he offered the St. Francis Center as the boycott headquarters; he never retreated when insulted or threatened; he insisted on justice for African American citizens.

At first, only a handful of people responded to Father Nathaniel's editorial. They began meeting at the St. Francis Center. "Every Sunday it [attendance] seemed to grow just a little bit," Father Nathaniel later said.[134] He was one of three clergymen selected to lead a new civil rights organization. The other two were African American—Reverend M. J. Black, pastor of Turner Chapel AME church, and Reverend William Wallace, pastor of Jennings Temple CME Church. None of these three had been involved with previous protests. Neither were they identified with any national civil rights organization. They could not be accused of being "outside agitators." They chose the name Greenwood Movement to emphasize the organization's local nature and its independence of all outside groups.

The goals of the Greenwood Movement can be summed up in two words: respect and jobs. *Respect* meant teaching Whites to use courtesy titles like Mister and Missus when addressing African Americans, not calling adults by their first names or, worse, using demeaning terms like "boy" or "auntie." It also meant advocating for stores' courteous treatment of customers on a first-come, first-served basis rather than waiting on White customers first while ignoring Blacks standing in line. *Jobs* meant hiring Blacks as cashiers and salespeople in stores, rather than relegating all Black employees to menial positions. Finding jobs for African Americans in the Greenwood city government carried especially great symbolic significance. No Black workers held any city jobs with significant responsibility. The complete absence of Black police officers and firefighters was especially galling. Improved city services—street paving, street lights, and sewers in Black neighborhoods—were additional demands of the movement.

To accomplish these goals, the Greenwood Movement initiated a boycott of all noncompliant merchants. The only establishments exempted from the boycott were banks, doctors' offices, drugstores for purchasing medicines, and a few stores that had promoted African American employees to responsi-

---

133. Alex Malouf Jr., in an interview with the author, August 17, 2010.
134. Machesky, interview by Conway.

ble positions. Boycotting White merchants had emerged as one of the most powerful tools of the civil rights movement. As early as the 1930s, in Harlem and other northern cities, African American leaders had led effective "Don't Buy Where You Can't Work" campaigns.[135] During the 1950s and 1960s, consumer boycotts were used successfully in conjunction with civil rights demonstrations in places like Montgomery and Birmingham, in Alabama, and Nashville, Tennessee. Closer to home, Mississippi NAACP leader Charles Evers organized effective boycotts in Natchez, Fayette, and Port Gibson.[136]

As King had proved in Montgomery, a consumer boycott could be an effective weapon wielded by people with few resources other than their combined purchasing power. Direct-action tactics like sit-ins left participants vulnerable to arrest, imprisonment, and physical violence; registering to vote was a public act that often led to economic reprisals. But selective buying was a private act that did not involve law breaking. A person could not be legally punished for failing to purchase goods at a store being boycotted. As long as protestors had alternative sources for needed supplies, a boycott was a difficult but viable weapon. The key to any boycott's success is maintaining a disciplined base of community support. If a significant number of consumers fail to honor a boycott, their friends and neighbors will likewise be unwilling to make the sacrifices a winning boycott requires.

The leaders of the Greenwood Movement believed that mounting an effective boycott could force White business leaders and politicians to make needed changes. The task would not be easy. Two earlier attempted boycotts had failed. Father Nathaniel knew that the key to success was a strong organization. He secured endorsements from three important Black civic groups: the Leflore County Voters League, the Greenwood Cooperative Club, and the Leflore County NAACP branch. The co-chairs announced that the boycott would begin on December 6, at the start of the 1967 Christmas shopping season, on which many merchants depended to push their ledgers into the black for the year. The boycotters targeted stores on the south side of town, ones that catered to an African American clientele. A couple businesses, including the Liberty Cash Market and Mid-West Dairy, responded by promoting Black workers to positions of greater responsibility and were removed from the boycott list. After engaging in strong early compliance, however,

---

135. For discussion of early boycotts, see Ralph L. Crowder, "'Don't Buy Where You Can't Work': An Investigation and Social Conflict within the Harlem Boycott of 1934," *Afro-Americans in New York Life and History* 15 (1991): 7–44; and Andor Skotnes, "'Buy Where You Can Work': Boycotting for Jobs in African American Baltimore, 1933–1934," *Journal of Social History* 27, no. 4 (Summer 1994): 735–61.

136. For discussion of the Port Gibson boycott, see Emilye Crosby, *A Little Taste of Freedom: The Black Freedom Struggle in Claiborne County, Mississippi* (Chapel Hill: University of North Carolina Press, 2005).

Black shoppers started drifting back to the stores. Kathleen Feyen observed, "After they got a few [Black] clerks in there, it kind of died out."[137] The Greenwood Movement continued drawing as many as fifty people to its Sunday meetings, but the boycott had lost most of its effectiveness.

On February 11, 1968, sanitation workers in Memphis, Tennessee, walked off their jobs in a strike for higher wages and better working conditions. Their action attracted national attention when Martin Luther King flew to Memphis to support their cause. Greenwood's proximity to Memphis made it easy for King to swing down to recruit local residents for his Poor People's Campaign. On March 19, 1968, King spoke at Jennings Temple AME church. Center Lady Micki Huber was in the church that night. "The church was so packed you could hardly move in there," she recalled in an interview. "People were crawling in and out of the windows just to hear him."[138] A standing-room-only crowd of 250 people heard King speak in person, while 200 more listened outside. The next day, King paid a visit to students at St. Francis School. Sister Chantal was thrilled when he walked into her classroom. In an interview, she recounted that he "asked everyone to be quiet and think of having one wish to be fulfilled. What would it be?" One small pupil named Jimmy stood up. He said, "He wished he could have a White friend to play with after school." As Sister Chantal recalled, Jimmy then related how he had been playing with a White boy who lived in the house next to his until the boy's father came out. The man took off his belt, beat his son, and told him "never to play again with that Black nigger. If he did, he would get a worse beating."[139] King bowed his head and prayed with the students.

News of King's assassination in Memphis on April 4, just two weeks later, hit Greenwood's Black residents especially hard because they had just heard him preach about struggle and freedom. On the morning of April 5, Sister Chantal's pupils ran off the school bus and into her classroom "angry and yelling," she explained, "upset like I never saw before. And then they started yelling hate words, even to us teachers. I remember looking at them in horror because I couldn't believe that the children I loved could do this."[140] Father Nathaniel canceled classes. Sister Chantal and Brother Adrian went to the art studio and began making signs to carry that afternoon on the march to the county courthouse. Later that day, together with two or three other sisters in full habits, Sister Chantal joined the demonstration. "I definitely wanted to be with the children because the National Guard had dogs, and the kids were

137. Kathleen Feyen, interview.
138. Micki Huber, interview with author, October 6, 2010.
139. Batten, interview.
140. Batten, interview.

terrified of these dogs," she recalled.[141] The march went off without incident, although there were reports of scattered window breaking and bottle throwing that night.

King's assassination revived the Greenwood Movement and breathed new life into the boycott. Its three leaders sought to channel the justifiable anger of Black citizens in a positive direction. Before calling for a resumption of the boycott, they tried to meet with city officials, but Mayor Sampson refused to confer with them. In addition, the *Greenwood Commonwealth* would not publish a paid ad requesting a meeting between representatives of the Black and White communities to discuss racial reconciliation. All channels of public communication were blocked.

On the day of King's funeral, four hundred movement members gathered at the St. Francis Center and voted to resume their boycott of White-owned stores. Their demands were spelled out in an open letter distributed to three thousand homes in the city. Their first and most important objective was opening communications between all people of Leflore County. They proposed establishing a permanent human relations commission to "mediate all problems of social concern." Their second demand was that "fair employment practices be adopted by all employers." Singled out for special mention were the city's police, fire, street, and sanitation departments. A third demand was that city services "be rendered to all citizens on a fair and impartial basis." Proposals included creating a city housing authority, integrating public schools, desegregating recreation facilities, and improving infrastructure and other services to the Black community such as street cleaning, sewer lines, garbage collection, and paved streets. To ensure that these changes happened, the Greenwood Movement insisted that "Black persons be appointed to all commissions providing health, educational, cultural, recreational, and other services." Underlying these demands was the desire to be treated with consideration and respect. Specific reforms mentioned in this area included the use of courtesy titles like Mister and Missus, "abandonment of all that smacks of condescension and paternalism," and "genuine regard for the feelings of others."[142]

Those attending the meeting also voted to rename the organization to the Greenwood Movement in Honor of Dr. Martin Luther King Jr. The new name announced to everyone that the movement was committed to following King's nonviolent philosophy. Mary Boothe, already a veteran activist at the age of twenty-three, explained, "When SNCC was in we didn't mind demonstrating; we didn't mind going to jail; but now we are not as militant as we were then. This movement is based on love and nonviolence, although SNCC

141. Batten, interview.
142. *The Greenwood Movement*, pamphlet, 27 June 1968, Archives of St. Francis Mission.

was nonviolent to a certain extent, but this movement is really based on love, law, and nonviolence."[143]

The Greenwood Movement's commitment to King's nonviolent principles won it a wide following in the African American community. During the early 1960s, only a small segment of the Black population had rallied behind SNCC's militant attack on White supremacy. Because the movement's new leaders had not been associated with the earlier protests and had avoided the rhetorical excesses of Black Power advocates, the movement now appealed to a wider constituency and won the backing of more conservative elements in the Black community. Activists from the SNCC/MFDP days accepted these changes, even if they did not wholeheartedly endorse them. Boothe became the movement's executive director; James Moore headed the picketing committee; and Jake McGhee was one of the most faithful picketers.

Movement leaders emphasized that their organization was an independent, homegrown entity, not affiliated with any national civil rights body. Given its clerical leadership, affiliation with King's Southern Christian Leadership Conference (SCLC) seemed like a natural alliance. When representatives of King's organization made overtures to the movement, they were politely but firmly rejected. The main reason given for this rebuff was SCLC's insistence on repeated mass demonstrations, which it had used without much success in Albany, Georgia, but more effectively in Birmingham, Alabama. According to Father Nathaniel, "[They wanted] us to march every single day—with or without a permit—and as many marched would be arrested. They wanted us to fill the jails completely."[144] He believed the Greenwood Movement could mount a successful protest without sending hundreds of people to jail.

The movement's three leaders understood that their boycott would not achieve its objectives without a solid foundation. They built a military-style organization of block captains who were responsible for visiting each home on their block, explaining the boycott, and urging people to observe the picket lines. They also learned which neighbors were not registered to vote and encouraged them to do so. Each block captain reported to a major in charge of one of twenty-two geographic areas. The majors, in turn, reported to five colonels.[145] The block captains became an essential communication link, keeping the movement's leadership aware of grassroots sentiment and informing residents of new developments. The movement also assembled a highly effective phone tree, capable of summoning hundreds of members to

---

143. "Interview with Miss Mary Booth," 7 August 1968, Ralph J. Bunche Oral Histories Collection on the Civil Rights Movement, Moorland-Spingarn Research Center, Howard University.

144. Machesky, quoted in Conway, "Mills of God," 68.

145. John Pearce, "Negro Boycott Shows Effect," *Memphis Commercial-Appeal*, April 28, 1968.

an emergency meeting in less than an hour. Mass meetings, held once a week at first and more often during the height of the boycott, featured speakers who roused the spirits of the movement's supporters, reinforced discipline among the troops, delivered news of merchants who had reached agreements with the movement's leaders, reminded boycotters which businesses remained on the boycott list, and reported developments in their efforts to meet with Greenwood's White establishment. A more controversial feature of these meetings was reading the names of persons seen violating the boycott. Father Nathaniel insisted this happened infrequently, but he could not stop movement supporters from informally circulating the names of Blacks observed shopping in White-owned stores.

Sunday meetings took place at the St. Francis Center. Later in the year, meetings also happened at Jennings Temple CME Church and other cooperating churches, but never in any Baptist churches. According to Reverend Wallace, the Baptists "really would not take any leadership in any of this movement."[146] He attributed their refusal to the fact that the Baptist pastors were hired by their congregations rather than being appointed by bishops, as Catholic and Methodist clergy were. Baptist deacon boards feared, with some justification, that their buildings might be burned by the Ku Klux Klan. No doubt, the memory of thirty-seven African American churches that were burned during Freedom Summer was fresh in their minds. In an interview, former teacher and Leflore County Voters League head David Jordan identified another factor behind the deacons' reluctance: dependence on white financial support. "When they [the Baptist deacons] got ready for an appreciation or anniversary, they would go downtown to certain business folks and get $200 to $300 to help them out," he said. The White merchants would then ask, "Well, you know, Reverend, I don't mind helping you out, but you ain't with that [civil rights] crowd?"[147]

In addition to his other duties, Father Nathaniel acted as the movement's publicist. He used the center's printing press to produce leaflets and a detailed brochure explaining the boycotters' demands. The *Center Light* newspaper was an important communication channel to reach those who could not attend the mass meetings. Father Nathaniel also used the paper to send messages to White Greenwood residents. In an editorial titled "Listen Greenwood," he expressed the accumulated frustrations of the city's African American community:

> Black people are trying to tell everyone that they have had enough of play-acting. They are trying to tell white people at last how it has hurt

---

146. William Wallace, in an interview with the author, August 19, 2010.
147. David Jordan, in an interview with the author, August 9, 2010.

all these years. They are trying to tell white people many things: that they know what is going on in the world; that they have watched TV and have seen people elsewhere treating people like them with courtesy and respect; that they are tired of having to see and feel all the symbols which remind them that Greenwood Negroes are considered second-class; that they are sick and tired of white people saying "nigras"; that they are tired of saccharine paternalism; that they are tired of white people acting as if they owned the country or this city; that they are tired of accepting hand-outs without a chance for a fair wage; that they are tired of white people treating them as children; that they are tired of white people thinking Black is synonymous with something dirty and ugly and immoral; that they have just had it, that's all.[148]

Writing in the *Mississippi Register*, the paper of Jackson's Catholic diocese, Father Nathaniel explained for White Catholic readers the fundamental reason for the boycott: "The Black people of Leflore County express it very simply: nobody will talk with us, the mayor won't talk, the merchants won't talk. What choice do we have?"[149]

Daily picketing was the most visible reminder telling shoppers that a boycott was in effect. Pickets marched back and forth in front of stores, carrying hand-lettered signs announcing the movement's grievances and proclaiming its objectives. Many were created at the center or in Brother Adrian's workshop at the mission. "I Have a Dream," "Shop Where You Are Respected," "Green Power," and "Equal Rights for All" were some common slogans. One particularly original sign read, "God Does Not Like To Be Insulted When He Is Wearing His Dark Suit." African American students picketed after school dismissal and on Saturdays. "When the kids were in school, the older people came out and walked the streets," Kathleen Feyen remembered. Pax Christi members joined the picket lines when they could get free from their regular duties. Picketers followed specific instructions—walk four to five feet apart, do not block the doorways, make about-face turns, keep moving continuously. "Go as close to the curb as you could get," Genevieve Feyen remembered. Her sister Kathleen added, "Keep moving and don't talk to anybody. You couldn't say [to someone], 'Don't go in there.' You could not talk to anybody. You had to keep moving."[150] The presence of White Center Ladies like the Feyen sisters ensured a racially integrated picket line, something rarely seen in Mississippi. "Dora Hollie [an African American] and I took the noon hour," Kathleen Feyen said. "She and I would walk the downtown White sec-

148. Nathanial Machesky, "Listen Greenwood," editorial, *Center Light*, June 21, 1968.
149. Nathanial Machesky, "Greenwood Boycott," *Mississippi Register*, May 7, 1968, 4.
150. Machesky, "Greenwood Boycott," 4.

tion of the streets from maybe 11:30 to 12:30 or 1:00." Usually there were no problems, but once, she said, "somebody came out of a store and threw a snake at us. . . . We screamed and hollered, and the man behind [us], I think it was Mr. Thomas, said 'Keep walking. Step over it.'"[151]

White Greenwood residents resented Whites' participation in the protest. David Jordan of the Leflore County Voters League remembered, "We did go downtown, and Kathleen Feyen and two of the other ladies was with us, and some of the local Whites did not like the idea that they were talking with us and we were always picketing and marching together. They would come back and say, 'Miss Feyen, you ought to be ashamed, you know better than this.' . . . but she wouldn't pay any attention, [she] just smiled at them and kept going."[152] Huber, another white Center Lady, reported similar difficulties when she appeared on picket duty: "We had lots of insults thrown at us. Of course, because we were White on a Black picket line, it was very rough for some people to handle."[153] Several Pax Christi members and six of the resident sisters took part in the picketing, but the visible participation of even one or two of them was enough to brand everyone associated with the St. Francis Mission and the center as agitators. Participating on the picket line was especially difficult for the priests "because they had friends in the White community," explained Kathleen Feyen. "The priests really thought before they got on the picket line. . . . I remember Father Fred [Kochan] and Father Dan [Nowak] walking with us."[154]

Spotters kept watch on city streets, jotting down names of shoppers not honoring the boycott. These violators were then visited in their homes and encouraged not to shop at the targeted stores. Peer pressure was the Greenwood Movement's most potent weapon. Mary Fluker described how boycotters dealt with those who continued patronizing White-owned businesses: "We talked about them like they were dogs in church and in class and in clubs. Now, we didn't call anybody's name, but we said, 'Now some of you folks are silly enough, foolish enough, or hate your race enough, to sneak in a back door and buy things.' That kind of cooled them down. Pride kept a lot of people out [of the stores]. They didn't want anyone to see them going in at all, so they stayed out."[155]

Greenwood police likewise kept close watch on the picketers, with at least one officer stationed on each block.[156] Huber recalled, "My first day [on the picket line] there was a policeman walking next to us clicking his gun. It was

---

151. Kathleen Feyen, interview.
152. David Jordan, interview.
153. Huber, interview.
154. Kathleen Feyen, interview.
155. Mary Fluker, interview by Mark Conway, January 28, 1980, in author's possession.
156. Overtime wages for police officers monitoring the boycott cost the city an estimated $10,000.

scary."[157] During the first month of picketing, however, only two people were arrested—one for disorderly conduct and another for profanity. Compared with their heavy-handed treatment of demonstrators a few years earlier, the conduct of the Greenwood police this time was relatively restrained.

Unlike earlier unsuccessful efforts, compliance with the renewed boycott was nearly complete. An account published in the *Memphis Commercial-Appeal* two weeks after the start of the boycott reported that merchants were feeling a major economic impact. The article described the scene one Saturday, normally the busiest shopping day of the week: "White merchants along Carrollton Street and Howard Street waited on white customers almost exclusively. There were no Negroes except those carrying signs and working in stores." The manager of an unnamed department store complained, "As far as I can tell it's 100 per cent effective. I don't mind telling you I'm down this month when I should be up because of Easter buying."[158] "They were killing us," recalled Malouf, who worked in his parents' furniture store on Carrollton Street.[159] Mayor Sampson, however, denied the boycott was having a serious impact on business: "We've got a lot of good Negroes in Greenwood who are going about their business shopping where they want to and in general conducting themselves like they should."[160] He placed primary responsibility for instigating the boycott on Father Nathaniel and his fellow Franciscans. "It's just a bunch of Catholic priests out there trying to run the whole country. We're not going to discuss it with them. They're just agitators sent in here. They've been sent here for just this purpose."[161]

Merchants on Johnson Street, who sold mostly to African American customers, also felt the full impact of the boycott. In a letter to the chamber of commerce, they complained, "for all practical purposes [the boycott is] 90% effective."[162] Seventeen of these merchants met with the movement's negotiating committee on April 24 and agreed to institute "fair and equal" hiring practices, to use courtesy titles with Black customers, and to petition the city council to negotiate with movement representatives.[163] On May 10 the mayor and city council met with four movement leaders to discuss a list of five demands. Sampson said the council would study and discuss the demands, but that their study would require "a good deal of time."[164] Since the city made no concessions, the boycott continued.

---

157. Huber, interview.
158. "Negro Boycott Shows Effect," *Memphis Commercial-Appeal*, April 28, 1968.
159. Malouf, interview.
160. "Boycott Story Disputed by Greenwood Mayor," *Jackson Daily News*, May 1, 1968.
161. "Greenwood Mayor Discounts Story," *Jackson Clarion-Ledger*.
162. Letter to chamber of commerce, quoted in Conway, "Mills of God," 70.
163. Conway, "Mills of God," 71.
164. Conway, "Mills of God," 72.

Extreme elements in the White community soon began harassing those they believed to be responsible for the boycott. Telephone threats were a daily occurrence at the St. Francis Center. Kathleen Feyen remembered, "We got telephone calls galore telling us where to go in no uncertain terms." She recalled one teenage girl working at the center, who asked Kate Foote Jordan how to respond to these threatening calls. Jordan advised, "Say thank you and God bless you." After two hours of responding to hostile callers, Kathleen Feyen said, the young woman begged for relief. "I God blessed everybody in Leflore County," she exclaimed.[165] Dealing with death threats became routine. One menacing voice asked Jordan where she wanted her bullet: "In the front or the back?" She calmly replied, "Wherever you want to put it."[166] One night during the boycott, the center was attacked. Unknown assailants drove past and tossed a firebomb on the roof of an adjacent building. Pax Christi members living a block away received a phone call from a neighbor who said, "There's a fire on your roof. Go check it out."[167] The fire was extinguished before it caused major damage.

Father Nathaniel was similarly abused over the phone and in writing. He took the threats seriously, and despite his advocacy of nonviolence, he began carrying a pistol for self-defense. "A Delta Discussion," an anonymous hate sheet, commonly believed to be the work of the Ku Klux Klan, printed a scurrilous denunciation of Father Nathaniel: "For years the negro ROMAN CATHOLIC CENTER ON Ave. I has been turning out huge quantities of anti-white, anti-Protestant, pro-communist literature and its so-called 'priest' FATHER NATHANAIL is known to have several negro 'girl friends' in his harem out there. His presence in Greenwood has long ago ceased to be necessary or desirable. The cesspool known as SAINT FRANCIS MISSION out on hiway 82 East is also a hotbed of integration and agitation. It could and should be removed from the scene and would never be missed."[168] In June, the attacks on Father Nathaniel escalated. The anonymous author of the next issue of "A Delta Discussion" wrote:

> The local arm of the communist Conspiracy has grouped itself into what it calls THE GREENWOOD MOVEMENT. This outfit is being led by a black hearted Catholic "priest" with a white face and a blood red political philosophy. His name—NATHANIEL MACHESKY—has appeared in previous bulletins. He has been allowed to carry on his revolutionary activities here in Greenwood much too long. He will one day leave here,

165. Kathleen Feyen, interview.
166. Kate Foote Jordan, quoted in Kathleen Feyen, interview by Mark Conway, January 24, 1980.
167. Genevieve Feyen and Kathleen Feyen, interviews.
168. "A Delta Discussion—V," n.d., Archives of St. Francis Mission.

one way or another. This also applies to his negro co-leader WILLIAM WALLACE. These so-called "religious leaders" are now promoting a vicious form of economic blackmail known as a boycott. As has been the case with all revolutionary activity by these "Civil Rights" groups; they first present a list of demands to the merchants and then attempt to force them to give by destroying their business. The more they get, the more they demand. This type of economic extortion was used very successfully in the Communist takeover of Russia.[169]

That summer, night riders shot into St. Francis Church, one bullet lodging in the wooden crucifix hanging above the altar. One day, Sister Chantal was walking on the grounds of the mission and saw bullet holes in the rear window of Father Nathaniel's car. He told her that "as he was driving home 'someone' had shot several bullets into the car, not to kill him, but to give him a warning."[170] Father Peter Machesky, OFM, Nathaniel's younger brother who also was a Franciscan friar, sometimes acted as his brother's bodyguard, patrolling with a rifle outside the church while Father Nathaniel celebrated Mass inside. The friars at the mission slept more soundly after they acquired a pair of Dobermans—Holly and Heidi—who barked at anyone coming onto the mission grounds.

Eventually, the Ku Klux Klan resolved to end Father Nathaniel's agitation for equal rights by putting out a contract for his murder. Bill Virden related this account as told to him by Father Peter Machesky:

One day there was this knock on the door of the rectory. Nathaniel goes out there, he opens the door, and this White dude is out there. The guy asked him, "Is Father Nathaniel around? I need to talk to him." Nathaniel says, "You're talking to him. Why don't you come in? I'll fix you a cup of coffee." And the guy said, "No, I just needed to be sure that I knew who you were because I've been paid $10,000 by the Ku Klux Klan to kill you. Sometime in the next thirty days, when you're walking back and forth between here and the church, I'm going to kill you deader than a hammer." Nathaniel asked him again, "Why don't you come in and we can talk about it?" He came back thirty days later; knocked on the door. Nathaniel happened to open the door again. Here's this same guy, and the guy told him, "I gave the money back." He said, "You're the bravest man I ever saw. I couldn't kill you."[171]

White Catholics operating businesses targeted by the boycott vented their anger at Father Nathaniel and his fellow Franciscans. Those business owners who had supported the priests and sisters ceased making their donations.

169. "A Delta Discussion—VI," 5 June 1968, Archives of St. Francis Mission.
170. Batten, interview.
171. Virden, interview.

Malouf described the dilemma of one such irate merchant: "I remember one of the guys who owned a shoe store. A nun had come in to get some shoes, and they never did charge them for shoes. Whatever you wanted you just got . . . two weeks later the nun was wearing the shoes he gave her [while] boycotting his store. All of these guys were getting very upset."[172]

One hundred thirty-six parishioners of Immaculate Heart of Mary Church signed a petition, which they sent to the bishop, saying they no longer wanted the Franciscan friars saying Mass for them. When the Sisters of St. Joseph reported to Immaculate Heart to teach their regular Confraternity of Christian Doctrine classes for children of the parish, they found the parents had kept them at home. The boycotters were being boycotted. Sidney Harris, a Greenwood lawyer, summarized the attitudes of White Catholics toward the priest leading the boycott: "Father Nathaniel was regarded as a trouble maker *par excellence*. And everybody would say how nice we were to him when he came down and established his mission and helped him and he turned on us. He was a traitor."[173] One anonymous letter writer ranted in the *Greenwood Commonwealth* that members of Immaculate Heart parish were "outraged by the attacks against us and fellow members of our community by Fr. Nathaniel Machesky and other intruder priests and nuns from St. Francis Mission. . . . As a result of his efforts to injure or ruin innocent persons by economic strangulation, many [White] Catholics view Father Nathaniel and his street-walker nuns and priests as public sinners who have violated the commandments of God."[174]

Bishop Joseph Brunini, who succeeded Bishop Gerow in 1967, wrote to Father Walter Maloney, pastor at Immaculate Heart of Mary, expressing his "full and complete support" for Father Nathaniel in "his struggle for the social and economic rights of all people of Greenwood. . . . this is not only a personal position but I am speaking in concert with the entire body of Catholic Bishops of the United States."[175]

St. Francis parishioners encountered more hostility in May 1968 when they attended a Catholic Youth Organization (CYO) spaghetti supper in the Knights of Columbus Hall. Father James Kircher escorted two African American CYO officers to the dinner. Midway through their meal, they were ordered out of the hall by Jesse J. Quinn, the Grand Knight of the Knights of Columbus, who told them they must leave now because "I promised the Knights no 'nigger' would come into this hall."[176]

172. Malouf, interview.
173. Sidney Harris, interview by Mark Conway, January 1980.
174. Anonymous, quoted in Mark Conway, "Mills of God," 75.
175. Joseph Brunini, to Walter Maloney, May 7, 1968.
176. Jesse J. Quinn, quoted in Daniel Nowak to Joseph B. Brunini, 14 June 1968, Diocese of Jackson Archives.

Greenwood city officials and merchants probably expected the renewed boycott to sputter and collapse as previous ones had, but that did not happen. Black customers stayed out of stores with remarkable determination. So given the suffering of uptown stores and no apparent weakening of African American resolve, on May 31 the all-White city council initiated legal action to halt the boycott. City attorney Lott rounded up sixty-one business owners and filed a motion on their behalf in chancery court, seeking an injunction against the leaders of the Greenwood Movement. Lott's petition accused Father Nathaniel and eleven other individuals of "creating an atmosphere of fear and terror in Greenwood's Negro community, and to a degree in Greenwood's white community." It stated that those named had "by force, violence, coercion, threats, abusive language, intimidation and other unlawful means prevented a great portion of Greenwood citizens, mostly Negro, from doing business with complainants."[177]

Chancery Judge William H. Bizzell sided with the complainants and issued a sweeping injunction aimed at crushing the boycott. His ruling enjoined Father Nathaniel and his associates from engaging in any activity to support the selective buying campaign. Specifically forbidden were

> Picketing or marching, or persuading or inducing any other person or persons from picketing or marching in any organized fashion whatsoever, with or without signs or placards. . . . Loitering or congregating, or persuading any person or persons to loiter or congregate. . . . Stationing themselves or anyone else as a lookout or lookouts for the purpose of observing customers entering, leaving, shopping, or doing other business. . . . Making, preparing, or causing to be made or prepared a record of the names, automobile license plate numbers, or other identification of person or persons. . . . Publishing, distributing, or announcing in any manner the name or names of person or persons who have entered or traded in . . . the business establishments. . . . Threatening, intimidating, coercing, or using force or violence on any person or persons.[178]

A hearing later that month in Bizzell's courtroom gave the merchants an opportunity to present evidence supporting their allegations. A parade of fifty-two witnesses testified that the movement's backers used violence and intimidation to enforce the boycott. Elvie Orlansky, who operated a dry goods store on Carrollton Avenue, testified that pickets lined the sidewalk in front of his establishment "three and four abreast, singing and hollering." He told of seeing a Black customer thrown to the ground by two demonstrators after

---

177. A. G. Abide et al., v. Nathaniel Machesky et al., Bill of Complaint, Chancery Court of Leflore County, Mississippi, June 5, 1968.

178. A. G. Abide et al., v. Nathaniel Machesky et al., Writ of Injunction, Chancery Court of Leflore County, Mississippi, June 5, 1968.

making a purchase in his establishment.[179] Black restaurant worker Ernestine Walker told of "mysterious night visitors to her home," who warned her not to testify in court. "Baby, we've got your number," they reportedly said. Frank Gunter said that an unknown person threw a bottle through his living room window after he purchased wire screen at a hardware store being boycotted. "I don't want glass flying in my house and for fear of that I don't go downtown," he testified. Eddie Archie reported that he and his wife were confronted after shopping in a White-owned store. "How would you like for something to happen to your family?" his wife was asked. Archie said that two bottles filled with flammable liquids, either kerosene or diesel fuel, were thrown at his home.[180] The most serious allegation involved Macy Jones, an employee of the Crystal Club, who was shot in the shoulder by an unknown assailant one day after testifying in court.[181]

Jonathan Shapiro, an attorney for the Lawyers' Committee for Civil Rights Under Law, represented the defendants. He sought to refute the charges of harassment, intimidation, and violent reprisals. When the hearing resumed on June 19, Father Nathaniel was the first defense witness. He testified for three hours, explaining the reasons for the boycott, its objectives, and the group's futile efforts to meet with city officials. "I have never condoned violence," he declared. He insisted that the Greenwood Movement desired peaceful and harmonious race relations. He also stated that "great emphasis was placed on the fact that violence was wrong." The friar admitted that the names of boycott violators had been read aloud "at one or two" mass meetings but that this practice was discontinued after the attempted arson at the Archie home.[182]

In his in-depth study of the Greenwood civil rights movement, sociologist Charles M. Payne offered some support for the merchants' claim of organized harassment. He reported that "a small secret group," known as Spirit, "was organized by a young man who moved to Greenwood from Hattiesburg." Members of this group targeted "people who repeatedly violated the boycott." They "might find that when they hung laundry out to dry, somehow it got thrown to the ground when they weren't looking. When they walked down the streets with bags of groceries, someone might bump into them spilling the groceries. People might have a brick thrown through their windshields."[183]

---

179. Jane Biggers, "Greenwood Boycott 'Roughing' Is Cited," *Jackson Clarion-Ledger*, June 14, 1968.

180. Frank Long, "Witnesses Tell Court of Intimidation Here," *Greenwood Commonwealth*, June 13, 1968.

181. Jane Biggers, "Witness Tells of Being Shot After Testifying," *Jackson Clarion-Ledger*, June 18, 1968.

182. Frank Long, "Machesky First Witness as Defense Is Opened," *Greenwood Commonwealth*, June 19, 1968.

183. Payne, *Light of Freedom*, 326–27.

Payne claimed that "at least one member of the [Movement's] board of directors knew about it [Spirit] and did not strongly disapprove."[184] In a 2010 interview, Reverend Wallace provided some support for this claim: "I'm sure there were those who were outside of the Movement who probably did things we did not agree with. . . . I never knew any of them."[185] In his 1968 court testimony, Father Nathaniel acknowledged hearing mention of a "Spirit Club," but denied he was familiar or associated with it.[186] It seems that the Greenwood Movement's leaders adopted a "don't ask, don't tell" policy regarding Spirit. Although they emphasized their dedication to nonviolence in public statements, they did not try very hard to discover who was responsible for violent incidents. In this way, they maintained the fragile coalition between moderate and militant elements in the African American community.

Judge Bizzell's injunction failed to cool the boycotters' enthusiasm. Instead, it seemed to have the opposite effect. Prior to the hearing, the number of picketers had dwindled. On some days only one or two patrolled downtown streets. After the injunction, however, the Black community responded with unity. Kathleen Feyen recalled: "I remember the injunction being the best thing that ever happened to us. . . . [the injunction] put us in the courtroom, and that courtroom was packed every day of the hearings. We couldn't have got that many folk on the street if we had given away free chickens. We didn't have to picket. There wasn't anybody going in those stores after the hearings."[187] Indeed, African American shoppers continued to honor the boycott despite the injunction. On July 13, 1968, Edward Noel reported from Greenwood, "The merchants here say you could throw a grenade down Main Street and nobody would be hit. What they mean is, the Negro-inspired boycott against white merchants has just about sounded a financial knell on retail cash register bells. A white Catholic priest has this town tied up in knots."[188] Instead of mass picketing, movement supporters strolled downtown streets wearing T-shirts emblazoned with "Greenwood Movement" to remind shoppers the boycott was still in force.

As the protest dragged on, Greenwood's uptown merchants sought a way to regain their lost customers. Malouf headed the Chamber of Commerce's committee of retail merchants. His parents were Lebanese Catholics who supported Father Nathaniel and the mission. Their twenty-six-year-old son knew and liked the forty-eight-year-old friar. "I was going out in the mornings and

---

184. Payne, *Light of Freedom*, 326–27.

185. Wallace, interview.

186. Frank Long, "Machesky First Witness as Defense Is Opened," *Greenwood Commonwealth*, June 19, 1968.

187. Kathleen Feyen, interview.

188. Edward Noel, "Greenwood Main Street Empty Despite Injunction," *Jackson Daily News*, July 13, 1968.

having coffee with Nat [Father Nathaniel]," he recalled in an interview. A group of store owners approached Malouf and said, "If you're in charge of the Retail Committee, and all the stores are going broke, it's up to you to fix it." He found two other business owners willing to serve on a negotiating committee: drugstore owner James "Jimmy" Hogue and Buddy Goodman, co-owner of Kantor's department store. Malouf assured the other merchants they would not make any concessions without first gaining their approval. He then sought guidance from Lott, the city attorney and former president of the Greenwood Citizens' Council. Lott offered this brusque advice: "Don't meet. When you go into discussions you have to compromise. We have nothing to compromise. We have nothing to give—nothing."[189] Malouf ignored his counsel. The three-person team met with the Greenwood Movement's negotiating committee. "We agreed on a few things and some things we couldn't agree on," he recalled. The first demand to be settled favorably was the use of courtesy titles for African American customers. A second issue was better jobs for Black employees. "In stores that had mostly Black customers, they wanted a few Black sales people," he said. This demand also was accepted. The third demand, to hire Black police officers and firefighters, was more difficult, because only the city government could do this. The merchants sent a letter to the mayor and city council recommending that Blacks be hired for these positions. When the city refused to take any action, the boycott continued.

Father Nathaniel did not participate in these negotiations. He was sensitive to the charge that a White man was preempting leadership of a Black protest movement. Whenever possible, he asked Reverend Wallace, who was Black, to speak on behalf of the movement. However, Greenwood's Whites continued to see Father Nathaniel as the main instigator of the boycott. There was considerable justification for this belief. He was the movement's chief strategist and most articulate publicist. His editorials in the *Center Light* eloquently summarized African American grievances. Pamphlets and letters defending the boycott and setting forth the movement's objectives bore the imprint of the former English teacher. In addition, he controlled access to the St. Francis Center, which served as the Greenwood Movement's command post. Most importantly, his eighteen years of selfless service had earned him the respect of all sectors of Greenwood's Black community.

By the spring of 1969, while boycotters waited for a decision on their appeal of Judge Bizzell's injunction, attention turned to the upcoming mayoral election. Mayor Sampson announced he would seek a fourth four-year term. His opponent was Thurman Henry, a former mayor, who was employed by the wealthy Billups family. His campaign slogan, "It's time for a change," suggested his willingness to depart from Sampson's hardline policies. When asked by a

---

189. Malouf, interview.

Center Light reporter if he would hire a Black police officer, he replied, "Yes, I would hire a competent man."[190] This response marked Henry as a moderate on race issues. Sampson responded with a full-page ad in the *Commonwealth* citing his success in maintaining law and order in the face of "determined opposition . . . by revolutionary forces to create racial strife and riots."[191] On Election Day, newly registered Black voters made their preference clear. In White North Greenwood, Sampson outpolled Henry 1,157 to 950. Mostly White West Greenwood gave the incumbent a smaller margin—741 to 689. In heavily Black East Greenwood, however, Henry trounced Sampson by nearly four to one—1,444 to 295.[192] The election result—3,083 to 2,193 in favor of Henry—decisively demonstrated the power of Greenwood's Black electorate.

Father Nathaniel scheduled a meeting with the mayor-elect. Before discussing pressing business, Henry requested that they pray together. The priest interpreted this as a sign that the new city administration was willing to break with the past.[193] On August 22, just six weeks after Henry was sworn in, the *Center Light* reported that Ernest Smith was hired as Greenwood's first African American police officer.[194] Two weeks later, another Black man, Austin Stancil, joined the force.[195]

One major issue remained unresolved. For more than a year, US District Judge William C. Keady had been considering the Greenwood Movement's appeal of Judge Bizzell's injunction. Finally, on November 20, 1969, Keady issued his ruling. He overturned the lower court's injunction and instead enjoined the merchants from interfering with "the plaintiff's right peacefully . . . to picket, march, demonstrate, protest, distribute leaflets or otherwise publicize their grievances of racial discrimination and denial of equal rights." Keady did admonish the boycotters not to demonstrate on private property, block public streets or sidewalks, make any threats, use any vile or profane language, or damage others' property.[196] The Greenwood Movement celebrated Keady's order as a signal victory. Father Nathaniel penned an editorial in the *Center Light* claiming that the drawn-out legal proceedings had a worthy result: "a precedent has now been established for the whole country, that it is completely legal to conduct a boycott and to picket on public property."[197]

190. "Henry Declares Candidacy," *Center Light*, March 21, 1969.
191. Charles Sampson, advertisement, *Greenwood Commonwealth*, May 12, 1969.
192. "Thurman Henry Voted Mayor of Greenwood," *Greenwood Commonwealth*, May 14, 1969.
193. Conway, "Mills of God," 88.
194. "City Council Hires First Black Officer," *Center Light*, August 22, 1969.
195. "Second Black Policeman Hired," *Center Light*, September 5, 1969.
196. *Machesky v. Bizzell*, U.S. District Court, Northern District of Mississippi, November 20, 1969.
197. Nathanial Machesky, editorial, *Center Light*, December 12, 1969.

With the injunction no longer hanging over their heads, the Greenwood Movement's leaders announced: "As of December 10, 1969, we officially call off our present boycott." Reverend Wallace explained, "One of the purposes of the boycott was to get dialogue. . . . the present administration will listen and be responsive to the needs of the community."[198] The Greenwood Movement continued holding weekly meetings; but with no urgent concerns on the agenda, attendance dwindled. The Leflore County Voters League, headed by David Jordan, soon emerged as the voice of Greenwood's African American community.

An Unhappy Ending

Father Nathaniel continued working in Greenwood for another decade. The mission flourished, but many of the programs he had established in the 1960s ceased. The St. Francis Center remained open but with reduced effectiveness, as Kate Foote Jordan aged and Pax Christi members left Greenwood for other missions. Bessie Wilburn ran the center singlehandedly until her retirement in February 2014.[199] St. Francis School's enrollment dropped significantly when a 1968 court order integrated Greenwood's public schools beyond token levels. The Sisters of St. Joseph gradually withdrew from St. Francis School as the numbers in their congregation declined. Sister Barbara Krakora, SSJ, began teaching fourth and fifth graders in 1986. The first thing she noticed was the dilapidated condition of the school. "Everything was second-hand," she recalled. "Desks were beat-up with screws missing, loose seats, mismatched everything. Books were so outdated. . . . Anything that came to the school came from the northern states, and it was from schools who were getting new books." Despite these limitations, however, she said she "just fell in love with everything down there. I felt in my heart this was truly a Franciscan place. This is where people live simply. They make do with what they have."[200] Sister Barbara left Greenwood ten years later, the last Sister of St. Joseph to teach at St. Francis School.

Today Franciscan Sisters of Christian Charity and lay teachers staff the school. In 2018, eighty-nine African American and Hispanic students were

---

198. "Boycott Officially Called Off," *Center Light*, December 12, 1969.

199. Kate Foote Jordan died in on December 17, 1984, at the age of seventy-two. In 2019 the Pax Christi Franciscans sold the St. Francis Center to Debra and Earnest Adams, who renovated the building. In 2021 they dedicated it for use as the Greenwood Community Center. Gerard Edic, "Community Center Ready to Serve," *Greenwood Commonwealth*, April 27, 2021.

200. Barbara Krakora, in an interview with the author, July 2, 2019.

enrolled. The school's financial condition was precarious; its future was described as "year-to-year."[201]

Father Nathaniel withdrew from public life. In 1997 Malouf observed, "Nathaniel became almost a recluse. After the boycott was over he wouldn't come downtown, didn't for years."[202] His rejection by Greenwood's White Catholics was a source of pain. "It hurt," Father Nathaniel later recalled. "My goodness, I had preached to these people. I heard their confessions. I prayed with them, went to funerals of their loved ones, took part in marriages of their loved ones. It hurt like crazy. I couldn't let them know, of course."[203]

In a 2010 interview, Mark Conway, who had volunteered at the mission as a college student during the late 1970s, described Father Nathaniel as worn down by his struggle: "He was tired. He had fought a hard battle. . . . I think in the end he really felt somewhat defeated." The friar's sleep was often interrupted by nightmares. "I think he had short nights. I don't think he slept well," Conway observed.[204] Father Conrad Targonski, OFM, then a newly ordained friar who occupied a rectory bedroom across the hall from Father Nathaniel, confirmed Conway's observations in a later interview. "His evenings were plagued," he remembered. "I would hear him at night walking up and down the hallway."[205]

In 1981, Farther Nathaniel was transferred from the mission he had established to Charleston, Mississippi, a change that wounded him deeply. Health problems afflicted his final years. He suffered from diabetes and required regular insulin injections. After a series of minor strokes, he left Mississippi for the Franciscan retirement home in Burlington, Wisconsin. Pat Claramunt, Father Nathaniel's niece, reflected on his deep distress. "You know, the credit union didn't work out as well as he had hoped it would, and the co-op. . . . When someone fell down on the job or something went askance, he was disappointed," she said. "I think he was lonely. His heart was in Greenwood."[206]

Steve Biggers visited Father Nathaniel in Wisconsin shortly before the priest's 1995 death. "He was not a happy camper being there," Biggers recalled. "He was angry. They wouldn't let him smoke; they wouldn't let him drink."[207] Brother Adrian remained in Greenwood until 1998, when his own

201. John Feister, "I (Still) Have a Dream: St. Francis School," *St. Anthony Messenger*, August 2018, 42.

202. Alex Malouf, quoted in Joe Atkins, "Memory of Machesky Lives in Greenwood," *Jackson Clarion-Ledger*, September 21, 1997.

203. Tim Kalich, "Father Nathaniel's Goodbye," *Greenwood Commonwealth*, April 11, 1993.

204. Mark Conway, in an interview with the author, November 24, 2010.

205. Conrad Targonski, in an interview with the author, August 16, 2012.

206. Pat Claramunt, in an interview with the author, January 5, 2011.

207. Steve Biggers, in an interview with the author, March 29, 2012.

failing health forced him to return to Queen of Peace Friary in Wisconsin. He remained there until his death in 2002.

During the early 1960s, Father Nathaniel watched the historic struggle for African American civil rights from the sidelines. He prayed that Greenwood's Whites would do the right thing and grant Black people the rights to which they were entitled. Once he had offered a hopeful assessment, but by 1967 his optimism vanished. Father Nathaniel realized that moral suasion and peaceful protest would never win concessions from Greenwood's White establishment. He recognized that White officials would not relinquish power unless forced to do so. Although Father Nathaniel never advocated violence, he did not shy away from harnessing the power of Black consumers in their quest for equality. Years later, he reflected on his decision to lead the boycott: "You know, it was the only thing left to do. It was a question of doing what was right or leaving town."[208] Father Nathaniel did not leave town.

During a difficult and dangerous time, Father Nathaniel spoke out for racial justice and social change. He did this fully aware of the likely consequences and without regard for his personal welfare. Today Father Nathaniel's legacy continues, not only in the church and school he established, but in the courageous example he set and in the hundreds of lives he profoundly influenced. Belated recognition of his contributions to the movement for racial equality came with the opening of the Mississippi Civil Rights Museum in December 2017.[209] A panel containing a portrait of the young Father Nathaniel reads in part: "When northern friends began bringing supplies, only Father Nathaniel made his facility available for food distribution."[210]

Steve Biggers's parents were among the few Greenwood Whites who had remained on friendly terms with Father Nathaniel. Biggers was troubled when he heard people making hateful remarks about the friar. When Father Nathaniel came to his home, Biggers asked him why he was doing things that would make his friends' parents say those kinds of things. Father Nathaniel replied, "A man's not worth his salt if he doesn't stand up for what he believes in."[211]

---

208. "St. Francis of Assisi Parish—Greenwood, Mississippi," *Mississippi Today*, January 9, 1987. Reprinted in *Sandalprints*, Assumption BVM Province, October 2001.

209. Maureen Smith, "History, Civil Rights Museums Open," *Mississippi Catholic*, December 12, 2017, https://www.mississippicatholic.com/2017/12/20/history-civil-rights-museums-open/

210. Jessica O'Connor (Mississippi Department of Archives and History), personal communication to author, February 9, 2021.

211. Biggers, interview.

Chapter 2

Sister Antona Ebo: To Selma and Beyond

Prior to March 10, 1965, Sister Mary Antona Ebo, FSM, lived in relative obscurity as a nurse and medical records administrator at St. Mary's Infirmary in St. Louis, Missouri. On that date everything changed. She was one of six Catholic sisters in an ecumenical delegation from St. Louis who flew to Selma, Alabama. They answered Dr. Martin Luther King's call to come to Selma to support the drive for African American voting rights and to protest "Bloody Sunday," the brutal assault on civil rights marchers that had occurred three days earlier. As the only African American sister among the demonstrators in the streets of Selma that day, Sister Antona was asked to explain her motive for coming to Selma. She complied with these memorable words: "I am a Negro and I am very proud of being a Negro. . . . Yesterday, being a Negro, I voted, and I would like to come here to say every Negro citizen, as well as the whites, should have the right to vote and be given the right to vote. That is why I'm here today."[1]

After eight hours in Alabama, she was on her way back to St. Louis. The next day she appeared in a photo on the front page of the *New York Times.* She was inundated by requests for interviews. "The phone was ringing off the hook," she said in an interview. "I even got a call from the Vatican newspaper."[2] For the rest of her life, Sister Antona was hailed as a hero of the civil rights movement.

Early Life

Sister Antona came from very humble beginnings. She was born Elizabeth Louise Ebo in 1924 in Bloomington, Illinois. Her parents called her Betty. Her childhood was "marked by great personal tragedies, crushing poverty and viru-

---

1. Mike Bush, "A Celebration of Sister Antona Ebo," NBC NewsChannel5, YouTube video, 5:41, https://www.youtube.com/watch?v=kDfMqo1kC_8.
2. Antona Ebo, in an interview with the author, December 21, 2012.

Sr. Antona Ebo speaking in Selma, Alabama, March 10, 1965. Photo used with permission of Getty Images.

lent anti-Black racism."[3] When she was four, her mother died during pregnancy. Two years later as the Great Depression took hold, her father lost his job as a janitor at the local public library. Unable to pay the mortgage on their home or support his children, he placed Betty and her two siblings in the McLean County Home for Colored Children, where she lived "off and on from 1930 to 1942."[4]

Raised a Baptist, Sister Antona first encountered Catholicism at age nine. She and a young friend nicknamed Bish were headed downtown to pick up day-old bread from a bakery. They passed St. Mary's Church, and Bish convinced Betty to enter the church with him. He knelt and prayed at the communion rail. According to author John Feister, this encounter left a lasting impression on young Betty Ebo: "She was fascinated and felt drawn to the Blessed Sacrament." As a teen, she contracted tuberculosis and twice was confined to a sanatorium. While being treated for tuberculosis, she requested religious instruction from a visiting priest and eventually became a Catholic.[5]

---

3. Shannen Dee Williams, "Sister Antona Ebo's Lifelong Struggle Against White Supremacy, Inside and Outside the Catholic Church," *America*, November 22, 2017, https://www.americamagazine.org/faith/2017/11/22/sister-antona-ebos-lifelong-struggle-against-white-supremacy-inside-and-outside.

4. Williams, "Ebo's Lifelong Struggle."

5. John Feister, "Antona Ebo, FSM: Brave Sister of Selma," *St. Anthony Messenger*, March 2007.

After recovering from her illness, she became the first African American student to graduate from Holy Trinity High School in Bloomington.

Becoming Sister Antona

After high school, Betty wanted to be a nurse. She applied to several Catholic nursing schools, but all rejected her because of her race. Then, in 1944, she was accepted at St. Mary's Infirmary Training School in St. Louis, "the nation's first and only Black Catholic nursing school." There she was part of the US Cadet Nurse Corps, a wartime government program to expand the number of nurses. Two years later, she was accepted as a postulant by the then Sisters of St. Mary and became one of the first three African American women in this historically German nursing order. She chose the religious name Antona after a Dominican sister who had taught her algebra and geometry in high school. Although the Sisters of St. Mary was technically integrated, Sister Antona and the other African American postulants resided in a separate novitiate "to ensure segregation in the dining, training, and social interactions of the community." She felt the sting of segregation most grievously when the all-White hospital where Sister Antona worked refused to admit her terminally ill father, even though he explained that his daughter had been granted permission to care for him. Despite these repeated rebuffs, Sister Antona "refused to abandon God's call on her life or accept white supremacy as normal in the church."[6] She continued working as a nurse until 1962, when she changed jobs to become a medical records administrator after earning a degree in this field.

Going to Selma

On the evening of March 7, 1965, television viewers across the United States tuned their sets to watch *Judgment at Nuremberg*, a drama about the trial of Nazi war criminals. The ABC broadcast was interrupted by a news bulletin from Selma, Alabama, showing African American civil rights marchers being viciously attacked by state police and sheriff's deputies. The demonstrators had attempted to march to the state capital, Montgomery, to protest the death of Jimmie Lee Jackson, shot by state police at a voting rights demonstration in nearby Marion, Alabama. That evening, Martin Luther King

---

6. Williams, "Ebo's Lifelong Struggle." In September 1947, newly appointed Archbishop Joseph Ritter ordered the integration of all St. Louis parochial schools. The integration of Catholic hospitals and other institutions soon followed. "Parents Protest After St. Louis Catholic Schools Are Integrated," *St. Louis Post-Dispatch*, September 21, 1947, https://www.stltoday.com/news/archives/sept-21-1947-parents-protest-after-st-louis-catholic-schools-are-integrated/article_fedc0718-1449-56ff-9c31-50115a468059.html.

Jr. sent an urgent telegram to leaders of religious denominations, saying that he planned to complete the march from Selma to Montgomery as a "matter of conscience and in an attempt to rouse the deepest concern of the nation."[7] He urged clergy to come to Selma with members of their congregations to support his drive to help African American citizens become registered voters. In Chicago, Mathew Ahmann, executive director of the National Catholic Conference for Interracial Justice, directed his staff to call their national network of Catholic Interracial Councils and to ask each to send a contingent to Alabama in support of King's voting rights campaign.[8]

The next day, Cardinal Joseph Ritter of St. Louis began organizing a group from his archdiocese. On March 10, two DC-3 planes chartered by Charles F. Vatterott Jr., a wealthy real estate developer and cofounder of the local Catholic Interracial Council, departed the St. Louis airport for Alabama. Aboard were forty-one Catholic, Protestant, and Jewish clergy, seven lay people, and six Catholic sisters.[9]

Sister Antona had gone to bed on March 7 unaware of the events that took place in Selma. When she came to work the next morning, she said, she was shocked when her employees "told me what had happened [in Selma] on Sunday afternoon." After hearing details of the assault on the nonviolent demonstrators, she casually remarked that if she didn't have so many responsibilities at St. Mary's Infirmary, she would be "down there with those people."[10] Little did she know that, as she spoke, Cardinal Ritter was making plans to send a group from St. Louis to Selma.

On Tuesday afternoon, March 9, Sister Antona received a call from Sister Eugene Marie Smith, SSM, administrator of the infirmary and her religious superior, who asked, "How would you like to go to Selma tomorrow?" Sister Antona recalled her initial reaction as stunned silence: "One side of me said, 'I don't want to be a martyr,' but the other side said, 'Put up or shut up.'" She felt that God was calling her bluff. Recovering from her surprise, she agreed to join the group making the trip. Word of her decision spread through the hospital. A friend advised her, "Now Sister, if you go down there, you don't know the Deep South. Stay with the group and keep your mouth shut." That night, Sister Antona learned the Reverend James Reeb, a White Unitarian minister from Boston, had been severely beaten by racist thugs. She asked

---

7. Martin Luther King Jr., quoted in Cornelia F. Sexauer, "A Well-Behaved Woman Who Made History: Sister Mary Antona's Journey to Selma," *American Catholic Studies* 115, no. 4 (2004): 38.

8. See Paul T. Murray, "From the Sidelines to the Front Lines: Mathew Ahmann Leads American Catholics into the Civil Rights Movement," *Journal of the Illinois State Historical Society* 107, no. 1 (Spring 2014): 100.

9. Sexauer, "Well-Behaved Woman," 45.

10. Mary Antona Ebo, quoted in Feister, "Brave Sister of Selma."

herself, "Are you outta your mind?" She later confessed she "didn't sleep too well that night."[11]

Witness for Civil Rights

The ecumenical mission gathered before dawn at Lambert Field for the two-and-a-half-hour flight to Selma. Arriving in Alabama, they were greeted by civil rights supporters, who advised them to stick together and ignore any racist provocations. Father Maurice Ouellet, SSE, pastor of St. Elizabeth's parish in Selma, was among the crowd who met their plane. On seeing Sister Antona, he later recalled, "She was as black as black could be. I said to myself, 'Oh my God, this is going to make a difference.'"[12] Years later, Sister Antona was struck by the realization that, as the only African American woman in the group, she faced greater dangers than the others. "I was in more jeopardy than I actually thought," she recounted in an interview. "If we had been arrested, and I had been in a separate part of the jail, anything could have happened to me and nobody would have known what was going on."[13]

Sister Antona and her companions were transported to Brown Chapel AME church, headquarters for the ongoing civil rights protests. As she walked through the George Washington Carver housing project across the street from the church, a young Black girl approached her. "She took one look at me and ran to me with her arms outstretched," Sister Antona described. "She had never seen a Black nun before. I embraced her and it was the kind of affirmation you can't get anywhere else in the world."[14]

The novel sight of six women religious dressed in full habits created a minor sensation when they entered the packed Brown Chapel. Reverend Andrew Young, one of King's key lieutenants in the Southern Christian Leadership Conference (SCLC), announced, "Ladies and gentlemen, one of the great moral forces of the world just walked in the door."[15] As the sisters were ushered to a place of honor in the front of the church, they heard murmuring

---

11. Ebo, quoted in Feister, "Brave Sister of Selma." Reverend James Reeb died two days later.

12. Maurice Ouellet, quoted in *Sisters of Selma: Bearing Witness for Change*, directed by Jayasi Hart (2007; Burbank, CA: Hartfilms, 2006), DVD.

13. Ebo, interview.

14. Norman Parish, "Sister Antona Ebo: God's Work in Living Color," *Liguorian Magazine*, February 2010. Residents of the George Washington Carver housing project had encountered White Catholic sisters on many occasions. Sisters of St. Joseph from Rochester, New York, staffed St. Elizabeth's elementary school and Good Samaritan Hospital, both part of the mission operated by the Edmundite Fathers from Vermont. See Amy Koehlinger, *The New Nuns: Racial Justice and Religious Reform in the 1960s* (Cambridge, MA: Harvard University Press, 2007).

15. Andrew Young, quoted in Feister, "Brave Sister of Selma."

from the crowd: "They brought the nuns. They brought the nuns." The presence of a Black sister was even more remarkable. Reverend L. L. Anderson, a Selma pastor who was presiding that morning, said, "This is the first time in my life I am seeing a Negro nun. To see her tells me you don't have to be white to be holy."[16] Sister Antona took the seat of honor, the pastor's chair, and joined in singing hymns she remembered from her Baptist childhood. She recalled, "I was having a good ol' relaxing time until someone asked me what my name was." She realized the organizers wanted her to address the congregation. Later she recalled, "I was so scared. In St. Louis everyone had told me not to say anything. I thought, 'This is the South. I can't do this.'"[17]

As she looked out over the assembly, Sister Antona saw people with bandaged heads, casts on limbs, and missing teeth—survivors of the Bloody Sunday violence. She summoned her courage and spoke into the microphone: "I am a Negro and a Catholic nun and I am here to witness to your rights to go register and vote. Just yesterday, in the City of St. Louis, I voted without having to go through what you are going through."[18] What she did not share with her audience was the fear she felt, how she had bargained with God, and how God had called her bluff. As she sat down, the crowd rose and gave her a standing ovation. Two weeks later, Sister Antona received a letter from Father Ouellet, pastor of the Selma mission. He wrote, "What you did [coming to Selma] is not only for the people of Selma, but for every American. I feel that this is a new beginning for our country and for the church here in the United States."[19]

When the rally concluded, the assembly filed out of Brown Chapel and prepared to march to the Dallas County courthouse, where they would demand that African American residents be allowed to register to vote. Reverend Young suggested that Sister Antona and the other sisters from St. Louis should lead the procession, a position that guaranteed news photographers would capture the remarkable sight of Catholic sisters leading a civil rights protest. A federal agent advised Sister Antona to remove her glasses if she could see well enough without them. That's when she thought, "Oh God, this is going to be real trouble. We're not here to play pick-up-sticks."[20] They

---

16. L. L. Anderson, quoted in Sexauer, "Well-Behaved Woman," 49. Three days after the St. Louis delegation departed from Selma, a similar contingent from Kansas City, Missouri, arrived. This group included Sister Ann Benedict Moore, a Sister of St. Joseph of Carondelet, the second African American sister to join the Selma protest. Shannen Dee Williams, "Black Nuns and the Struggle to Desegregate Catholic America after World War I" (PhD diss., Rutgers University, 2013), 181.

17. "Sister Antona Ebo," *SSM Health Care*, October 4, 2011.

18. Mary Antona Ebo, quoted in Williams, "Ebo's Lifelong Struggle."

19. Maurice Ouellet, quoted in Sexauer, "Well-Behaved Woman," 48–50.

20. Feister, "Brave Sister of Selma," 24.

had advanced only half a block when Selma's director of public safety, Wilson Baker, announced, "There will be no march today."[21] To make sure his order was obeyed, Baker was backed by a force of three hundred helmeted state troopers and local police officers. Stalled in the middle of the street, Reverend Anderson called on the out-of-town visitors to state their reasons for coming to Selma. First to speak was Sister Antona. She repeated the message she had proclaimed earlier in Brown Chapel. The next day, the *New York Times* quoted her words in a front-page story.

Back in St. Louis

The demonstrators knelt to pray the Our Father and then returned to Brown Chapel without incident. The St. Louis party returned to their waiting planes, and by 7:00 p.m. they were back in St. Louis. They had been gone for no more than twelve hours. The next afternoon, two of the sisters who had been in Selma appeared on a local call-in radio show. The station was swamped with calls. About half of the callers approved of their mission, but the sisters discovered that many St. Louis residents opposed their participation in the Selma demonstration. One caller stated, "You have violated the code of Christianity by going down to Selma [because] there was a federal and state order not to march." Another disparaged them: "I don't have any respect for those nuns at all. I think they should stay in their chapels and churches and do their praying there."[22] In an interview, Sister Antona gave another example of the negative reaction she encountered: "We were accused of being dupes of the communists. The John Birch Society sent me a [critical] letter."[23] Disapproval also came from the Catholic hierarchy. Archbishop Thomas J. Toolen of the then Diocese of Mobile-Birmingham pointedly objected to the participation of out-of-town priests and nuns in racial demonstrations. Those who came from other areas should be at home "doing God's work," he declared. He forbade priests and religious who lived in Selma from taking part in protests or marches.[24]

Some observers saw the sisters' role in the Selma demonstrations as a catalyst for the feminist movement. Sister Antona took issue with this view:

---

21. Sexauer, "Well-Behaved Woman," 51.
22. Callers quoted in Sexauer, "Well-Behaved Woman," 54.
23. Ebo, interview.
24. Thomas J. Toolen, quoted in Donald Janson, "Catholics Firm on Role in Selma," *New York Times*, March 24, 1965. Weeks after the successful completion of the march from Selma to Montgomery, Toolen ordered Father Maurice Ouellet, who had fed and housed out-of-town demonstrators in Selma, to leave his diocese. "I want Ouellet out of Selma," Toolen wrote the head of the Edmundite order. "He is a good priest but crazy on this subject [civil rights]." Toolen, quoted in Paul T. Murray, "'The Most Righteous White Man in Selma': Father Maurice Ouellet and the Struggle for Voting Rights in Selma," *Alabama Review* 68, no. 1 (January 2015): 62.

"Maybe others may have known what the feminist movement was, but I didn't . . . not at that time. I had no idea about the feminist movement." She learned about feminism in the 1980s, but she said in an interview, "I did not see it as inclusive of Black women. . . . I don't see myself included as a feminist."[25]

In 1985, on the twentieth anniversary of Bloody Sunday, Sister Antona returned to Selma. At this occasion she received a key to the city from Mayor Joe Smitherman, who had been mayor in 1965. He expressed his surprise on meeting the diminutive sister. "We often wondered what became of that little colored lady they dressed up like a nun," he told her.[26] Selma Whites could not believe that a Black woman could be a Catholic sister.

Later Career

Sister Antona's brief trip to Selma in 1965 was the beginning of a major shift in her career path. She moved from a relatively insulated position in St. Louis to a broader national stage. In 1967 she was appointed chief administrator of her order's St. Clare's Hospital, a hundred-bed facility in Baraboo, Wisconsin. She became the first African American woman to head a US health care facility, serving in this capacity for five years. She then moved to Madison, Wisconsin, where she became executive director of the Wisconsin Conference of Catholic Hospitals and assistant director of St. Mary's Hospital.

Eager to get out of "the paper-pushing business," Sister Antona embarked on a new career as a hospital chaplain. After gaining certification in clinical pastoral education and earning a master's degree in theology of health care, she returned to St. Mary's Hospital to be its chaplain. In 1981 Bishop Joseph Brunini of the Diocese of Jackson, Mississippi, recruited her to be a chaplain at the University of Mississippi Medical Center. During six years in Mississippi, Sister Antona formed a close friendship with Sister Thea Bowman, FSPA, another pioneering Black sister then working for the Jackson diocese (see chapter four below for more on Sister Thea Bowman).[27]

Much earlier in her career in August 1968, Sister Antona was among 154 African American Catholic sisters who attended the founding gathering of the National Black Sisters' Conference (NBSC) at Mount Mercy College (now Carlow University) in Pittsburgh. For a week, the sisters discussed "their place in the burgeoning Black revolution" and strategies "to confront longstanding racism in their church." She was elected to the NBSC's first executive board

---

25. Ebo, interview.
26. Ebo, interview.
27. Ebo, interview.

and from 1979 to 1982 served as its president.[28] Sister Mary Callista Robinson, OSF, was a young sister attending that first conference. Sister Antona "was a great organizer," she remembered in an interview. "During the early years of the NBSC she helped with us with the constitution. We really appreciated her expertise in that." In addition, "She always let us know that she had a segregated novitiate. She never let go of that."[29]

In 1987, Sister Antona returned to St. Louis and was chosen to lead her congregation. She presided over the reunification of the Sisters of St. Mary and the Sisters of St. Francis of Maryville, Missouri. The reunified order chose the name Franciscan Sisters of Mary for its merged community. Sister Antona continued in that leadership position through 1991. She remained in St. Louis for the rest of her career, serving on the archdiocesan human rights commission and the Missouri Catholic Conference on Social Concerns, as well as being a pastoral associate at St. Nicholas parish.[30]

Sister Antona received many awards, including honorary degrees from six universities. In 1989, the NBSC named her the recipient of the organization's Harriet Tubman Award for being "called to be a Moses to the people." When Pope St. John Paul II toured the United States in 1995, she and Rosa Parks received Communion directly from his hand.

In 2007, Sister Antona was featured in the PBS documentary *Sisters of Selma: Bearing Witness to Change*. The program's director, Jayasri Hart, had come from India to study filmmaking at the University of Southern California. While looking for a story to illustrate how the changes begun by the Second Vatican Council had affected women religious, Hart heard about the nuns who went to Selma. She spent the next five years researching and filming *Sisters of Selma*. Hart considered Sister Antona the star of her film: "As she [Sister Antona] says, suddenly, it became important that she was Black. I think that mobilized the whole story."[31] One enthusiastic Amazon reviewer wrote, "This documentary captures for all time the compelling courage of those individuals who would burst the social or institutional restrictions of their lives to stand up for what is right."[32] Two years later, Sister Antona spoke to an audience at St. Augustine Catholic School in Washington, DC. After viewing the film, Paul A. Thomas, a Black Catholic from Maryland, commented, "To have

---

28. Williams, "Ebo's Lifelong Struggle." Williams also reports that Sister Antona's superiors at the sisters of St. Mary received the invitation to send their Black members to the initial meeting, but "they chose not to inform their eight Black members."

29. Mary Callista Robinson, in an interview with the author, June 24, 2020.

30. "Obituary: Sister Antona Ebo, FSM," *St. Louis Review*, November 17, 2017, https://www.archstl.org/obituary-sister-mary-antona-ebo-fsm-1499.

31. Jayasri Hart, quoted in Feister, "Brave Sister of Selma," 25.

32. Ed, "One of the most compelling messages for our time," Amazon, April 3, 2012, review for *Sisters of Selma*, https://www.amazon.com/sisters-Selma-Jayasri-Majumdar-Hart/dp/B000ND91ZO#customerReviews.

someone right in front of me who was actually in Selma, who put her faith in Jesus Christ to carry her through such a dangerous situation, really drives the point home for me. It's our responsibility to try and right our wrongs."[33]

By that time, Sister Antona no longer held a formal position in any organization, but she hardly could be considered retired. Her lively spirit was unquenchable. She delighted in speaking to younger audiences about her experience in Selma and encouraging their activism. In 2005 she was diagnosed with lymphoma. "My faith told me, you are in control of this," she said. "I refused to fall apart." Twelve months later, her doctor announced that her cancer was in remission.[34]

In 2014, the age of ninety, she asked a friend to drive her to nearby Ferguson, Missouri, where African Americans were protesting the police shooting of Michael Brown. There she encouraged a reporter to deeply examine the situation. "You are not here to take a superficial picture," she said. "The mistake I think many of us made in the '60s is we were taking somebody else's word for it; you have to look under the rug."[35]

Three months before her death in 2017, Sister Antona's life was celebrated in a presentation at the Missouri History Museum. Although she could not be present, the event was streamed to her apartment, where she watched with family and friends. The two-hour program included music, poetry, acting, and video interviews. Her friend and fellow parishioner, Frederick Scurloch, offered this tribute: "She lives up to what Jesus told us to do—to go into the world and show love to our brothers and sisters."[36]

Sister Antona's Legacy

News of Sister Antona's death brought an outpouring of tributes to her accomplishments and her spirited personality. St. Louis Archbishop Robert J. Carlson stated, "We will miss her living example of working for justice in the context of our Catholic faith."[37] Father Manuel Williams, CR, a close friend,

33. Paul A. Thomas, quoted in Chaz Muth, "Black Catholic Nun Discusses Her Role in 1960s Civil Rights Movement," *Catholic San Francisco*, February 20, 2009, https://issuu.com/productioncsf/docs/csf-2-20-09.

34. Mary Antona Ebo, quoted in Parish, "In Living Color," 24.

35. Mary Antona Ebo, quoted in Gloria Ross, "Beloved Civil Rights Figure Sister Mary Antona Ebo Passes at 93," *St. Louis American*, November 11, 2017, http://www.stlamerican.com/news/local_news/beloved-civil-rights-figure-sister-mary-antona-ebo-passes-at-93/article_b5037cd4-c74a-11e7-8658-dfd011b81f6a.html.

36. Frederick Scurloch, quoted in Jennifer Brinker, "Sister Antona Ebo Feted as Example of Living the Gospel Message," *St. Louis Review*, August 2, 2017, https://www.archstl.org/sister-antona-ebo-feted-as-example-of-living-the-gospel-message-1514.

37. Robert J. Carlson, quoted in "Obituary: Sister Mary Antona Ebo, FSM," *St. Louis Review*.

First African American Postulants of the Franciscan Sisters of Mary, St. Louis, 1946. Pictured from left are Sister Antona Ebo, Sister Marie Therese Townsend, Sister Hilda Brickus. Photo courtesy of Franciscan Sisters of Mary archives.

delivered the homily at Sister Antona's funeral. He began by singing lines from an African American spiritual, "Ain't Got Time to Die": "I've been too busy working for the kingdom / I ain't got time to die." He said Sister Antona "modeled that spiritual as a disciple of Jesus, working for His kingdom throughout her life. . . . She did it all with the grace that came from a heart centered on love—a vine attached to Jesus." He closed with his memory of talking with her at the fiftieth anniversary of the Selma march. He asked how it felt to be there five decades later, "knowing all that you did." She replied by gently shaking her head and saying with characteristic humility, "Oh Manny, we have so much more to do."[38]

---

38. Manuel Williams, quoted in Mary C. Weisenburger, "Sr. Mary Antona Ebo: Selma's Beacon of Hope," *Minute Meditations with Mary* (blog), January 15, 2018, https://minutemeditationswithmary.weebly.com/minute-meditations/sr-mary-antona-ebo-selmas-beacon-of-hope.

Chapter 3
Brother Booker Ashe and the House of Peace

B rother Booker Ashe, OFM Cap, was many things to many people. According to friends, colleagues, elected officials, students, celebrities, his fellow Capuchins, and guests at the inner-city mission he founded and then directed for twenty-seven years, Booker was talented and flawed; full of faith, hope, and love; gregarious and charismatic; very demanding; a positive role model; honest and loving; a modern-day Gandhi, a Black Santa Claus, a modern Friar Tuck, a Mother Theresa type, and the pope of Milwaukee; robust and portly; African American; Catholic, spiritual, and religious; theatrical and schooled in the arts; jovial, unselfish, and liked by everybody; a voice of conscience; a champion of the poor and minister to the needy; a selfless lover of humanity; deeply compassionate; able to motivate people; a good public relations man; highly effective; a chain smoker; insightful, direct, and cunning; a bridge builder; and kindly, savvy, generous, gentle, irrepressible, nationally known, sincere, honest, affable, jolly, gifted, affirming, dedicated, caring. These words, compiled by Willy Thorn, author of *Brother Booker Ashe: It's Amazing What the Lord Can Do*, document both the high regard in which he was held and the aspects of his multifaceted personality.[1]

Brother Booker was the first African American member of the Capuchin Franciscans, a religious order known for its concern for the poor. As a champion of racial justice and an advocate for the downtrodden, he made a lasting impact on the city of Milwaukee, Wisconsin, during the last decades of the twentieth century. His biography is studded with superlatives, but he was not without his flaws. Fully human, passionately committed, Brother Booker was a true disciple of St. Francis of Assisi.

Early Years

Booker Taliaferro Ashe Jr., bearing the name of the famous African American educator Booker T. Washington, was the fourth of six children born to his

---

1. Willy Thorn, *Brother Booker Ashe: It's Amazing What the Lord Can Do* (Milwaukee, WI: Marquette University Press, 2011).

family in Columbia, South Carolina, in 1932. The professional tennis star Arthur Ashe was a first cousin. His father, Booker T. Ashe Sr., was trained as a lawyer, but he became a store keeper during the Depression when he was unable to support his family with the legal profession. After World War II, Evelyn Livingston Ashe, his mother, moved with her children to Evanston, Illinois, a mostly White, middle-class Chicago suburb. She had been an elementary school teacher in South Carolina and never discussed the reason for her separation from Booker's father, who remained in South Carolina. After coming to Illinois, she worked in the Chicago restaurant operated by her son Ernest.

Growing up in Evanston, Booker was sheltered from extreme bigotry and prejudice. Although the Ashe family was not wealthy, neither were they extremely poor. As an adult, Brother Booker reflected, "I did not understand the kind of poverty that exists in the poorest of communities. I never knew what it was like to never have food in the house."[2] Booker's exuberant personality was evident at a young age. At family gatherings he eagerly recited poems he learned in his grade school classes. In high school he gravitated toward acting and public speaking.

His mother was a Catholic convert, and Booker was baptized into her faith at age sixteen. He took religion seriously and began investigating various religious orders. He sent a card to the Capuchin religious order indicating his interest in religious life. Father Flavian Blong, OFM Cap, vocation director of the Province of St. Joseph, visited the Ashe home to recruit Booker. His mother redirected the friar to find her son in a pool hall across town: "Remember, Father, it's a tough crowd and it is smoky in there," she reportedly cautioned him.[3] The priest waited patiently at the pool hall until Booker was ready to leave and then revealed his reason for coming. The Capuchins were dedicated to serving the poor, Father Blong explained. Booker was impressed that the friar had sought him out. He also found the traditional Capuchin mission of "prayer and contemplation, preaching, and physical care of the needy" attuned to his own desires.[4] However, Booker had other priorities; he was not yet ready to join a religious community.

After graduating from St. Malachy's High School in Chicago, Booker trained to become a professional actor, a career he had been dreaming about since fourth grade. He enrolled in the acting program at Chicago's prestigious Goodman Theatre. Those who knew Booker in those days envisioned a future

---

2. Michael Holt, "Brother Booker Ashe: Personality of the Year," *Milwaukee Community Journal*, March 25-April 5, 1978.

3. Flavian Blong, quoted in Timon Costello, "Brother Booker Story," cited in Perry McDonald, *House of Peace: A History* (Milwaukee, WI: Province of St. Joseph of the Capuchin Order, 2016), 65.

4. Capuchin Franciscan Province of St. Joseph, "History of the Capuchins," https://www.thecapuchins.org/who-we-are/history-of-the-capuchins.

that would lead to starring roles on Broadway. His hoped-for career as a thespian came to an abrupt end, however, when he foresaw potential conflicts, because actors sometimes are called to portray morally questionable characters. In later years he related, "I asked myself, 'If I'm ever offered a condemned part would I take it?' The answer was yes, and I decided 'This is not the place for me.'"[5]

Becoming a Capuchin

On his application to the Capuchin order in 1951, the young Booker wrote, "I like it [the order], and want to save my soul, and work for God on this earth."[6] He was accepted as a candidate, and at the age of nineteen he began his training at St. Felix Friary in Huntington, Indiana. Entering the mostly German St. Joseph's Province, he became the first Black Capuchin in the United States. He took the name Agathangelus in honor of a Capuchin martyr. His fellow friars called him Brother Aggy. (By 1967 he had returned to using his birth name, Booker, and this chapter follows that preference.) Brother Booker did not seek ordination as a priest; he preferred being a brother. "I felt my talents lay more in working with my hands than in sacramental ministry," he told an interviewer. "My intention was to do skillful things . . . in physical labor."[7] His evaluation at the end of his novice year praised Brother Booker's "cheerfulness, his respect for the priesthood, and his punctuality at religious exercises." The only negative note was "some difficulty observing the rules of silence."[8]

Brother Booker continued his training in Indiana from 1952 to 1956. There he served as secretary to Father Solanus Casey, OFM Cap, a renowned Capuchin holy man. At the time Brother Booker knew him, Father Casey was more than eighty years old. As an Irishman in a German order, he had experienced much discrimination in his religious life. Due to poor seminary grades, he was not allowed to preach or hear confessions. For most of his life he did tasks usually performed by religious brothers, not priests. Nevertheless, he gained a reputation as a mystic. According to Thorn, Father Casey "cured diseases, solved domestic problems, sorted business affairs, resolved strife and brought people to the faith through vision and works."[9] Father Casey received more than two hundred letters a day. Part of Brother Booker's job was helping

---

5. Holt, "Brother Booker Ashe."
6. Matthew Gottschalk, "Necrology: Booker T. Ashe, 1932–2000," http://www.sjp-communications.org/images/uploads/documents/nec-ashe.pdf.
7. Eugene Horn, "Work of the Lord Never Ends for Br. Booker Ashe," *Catholic Herald*, February 27, 1992.
8. Gottschalk, "Necrology."
9. Thorn, *Brother Booker Ashe*, 19.

the elderly friar keep up with this correspondence. Before leaving Indiana, Brother Booker remembered, his mentor prophesied "that I would make my solemn profession, that I would see my twenty-fifth jubilee, and that I would help to bring about a lot of changes in the province. He even told me that I would do things that no other brother had done."[10] Each of these predictions came true in Brother Booker's subsequent career.

As the first, and for several years the only, Black Capuchin in the United States, Brother Booker experienced racial prejudice and discrimination. Many students, faculty, and staff at Capuchin institutions came from rural areas of Wisconsin, Indiana, and Michigan. Most had never interacted with an African American person. A blind, elderly Capuchin once asked Brother Booker for his last name. When Booker replied that his family name was Ashe, the old priest said, "That's not German." Booker explained he was Black. The priest laughed and said, "You can't be serious. The Capuchins would never let a darkey in."[11] Brother Booker's nephew, Bob Smith, who entered the Capuchin order twenty years after his uncle, described some of the abuse his uncle endured: "He was alone. He suffered a lot. He still never complained. . . . He didn't have anybody he could go off and talk with. . . . In the seminary, think of being Black and being alone. . . . Some of your teachers were racist. You had kitchen staff that were racist. You had other students that were racist. You had people in the town that were racist." According to Smith, Brother Booker suffered all this abuse in silence.[12]

Brother Booker's Early Capuchin Career

Brother Booker professed his final vows on February 2, 1956. His next stop was St. Anthony Friary in Marathon, Wisconsin, where he trained as a receptionist and cook for three additional years. He did not enjoy cooking for the large community of friars. He wrote to his provincial superior: "I do not like cooking, and I always try to get out of this job if I can. . . . I don't like cooking now, and I know that I will never like it."[13] In later years, his fellow friars found this statement highly ironic, because Brother Booker eventually became famous for the excellent dishes he concocted and for his delight in preparing special recipes for friends and guests. In this he benefited from advice from his mother and from his brothers Ernest and Herbert, both of whom were well-known chefs.

---

10. Michael Crosby, ed., *Solanus Casey: The Official Account of a Virtuous Life* (Chestnut Ridge, NY: Crossroad Publishing Company, 2000), 119–20. Solanus Casey was declared a Servant of God in 1995. His cause for sainthood is now being investigated by the Church.

11. McDonald, *House of Peace*, 76.

12. Bob Smith, in an interview with the author, June 11, 2020.

13. Gottschalk, "Necrology."

Brother Booker was assigned to serve St. Elizabeth's Capuchin parish in Milwaukee from 1959 to 1962. Then a thriving, mostly White congregation, it soon became depleted by so-called White flight to the suburbs. Brother Booker served the parish as sacristan, porter, and cook. He was popular with young and older parishioners, and he enjoyed participating in their numerous activities and societies. St. Elizabeth's was a welcome change from the rural isolation of St. Anthony's. In the friary kitchen, he frequently called his mother to consult on recipes. His colleagues later said that they often saw him in the kitchen holding a telephone receiver in one hand and stirring a pot on the stove with a spoon in the other hand.[14]

Another change in assignment in 1962 brought Brother Booker to rural Mount Calvary, Wisconsin. There he worked as secretary to the director of vocations at the Holy Cross Friary, and then he filled the same role for the rector of the Capuchins' St. Lawrence Seminary. During his five years in this isolated setting, race relations in the United States were undergoing a profound transformation. The modern civil rights movement, begun in the 1950s, gained momentum as African Americans demanded an end to persistent inequalities, not only in the South but also in northern cities. Nonviolent demonstrations led by Martin Luther King Jr. in places like Birmingham, Alabama, as well as the 1963 March on Washington, pressured lawmakers to pass needed legislation. The 1964 Civil Rights Act mandated desegregation of public accommodations across the South. In 1965, the Voting Rights Act struck down barriers to Black voter registration.

During his time at Mount Calvary, Brother Booker began his career as a public speaker. He shared a message of racial pride and interracial understanding with audiences throughout the state of Wisconsin. In 1964 and 1965, as the civil rights movement commanded national attention, Brother Booker accepted more than a hundred speaking engagements. Many of these lectures were delivered to Catholic groups in mostly White Wisconsin towns like Appleton, Fond du Lac, Manitowoc, Oshkosh, Racine, Sun Prairie, and Tomahawk. He also spoke at larger metropolitan venues in cities like Baltimore, Detroit, and Milwaukee. In his early engagements, he addressed the racial crisis in American society, the economic and social challenges facing African Americans, Black history, Black culture, and the experience of being Black and Catholic. Titles of his lectures during this time included "Black Power: Build or Burn," "Getting to Know the Negro," "On Inner City Problems," and "Prejudice Is Everywhere." Over time, however, his message changed. Apparently he learned he could make a more positive impact by emphasizing universal goals such as love, peace, brotherhood, and Christian unity rather than by articulating Black grievances. Some lecture titles from this later period

---

14. Gottschalk, "Necrology."

Brother Booker Ashe. Photo courtesy of St. Joseph Capuchin Province Archives.

include "The Way Catholic Christians, White and Negro, Should Live Together," "On Christian Concern," and "We Are All God's Children."[15]

The combination of a timely message and a compelling delivery contributed to Brother Booker's popularity as a speaker. "He had an amazing way, during critical times, of enabling white people to bridge that gap and find common ground," said Father Michael Crosby, OFM Cap. "When Brother Booker came round and was preaching, he had the people in the palm of his hand."[16] While preaching, he drew on his theatrical training. "He was a grand communicator," recalled Father Alan Veik, OFM Cap, in an interview. "He knew how to present in a dramatic way. . . . He was very good at play acting. He read a lot of poetry. He used it in his talks."[17]

Brother Booker's friend Bishop Joseph Perry, auxiliary bishop of Chicago, observed, "He could command an audience. He was piercing and consoling. He reminded them how good they really were and how good they could be."[18] Bob Smith, Booker's nephew, heard his uncle preach many times. "I would pay to hear him preach," he declared in an interview. "When he fin-

15. Thorn, *Brother Booker Ashe*, 110.
16. Michael Crosby, quoted in Thorn, *Brother Booker Ashe*, 110.
17. Alan Veik, in an interview with the author, June 23, 2020.
18. Joseph Perry, quoted in Thorn, *Brother Booker Ashe*, 107.

ished, you wanted more, not less. He never gave same talk twice and never used notes." "His knowledge of the Gospels and his ability to apply them to daily life was remarkable," Smith continued. "He had a saying: 'Mary, barefoot, homeless, and pregnant.' He talked about the Mother of Jesus being unwed. All of a sudden, people understood the plight of people in the Black and Mexican communities."[19]

Despite the historic gains won by the civil rights movement, many African Americans remained segregated and mired in poverty. Pent-up frustrations boiled over into rioting in the Watts section of Los Angeles in 1965. Similar disturbances took place in cities across the United States during the summers of 1966 and 1967. Brother Booker felt increasingly confined as the only Black friar in the nearly all-White environment of Mount Calvary. According to Father Timon Costello, OFM Cap, Brother Booker approached the Capuchin provincial minister, Father Rupert Dorn, OFM Cap, and requested a transfer. "I feel a need to be with Black people," he said. Father Dorn granted Booker's request and sent him back to Milwaukee, thereby launching the most eventful phase of Brother Booker's career.[20]

During his time as Father Casey's secretary, Brother Booker had learned about the Capuchin soup kitchen in Detroit, which Father Casey had helped found in 1929. Unemployed workers, looking for food, would knock on the monastery's back door. "They are hungry; get them some soup and sandwiches," Father Casey urged his fellow friars. As the lines grew to two thousand people and more, the friars realized they had to do more. Working with men and women of the Secular Franciscans, they collected food from farms, baked bread, cooked soup, and served meals in the hall next to the monastery. To this day, the same Capuchin soup kitchen continues serving the poor in Detroit.[21] No doubt, Brother Booker had this example of Franciscan hospitality in mind when he returned to Milwaukee in 1967.

Capuchin Missions in Milwaukee

Capuchins had ministered to Milwaukee's African American population since the first decade of the twentieth century, when friars from St. Francis and St. Elizabeth parishes took responsibility for St. Benedict the Moor Mission.[22]

---

19. Smith, interview.

20. Costello, "Brother Booker Story," cited in Gottschalk, "Necrology."

21. Capuchin Soup Kitchen, "History," https://www.cskdetroit.org/about_us/history/.

22. For more on the early years of St. Benedict's parish, see David J. Endres, "Door to Door: The African American Apostolate of St. Benedict the Moor, Milwaukee, Wisconsin, 1908–1923," in *Many Tongues, One Faith: A History of Franciscan Parish Life in the United States* (Oceanside, CA: Academy of American Franciscan History, 2018), 126–32.

Father Stephen Eckert, OFM Cap, first pastor of St. Benedict's, enlarged the congregation by going door-to-door seeking new members. The second pastor, Father Philip Steffes, OFM Cap, established a small boarding school for African American Catholic youth. The school "commemorated Black History month in February, accentuated the role of African Americans in U.S. History, and brought in an array of accomplished African American speakers."[23] In 1931, the Capuchins opened the forty-two-bed St. Anthony Hospital for African American patients, although Whites were accepted as well. The order also operated Father Stephen's Day Camp, a summer camp for youngsters from the Hillside Housing Project, from 1953 to the early 1960s. The gentle and soft-spoken Father Matthew Gottschalk, OFM Cap, was a role model for the young seminarians who staffed the camp. According to historian Steven Avella, Father Gottschalk "was as sure as any priest of his day that racism was morally repugnant and had to be opposed."[24] He worked with other Catholic activists seeking to ameliorate the city's racial problems.

Among those Father Gottschalk mentored during the 1950s were Fathers James Groppi and Patrick Flood. Flood recalled Father Gottschalk as a "young priest with a beard down to his belly button who used to walk the streets all the time. He knew the inner city as a sociologist as well as a clergyman. He knew all the [Black] families. Everybody knew him. . . . he was really an authority on that population in Milwaukee." Father Gottschalk learned more about the cultural roots of Milwaukee's Black migrants and the emerging movement for African American rights by touring Catholic missions in the Deep South. In 1961 and again in 1963, accompanied by Flood, Groppi, and Father Austin Schlaefer, OFM, Father Gottschalk traveled to Alabama, Mississippi, and Louisiana. In 1965, the four drove to Selma, Alabama, where they joined the voting rights demonstrations. The clergymen returned north more committed to the struggle for civil rights in Milwaukee.[25]

Racial Inequality and Unrest in Milwaukee

Brother Booker arrived in Milwaukee during a time of intense racial conflict. In cities across the United States, encounters between police and African American residents escalated into widespread rioting, looting, burning, and occasional sniper fire, until these conflicts were quelled by local police or, in more serious clashes, by the intervention of the National Guard or federal troops. Depending on their political orientation, observers characterized these

23. Steven Avella, *Confidence and Crisis: A History of the Archdiocese of Milwaukee, 1959–1977* (Milwaukee: Marquette University Press, 2014), 87.
24. Avella, *Confidence and Crisis*, 110.
25. Patrick D. Jones, *The Selma of the North: Civil Rights Insurgency in Milwaukee* (Cambridge, MA: Harvard University Press, 2009), 94–96.

outbursts as riots, civil disturbances, rebellions, or insurrections. The Kerner Commission, appointed in 1967 by President Lyndon Johnson to investigate the causes of urban racial violence, reported that White racism was the underlying reason for such violence. The commission's report famously concluded that the Unites States was "moving toward two societies, one black, one white—separate and unequal."[26]

Milwaukee municipal officials were alarmed, but not surprised, when a riot erupted in their city on July 31, 1967. Indeed, they had been preparing for such an eventuality. The city's African American population was quite small during the first decades of the twentieth century, but the migration of Southern Blacks seeking industrial jobs during and after World War II swelled that number. The 1940 census counted only 8,821 Blacks residing in Milwaukee; by 1960 that number had soared to 62,458, an increase of 700 percent.[27] Racial discrimination and residential isolation confined most African Americans in the near north side district known as the "inner core." The city enjoyed the dubious distinction of being one of the most segregated cities in the United States. The intersection of Third and Walnut Streets once had been the hub of a thriving African American community. However, according to historian Patrick D. Jones, by the 1960s "the nightclubs, restaurants, movie theatres, offices, and retail stores that once flourished had deteriorated and given way to a disparate collection of bars, discount stores, small groceries, relief agencies, a Nation of Islam temple, and a growing association of vacancies."[28] The impact of segregation was compounded by years of neglect by the city's White power structure. Longtime *Milwaukee Journal* reporter Frank Aukofer wrote that Mayor Henry Maier and other political officials "were downright callous in ignoring and downplaying the problems of black Milwaukee."[29]

African American leaders and civil rights organizations protested this unequal treatment, to little avail. Val Phillips, then the lone Black member of Milwaukee's city council, repeatedly proposed an open housing ordinance, and each time it was voted down eighteen to one, with hers being the only vote in favor. In 1964, the Milwaukee United School Integration Committee (MUSIC), a coalition of religious, civil rights, and labor organizations, staged a one-day boycott of public schools to protest de facto segregation. Renewed

---

26. Kerner Commission, "Report of the National Advisory Commission on Civil Disorders" (Washington, DC: Government Printing Office, 1968), 1.

27. Campbell Gibson and Kay Jung, "Historical Census Statistics on Population Totals by Race, 1790 to 1990, and by Hispanic Origin, 1970 to 1990, for Large Cities and Other Urban Places in the United States: Table 50 Wisconsin," 113, US Census Bureau, https://www.census.gov/history/pdf/pop-twps0056102020.pdf.

28. Jones, *Selma of the North*, 143.

29. Frank Aukofer, quoted in McDonald, *House of Peace*, 4.

protests in 1966 focused on the racially restrictive membership policy of the all-White Eagles Club, to which many judges and other elected officials belonged. Nightly picketing outside the club, led by the NAACP Youth Council and its outspoken advisor, Father Groppi, then assistant pastor of St. Boniface Catholic Church, attracted limited attention. When the Youth Council switched its target and began picketing the homes of prominent Eagles Club members, throngs of hostile White counterdemonstrators turned out, hurling rocks and screaming obscenities.[30]

Concentrated poverty, ongoing discrimination, and tensions between the police and young African Americans fueled a major riot starting on the evening of July 30, 1967. Crowds began gathering in the neighborhood around Third and Walnut Streets. Soon police reported that a mob of three hundred Blacks were throwing rocks at passing motorists and breaking windows of White-owned businesses. This activity was followed by looting and arson. Accounts do not agree on a specific incident that sparked the violence, but residents reported hearing a rumor that police had beaten a Black child. "The rumor we got," recalled one African American youth, "was that police had beaten up a kid pretty bad over on Third and Walnut."[31] The disorder spread along Third Street near St. Francis Church. Father Gottschalk tried to reason with the rioters and was attacked by an irate member of the mob. Others at the scene pulled the assailant off Father Gottschalk and hustled the friar to safety.[32] Around 2:00 a.m. on July 31, a confrontation between plainclothes police officers and a Black resident armed with a shotgun resulted in the deaths of one officer and a Black bystander and the wounding of four other officers. Mayor Maier imposed a curfew; Governor Warren Knowles dispatched National Guard troops. When the rioting subsided four days later, five people were dead, one hundred were injured, 1,740 were arrested, and more than $500,000 of property damage was reported.[33]

Establishing the House of Peace

Thirty-five-year-old Brother Booker had arrived in Milwaukee at a critical time in 1967—only weeks before the rioting began. He was no longer known as Brother Agathangelus, as he had resumed using his birth name. He was assigned to St. Francis parish. The city was already a racial tinderbox, and the Capuchin parishes were at the heart of the danger zone. The Capuchin friars

30. See materials found at University of Wisconsin–Milwaukee Libraries, "March on Milwaukee," https://collections.lib.uwm.edu/digital/collection/march/search/search term/Picketing%20the%20Eagles%20Club/field/event/mode/all/conn/and/order/title.

31. Jones, *Selma of the North*, 144.

32. McDonald, *House of Peace*, 6.

33. Jones, *Selma of the North*, 148.

responded by establishing an important source of assistance for residents of the riot-torn inner core.

Father Gottschalk, then the pastor of St. Francis parish, admitted that he was "not quite sure what he [Brother Booker] was going to do when he was assigned to the parish."[34] Not long after his arrival in the city, Brother Booker participated in preliminary meetings for a community center being planned for the near north side riot zone. The as-yet unnamed agency was conceived as an extension of St. Francis parish. On New Year's Eve, 1967, the parish bulletin announced, "In the planning is an experimental extension of the parish. In the near future, a small, accessible community center will be established in an area that is comparatively remote from the more established parishes."[35] Father Gottschalk was closely involved with the center for decades to come. He understood that the center could not be successful unless a Black person was at the helm. "When we first talked about it, we didn't know who would be the director," Brother Booker later recalled. "They felt as a group it would be better if a Black person did it. In those days I was the only Black person around."[36] In retrospect, this turned out a providential choice.

After months of discussion and planning, Brother Booker and Father Wilbert Lanser, OFM Cap, associate pastor at St. Francis, located a vacant storefront on the corner of West Walnut and 19th Streets. It consisted of a large main room and two smaller rear rooms suitable for offices. They leased the building for one hundred dollars a month. Four rental apartments on the second floor housed Brother Booker and a rotating roster of other Capuchins. In 1969, another small building nearby was acquired for use as the center's library.

Although sponsored and staffed by religious personnel, the center was never intended as a base for evangelization. The Capuchins assured pastors of nearby Protestant churches that the proposed center would not be a rival storefront Catholic church. Its services would be available to all community residents regardless of religious affiliation. "We don't preach to them," Brother Booker told a reporter. "Nor are we trying to get them into the Catholic Church or any other church. We are merely concerned Christians with a mission to help people without expecting a return."[37] The Capuchin friars have continued this policy to the present day.

The center did not start with any predetermined set of objectives other than being of service to people living in the area. Before it opened, Brother

---

34. Matthew Gottschalk, quoted in Thorn, *Brother Booker Ashe*, 41.

35. Matthew Gottschalk, "A History of Caring: The House of Peace Celebrates 25 Years," *Re: Caps* 8, no. 1 (April 1993): 10.

36. Holt, "Brother Booker Ashe."

37. Joan Schaupp, "Spontaneous Racial Understanding," *Green Bay Register*, June 5, 1970, quoted in Thorn, *Brother Booker Ashe*, 55.

Booker "spent several weeks on the streets getting to know the people."[38] He stated, "If we were to work with the people we had to have knowledge of them and find out what their needs were."[39] Trained volunteers spent weeks canvassing the neighborhood, informing residents about the new center, and inquiring about their needs.

The renovated storefront at 1835 W. Walnut St. opened its doors as the House of Peace on February 25, 1968. Brother Booker explained the significance of the name: "We felt a House rather than just sort of an agency building would be better. And Peace, because of what it says, a house of friendship and love and understanding."[40] The House of Peace also became Booker's home; he lived in one of the second-floor apartments. "We felt if we really were going to be part of the community, we couldn't drive off at night," he explained. "[If we did that] we would be just like those do-gooders who go back to their safe places."[41] The House of Peace attracted hundreds of curious people from the neighborhood. Among the first services it offered were the distribution of food items and clothing. Free day-old bread, collected from local bakeries, was handed out twice a week. Clean used and new clothing from the Capuchin Closet was sold at modest prices. Now, fifty years later, these basic services continue.

An early program aiding pregnant teenage girls illustrates the House of Peace's ability to respond to community needs. One young woman coming to the center instigated the outreach. She told Brother Booker she was having a baby but did not know where to go for aid. He said, "Go out and find other gals facing the same problem and we'll get an expert to help you." She returned with fifteen other pregnant teens, and a group counseling program was born.[42] Other early services included referrals for employment, job training, educational opportunities, and assistance securing adequate housing. Friar Charles Mueller, OFM Cap, trained as an alcohol counselor so he could run an Alcoholics Anonymous group at the center.[43]

The House of Peace worked with a set of operating principles that set it apart from many traditional social welfare agencies. First, it accepted no government funding. Brother Booker believed that government assistance encouraged dependence and imposed too many arbitrary rules. The House

---

38. "Brother Booker—A Real Santa for Inner City Blacks," *Catholic Herald Citizen,* December 9, 1976, quoted in Thorn, *Brother Booker Ashe,* 47.
39. Booker Ashe, quoted in McDonald, *House of Peace,* 8.
40. Booker Ashe, quoted in Holt, "Brother Booker Ashe." Although the Vietnam War was raging at this time, the House of Peace was not involved in the anti-war movement.
41. Barbara Schmoll, "Core Library Sheds Light on Black Past," *Milwaukee Journal,* July 21, 1968.
42. Schmoll, "Core Library Sheds Light."
43. McDonald, *House of Peace,* 15.

of Peace guests, as those receiving assistance were known, did not have to fill out lengthy applications or answer embarrassing personal questions to qualify for benefits. As a result, there were few statistics to demonstrate program effectiveness. No one who showed up at the door seeking aid was turned away. Adhering to these principles meant that Brother Booker was constantly soliciting funds and could not always account for how donated dollars were spent. It also gave him flexibility that other agencies lacked. He carried a roll of bills in his pocket. When he encountered individuals or families with urgent needs, he could offer immediate financial assistance without waiting days or weeks for a government-funded agency to determine an applicant's eligibility.

Initially, the Milwaukee archdiocese contributed $1,000 per year toward the House of Peace's operating expenses; this amount declined over the years. The Capuchin St. Joseph Province was a primary source of support, especially for major capital improvements, but the ministry was expected to raise most of its own funds for ongoing operations. The first fundraising event for the House of Peace was an April 1968 concert by Father Clarence Rivers, an African American priest of the Cincinnati diocese, leading liturgist, and a pioneering composer of Black liturgical music.[44] It drew a large audience to the Marquette University High School auditorium and raised nearly $1,000. Brother Booker also mailed out fundraising appeals four or five times a year. In one letter, he stated, "Our purpose is to be a living witness of Christ's love for the poorest of the poor by living and working among them."[45] He also cultivated a network of wealthy Milwaukee residents who could be counted on to donate for special projects and emergencies. The most important of these individuals was Harry John, heir to the Miller brewing fortune, who supported several of Brother Booker's projects through the DeRance Foundation.

By the fall of 1969, the House of Peace staff had grown to nine: four Capuchins and five lay people. Their efforts were supplemented by a steady flow of volunteers, many of whom came from suburban Catholic parishes. On a normal week, twenty-five to thirty volunteers participated. During some peak periods—Thanksgiving and Christmas were especially busy times for distributing food parcels and children's gifts—the volunteer count was as high as seventy-five.[46] Brother Booker emphasized that the volunteers benefited as

---

44. Throughout his priestly career, Father Clarence Rivers worked "to bring the riches of African American religious tradition and music to the Catholic Church." St. Joseph Catholic Church (Cincinnati, OH), "The Legacy of Father Clarence Rivers," https://stjosephcincinnati.org/our-team/. See also Clarence-Rufus J. Rivers, "Freeing the Spirit: Very Personal Reflections on One Man's Search for the Spirit in Worship," *U.S. Catholic Historian* 19 (2001), 95–143.

45. Ashe, quoted in McDonald, *House of Peace*, 14.

46. McDonald, *House of Peace*, 14.

well as the guests. "The poor need us. But we also need the poor and needy for our own salvation," he often said.[47]

Brother Booker was a proud Black man who sought to engender the same pride in those he served, especially the young. "Black is beautiful" was an important message conveyed by the House of Peace. From the beginning, the House of Peace placed a strong emphasis on African American history and culture. Black American and African art hung on the walls of the building. Its Triple B Library—that is, Black Beautiful Books—occupied a prominent place at the early House of Peace. It contained seven hundred volumes, available for use by community residents, on race-related topics such as history, art, music, theater, and politics. The library was hailed as an important community resource, but it remained open for only a few years.[48]

Despite being faithful to the Church's teachings, Brother Booker criticized the Church's failure to empower African American Catholics and neglecting the needs of Black communities. Speaking at the founding meeting of the Black Catholic Clergy Caucus in 1968, he said, "The Catholic Church is in peril in the Black community unless more Black men are recruited for the priesthood, more laymen are allowed to serve as deacons, and the Black priests we have are given more power."[49] Addressing the National Catholic Education Association, he stressed the critical importance of keeping inner-city Catholic schools open. He told educators in the audience, "We are the Church of the Poor, or we are not the Church of Christ. Education is the total cure for poverty. Yet 90 percent of diocesan funds go to affluent areas. . . . Meanwhile, the largest percentage of Catholic schools closing are in the inner city. It's essentially stealing from the poor."[50]

Working with Young People

From the beginning, Brother Booker worked with the young people of the surrounding community, and he made sure the House of Peace strongly emphasized children's programming.

This emphasis was especially true of the summer months. Thorn wrote, "Brother Booker opened the House of Peace's doors wide to the neighborhood youth. It offered a constructive atmosphere; someplace to be chal-

---

47. Booker Ashe, quoted in Schmoll, "Core Library Sheds Light."
48. At some point, the Triple B Library was no longer listed among the House of Peace's resources. It may be that the library did not survive the 1973 move to 1702 W. Walnut.
49. Booker Ashe, quoted in Thorn, *Brother Booker Ashe*, 128.
50. Ashe, quoted in Thorn, *Brother Booker Ashe*, 127.

Brother Booker with students in class. Photo courtesy St. Joseph Capuchin Province Archives.

lenged, and an environment more positive than the streets. . . . He enlisted Capuchins and relatives to supervise, and hired older kids to help and clean up."[51] For many years, Booker's sister, Dorothy V. Johnson, traveled to Milwaukee from her retirement home in Delray Beach, Florida, to take over as director of the summer school.

The summer program began after the public schools closed in June and ran for seven weeks through the end of July. It offered a strong academic component with classes in reading and math but also included "a heavy emphasis on cultural enrichment."[52] Nathaniel Gillon, who volunteered to work with the children, recalled, "You had 75 kids, all in the House of Peace. All in the upper room and lower room. I had to create a learning space. You've got to do all these activities: recreation, academic, lunchroom, resting. Take them to the park."[53] Teenagers from the House of Peace youth leadership program helped supervise the youngsters. Students were selected for this program based on their leadership potential and communication skills. Participants—

---

51. Thorn, *Brother Booker Ashe*, 65.
52. Thorn, *Brother Booker Ashe*, 69.
53. Nathaniel Gillon, quoted in Thorn, *Brother Booker Ashe*, 66.

as many as fifty a year—were chosen by a panel of educators. Brother Booker arranged to pay their tuition at the Catholic Messmer High School. In return, recipients agreed to maintain a minimum 2.5 grade point average and to volunteer for fifty hours at the House of Peace during the school year. On Saturdays, young people reported to the House of Peace, where they received academic support and guidance from speakers who discussed topics such as effective study habits, applying for college financial aid, and conducting job searches. When the school year ended, they in turn provided supervision and direction for younger children enrolled in the summer enrichment program, in addition to acting as role models. A 1994 report concluded that the House of Peace summer experience "provides pride, enjoyment and self-esteem to the teens, but also exposes the teens to the difficulties and seriousness of caring for children. In this controlled environment the teens have an opportunity to understand more clearly what parenting and child care are all about."[54]

Each year the summer program culminated in an all-expense-paid trip to an out-of-state destination of cultural or historic significance. Brother Booker chose a different location each year. For the 1976 bicentennial, he took program participants to Washington, DC, where they toured the White House. Another year they went to New York, where he shepherded ninety-six young people to a Broadway performance of *The Wiz.* "There always was some element of the arts that'd be involved," Gillon reported. "In New York, the kids all went to three or four plays. They'd get dressed up, go out to the restaurants."[55] Brother Booker believed it was important to take neighborhood children out of their circumscribed environment and to expose them to some of the sites and experiences that were part of a middle-class upbringing. Brother Booker also used these trips to teach social skills such as how to dress, use tableware at a restaurant, greet others, and thank them. Smith explained, "The program taught the skills that other youth learned from parents at an early age."[56] Funding for these trips was ensured by a bequest to Brother Booker in his sister Dorothy's will.

Brother Booker's involvement with young people continued during the school year. He believed strongly in the value of a Catholic education for inner-city students, so he raised money to pay for tuition and uniforms for neighborhood children attending parochial schools. Students in need received full-tuition scholarships at Messmer High School and other Catholic secondary schools like Dominican, Marquette, and St. Joan Antida. Over its first twenty-five years, the House of Peace awarded nearly two million dollars in scholarships to students in need.[57]

---

54. Quoted in McDonald, *House of Peace*, 30.
55. Gillon, quoted in Thorn, *Brother Booker Ashe*, 69.
56. Bob Smith, email message to author, July 6, 2020.
57. Gottschalk, "History of Caring," 12.

In 1984, Brother Booker got involved in promoting Catholic education in a major way. Milwaukee's Archbishop Rembert Weakland announced that Messmer High School, the only Catholic secondary school serving the city's inner core, would close due to declining enrollment and growing financial deficits. Brother Booker was prominent among a group of alumni, parents, and community residents who formed a Save Messmer committee to keep the school open. A substantial grant from the DeRance Foundation enabled Messmer supporters to purchase the school from the diocese and rebrand it as an independent private institution. Brother Booker worked closely with Wisconsin's Governor Tommy Thompson to pass the Milwaukee Parental Choice program in the state legislature, which helped low-income families to pay the tuition at Messmer and other private schools. Smith, by then a twenty-seven-year-old Capuchin brother, took over as the school's principal and continued in this role for eight years. Later, he served as its president. In 1998, Messmer was officially recognized as an independent Catholic school by the Milwaukee archdiocese.

A New Home for the House of Peace

The planned widening of Walnut St. and resulting destruction of the original House of Peace building in 1973 forced Brother Booker to search for a new home for the center. Fortunately, a vacant grocery store across the street and down the block at 1702 W. Walnut Street was for sale. Members of the Klamit family who owned the market agreed on a purchase price of $15,000, which was provided by a grant from the DeRance Foundation. Renovating the building to bring it up to code required an additional $4,000, with much of the carpentry work done by two Capuchin brothers. The new, larger home of the House of Peace, with basement storage space and a second-story residence, was much more suitable for its expanded operations.

The refurbished building opened to the public on May 27, 1973.[58] Distribution of food items such as day-old bread and food vouchers continued in the new building, as well as the sale of gently used clothing. African art and pictures of African American leaders continued to decorate interior walls. The increased space allowed the House of Peace to serve as a meeting place for community groups including Frontiers International, Knights and Ladies of St. Peter Claver, the Heritage Chorale, Friends of the House of Peace, and the Walnut Street Gathering Club.[59] The following year, Brother Booker purchased a nearby building, which provided additional office space and temporary housing for families displaced from their homes by fire or eviction. Later,

---

58. Gottschalk, "History of Caring," 23–24.
59. Gottschalk, "History of Caring," 31–32.

it accommodated a medical clinic run by a registered nurse as well as an office for the Women, Infants, and Children (WIC) nutrition program. By 1975, a staff of eleven people was responsible for multiple social service programs. Young Capuchins rotated through the House of Peace as an important part of their formation. Other friars joined the staff for longer stints, but none stayed as long as Brother Booker.

Brother Booker, Thespian

Brother Booker never lost his love of theater. In 1975, he formed a partnership with Arlene Skwierawski, a former nun and talented music teacher at North Division High School. North Division, with a mostly Black enrollment, was considered one of Milwaukee's most "difficult" schools. "He had public school kids; kids that were poor. They were kids who were talented. He knew they needed an outlet to keep them focused on school," said Smith in an interview.[60] "He wanted the kids to shine," recounted Shirley Patterson-Bordeaux. "He wanted them to be their best. The kids knew it and they'd get mad at him. But he gave rewards too. . . . The kids loved him. They just loved him."[61]

Brother Booker and Skwierawski discovered and cultivated a wealth of talent among North Division students. Over a span of nearly twenty years, they staged a series of musicals with Brother Booker as director and producer and Skwierawski in charge of the music. Their initial production, *Purlie Victorious*, was the first Milwaukee staging of the Broadway hit. There followed a number of popular productions, including *Amen Corner*, *Don't Bother Me I Can't Cope*, *Godspell*, *Hello Dolly*, and *Two Gentlemen of Verona*. Their most acclaimed production was *The Wiz*, featuring Brother Booker in the role of the Cowardly Lion. "We were the first school to do it in Milwaukee," related Skwierawski. "We did that show three times. He was the Lion. He was phenomenal." A local television station broadcast the play in prime time.[62] It is easy to picture the rotund Brother Booker roaring and cavorting around the stage dressed in a furry lion's costume.

Brother Booker used the productions to teach the cast members discipline and presentation skills. "He was a fantastic director. He got things out of the kids nobody could get. They feared him, but respected him and loved him," said Skwierawski.[63] Proceeds from the shows funded college scholarships for the students. In 1990, Brother Booker, Skwierawski, and two others founded

---

60. Smith, interview.
61. Shirley Patterson-Bordeaux, quoted in Thorn, *Brother Booker Ashe*, 138.
62. Arlene Skwierawski, quoted in Thorn, *Brother Booker Ashe*, 142.
63. Skwierawski, quoted in Thorn, *Brother Booker Ashe*, 138.

City at Peace in the Arts (CAPITA), a nonprofit adult community theater group that produced popular shows like *West Side Story*, *Jesus Christ Superstar*, and *Fiddler on the Roof*.[64]

Thanksgiving and Christmas Celebrations

Brother Booker loved a celebration. He made sure that guests of the House of Peace, especially children, received food and presents for the holidays. At Thanksgiving in 1975, the House of Peace distributed more than thirteen hundred turkeys and baskets of food. The following year, Brother Booker gave out more than one thousand food certificates. He decided that gift certificates to local grocery stores were more appropriate because some families lacked an oven in which to cook a big bird, and others preferred food other than turkey.[65] At Christmas, Brother Booker distributed toys for children in addition to providing food for the holiday. He insisted that mothers come to the House of Peace without their children to select one new toy for each child. "He never wanted kids to see their parents begging," Patterson-Bordeaux stated.[66] He also refused to give out toy guns. If they were donated, he would accept them politely; but later, when the donor was out of sight, "he'd break them. He'd step on water guns and break them."[67] To friends and staff of the House of Peace, Brother Booker gave his homemade fudge. "He'd be going out to Sam's Club and buying marshmallows, and big blocks of fudge, and nuts," recalled Father Veik. "He'd be stewing up this fudge, all different types, boxing it up and handing it out to everybody under the sun."[68] On its first Christmas, Father Gottschalk later described, the House of Peace "helped 120 families with food and provided 160 with toys."[69] The number of families receiving Christmas gifts increased each year after that. In 1973, 1,206 families received food and clothing, and 4,000 children got toys. During Christmas 1976, 3,115 families were served; in 1978, that number rose to 3,900.[70]

Easter was the occasion for a massive Easter egg hunt. "He'd just buy cases of eggs," reported Patterson-Bordeaux. "He'd get the massive crates that held dozens of cartons within the big box. We had to dye them. Dye them all."[71]

---

64. McDonald, *House of Peace*, 73.
65. McDonald, *House of Peace*, 28.
66. Patterson-Bordeaux, quoted in Thorn, *Brother Booker Ashe*, 80.
67. Thorn, *Brother Booker Ashe*, 79.
68. Alan Veik, quoted in Thorn, *Brother Booker Ashe*, 78.
69. Gottschalk, "History of Caring," 12.
70. McDonald, *House of Peace*, 28.
71. Patterson-Bordeaux, quoted in Thorn, *Brother Booker Ashe*, 64.

Capuchin Leader

Brother Booker's energetic leadership of the House of Peace and his reputation as an articulate proponent of racial justice contributed to his growing stature in the Capuchins' St. Joseph Province. In 1970 his fellow Capuchins recognized his talents and elected him to the provincial council, an advisory board to the provincial minister and a leadership body for the province's four hundred priests and brothers. They reelected him to a second three-year term in 1973. His election as a brother, not an ordained member of the clergy, broke a longstanding tradition of placing only priests on the council. He also was selected to represent the North American Capuchin Conference at an international Capuchin gathering in Taize, France.[72]

Dealing with Disaster

In addition to the challenges of serving a high-needs population, the House of Peace staff had to cope with two major disasters. In September 1983, a fire broke out in the next-door building that housed the medical clinic. Occupants of the building, including a family of four living upstairs, escaped with minor injuries. But the fire spread, doing extensive damage to the House of Peace itself. Brother Booker launched a fundraising campaign that secured more than $400,000 in donations from friends and local organizations to renovate the spaces damaged by the fire and to build an addition onto the main building. Among the facilities added during the renovation were rooms for an emergency refuge for battered women.[73]

A second disaster hit the House of Peace in December 1994, when a flatbed truck loaded with heavy construction equipment crashed into the building. The cab of the truck went through the chapel and ended up in the social worker's office in the rear of the building. The truck driver and volunteers who were preparing Christmas gifts were injured, but none of them were seriously hurt. Brother Booker escaped unhurt, but nearly every part of the building was damaged. Toys and clothing being readied for Christmas distribution were destroyed. Community members responded with generous donations to replenish the Christmas gifts and to repair the extensively damaged building.[74] Murals were painted on the south and east sides of the building to apply a finishing touch to the restoration. One panel depicted seven local African American leaders in public service. The second panel portrayed seven other African Americans prominent in community activism. A third panel was

---

72. McDonald, *House of Peace*, 78–80.
73. McDonald, *House of Peace*, 38.
74. McDonald, *House of Peace*, 50–51.

dedicated to religious leaders, displaying portraits of Brother Booker flanked by Reverend Joseph Ellwanger, pastor of Holy Cross Lutheran church, and Reverend Ernest Glenn, pastor of Christ Presbyterian church.

New Programs Added

One of the most serious problems facing people living in poverty, in Milwaukee and elsewhere, is the unmet need for medical care. In 1990, Brother Booker took an important step to deal with this issue by reaching an agreement with the University of Wisconsin's Milwaukee College of Nursing. Dr. Sandra Underwood, a newly hired nursing professor, approached Brother Booker with a proposal to open a two-day-a-week clinic at the House of Peace. Her students would gain experience working with clients underserved by the medical profession, and guests at the House of Peace would receive medical services they could not otherwise afford. Clients who arrived at the basement offices, most of them women, received screening and education for diabetes, hypertension, high cholesterol, and other health conditions prevalent in low-income communities. As the availability of this free service became more widely known, the number of clients steadily increased; nurse practitioners saw patients four days a week. Starting in 1992, instructors from the university offered regular health education classes. Brother Booker made room for a permanent clinic, and the college of nursing provided all needed staff, equipment, and supplies.[75] Among the staff was Pang Vang, a nurse clinician and health educator, who reached out to the neighborhood's growing Hmong refugee population. The American Cancer Society operated the Loan and Gift Closet, which provided equipment and supplies for cancer patients such as wigs, walkers, shower stools, and breast prostheses. In a typical year the clinic served about 650 individuals.[76]

One of the most unusual ventures at the House of Peace was the United Parcel Service (UPS) internship program, which ran from 1994 to 1996. It was the brainchild of a retired UPS executive who felt that the company's White drivers needed sensitivity training to avoid misunderstandings when making deliveries in minority areas. Brother Booker and Father David Boyd, an Episcopal priest, put together a five-day curriculum for UPS employees that exposed them to a variety of experiences in the inner city as well as talks by Brother Booker, Father Boyd, and members of the House of Peace staff.[77]

---

75. McDonald, *House of Peace*, 45–46.
76. McDonald, *House of Peace*, 121–22.
77. McDonald, *House of Peace*, 49.

Leader of Black Catholics

Brother Booker's fame was not limited to Milwaukee or Wisconsin. He emerged as a prominent figure on the national stage through his leadership of the National Black Catholic Clergy Caucus (NBCCC). This fraternity of African American priests, brothers, and deacons had a dual mission. First, it served as a support group for Black clergy as they struggled against racism within the US Catholic Church. Second, it worked as an advocacy organization, striving to reshape the institutional Church by opening it to the needs of Black communities and expressions of Black spirituality.

Brother Booker assumed a prominent role in the NBCCC from its founding meeting, serving as its president or co-president for six years and a board member in other years. Pressure from the NBCCC and parallel organizations of Black sisters, seminarians, and lay people helped prod leaders of the Catholic Church in the United States to establish the National Office for Black Catholics (NOBC) with offices in Washington, DC. Brother Booker chaired the NOBC board for three years. Two important projects that both the NBCCC and the NOBC supported were the creation of the Institute for Black Catholic Studies at Xavier University in New Orleans and the 1987 publication of *Lead Me, Guide Me*, the Black Catholic hymnal.[78]

For many years, the House of Peace was the meeting place for Black Catholic clergy, deacons, seminarians, and sisters from the Milwaukee area. Brother Booker hosted their monthly gatherings and shared the chair duties with a Black sister. Sister Mary Callista Robinson, OSF, a member of the Little Falls, Minnesota, Franciscan community, began attending these meetings while a student at Edgewood College in Madison, Wisconsin. When she moved to Milwaukee to teach in the Harambee Community School, she continued her participation. In an interview, she reminisced that their meetings always included a meal prepared by their host: "He would call that a snack, but to us it was a meal. . . . We're talking about meat, some kind of potato or rice or beans, and dessert. A real meal."[79] As Brother Booker matured in his mission, cooking meals for large groups became a form of hospitality rather than the chore he had disliked in his early years as a Capuchin. He was known for his bread pudding, gumbo, jambalaya, and red beans and rice. Bob Smith claimed in an interview that Brother Booker never cooked a dish the same way twice and never consulted a written recipe.[80]

These gatherings fostered social bonds among Black religious men and women in addition to dealing with more serious business. According to Sister

78. *Lead Me, Guide Me* (Chicago: GIA Publications, 1987).
79. Mary Callista Robinson, in an interview with the author, June 24, 2020.
80. Smith, interview.

Brother Booker Ashe, in the kitchen. Photo courtesy of St. Joseph Capuchin Province archives.

Callista, the meetings were especially valuable for those in "formative religious life like postulants, novices, seminarians. We would be a group that would support them as they were forming to become a priest or religious in their order."[81]

Brother Booker's Later Years

A major celebration marking the twenty-fifth anniversary of the House of Peace took place in September 1993. Four hundred fifty guests, including members of Brother Booker's family and friends from around the country, attended a fundraising brunch at the Milwaukee Convention Center. Richard Artison, the African American sheriff of Milwaukee County, was the master of ceremonies. Father Gottschalk presented a history of the House of Peace with a special tribute to its founder and guiding light, Brother Booker.[82]

Unfortunately, a marked decline in Brother Booker's health followed this joyful milestone. Brother Booker had never taken good care of himself. His friends had urged him to control his weight, eat a healthy diet, and stop smok-

---

81. Robinson, interview.
82. McDonald, *House of Peace*, 43–44.

ing, but he did not comply. He worked late into the night and rose at four each morning for prayer and Mass at a Franciscan parish. His colleagues tried without success to persuade him to take a vacation. "He was so intent on looking at the needs of other people that he neglected himself," said Sister Callista.[83] "He worked himself to death," observed his nephew, Bob Smith; "He once told me that he'd rather burn out than rust out."[84]

Brother Booker suffered from high blood pressure and diabetes. A series of transient ischemic attacks (commonly known as mini-strokes) began to affect his mental functioning. "There's no question . . . we could see toward the end there was something wrong," Bob Smith recalled. "Because he was so skilled of an actor, he could sometimes fool you. We would talk among ourselves, 'What's wrong with Uncle Booker?'"[85] His brother Capuchins also noticed "some slippage" in Brother Booker's functioning by 1993. "Mail was not processed. . . . Things weren't followed up on. It became obvious that something was happening to him," said Father Veik, who at that time lived with Brother Booker at the House of Peace.[86]

Brother Booker ran the House of Peace using a family-style management system. All staff members reported directly to him, the family's head; he made all decisions of any consequence. Employees and volunteers were loyal to their leader, so none were willing or able to step in when he began to exhibit signs of impairment. Ultimately, a pending newspaper exposé threatened to make public the deteriorating state of affairs at the House of Peace. This convinced the Capuchin leadership to replace Brother Booker as director of the program he had created. When he refused to resign, the Capuchins felt they had no alternative but to remove him against his will. Father Veik turned to Brother Booker's friend, Sheriff Artison, for advice. The sheriff recommended a forcible intervention.

On September 28, 1995, Father Anthony Scannell, OFM Cap, provincial minister of the St. Joseph Province, issued a press release stating that "Brother Booker Ashe has given up his administrative duties as Director of the House of Peace."[87] A more accurate statement would have said that Brother Booker was spirited away from the House of Peace under duress. That morning, when Brother Booker climbed into his van to be driven to his regular chiropractic appointment, three of his Capuchin associates commandeered the vehicle and drove him to the St. Fidelis Friary, the order's retirement facility in Appleton, Wisconsin. According to Father Veik, it was an extremely tense encounter. Once the van was underway, "not another word was spoken by anyone in the

---

83. Mary Callista Robinson, quoted in Thorn, *Brother Booker Ashe*, 221.
84. Smith, interview.
85. Smith, interview.
86. Veik, interview.
87. Anthony Scannell, quoted in McDonald, *House of Peace*, 53.

vehicle during the two-hour drive to Appleton." When they reached their destination, one hundred miles from Milwaukee, Brother Booker protested: "You did this without talking to me. You did this without my permission. This is like the ships from Africa."[88]

Appleton was hardly an ideal location to treat Brother Booker's multiple medical problems. Bob Smith observed, "You took him totally out of the environment that he lived in forever and put him back in a place that had bad memories from his formation. You could see his health drop daily when he was up there."[89] Months later, Brother Booker was transferred to the Family House, an assisted-living facility in Milwaukee. This setting was a better situation where he could be treated by other Black people and visit with people he had served for years at the House of Peace. But Brother Booker's forced removal led to hard feelings in Milwaukee's African American community. Father Veik recalled that "the civic community never really understood that the House of Peace was connected and managed by a landlord across the lake—the province of the St. Joseph Capuchins," headquartered in Detroit.[90] Bob Smith, now a former Capuchin, agreed that in light of his uncle's serious medical problems, the decision to oust Brother Booker from leadership at the House of Peace was correct, but that the heavy-handed manner in which his dismissal was accomplished was wrong.[91]

Brother Booker's health continued to deteriorate at Family House. A serious stroke around Christmas 1996 left him paralyzed on his left side and resulted in his transfer to St. Mary's Nursing Home, where he lived during his final years. Being restricted in the nursing home was a very difficult adjustment. "He had to accept being totally ministered to," recalled Father Lloyd Thiel, OFM Cap; "it was so hard, so hard, because he was always ministering to others."[92] Brother Booker's friend Nathaniel Gillon was a frequent visitor. He described Brother Booker as a rebellious patient. "We were always doing something illegal," he said. "You're not supposed to smoke [in the nursing home]. So he'd say 'Take me out of this room so I can get a cigarette.' Or you're not supposed to eat, so he'd ask me to go get food anyway."[93]

Brother Booker Ashe died on Christmas Eve 2000 at age sixty-two. His funeral was held at St. Francis Church in Milwaukee on December 30. The Midwest was hit by a major snowstorm the night before the service. His friend Bishop Perry of Chicago drove ninety miles through unplowed roads to reach Brother Booker's final rites. He was one of three bishops in attendance. Black

88. Veik, interview.
89. Smith, interview.
90. Smith, interview.
91. Smith, interview.
92. Thorn, *Brother Booker Ashe*, 260.
93. Gillon, quoted in Thorn, *Brother Booker Ashe*, 260.

clergy and religious came from around the country. Bishop Perry remembered the funeral as "a fitting tribute for a religious brother who made his mark on so many of us."[94]

In the obituary he wrote for Brother Booker, Father Gottschalk, his Capuchin associate for more than three decades, wrote that his friend's personality had many aspects. Consequently, each person who knew Brother Booker came away with a different impression. One side that few people knew was the suffering Brother Booker, "his body bent with pain," and the friar who was "misunderstood and even rejected by some he served." Father Gottschalk extolled Brother Booker as modern example of a man who followed Jesus's admonition to "go and sell what you have and give to the poor."[95]

The House of Peace After Brother Booker

The Capuchins faced the difficult task of restructuring the House of Peace to face the future without its founder and longtime charismatic leader. Fathers Gottschalk and Veik took over as interim directors. Although the House of Peace continued to provide essential services after Brother Booker's ouster, its operation underwent significant changes. One of the administrative team's first actions was to form a task force "to discuss the relationship of the House of Peace to the province, to evaluate the House of Peace, to clarify its mission, and to consider administrative/management structure questions."[96] The task force recommended that job descriptions for all employees be formalized, that regular staff meetings be held, and that performance reviews should begin.[97] They also installed an improved recordkeeping system and implemented bookkeeping procedures. Brother Booker had seldom been able to satisfactorily account for the money he received; he often dispensed cash to people in need he encountered on the street. (This resulted in his being robbed at gunpoint on one occasion.) "Booker couldn't tell us where the money went or how it got there," Father Perry McDonald, OFM Cap, observed. This vague accounting caused problems with the Capuchin province, which was trying to keep better track of the money he received and how it was dispensed.[98] "There never was the capacity to have an audit until Brother Booker left," Father Veik agreed.[99]

In 1997, Charles "Chuck" Holton, a retired African American social worker, took over as director of the House of Peace, replacing the interim

---

94. Joseph Perry, email message to the author, June 6, 2020.
95. Matt. 19:21–22, quoted in Gottschalk, "Necrology."
96. McDonald, *House of Peace*, 93.
97. McDonald, *House of Peace*, 93.
98. Perry McDonald, in an interview with the author, April 27, 2018.
99. Veik, interview.

leadership team. He was hired with the understanding that he would serve only until a replacement could be hired. Father Gottschalk remained as spiritual director. Holton introduced drug and alcohol counseling services and a computer literacy program that linked young people and senior citizens. Charles Clausen, a lawyer and former law professor, was hired as director when Holton retired. One important program established during Clausen's tenure was the Marquette University Legal Clinic. Students from the Marquette University Law School would interview an assigned client, and then student and client met together with a practicing lawyer to discuss how to proceed with the case. Originally located at the St. Francis Friary, the program moved to the basement of the House of Peace in 2003. During 2011, it served 2,917 people.[100] As part of his push to professionalize operations at the center, Clausen also decided to end the summer enrichment program begun by Brother Booker. He believed that supervising the children pulled staff away from their normal responsibilities, making it difficult to adequately serve the adult guests. Clausen also cited the expense of the end-of-summer trips that students took as part of the program.[101]

In March 2003, Brother Mark Carrico, OFM Cap, became executive director of the House of Peace, replacing Clausen. According to Father McDonald, "Mark did not consider himself an initiator of new programs but knew his strength lay in administration."[102] He continued the staff professionalization efforts begun under Clausen. Among the features he introduced were job descriptions for all staff members, regular performance reviews, and pay raises based on salaries prevailing in the region.

Father McDonald, who served as pastoral director at the House of Peace from 1996 to 2004, identified another significant innovation: establishing a development office. As director, Brother Booker had done much of the fundraising through his personal contacts with business and political leaders and with the heads of charitable agencies and foundations. He had formed relationships with these influential individuals while serving on the boards of numerous civic organizations, including a stint as chair of the Milwaukee Commission on Human Relations. "I don't know how he managed the time with all else that commanded his presence and direction at the House of Peace," his friend Bishop Perry marveled, "but his wisdom and direction and insight were appreciated by the many social agencies that worked in the city of Milwaukee."[103] His success in winning donations from wealthy individuals led some to compare Brother Booker to Robin Hood. To fund major capital

---

100. McDonald, *House of Peace*, 120–21.
101. McDonald, *House of Peace*, 116–17.
102. McDonald, *House of Peace*, 127.
103. Perry, email.

improvements, he had depended on grants from philanthropist friends and loans from the Capuchin province. In 2005, all fundraising and public relations efforts were consolidated in the hands of professional staff people in the newly created development office.[104]

In 2015, St. Joseph's Province launched Capuchin Community Services to provide management and support services for its two programs serving Milwaukee's poor and needy: the House of Peace and St. Ben's Meals. The origins of St. Ben's Meals can be traced to Casa Maria House, founded by a Catholic Worker couple, Michael and Nettie Cullen. In 1966, they began providing a daily meal for Milwaukee's homeless. Growing numbers of hungry people soon overwhelmed the Cullens' small space. In 1970 the service moved to its present location at St. Benedict the Moor parish and adopted the name St. Ben's Community Meal. In 2016, it served hot meals six evenings a week to more than a hundred thousand individuals.[105] Another component of St. Ben's Meals is the renovated former St. Anthony Hospital building, which contains sixty housing units for formerly homeless individuals. St. Ben's Meals and the House of Peace, both financed and maintained by the Capuchin St. Joseph Province, operate in close proximity. Although they serve different populations, some sharing of resources became reasonable. Capuchin Community Services therefore provides fiscal oversight for both programs, including regular audits. The name of Capuchin Community Services also serves as a label for marketing purposes. With the word "Capuchin" in its name, a single development office raises money for both charities.[106]

Brother Booker's Legacy

After Brother Booker's death, many public figures offered tributes to his good works; government bodies passed resolutions honoring his accomplishments. A Milwaukee housing development bears his name, and the Brother Booker Ashe Lecture is delivered each year at Cardinal Stritch University. But perhaps the most fitting recognition of his life was the 2007 creation of the Brother Booker Ashe Lay Leadership Program of the Archdiocese of Milwaukee. Sister Callista, its director and Brother Booker's longtime friend, explained that the program "is designed to engage, enrich and celebrate the traditions of the church as well as the reality of being a Black Catholic from a theological, spiritual, historical, social, philosophical and psychological perspective as these impact contemporary pastoral practice and life." Graduates

---

104. McDonald, *House of Peace*, 130.
105. Colleen Jurkiewicz, "A Ministry of Presence," *St. Anthony Messenger*, October 2018, 16.
106. Veik, interview.

of the three-and-a-half-year course of studies are prepared to enter a "meaningful and effective ministry with the Black community."[107]

Though the House of Peace continues to provide crucial services to the needy population of Milwaukee's inner core, it is a much different organization from the one Brother Booker envisioned in 1968. If he were to return, he would remark on the absence of young people. The summer enrichment program for neighborhood children was discontinued in 2002; the teen leadership initiative disappeared soon afterwards. The wonderful excursions to New York, Atlanta, Washington, DC, and elsewhere are a distant memory. Today the House of Peace serves adults almost exclusively. The task of inspiring and cultivating future leaders has been left to others.

Racial uplift and interracial understanding are two other elements of Brother Booker's agenda that have receded over the decades. The Triple B Library did not survive for long; apparently other needs were more pressing. During the 1960s and 1970s, Brother Booker frequently addressed White audiences around the state, articulating African American demands for equal treatment and making the case for a Christian approach to racial justice. He initiated exchanges between city youth and their suburban counterparts to promote interracial harmony. He welcomed college students seeking a deeper understanding of the causes of urban problems. The House of Peace still brings Whites from suburban Catholic parishes into contact with inner-city residents, but their interactions are limited, with the Whites dispensing charity that is received by African Americans and Asian immigrants. African and African American art decorates both the interior and exterior of the building, but educational programs celebrating Black history and culture no longer take place. Bob Smith, who has been involved with the House of Peace since his youth, recently observed, "When the House started in '68, it was because of the effects of the riots and segregation, etcetera. The House of Peace is perfectly situated to address exactly what's going on in our country today. The only problem is that you don't have a person with the experience to reenergize what was started."[108]

Everyone who encountered Brother Booker in his prime can testify to what a dynamic and gifted individual he was—truly someone who comes along once in a lifetime. Social scientists who study movements for social change have documented numerous examples of organizations that foundered following the death of a charismatic leader like Brother Booker. The decline of the Southern Christian Leadership Conference (SCLC) after the assassina-

---

107. Mary Callista Robinson, quoted in Karen Mahoney, "Program Develops Leaders for Black Community," *Catholic Herald*, October 14, 2010, https://catholicherald.org/news/local/program-develops-leaders-for-black-community/.

108. Smith, interview.

tion of Martin Luther King is an illustrative example. After Brother Booker's departure, Capuchin administrators at the House of Peace felt they must install a bureaucratic structure to replace Brother Booker's informal, family-style management practices. Today the House of Peace continues to provide vital social services in an area with abundant pressing problems. Its durability is a testament to both Brother Booker's initial vision and the dedication of his Capuchin colleagues.

Bob Smith summarized Brother Booker's legacy as "one of Peace, Courage, Heart, Giving, Sacrifice, Fraternity, Education, and love of God and neighbor. He was a lion."[109]

---

109. Bob Smith, email message to the author, July 6, 2020.

Chapter 4

Sister Thea Bowman and Franciscan Sisters of Perpetual Adoration: Working for Racial Justice

wo hundred Catholic bishops gathered on the campus of Seton Hall University in June 1989 for the semiannual meeting of the then National Conference of Catholic Bishops. At the plenary session on the morning of June 17, the topic was evangelization among Black Catholics. For the first time in its history, this organization of mostly gray-haired, White men was addressed by an African American woman: Sister Thea Bowman, FSPA. Dressed in a colorful batik robe, she spoke from a wheelchair because of the cancer that would end her life nine months later. However, she refused to let the pain from her illness quench her indomitable spirit. Wasting no time, she began by posing a pointed question to the bishops: "What does it mean to be Black in the Church and society?" Then she sang, as she often did in her presentations. Her voice soared over audience members, who listened in awed silence to her rendition of the African American spiritual "Sometimes I Feel Like a Motherless Child."[1]

For the next thirty minutes, Sister Thea delivered an incisive discourse on the African American experience. She answered her initial query with a ringing declaration: "I come to my Church fully functioning. . . . I bring my whole history, my traditions, my experience, my culture . . . as a gift to the Church."[2] She urged the assembled bishops to accept and respect distinctive forms of Black spirituality, to train White priests so they would be comfortable interacting with their African American parishioners, to involve Black Catholics in making decisions that affect their lives, to rid the Church of paternalism, and to include Black cultural practices in the liturgy. Bishop William Houck of the Jackson, Mississippi, diocese recalled, "She was challenging the bishops to understand the different cultures and to be open to that in the

---

1. Thea Bowman, "Sister Thea Bowman Speech to U.S. Catholic Bishops," June 1989, YouTube video, 35:02, https://www.youtube.com/watch?v=uOV0nQkjuoA.
2. Thea Bowman, "Sister Thea Bowman Speech."

Church."[3] Sister Thea made a special plea to preserve Black educational institutions like Holy Child Jesus School, which she attended as a child in Canton,
Mississippi, and where she later taught. In her closing, she asked the bishops
to stand, join their hands, and sing with her. Unaccustomed to taking orders
from a woman, the bishops slowly rose to their feet, self-consciously reached
out to take the hands of the men on either side of them, and sang "We Shall
Overcome," the anthem of the civil rights movement.

Franciscan Sisters of Perpetual Adoration

Franciscan Sisters of Perpetual Adoration (FSPAs) taught Sister Thea
(then Bertha Bowman) at Holy Child Jesus School in Canton. At the age of
fifteen, she left her home and family and traveled to La Crosse, Wisconsin,
where she became the first African American member of this religious community. Because both the school and the order were essential to who Thea
Bowman became, they merit extensive discussion here.

The FSPA founders, six Bavarian women, came to the United States a
century earlier, first settling in Milwaukee, Wisconsin. They planned to minister to German immigrants by "educating children, caring for the disadvantaged, and, when possible, establishing perpetual adoration of the Blessed
Sacrament." The sisters opened an orphanage in Milwaukee, but during their
early years, they spent most of their energies cooking and cleaning for priests
and seminarians at the diocesan seminary. They were called "seminary maids,"
and at times they were ordered to gather crops in the fields.[4] They felt overwhelmed by the physical labor and found themselves unable to develop a truly
religious life. In 1864, they moved their motherhouse to Jefferson, Wisconsin.
In this locale they were able to teach in rural Catholic schools, which they
considered a much more satisfactory arrangement. Seven years later, they
moved again, this time to the newly established Diocese of La Crosse on the
banks of the Mississippi River. There, on August 1, 1878, the sisters began
their adoration of the Blessed Sacrament, a devotion they have continued
twenty-four hours a day without interruption for more than 140 years.[5]

Education at the elementary and secondary levels has been the FSPAs'
primary mission for much of their history. At their peak membership in the
1960s, they staffed ninety elementary schools and twenty high schools. Most

3. William Houck, quoted in Charlene Smith and John Feister, *Thea's Song* (Maryknoll, NY: Orbis Books, 2009), 263.

4. M. Mileta Ludwig, *A Chapter of Franciscan History: The Sisters of the Third Order
of St. Francis of Perpetual Adoration, 1849–1949* (New York: Bookman Associates, 1950),
103–29.

5. Franciscan Sisters of Perpetual Adoration, "FSPA History," https://www.fspa.org/
content/about/history.

were located in the Midwest, with some in western states. In 1883, the sisters entered the nursing field, founding St. Francis Hospital in La Crosse, and opening an affiliated nursing school. To train sisters as teachers, the FSPAs established St. Rose Normal School in La Crosse in 1890. Over the years, it evolved into present-day Viterbo University. The sisters have also done missionary work in China, Guam, El Salvador, and Zimbabwe.[6]

Mission to the Chippewa People

The FSPAs entered the domestic missionary field in 1883 when they began educating members of the Chippewa tribe living on the shores of Lake Superior in remote northern Wisconsin. On March 28, after a harrowing bobsled trip over the frozen waters of Chequamegon Bay, Sisters Cunigunda Urbany, FSPA, and Emmanuela Klaus, FSPA, arrived at Odanah, a small settlement on the Bad River reservation. There they established St. Mary's Indian School to educate young Native American people.[7]

The order's historian reported that many Native Americans "gathered around [the newly arrived sisters], ostensibly to help, but really to stare." That first meeting was awkward for both the sisters and the Native Americans, "since the former could not speak Chippewa and many of the latter knew little or no English." The sisters' residence, recently built by the men of the tribe, was "an unplastered log house with a kitchen, a living room, a small chapel, and a large classroom on the first floor and with two dormitories on the second." Because the Native American population was scattered across the 125,000-acre reservation, the school was, of necessity, a boarding institution. When Sister Emmanuela began the first day of school on April 3, twenty-five students showed up for classes; that number soon increased to forty. Sister Cunigunda instructed older girls in cooking and "household arts."[8]

Living conditions in northern Wisconsin at the time were primitive. The nearest store was fourteen miles away, accessible only by canoe or a narrow trail through the forest. The sisters' food consisted mostly of game, smoked fish, and produce donated by their pupils' parents. The harsh environment—heavy snow in the winter, frequent flooding in the spring, and high humidity during the short summer season—took its toll on the sisters' health. Sister Mechtild Schuler, FSPA, who replaced Sister Emmanuela, died after just one year in Odanah. Twenty-year-old Sister Thaddea Hageman, FSPA, who came to assist Sister Cunigunda, contracted pneumonia and died in December 1886.[9]

---

6. Franciscan Sisters of Perpetual Adoration, "FSPA History."
7. Ludwig, *Chapter of Franciscan History*, 238.
8. Ludwig, *Chapter of Franciscan History*, 238–39.
9. Ludwig, *Chapter of Franciscan History*, 239–41.

Katherine Drexel, the Philadelphia Catholic heiress (now St. Katherine), visited St. Mary's Indian School in 1888. It created such a favorable impression that she donated $8,000, which enabled the sisters to purchase the vacant school building of a former Presbyterian mission. Three years later, she contributed another $5,000 to construct an annex that nearly doubled the school's capacity.[10] Mother Drexel later founded the Sisters of the Blessed Sacrament to do missionary work among Native Americans and African Americans.

By 1949, thanks to an improved standard of living and better transportation, St. Mary's was almost entirely a day school. Of the 250 students enrolled, only twenty were boarders. In 1968, the FSPAs turned control of the school over to the Chippewa tribe. St. Mary's closed the following year.[11]

Holy Child Jesus Mission

As the FSPAs wound down their work among the Chippewa people, they embarked on another equally challenging mission project among African Americans in Mississippi. In 1946, Bishop Richard O. Gerow of the Diocese of Natchez invited the Missionary Servants of the Most Holy Trinity (Trinity Missionaries) to establish a mission in Canton, a town of eight thousand people located twenty-five miles north of Jackson. The Trinity Missionaries are an order dedicated to spreading the Gospel among poor and marginalized communities. Like all of Mississippi at that time, Canton was rigidly segregated. Many of its African American residents lived in abject poverty. It had one Catholic church, but African Americans were not welcome there.

Father Andrew Lawrence, MSSST, searched for a property suitable for a mission to Black people, but he soon learned that Whites in Canton were reluctant to sell land to create a Catholic church serving African Americans. Eventually, he purchased an undeveloped three-acre swampy parcel known as Frog Hollow. "It was not an ideal spot," Father Gilbert Hay, MSSST, conceded, "but it was the only one available, and we feel with proper planning, grading, and landscaping, much can be done with it."[12] Father Justin Furman, MSSST, the first pastor of what was named Holy Child Jesus Mission, salvaged two surplus barracks from a decommissioned Army Air Corps base and had them reassembled on this site. One building served as a combination church and clinic, the other as a school. An existing house on the property was con-

---

10. Ludwig, *Chapter of Franciscan History*, 243–44.

11. Grace McDonald, *A Chapter of Franciscan History, Volume II: The Sisters of the Third Order of Saint Francis of Perpetual Adoration, 1949–1989* (La Crosse, Wisconsin: St. Rose Convent, 2010), 388.

12. Gilbert Hay, "A Brief History of Holy Child Jesus Mission at Canton Mississippi," talk given at a Chancery Meeting, 1948, Franciscan Sisters of Perpetual Adoration Archives, La Crosse, WI, hereafter cited as FSPA Archives.

verted to serve as a convent for two sisters from the Missionary Servants of the Most Blessed Trinity who assisted Father Furman. Sister Marie Jean, MSBT, began doing home visits, distributing food and clothing to the poor, and dispensing medicine from the small clinic. Sister Francis Marie, MSBT, taught eighteen children in a kindergarten class. The following year, Sisters Noreen, MSBT, and Marie Vincent, MSBT, replaced Sister Francis Marie and expanded the school to include first and second grades.[13]

Because the sisters were not trained educators, Father Lawrence searched for an order of teaching sisters to take over Holy Child Jesus School. In May 1942, he had presented an illustrated lecture about the Missionary Servants' missionary work in the South at the FSPAs' St. Rose motherhouse. In subsequent years, he corresponded with the order's mother superior, expressing his hope that her order "would accept charge of a school in one of the centers served by his community."[14]

In December 1946, Mother Rose Kreibich, FSPA, stopped to visit the Canton school on her way to inspect the FSPA's mission in China. She met with Father Lawrence and promised to send FSPA sisters to staff Holy Child Jesus School as soon as possible. Eight months later, he wrote Mother Kreibich, pleading with her for "definite assurance that we may expect three or four of your own sisters this coming year to teach at Holy Child Jesus Mission." Father Hay, newly installed as pastor of the mission, explained the specific need: "We now have a two-room school, one room of which is being used as a kindergarten, the other as a combined first and second grade." The Missionary Servants of the Most Blessed Trinity taught fifty-eight students, but Father Hay pointed out, "Their assignment is only a temporary one to help us get started." He acknowledged the "opposition to the Church and her teachings in this part of the country" but promised that the sisters would "like working with our children here. They are eager and affectionate, and religious at heart."[15]

In early 1948, Mother Kreibich finalized plans to send four FSPAs to Mississippi. Sister Vita Berger, FSPA, became the principal and was to teach grades five and six; Sister Vincenza Naumann, FSPA, would teach grades three and four; Sister Judith Quinn, FSPA, would teach grades one and two. Sister Genedine Melder, FSPA, a registered nurse, was to serve as cook and housekeeper for the convent in addition to operating the dispensary. Mother Kreibich realized that Mississippi's high rate of infant mortality and limited medical facilities for African Americans made health care as much of a priority as education.[16]

---

13. No surnames could be found in the archives for these women religious.
14. Andrew Lawrence, quoted in Ludwig, *Chapter of Franciscan History*, 254.
15. Gilbert Hay, quoted in Ludwig, *Chapter of Franciscan History*, 255.
16. Ludwig, *Chapter of Franciscan History*, 255.

Mother Albertine Semsch, FSPA, and Sister Regina Koehler, FSPA, rode the overnight Panama Limited train to Mississippi in May 1948. Their objective was to make final arrangements for the FSPAs who were to staff Holy Child Jesus School later that summer. When they stepped off the train at Canton's Illinois Central station, they encountered conditions unlike any they had previously experienced. Canton was the county seat of Madison County, where seventy-eight percent of the population was African American. The homes the sisters passed on their way to the mission exposed the wide divide between Blacks and Whites. Those occupied by White families were, for the most part, well maintained and neatly painted with carefully tended lawns and flower gardens. African American homes, in many cases, were later described as "dilapidated shacks" of one or two rooms crowded together on small lots and "occupied by six, eight, or more people." The walls and floors of these crude structures had cracks "through which the wind can blow." Most Black adults, many of them day laborers and former sharecroppers, had little formal education. Public schools for African Americans were ill equipped and overcrowded, and they had a shortened school year because students were excused from classes when planters needed them to help cultivate and harvest cotton. The need for better educational opportunities for African American youth in this community was undeniable.[17]

Facing Many Challenges

Living and working in the Deep South required the sisters from Wisconsin to make many adjustments. First, they faced the inescapable heat. The sisters sweated profusely as they toiled in non-air-conditioned buildings wearing their floor-length habits and stiffly starched wimples. Sister Mary Avila Wittig, FSPA, described her first day in Mississippi: "Sister Maureen took me outside [the convent] and explained about the buildings and the area around [the school]. We stood in the hot, hot sun. I thought my brains would fry."[18] The sister housekeeper had to do several loads of sweat-soaked laundry each day to keep the sisters' white summer habits fresh and clean. Sister Theone Beres, FSPA, assisted Sister Enrico Pudenz, FSPA, with selling used clothing shipped from the North. The garments were kept in a stifling storage shed known as the Emporium, one of the mission's most popular features. Catholic congregations in the North sent regular shipments of donated clothing, which the sisters inspected and sorted. Only clean garments free of holes and tears were

---

17. "An Account Gleaned from Mother Assistant's Diary and from Her Talks to Various Groups," *Sisters' Newsletter*, June 1948, FSPA Archives.
18. Mary Avila Wittig, group interview with Canton (MS) FSPAs, 7 May 2004, FSPA Archives.

offered for sale. Prices were set low out of consideration for the limited incomes of most African American families. Funds realized from clothing sales helped support the mission. Mothers could clothe all their children for only two or three dollars. Sister Theone remembered, "I used to perspire so much that the perspiration would run off my face," soaking the paper she used to wrap bundles of secondhand clothes.[19]

Another difficulty the sisters faced was interpreting the thick Southern drawls of Canton residents and Holy Child students. Sister Rita Mae Fischer, FSPA, who came to Canton in 1961, recalled listening to youngsters on the playground on her first day. "I couldn't understand a word they were saying," she said in an interview. "I thought, 'How am I ever going to teach these children?'"[20] Sister Sarah Wiesneske, FSPA, related an incident when a young girl inquired of her, "Tammy got?" Puzzled, she asked the student to repeat her question. After several repetitions, she finally grasped that the child was asking, "What time you got?"[21] A challenge all the sisters shared was teaching the children to speak what they considered standard English. Students would say, "I be's tired" or "I be's here tomorrow," Sister Theone recalled. Through frequent drill, the young people learned to use the sisters' standard English in their schoolwork.[22]

The sisters also had to learn new meanings for seemingly familiar words. A woman from the neighborhood once asked Sister Delberta Schmitz, FSPA, if the used clothing store was "going to be open this evening." Sister Delberta answered, "No, but it will be open this afternoon." From the woman's puzzled expression, Sister Delberta realized a communication problem existed. She rephrased her reply: "It will be open at 1 o'clock," she said. "Oh, then it will be open this evening," the woman deduced.[23] Sister Theone once heard a neighborhood woman remark about an elderly friend, "She'll be passin' soon." "I looked to the right and to the left to see if anyone was coming, but I never could see anyone coming," sister said. Finally, she grasped that the expression meant that someone was dying.[24]

A more serious challenge the sisters faced was the wide range of abilities among their students. If a pupil recently transferred from public school, she might be placed in fourth grade by age, but she might be reading at only a first-grade level. One of the first FSPAs in Canton observed, "Some [students] who are already ten or twelve cannot write their names."[25] Sister Sarah remem-

---

19. Theone Beres, "Recollections of My Experiences While Working in Canton, Mississippi," n.d., FSPA Archives.
20. Rita Mae Fischer, in an interview with the author, April 29, 2019.
21. Sarah Wiesneske, group interview with Canton FSPAs, FSPA Archives.
22. Beres, "Recollections."
23. Delberta Schmitz, group interview with Canton FSPAs, FSPA Archives.
24. Beres, "Recollections."
25. "Account Gleaned," FSPA Archives.

bered, "I really taught all the grades from primer to fifth because they were at so many different levels."[26] The sisters compensated for their students' poor preparation with extra effort and individual attention. Sister Dorothy Peiper, FSPA, explained, "We were with the children from the time they got there until they left. There were no substitutes for playground duty, lunchroom duty. I remember working a lot on projects to help the children learn in areas that they were deficient in, such as math."[27]

Encounters with Segregation

Perhaps the sisters' most difficult adjustment was learning to live in a segregated society, where encounters with racism were routine experiences. In July 1948, the first FSPAs in Canton went shopping in Jackson, Mississippi, where they discovered "two drinking fountains about a foot and a half apart along a wall with the word COLORED in bold print aside of one and WHITES next to the other." In a letter to sisters back in Wisconsin, they added, "Undoubtedly, there are many similar regulations."[28] As long as they remained on the grounds of the mission, they could safely ignore most restrictions of the Jim Crow code. When they ventured into the surrounding community, however, they had to be on their guard.

The sisters saw firsthand how racism perpetuates inequality. Sister Theone visited elderly people and young mothers in their homes, where she regularly observed the unhealthy conditions endured by residents in the dilapidated rental houses. "The walls were not painted or papered," she reported. "Sometimes when one looked at the wall, grass could be seen through the holes. Many times the roof leaked and sometimes the people would chop a hole in the floor to let the water run through." Despite these miserable conditions, she said, the White owners "did charge quite a bit of rent for these homes." "If the renter did not pay the rent . . . on the first day of the month, they were immediately evicted."[29] At one home, a concerned mother who had no phone asked Sister Theone to call a White doctor about her sick baby. Sister Theone returned to the convent and placed a call to the doctor's office. "I started out by saying that Mrs. ___ wanted . . ." she related. The physician did not let her complete the sentence. He angrily interrupted: "We don't call those niggers by the name of Mrs. They aren't worth it and I won't stand for it." Sister Theone later commented, "I never have heard anyone that angry

26. Wiesneske, group interview with Canton FSPAs, FSPA Archives.

27. Dorothy Peiper, group interview with Canton FSPAs, FSPA Archives.

28. Your Sunkist Missionaries, letter to Reverend Mother, 19 July 1948, FSPA Archives.

29. Beres, "Recollections."

over the phone before or since. I just felt as though there were sparks of fire coming over that telephone line."[30]

Because health problems were so prevalent and health care was not readily available for African Americans, Sister Theone began teaching community members how to care for sick family members in their homes. She started with a group of older women. Then she opened a class for girls from Holy Child Jesus School and a second class for public school girls. "I sometimes took the girls with me to give them practical experience in giving baths, cleaning a room, cooking breakfast, feeding patients, taking temperatures, noting symptoms of the patient, and noting important facts in case a doctor had to be called," she explained. Her classes proved so popular that she offered one in the evening for working women and another for boys who asked to be included.[31]

The teaching sisters were appalled by the deplorable conditions in Madison County's schools for people of color. Sister Mary Walter Heires, FSPA, reported visiting an African American school in an "old abandoned church" in the country, where "the children had to sit on the floor and write on the seat of the benches for a desk." At another rural school, instead of a blackboard, "the walls were painted black so the children can write on them." She recalled that a teacher at a city school told her, "If all the students come on any one day there would never be enough desks." If that happened, some students would have to sit on the floor.[32]

Sister Mary Walter taught English and soon needed additional books for her pupils' book reports. She related, "I went to the public library to check out as many books as I could conveniently carry. These were the days of segregation and it was daring for me to take books and slip them to our students." On one of her visits, the White librarian suggested, "Here is a book I think your boys will like." Sister Mary Walter realized the sympathetic woman knew that she was borrowing the books for her African American students. Sister Mary Walter grew bolder, asking if she could bring her students to the library "to show them a real card catalog and how it was used." The librarian forwarded this request to the public school board, which was in charge of the public library. She soon heard back from the board president, who sternly warned, "In the South we have some traditions and we would close this library if a Black person stepped across the sill." However, in a small concession, the board did allow Sister Mary Walter to continue checking out books for her students. Eventually, Holy Child Jesus School opened its own library with books donated by northern support-

30. Beres, "Recollections."
31. Beres, "Recollections."
32. Mary Walter Heires, "Memories of Canton, MS," speech, Catholic Schools Week, n.d., FSPA Archives.

ers. For many years, the school's library was the only place in Madison County where Black children could borrow books.[33]

Not only public institutions were segregated. Catholic churches in Mississippi also were restricted by race. Years before Holy Child Jesus Mission opened, Sacred Heart parish was established to minister to White Catholics. Although Church doctrine maintained that worship services must be open to all believers, this mandate was widely ignored in the Deep South. At best, a back pew was reserved for worshippers who were Black. In Canton, Black Catholics were forbidden to set foot in Sacred Heart church. On one occasion, the FSPAs brought a group of Holy Child students to the church to attend the funeral Mass for a local merchant who had befriended the sisters and treated African American customers with respect. White Sacred Heart parishioners allowed the sisters to enter but refused to permit their students inside the church. "We sisters did get up and leave with them, feeling it was not a very good example of Christianity, much less Catholicity," Sister Theone reported.[34]

Once in a great while, the sisters were able to overcome or circumvent Jim Crow barriers. One day in August, before classes began, Sister Vita and Sister Mary Walter visited the Mississippi Department of Education's Canton office to pick up books to use in math classes. Black schools routinely received used textbooks in poor condition that the White schools had discarded. When Sister Vita was offered the used texts, she confronted the superintendent: "How can we train the children to take care of books when they are dirty, torn and scribbled over?" Later that day, the superintendent appeared unannounced at Holy Child Jesus School. "He asked to see our books from previous years," Sister Mary Walter recalled. "He handled them—last year's algebra texts. Not a mark in them—used but clean. He said, 'I'll see what I can do.' Before school started, our new books arrived."[35]

Despite their white skin, the FSPAs in Canton sometimes experienced discrimination because they were northerners and Catholic. Sister Ruth Winnike, FSPA, described going to register to vote at the Madison County courthouse. The registrar asked her, "Why don't you damn Yankees stay up North and take care of your own backyard?"[36] Sister Mary Avila reported a similar encounter took place when she tried to register. When she and other sisters walked into the registrar's office, he opened a desk drawer containing several pistols. Once the sisters told him they had come to register to vote, he angrily slammed the drawer shut and announced, "We're finished for the day."[37]

33. Heires, "Memories of Canton, MS," FSPA Archives.
34. Beres, "Recollections."
35. Heires, "Memories of Canton, MS," FSPA Archives.
36. Ruth Winnike, group interview with Canton FSPAs, FSPA Archives.
37. Wittig, group interview with Canton FSPAs, FSPA Archives.

A Twofold Mission

Many of the FSPAs sent to Canton had volunteered for this demanding mission. Sister Mary Walter remembered that she "really had to work" to be assigned to Holy Child Jesus School. "I kept asking Mother Rose," she said, and Mother Kreibich eventually gave in.[38] Few of the sisters had any previous contact with African Americans; and some, no doubt, harbored prevalent racial prejudices and stereotypes of their own. Before leaving for Canton, colleagues warned Sister Sarah, "You are really going to have problems with the odor of the Black people. You won't be able to take it." After a few weeks at Holy Child, she realized, "Black people's body odor is not any different than ours."[39] Living in close proximity to African American families and interacting with African American youth on a daily basis soon put many biased beliefs to rest.

What motivated these religious women to exchange familiar surroundings in the Midwest for life in a poverty-stricken African American community? To be sure, the sisters' primary reason for going to Mississippi was winning souls for Christ. They prayed, as Mother Semsch did, that by providing a Catholic education to African American youngsters they could "lead them to Him who suffered and died for them as well as for us." However, this was not their only motive. Mother Semsch also stated in a later account that the sisters were expected to aim to improve "the social and economic conditions of these poor people in order that they may take their place as true loyal citizens of this country." In addition, she hoped that by their example the FSPAs would be able to "break down the bigotry which is rampant in the South." Perhaps not all sisters shared their leader's noble goals, but these views were expressed often enough that they represented the order's official stance.[40]

The existence of Holy Child Jesus Mission and School was a public statement on behalf of African American civil rights. Seeing White priests and nuns living in an African American community was an affront to segregationists who opposed racial integration in any form. During the years when Sister Thea taught at Holy Child, the sisters lived in an integrated convent. In the classrooms by that time, Black children received an education from teachers, all but one of whom were White, which was superior to that provided in the segregated Black public schools. It also was equal to, if not better than, the education that even White children in Canton received. The sisters dedicated their lives to preparing their students to compete successfully for the advanced educational and employment opportunities that they hoped would someday open for them. Many of the sisters taught at Holy Child for decades. Their

38. Heires, "Memories of Canton, MS," FSPA Archives.
39. Wiesneske, group interview with Canton FSPAs, FSPA Archives.
40. "Account Gleaned," FSPA Archives.

pupils knew that these teachers cared deeply about them. Holy Child alumna Nola Jo Starling-Ratliff likened the Holy Child Jesus community to a family: "a strong family built on values. . . . For the Catholic nuns that were there, we were their children in essence because they didn't have children [of their own]. They looked upon us *as if we were theirs*, and they wanted us to be the best because we were theirs."[41]

Bertha Bowman Meets the FSPAs at Holy Child Jesus School

When the first resident FSPA sisters arrived in Canton in mid-July 1948, they had much work to do to get ready for the opening of school. Fortunately, they had the assistance of eager young African Americans from the neighboring community. Among these willing workers was ten-year-old Bertha Bowman, who lived at 136 Hill Street, one block from the mission. One year earlier, Bertha had been baptized a Catholic at the Holy Child Jesus Mission. A precocious child with a strong interest in religion, she had investigated all the churches in her community—Methodist, Baptist, Episcopalian, Adventist, AME, and AME Zion. "But once I went to the Catholic Church, my wanderings ceased," she wrote. She gravitated to the White sisters preparing the school. Forty years later, Bertha, by then known as Sister Thea Bowman, FSPA, recalled how she and other children "helped clean up the old army barracks, haul the desks, unpack the books, cut up the scrap paper, line up the chairs, polish the tables, wash the windows, and pretty-up the makeshift bulletin boards."[42]

The Trinity Missionary fathers posted notices in the African American community to inform parents about the new teachers and the expanded classes soon to commence at Holy Child Jesus School:

FATHER GILBERT
Announces the opening of
HOLY CHILD JESUS
ELEMENTARY SCHOOL
FOR COLORED PUPILS
To be conducted by the
SISTERS OF THE THIRD ORDER
OF ST. FRANCIS
OF PERPETUAL ADORATION
Grades 1 to 6

41. Nola Jo Starling-Ratliff, in an interview with the author, September 6, 2019, emphasis added.
42. Thea Bowman, "Holy Child Jesus School—Then and Now," *Holy Child Jesus School Newsletter*, March 28, 1989, 2, FSPA Archives.

TUITION $2.00 per month each child
Special rates for more than one child in family[43]

Sister Thea described the mixture of children who greeted the sisters on the first day of school: "We came, about 70 of us, grades 1 through 6, in white blouses and blue uniforms. . . . Some hungry; some afraid; some eager and inquisitive; some shy; some so far behind to ever catch up academically; some far too old, even for sixth grade; most already discouraged with school and learning; some too poor to pay even the $2.00 per month tuition that was asked but not required."[44]

For young Bertha Bowman, the classes and teachers at Holy Child were a welcome improvement over the conditions she experienced at the "under-staffed, under-financed, segregated public school" she previously attended. Because class size at Holy Child was limited to twenty-seven students, Sister Thea later wrote, "There was no more overcrowding. There were no more classes of sixty little children, two occupying the space really intended for one small body." Attendance was strictly enforced: "There was no skipping school. Sister would come to your house to see your mother, or Father would just come and get you." The sisters were serious about education. Sister Thea recounted: "There was no time for playing tic-tac-toe in school, no time for fooling around, no time for fighting or the dozens [a popular game involving the exchange of verbal insults]. There was no more meaningless homework like copying the reading lesson or copying spelling words. Homework had a purpose, and you'd better do it at home or you would find yourself the next day doing it in the classroom after school." Even the textbooks were better: "Everybody had books to use. They were clean and neat. At the public school, Black children got the books White children had used for five years. . . . And at the public school there had never been enough books to go around."[45] Holy Child Jesus School added one grade in each subsequent year until it offered a full curriculum from kindergarten through twelfth grade.

All the pupils at Holy Child Jesus School were African American, but this demographic was not due to any deliberate exclusion of White pupils. Sister Mary Walter insisted, "We always had our arms open to white children and they told us they would come but were afraid."[46] Sister Mary Eve Hytry, FSPA, recalled that one White student did attend Holy Child for a short time: "One year I had one little White girl [in class]. She was there for a while and

---

43. Quoted in "Interesting Things Reverend Mother Told Us About Her Trip to Canton," November 1948, FSPA Archives.

44. Bowman, "Holy Child Jesus School," 2, FSPA Archives.

45. Bowman, "Holy Child Jesus School," 2, FSPA Archives.

46. Heires, "Memories of Canton, MS," FSPA Archives.

then, all of a sudden, she left." According to Sister Mary Eve, White Canto-
nians were boycotting the business of the girl's father "because he was sending
his child to the Black school." Soon after that, the family moved out of town.[47]

Because Bertha's father, Theon Bowman, was a physician and her mother,
Mary Esther Bowman, and maternal grandmother, Lizzie Williams Coleman,
were teachers, she appreciated a quality education more than most of her
youthful contemporaries. "We had solid teaching and solid study, reading, writing, arithmetic, religion, drill and drill and drill and more drill," she noted. In
addition to the standard academic subjects, her education included several nontraditional skills: "We helped make library shelves from orange crates and poster
paper. We helped prepare school lunch. We wrote letters to benefactors all over
the country who helped keep our school alive. We cleaned the school, sanded
desks, cut the grass, painted beaverboard walls. We worked in groups. Ada
helped me with math. I helped Walter and Willie with reading. . . . We older
children supervised the younger children on the playground. We taught them
games and songs and dances. We wiped their noses and dried their tears."[48]

The influence of the Franciscan sister-teachers extended beyond the classroom. Sister Thea's childhood friend Flonzie Brown-Wright fondly remembered the tantalizing aromas coming from the sisters' kitchen. Sister Enrico,
who served as cook for the convent, "baked cookies for the children. She
would even allow us to come in the kitchen while she baked the delicious
treats. We thought that was just so fantastic. We were in the kitchen with the
nuns while they were baking us cookies and fixing us lemonade and ice cream
cones." At play, the two girls pretended to be nuns, using long scarves as veils
in imitation of the sisters who taught them.[49]

Perhaps the most significant effect of Bertha's education at Holy Child
Jesus School was the strong bond she formed with the Franciscan sisters who
taught there. Long after she left Canton, she recalled, "As a ten-year-old, I
had my first real meeting with people who were White—the priest and sisters
at Canton. At first I mistrusted them; but when I got to know them, I learned
to love them."[50] Many years later, Sister Thea wrote about their influence: "I
was drawn to examine and accept the Catholic faith because of the day-to-
day lived witness of Catholic Christians who first loved me, then shared with
me their story, their values, their beliefs; who first loved me, then invited me
to share with them in community, prayer and mission."[51] Brown-Wright stated

---

47. Mary Eve Hytry, in an interview with the author, April 29, 2019.
48. Hytry, interview.
49. Flonzie Brown-Wright, in an interview with the author, June 23, 2010.
50. Charles D. Burns, "Deep in Their Hearts, Lord, They Do Believe," *Divine Word
Messenger*, March/April 1965, 41.
51. Thea Bowman, *Thea Bowman: In My Own Words* (Liguori, MO: Liguori Publications, 2009), 26.

in an interview that the caring example the sisters provided had a greater influence on Bertha's determination to become a sister than the religious doctrines they imparted. She "was intrigued with their compassion," Brown-Wright remembered: "She was intrigued with how they would come into the homes and help families cook or how they would pick up kids whose noses were running and wipe the noses."[52]

Bertha was so enamored of the sisters that she resolved to become one. Her parents opposed this decision. They did not want their teenage daughter and only child to leave home for far-off Wisconsin. Her father reportedly warned her, "They're not going to like you up there, the only Black in the middle of all the whites."[53] But Bertha was stubborn; she staged a hunger strike in protest. Her childhood friend Doris Jones O'Leary recalled, "She wouldn't eat a thing and became so thin. Her poor parents were so troubled by her refusal to eat that they agreed to let her go to the convent."[54] In August 1953, Bertha's parents reluctantly said goodbye as their precious child boarded an Illinois Central train taking her north to commence the lengthy process of becoming a Franciscan sister.

Bertha Bowman Becomes Sister Thea

As fifteen-year-old Bertha Bowman prepared to depart Canton to begin the long journey to the FSPA motherhouse in La Crosse, she won a rare victory over Jim Crow restrictions. By law, she was supposed to ride segregated from the White passengers, which meant being separated from the sisters who were accompanying her. However, Sister Vita protested to the conductor, who finally relented and agreed to allow Bertha to ride in the White coach "after being firmly reassured that it was all right with each one of us."[55]

As a student at St. Rose High School in La Crosse, Bertha had needed to adjust to a radically different lifestyle. There was the unfamiliar cuisine, lacking the fried chicken, catfish, collard greens, pecan pies, sweet potatoes, and okra that were staples of the Southern menu she was used to. Coping with the Wisconsin winter—five months of ice and snow—was another challenge. But the greatest difference lay in living in an exclusively White environment—being the only Black among nearly two hundred aspirants, postulants, and novices living in the five-story convent. Sometimes she remarked to trusted friends, "You all are so pale around here."[56] For many of the White sisters, who came

52. Brown-Wright, interview.
53. Smith and Feister, *Thea's Song*, 37–38.
54. Doris Jones O'Leary, quoted in Maurice J. Nutt, *Thea Bowman: Faithful and Free* (Collegeville, MN: Liturgical Press, 2019), 28.
55. Heires, "Memories of Canton, MS," FSPA Archives.
56. Smith and Feister, *Thea's Song*, 52.

Sister Thea Bowman at St. Rose Convent, La Crosse, Wisconsin, 1968. Photo courtesy of Franciscan Sisters of Perpetual Adoration archives.

from small towns in the Midwest, teenage Bertha was the first African American they ever met. Most were ignorant about Black people and shared the prejudices and stereotyped notions common among Whites of that time.

Bertha soon distinguished herself by excelling in academic pursuits, especially English, and winning awards for her written compositions. In January 1955, she began taking courses at Viterbo College, and the following month she was accepted by the order as a postulant. However, her academic progress was put on hold that April when she was diagnosed with tuberculosis. Bertha was hospitalized for the next twelve months, which put her a year behind her classmates. By August 1956, she was fully recovered and became a novice sister, taking the religious name Thea, the feminine version of her father's name. Two years later, an article in the *La Crosse Tribune* announced that Sister Thea had been accepted as the first professed Black member of her religious community.[57]

After another year as a full-time college student, Sister Thea began her teaching career at Blessed Sacrament School in La Crosse, where she instructed fifth and sixth graders, all of them White. At first, some parents objected to having a Black sister teaching their children, but after meeting

---

57. Smith and Feister, *Thea's Song*, 74.

Sister Thea their complaints evaporated. When it was time for music instruction, Sister Thea shared songs from her African American heritage, leading students in the spirituals she had learned as a child. In February 1961, she wrote her parents, "This week in music class I taught my children, 'Couldn't Hear Nobody Pray.' Now they are clamoring for more. There are only two more [spirituals] in our book, so that will have to suffice."[58]

Later in 1961, twenty-one-year-old Sister Thea returned to Canton to teach at Holy Child Jesus School. In the South again, she had to be aware of the prevalent segregation norms. Her residence in the convent with White sisters violated the Jim Crow code. Mary Terwey, a visitor at the Holy Child convent, remembered, "For safety sake Sister Thea would not answer the door bell at the convent."[59] When traveling by car with other sisters, Sister Thea later recalled, "I would duck down in the car when we passed white people in the streets or on the road—and especially when we passed the white police."[60]

Sister Thea brought the gift of Black pride to her Black students at Holy Child Jesus School, something the White FSPAs were unable to convey. Walter C. Jones, who attended Holy Child from kindergarten through high school, considered Sister Thea his idol. "Sister Thea was a beautiful, richly talented Black woman," he recalled. "Sister Thea kind of got us started in a cultural movement, in that we would sing. We started a choir. She taught us to sing and taught us Black values, self-esteem."[61] Her emphasis on Black culture extended beyond music. "Sister Thea was really into Black literature," Starling-Ratliff recalled in an interview; she emphasized "all the [Black] authors, not only music. Instilling in us the desire to read those books that are profound in our culture."[62] Sister Thea was a demanding teacher, insisting that her pupils concentrate their full effort on their studies, but she coupled that firmness with love. Sister Thea's teaching inspired Cornelia Johnson, another of her students. "She spoke to us not like children but as if we were her sisters and brothers. The students at Holy Child Jesus really knew that she cared about us," Johnson reminisced.[63] Sister Thea insisted, "It is so important that they learn to value themselves before the world had had a chance to beat them down."[64]

Early on, Sister Thea formed the Holy Child Jesus Singers, using spirituals and gospel songs to transmit to her students the cultural legacy passed

58. Bowman, quoted in Smith and Feister, *Thea's Song*, 77.
59. Mary Terwey, group interview with Canton FSPAs, FSPA Archives.
60. Bowman, quoted in Smith and Feister, *Thea's Song*, 90.
61. "Mississippi—Canton: Walter C. Jones Interviewee, Part 1," sound recording, 17 November 1991, Tulane University Digital Archive, https://digitallibrary.tulane.edu/islandora/object/tulane%3A54087.
62. Starling-Ratliff, interview.
63. Cornelia Johnson, quoted in Nutt, *Thea Bowman*, 46.
64. Thea Bowman, quoted in Nutt, *Thea Bowman*, 49.

Sister Thea Bowman leading the Holy Child Jesus Singers, Canton, Mississippi. Photo courtesy of the Catholic Diocese of Jackson, Mississippi.

down by their elders. In 1965, she and her choir recorded an album of thirteen spirituals titled *The Voice of Negro America*. The students sold copies of the record, raising $16,000 toward the construction of the new church. In addition to their songs, Sister Thea recorded a personal message on their value: "While the world is full of hate, strife, vengeance, we sing songs of love, laughter, worship, wisdom, justice, and peace because we are free. Though our forefathers bent to bear the heat of the sun, the strike of the lash, the chain of slavery, we are free. No man can enslave us. We are too strong, too unafraid. America needs our strength, our voices to drown out her sorrows."[65] Starling-Ratliff was one of the singers who soloed on the record. She remembered Sister Thea's message about the music they performed: "Sister Thea showed us how important singing spirituals was—going in depth with our music and our culture—that we had a lot to share, that we needed to share and take pride in."[66]

---

65. Bowman, quoted in Nutt, *Thea Bowman*, 93.
66. Starling-Ratliff, interview.

Fighting City Hall

The mission's most frustrating encounter with Jim Crow restrictions involved a prolonged feud with Canton city officials over the construction of a new church building. In 1953, the pastor, Father Furman, purchased lots adjoining the mission facing South Union Street, which ran through the White community. He planned to use this land as the site of a permanent church building to replace the temporary structure erected in 1946, which held no more than fifty worshippers. According to Sister Mary Walter, "Our little wooden barracks church got to be too small for our parishioners and student body." The White owners sold the property, she said, "thinking that Father Justin was going to live there. When word got around that there were plans to build a church things got hot!" White residents living nearby objected: "Threats were made that if the church were built it would not be protected."[67] Bishop Gerow advised Father Furman not to antagonize his White neighbors and instead to shelve his plans for a new church. A combination gymnasium-auditorium constructed on the Holy Child Jesus grounds in 1956 subsequently became the site for Sunday Mass. On Saturdays, chairs were set up in the gym for worship. Then on Monday mornings, students folded the chairs away so the gym could be used for classes and athletic events.[68]

In 1963, Father Luke Mikschl, MSSST, the mission's new pastor, had the old house facing Union Street demolished in anticipation of constructing a new church. He began negotiating with the mayor and city council about the long-delayed building project. He agreed to locate the church two hundred feet back from Union Street and not to have the structure face the street. In return, city officials promised they would issue a building permit. However, in February 1965, when Father Mikschl submitted blueprints for the new church, the permit was not forthcoming. The pastor was told to wait. A petition bearing two hundred signatures from White residents opposing construction of the church then persuaded city leaders to renege on their pledge. The city rezoned the land and denied the permit.

Frustrated by repeated delays and lack of good faith, Father Mikschl resolved to take action. In an open letter addressed to "Fellow Citizens of Canton," he explained, "Because we do not have a church, but especially since we are unable to build one . . . we now feel we have no other choice but to attend services at Sacred Heart Church."[69] On Sunday, May 23, 1965, after obtaining approval from Bishop Gerow, Father Mikschl led a procession of

---

67. Heires, "Memories of Canton, MS," FSPA Archives.

68. Sarah Wiesneske, "A History of the Struggle of Holy Child Jesus Church, Canton, Mississippi," n.d., FSPA Archives.

69. Luke Mikschl, to Fellow Citizens of Canton, May 1965, Mississippi Department of Archives and History, Mississippi State Sovereignty Commission Online, 10-55-0-51-1-1-1.

Holy Child Jesus parishioners and FSPAs to Sacred Heart church, where he celebrated Mass. He had notified Father Patrick Moran, Sacred Heart's pastor, that he and his flock would be coming at 2:00 p.m. that afternoon. The bishop sent a letter to be read at Sacred Heart church, in which he said he was "very much disturbed at the refusal of the city to grant a permit for the building of a church in which our colored Catholics can attend mass and receive spiritual attention."[70] Father Mikschl celebrated the Mass in the afternoon to avoid conflict with scheduled events at Sacred Heart.

The service went off without incident. Not long afterwards, the city issued the desired building permit with one condition—that the mission erect a seven-foot brick wall to shield White properties from the new church. "We refused to put up the brick wall unless the city supplied the brick and paid for the labor," Sister Mary Walter declared.[71] Instead, the mission erected a five-foot wooden fence as a compromise. Bishop Gerow dedicated the modern Holy Child Jesus church on April 17, 1966. Months after the new building was completed, sisters and parishioners, "under cover of darkness," pulled sections of fence out of the ground and "hid them behind Father's garage." "We went like thieves in the night," said Terwey, one of the raiding party.[72] Sister Mary Walter reported, "No one ever said a word or even noticed" their act of civil disobedience.[73]

The Civil Rights Movement Comes to Canton

Meanwhile, in the early to middle 1960s, the civil rights movement was rocking Mississippi's segregated society, first with the Freedom Rides protesting segregated transportation facilities, and then with a coordinated campaign against discriminatory voter registration practices. Because only a handful of Madison County's majority Black population were registered voters, civil rights organizations, primarily the Congress of Racial Equality, organized demonstrations that focused on gaining the right to vote. On February 28, 1964, four hundred African American residents stood in line outside the county courthouse for five hours in chilly weather waiting to register. Fifty law enforcement officers armed with shotguns and tear gas harassed and threatened them. Only five individuals from the line were allowed to complete the registration application.[74]

---

70. Richard O. Gerow, quoted in W. F. Minor, "Miss. Priest Leads Flock to 'White' Catholic Church," *New Orleans Times-Picayune*, May 24, 1965, Mississippi Department of Archives and History, Mississippi State Sovereignty Commission Online, 10-55-0-54-1-1-1.
71. Heires, "Memories of Canton, MS," FSPA Archives.
72. Terwey, group interview with Canton FSPAs, FSPA Archives.
73. Heires, "Memories of Canton, MS," FSPA Archives.
74. Civil Rights Movement Archive, "Freedom Day in Canton (Feb [1964])," http://www.crmvet.org/tim/timhis64.htm#1964canton.

Father Mikschl encouraged members of his congregation to become registered voters, but the priests and sisters at Holy Child Jesus Mission were not involved in organizing this or other similar demonstrations. Bishop Gerow believed that engaging in public protests was not an appropriate role for Catholic clergy and religious, a belief that was widely shared by American Catholics of this time.[75] The elderly bishop frowned on civil rights activism by clergy and religious. He feared that if priests, brothers, or sisters of his diocese participated in demonstrations, they might be harmed or even killed. The FSPAs saw their role as preparing their pupils to take an active role as citizens of their community. They knew they risked violent reprisals if they openly advocated for equal rights.[76]

Although Father Mikschl endorsed the goals of the civil rights movement and remained active behind the scenes, he avoided participating in any demonstrations or marches, with the one exception being the procession to Sacred Heart church. Although he had testified at a hearing conducted by the US Civil Rights Commission in Jackson in February 1965, he denied being involved in the movement. "I am aware of the movement, but I have never attempted to take any leadership in it," he told reporter W. F. Minor.[77] Father Luke found other ways to support African American advancement. In 1965, he allowed the Child Development Group of Mississippi, a Head Start program closely allied with the civil rights movement, to use Holy Child Jesus Mission facilities for one summer session. The mission also hosted STAR, the adult education and job-training program supported by the Mississippi Catholic diocese. Mississippi segregationists opposed both of these antipoverty efforts, which were funded by the federal government as part of the Johnson administration's War on Poverty. They objected to Black and White adults learning together in the same classrooms and the racially mixed staff that taught them. Equally objectionable was the federal money flowing into the African American community without the approval or control of local White politicians.

The summer of 1966 proved to be a violent turning point for the civil rights movement in Canton. For a few days in June, Holy Child Jesus Mission became the focal point of a national protest. On June 5, James Meredith, the

---

75. Apparently Bishop Gerow did not consider the procession of Holy Child parishioners to Sacred Heart church to be a civil rights demonstration.

76. When two Josephite priests, Fathers Philip Berrigan and Richard Wagner, attempted to join a 1961 sit-in demonstration at the Jackson, MS, airport, Bishop Gerow threatened to expel all Josephites from Mississippi if their superior did not order them to desist. "2 Priests Stopped from Joining Riders," *New York Times*, August 23, 1961, 31. Bishop Joseph Brunini, who succeeded Gerow in 1967, took a more permissive view of religious civil rights activism.

77. Minor, "Miss. Priest Leads Flock."

first African American to attend the University of Mississippi, announced his intention to walk 250 miles from Memphis, Tennessee, to the Mississippi state capitol in Jackson. He dubbed this effort the March Against Fear. His avowed purpose was "to challenge the all-pervasive and overriding fear" still prevalent among Black Mississippians.[78] Decked out in a jaunty pith helmet and carrying an African walking stick, he set off down Highway 51. On the second day of his trek, near the small town of Hernando, Mississippi, fifteen miles south of the Tennessee border, a would-be assassin shot Meredith in the back. Fortunately, his wounds were not fatal.

National civil rights leaders including Martin Luther King Jr. and Stokely Carmichael, the newly elected head of the Student Nonviolent Coordinating Committee, flew to Meredith's bedside and pledged to continue his crusade. Several hundred volunteers rallied to the cause. Hiking from town to town, they urged African Americans to take advantage of the recently passed Voting Rights Act to become registered voters. When the march reached Greenwood, Carmichael electrified a crowd of 600 when he angrily shouted, "We been saying freedom for six years now and we ain't got nothin'. What we gonna start saying now is Black Power!" The crowd answered back, "Black Power! Black Power!"[79] Reporters seized on this new slogan as an ominous sign. Some saw it as a shift toward the Black nationalism of Malcolm X and the Black Muslims. Others claimed it repudiated King's philosophy of nonviolent protest. For the remainder of the march, Black Power supplanted voter registration as its dominant theme.

Two days before the Meredith March reached Canton, Sister Thea's childhood friend Brown-Wright, now a leader of the local NAACP chapter, received an urgent phone call from King. "Can you provide housing and food for about three thousand people?" she recalled him asking. Once she recovered from her surprise, Brown-Wright agreed to take on this staggering assignment. The first person she contacted was Father Mikschl. She remembered, "I told him Dr. King had called and was bringing all the tired, hungry marchers to Canton. They'd be getting into Canton in a couple of days and could we use the gym to sleep people." The Holy Child Jesus gymnasium was the only private facility in the Black community large enough to accommodate a crowd of that size. That the request came from King himself was enough to convince Father Mikschl. "He was on board right away," Brown-Wright recalled in an interview. "We could go to the [Holy Child Jesus] gym and to the church when we couldn't go anyplace else."[80]

78. Goudsouzian, *Down to the Crossroads*, 7.
79. Stokely Carmichael, quoted in Goudsouzian, *Down to the Crossroads*, 143.
80. Brown-Wright, interview.

When King arrived in Canton on the afternoon of Thursday, June 23, he chatted with adults enrolled in STAR classes and posed for photos outside Holy Child Jesus School. "His presence was electrifying," reported Father Mikschl, who bestowed a priestly blessing on the smiling Baptist minister.[81] The demonstrators who came with King rested in the Holy Child Jesus gym and camped on the mission grounds. The FSPAs assisted medics from the Medical Committee for Human Rights in providing first aid for the footsore marchers. "We took all our pails from school, from the convent, dishpans, any kind of thing you could soak a foot in," recalled Sister Sarah. "We even used our electric roaster for people to soak their feet in." The sisters also helped make sandwiches for the multitude gathered at the mission. "We put two pieces of bread and a piece of bologna [together] and gave them to the people," Sister Sarah added. "I don't know how many people we fed, but there were hundreds of them." King himself dozed in an easy chair in the sisters' living room. According to Sister Sarah, the chair later became a treasured relic in the Bowmans' home.[82]

Tension between the Mississippi Highway Patrol and the marchers reached a boiling point in Canton. Civil rights forces were determined to pitch their tents in a public space. Canton officials refused to permit use of a city park, so march leaders instead chose McNeal Elementary School, which had an all-Black enrollment and faculty. Local activist and Holy Child Jesus congregant Robert "Junior" Chinn recalled, "We felt like since we were paying taxes here and our children were going to school here, we had a right to use these grounds."[83] The superintendent of schools rejected their request. Despite his veto, civil rights forces resolved to go ahead and pitch their tents at the school.

That evening, as marchers began raising the first tent, the highway patrol, aided by sheriff's deputies and Mississippi fish and game officers, launched a tear gas attack. "We started to go up with the ropes and all hell broke loose," Chinn recounted. "We was just lucky that nobody didn't get killed."[84] Veteran journalist Paul Good reported that more than sixty state troopers "came stomping in behind the gas, gun-butting and kicking the men, women, and children. They were not arresting, they were punishing."[85]

Civil rights workers and their local followers scattered in all directions. Many, especially those from out of town, found their way back to Holy Child Jesus Mission. The FSPAs assisted Medical Committee for Human Rights per-

81. "Holy Child Jesus Mission and 'The March,'" n.d., FSPA Archives.

82. Wiesneske, group interview with Canton FSPAs, FSPA Archives.

83. Robert "Junior" Chinn, in Paul Murray, "Return to Mississippi," August 4, 2018, YouTube video, 26:07, https://youtu.be/r0JgdASioW0.

84. Chinn, in Murray, "Return to Mississippi."

85. Paul Good, *The Trouble I've Seen: White Journalist/Black Movement* (Washington, DC: Howard University Press, 1975), 261.

sonnel in setting up an emergency first aid station in their convent. Sister Rita Heires, FSPA, described what happened that night:

> People who were injured, primarily by tear gassing, were brought to the convent. We used a lot of Murine for eye burns and cleansed wounds. I never realized that gassing had cartridges, but people got burned by the cartridges as well as the tear gas. [Sisters] Cecelia Lonsdorf, Sarah, and Erna [Farni], and myself were just receiving whoever came in. Usually, for most of them, it was just a matter of sitting there and wash out their eyes and until they felt comfortable enough to go. But one woman was brought in . . . on a stretcher and she was in such pain. I remember Sister Cecelia took her to her bedroom and put her in bed and she stayed with her. Finally, they called the ambulance to take her to the hospital. She had been kicked by one of the guards.[86]

Among the injured, the sister remembered one African American girl:

> There was a young girl, I'd say twelve or thirteen [years old], who some-how latched herself with the march and came along. She was Black. Because it was not really safe for her to be among the whole crowd, and she was probably very tired, they brought her to the convent, and we had a roll-away bed there set up so she could get some rest, and she took a bath and got some clothes from the secondhand store and was sleeping in bed. My sister [Sister Mary Walter] called me over, I remember so dis-tinctly, her little black leg was sticking out. On her leg she had written with a ballpoint pen, or someone had written, "Black Power."[87]

Around 2:00 a.m., Sister Rita left the convent and walked back to the garage apartment where she was staying. She was startled to see a large Black man approaching out of the darkness. He wrapped his arm around her. "Sister, I'll protect you," she remembered he said. "You look like the Klan." She explained, "We were wearing white habits and, of course, that had never entered my head."[88]

Sister Mary Eve recalled how everyone who worked at the Holy Child Jesus Mission was aware of threats by the Ku Klux Klan. Father Mikschl had told the sisters "how the Klan would call and say, 'I'm coming to get you.' And he'd say, 'Good. I'll be waiting for you.' He would sit on the porch with a neighbor with a gun in his lap. They never showed up," Sister Mary Eve remembered in an interview.[89]

---

86. Rita Heires, in an interview with the author, April 30, 2019.
87. Rita Heires, interview.
88. Rita Heires, interview.
89. Hytry, interview. Sister Rita Mae Fischer, FSPA, offered an alternative version. "The way I heard the story of the Klan calling, Father Luke's response was briefly, 'God bless you.' Then, being somewhat fearful, he spent the night in the convent parlor." Rita Mae Fischer, personal communication to the author, March 4, 2020.

Even so, these were not idle threats. Adding to the atmosphere of terror in Canton during June 1966 was the news that St. Joachim's school for African American children, operated by the Trinity Missionaries in nearby Leake County, had been bombed and burned to the ground by the Klan on the same night as the Canton tear gas attack. Sister Rita, together with Father Mikschl and other sisters, drove there to inspect the ruins a few days later. In an interview she described what she observed:

> We saw the big canisters of gas, empty of course, that they [the Klan] used to put around the building so it would go up in a very hot blaze. It was so hot that the glass was melted. Even the iron was twisted as it melted. Everything was gone except maybe two to three feet of brick on the bottom. It was very eerie. The bus that was nearby was seared; the trees were scared from the heat. Luckily, Father Maurice [the pastor] was away on retreat; the sisters were away on vacation, so no one was injured.[90]

After the Canton tear gas attack on June 23, five hundred marchers with nowhere else to go unrolled their bedrolls in the Holy Child Jesus gymnasium or outside on the lawn. The following day, they lounged on the grounds, consuming sandwiches, milk, Kool-Aid, and soup served by the sisters and Wisconsin high school girls teaching summer school classes at the mission. "Fortunately, we had considerable food on hand," wrote an anonymous sister, "since we make sandwiches for the STAR people every afternoon."[91] That evening, the throng again marched to McNeal School, only to be told that the tents had been moved to Tougaloo College, the next-to-last stop for the Meredith March. Thus the civil rights demonstrators avoided a second confrontation with Mississippi law enforcement.

On Sunday, June 26, Father Mikschl drove a station wagon filled with sisters, some of the White students from Wisconsin, and Holy Child Jesus student Nola Jo Starling to Jackson for the rally at the state capitol building concluding the Meredith March. The crowd that assembled for the gathering was split, with hostile Whites on one side of the street and supportive Blacks on the opposite side. Sister Rita recalled, "As long as we were on the White side, the girls were very popular, whistled at and so forth. As soon as we crossed the street to get to the Black side, the catcalls changed to very divisive things and that was a great concern. Sister had them [the high school girls] get inside the wall of our habits. We were very conspicuous."[92] Father Mikschl confirmed, "The TV cameras zoomed in on the sisters in their white habits in the crowd."[93]

---

90. Heires, interview.
91. Dear _____, June 1966, FSPA Archives.
92. Heires, interview.
93. Luke Mikschl, "Holy Child Jesus and the Mississippi Freedom March," *Maryknoll Magazine*, July 1966, 108.

Sister Thea's Growing Fame

Sister Thea missed the excitement at Holy Child Jesus Mission that summer; she was taking graduate classes at the Catholic University of America in Washington, DC, beginning work on her master's degree in English. The rapidly evolving civil rights movement and the intellectual stimulus of her studies contributed to "a growing Black consciousness" in the young Franciscan sister. At a time when many White liberals insisted that Blacks and Whites were basically the same, Sister Thea pointed to fundamental differences. In 1965 she wrote, "The Negro really is different from the white man. He has a different way of thinking, a different kind of endurance. But differences should not cause conflict; they should complement each other. And so it is wise that we do not destroy what is good in Negro culture, but develop it to harmonize it with other traditions. In this way we build a new and better way of life."[94]

That fall, she returned to Canton to teach at Holy Child Jesus School, where she remained for two more years. Sister Thea left Canton in 1968 to begin full-time PhD studies at Catholic University of America in Washington, DC. There she was "welcomed into the Black Catholic community" and "met many members of the international Black community." According to her biographers, Charlene Smith and John Feister, Sister Thea "experienced an awakening" during her years at Catholic University. "She would be herself. She would integrate her natural soul into all her relationships. She decided to be as bold as she had been as a child in Canton, to be daring, to have fun."[95]

That summer Sister Thea participated in the founding convocation of the National Black Sisters Conference at Mount Mercy College (now Carlow University) in Pittsburgh. At one session, she led 150 African American women religious in singing a gospel hymn. After that session, all the sisters at the assembly knew who Sister Thea was. She completed the coursework for her doctoral degree in English literature in 1971 and returned to Wisconsin to teach at Viterbo College, where she soon became chairperson of the English department. In addition to teaching, Sister Thea organized a choir called the Hallelujah Singers to sing the spirituals that were dear to her heart. A reviewer at one performance by the group observed, "With hand-clapping, call-and-response techniques, and a general sort of conversational approach, they suggested the uninhibited joy in music and religion that seems characteristic of many Black people."[96]

Although she now resided in Wisconsin, Sister Thea's ties to her home state remained strong. She returned to Canton on a regular basis to spend

---

94. Bowman, quoted in Burns, "Deep in Their Hearts," 40.
95. Smith and Feister, *Thea's Song*, 100.
96. Quoted in Smith and Feister, *Thea's Song*, 136.

time with her elderly parents. These visits always included a stop at Holy Child Jesus School, where students and teachers regarded her as celebrity—a native daughter who had achieved success in the world outside Mississippi. Deborah Jackson Pembleton attended Holy Child Jesus School during those years. She treasured Sister Thea's appearances at the school, as she recalled in an interview: "She would come back to campus to the school, and she would teach a singing class. We would learn a song. She would come in maybe three or four times during the week she was visiting, and at the end of the week we would do a performance for the school. When we were selected, we were delighted, and [we were] highly disappointed when she would select another class."[97] Sister Thea's contagious enthusiasm left a lasting impression on Pembleton. "It would be like a breath of fresh air," she recalled. "We would be able to see that so many things were possible. . . . She would tell us how we could be empowered, how we could go anywhere."[98]

In 1978, Sister Thea left her position at Viterbo College and returned to Canton to care for her ailing parents. Her mother had been ill for several years, and her father was too frail to aid in her care. But Sister Thea was too gifted, and her talents were too much in demand, for her to sit home in Canton for long. Bishop Joseph Brunini, who had succeeded Bishop Gerow in 1967, invited Sister Thea to work for the Diocese of Jackson to establish an Office of Intercultural Awareness. At first, she was a consultant, but soon she was named its director. In this capacity, Sister Thea worked with clergy and faculty at Catholic schools as well as with Black and White parishioners in the diocese to promote multicultural understanding. Given Mississippi's history of state-sponsored racism and extreme African American poverty, her job was doubly challenging. Not only did she have to persuade White Catholics to accept Blacks as their equals, but she had to convince African Americans to lower the social and emotional walls they had built to protect themselves from racial insult.

Sister Thea identified three primary objectives in her work for the diocese: improving interracial relations in the diocese, helping Black Catholic schools in their self-help programs, and fostering Black vocations.[99] She kept a demanding schedule, traveling back and forth from Canton to Jackson and to far-flung parishes across the state. In their biography of Sister Thea, Smith and Feister reprinted her calendar for September 1978. It included liturgies and poetry readings; meetings with priests, sisters, and the bishop; planning meetings and a staff meeting; meetings with diocesan councils; workshop presentations on

---

97. Deborah Jackson Pembleton, in an interview with the author, July 19, 2019.

98. Deborah Jackson Pembleton, quoted in John Davis, "The Life and Legacy of Sister Thea Bowman," Wisconsin Public Radio, February 26, 2015, https://www.wpr.org/life-and-legacy-sister-thea-bowman.

99. Nutt, *Thea Bowman*, 71.

multicultural pluralism; and music rehearsals and much more.[100] She addressed parents at Catholic schools and brought the Holy Child Jesus choir to perform at White parishes. Her former student, Walter Jones, described Sister Thea's impact on Catholic audiences: "She was bringing in this whole new consciousness that you don't have to be so cold; you don't have to be so orthodox. You can praise God. You can lift your voices."[101] Sister Thea helped organize a Mississippi chapter of the National Office for Black Catholics (NOBC). She also assisted in planning the 1983 joint meeting of the National Black Catholic Clergy Caucus (NBCCC), the National Black Sisters' Conference (NBSC), and the National Black Seminarians' Association, held in Jackson. When the delegates came to Jackson, they were welcomed by Governor William Winter at the Mississippi governor's mansion at a reception arranged by Sister Thea.[102]

Sister Thea's growing fame brought a flood of invitations to speak and lead workshops across the United States. She accepted speaking engagements in places as widely scattered as San Francisco, Minneapolis, Houston, Cleveland, Chicago, and Louisville. In some years she gave as many as one hundred speeches and workshops. Her presentations were described as "dynamic, scholarly, spell-binding, provocative, infectious, challenging."[103] Her friend, Redemptorist Father Maurice Nutt, CSsR, identified two common themes in many of Sister Thea's speeches: "to encourage people to use their God-given gifts and talents for the betterment of their churches and community and to build the kingdom of God wherever they find themselves."[104] By the early 1980s, she had exchanged her nun's habit for distinctive robes inspired by African styles. She told author Feister, "The clothes are an expression of my personality, an expression of my values, and expression of my history and culture, and my tradition."[105] Audience members embraced her inspirational words and considered themselves privileged to have heard her message. In later years, they fondly retold their memories of meeting Sister Thea.

Sister Thea also maintained her ties to the academic community. She lectured at the University of Mississippi's annual William Faulkner conference, presenting nine scholarly papers on various themes in Faulkner's novels and stories. She praised the author for his "sympathetic, enlightened, and objective approach to Negro character, a keen awareness of Southern white mentality, a tremendous emphasis on the brotherhood of man concept, and a scathing

---

100. Smith and Feister, *Thea's Song*, 157–58.
101. "Mississippi—Canton: Walter C. Jones Interviewee, Part 1," Tulane University Digital Archive.
102. Nutt, *Thea Bowman*, 82–83.
103. Nutt, *Thea Bowman*, 169.
104. Nutt, *Thea Bowman*, 78.
105. Bowman, quoted in Smith and Feister, *Thea's Song*, 178, quoted in Nutt, *Thea Bowman*, 84.

condemnation of grasping, materialistic aggressiveness."[106] Sister Thea was among the thirty-three founding members of the Black Catholic Theological Symposium. She also was a charter faculty member at the Institute for Black Catholic Studies at Xavier University in New Orleans, where she regularly taught courses on the spirituality of Black literature, Black religion and the arts, and two levels of preaching courses. Each summer from 1980 to 1988, she conducted workshops on liturgical worship and preaching for priests, sisters, and brothers who ministered in Black parishes.[107]

During the early 1980s, Sister Thea was among the group of African American scholars, musicians, and liturgical experts who created the first African American Catholic hymnal, *Lead Me, Guide Me*. The impetus for this songbook came from the NOBC and the National Black Clergy Caucus. The first edition, which appeared in 1987, contained an essay by Sister Thea explaining the origins and significance of Black sacred song. She outlined five essential characteristics: holistic, participatory, real, spirit-filled, life-giving. She emphasized that Black sacred song "is in a very real sense, the song of the people." She closed her essay by reminding her readers that "Black sacred song has been at once a source and expression of Black faith, spirituality, and devotion. By song, our people have called the Spirit into our hearts, homes, churches, and communities."[108] The publication of *Lead Me, Guide Me* filled an urgent need for Catholic worshippers, as evidenced by the sale of one hundred thousand copies in its first four years in print. Today a revised and expanded edition of *Lead Me, Guide Me* is still widely used in Catholic congregations across the United States.

Sister Thea's celebrity status rose to superstar level on May 3, 1987, when she appeared in a segment of the CBS news program *60 Minutes*. Camera crews had followed her for two years, recording Sister Thea in action in Washington, DC; New Orleans; Raymond, Mississippi; and several locations in Canton. Anchor Mike Wallace, often portrayed as a hardnosed reporter, was charmed by Sister Thea. In the foreword he later wrote for *Shooting Star*, a collection of Sister Thea's writings and speeches, he gushed: "I don't remember when I've been more moved, more enchanted by a person whom I've profiled than by Sister Thea Bowman. . . . her openness, her compassion, her intelligence, her optimism, her humor captured me."[109] Wallace introduced

---

106. Smith and Feister, *Thea's Song*, 87.
107. Nutt, *Thea Bowman*, 92.
108. Thea Bowman, "The Gift of African American Sacred Song," United States Conference of Catholic Bishops, http://usccb.org/issues-and-action/cultural-diversity/african-american/resources/upload/The-Gift-of-African-American-Sacred-Song-Sr-Thea-Bowman.pdf.
109. Mike Wallace, foreword, in Thea Bowman, *Shooting Star* (Winona, MN: Saint Mary's Press, 1993), 9.

the broadcast with these words: "Today at forty-nine, Sister Thea is still shaking people up, preaching in her African robes, not the traditional white Catholic litany, but a new Black Catholic Gospel powered by the conviction that when something is wrong you change it." When Wallace asked what set her apart from other activists, Sister Thea replied, "I think one difference between me and some other people is that I'm content to do my little bit. Sometimes people think they have to do big things in order to make change, but if each one of us would light a candle we'd have a tremendous light."[110]

In 1984, Sister Thea suffered a series of emotional blows. First, she was diagnosed with breast cancer and had a modified radical mastectomy followed by chemotherapy. Eight months later, her mother, who had been in declining health for several years, passed away. Her father then suffered a stroke and died one month after his wife. Despite the cancer and her grief, Sister Thea soon resumed her schedule of speaking engagements and national commitments. According to Smith and Feister, "Her spirit, mind, and voice would remain strong and her life would go on full tilt, until January of 1988," when her cancer returned.[111] In her battle with the dread disease, Sister Thea was an inspiration for others struggling with incurable illnesses. "I'm going to live until I die," was her oft-repeated motto.

Closing Holy Child Jesus School

Sister Nancy Lafferty, FSPA, had come to Canton in 1979 to be principal of Holy Child Jesus High School. It was her unhappy duty to close the school. She recalled in an interview, "We had an elderly faculty, especially in the high school, and they were needing to retire. I was called and asked if I would come and run the high school for one more year because the finances were such that we could see the handwriting on the wall." She formed a school board of parents and shared the school's financial picture with them. They agreed that the high school could not continue to operate. Academically, the students were in good shape. "They had good study habits and well-organized study halls, so they were ready" for the next grade, Sister Nancy recalled in an interview. Those in the rising senior class were highly motivated; they wanted to be the last class to graduate from Holy Child Jesus, so the school board decided to keep the high school open for one more year.[112] Holy Child Jesus Elementary School continued operating for three more decades, although the last FSPAs left in 1989. In April 2012, the Diocese of Jackson announced that Holy Child Jesus Elementary would also close its doors after

---

110. Bowman, cited in Wallace, foreword, in Bowman, *Shooting Star*, 10.
111. Smith and Feister, *Thea's Song*, 187.
112. Nancy Lafferty, in an interview with the author, April 29, 2019.

sixty-five years, citing declining enrollment and insufficient financial aid for students from low-income families.[113]

Accomplishments of the FSPAs and Sister Thea

When the FSPAs came to Canton in 1948, they embarked on a twofold mission: winning souls for Christ, and bringing badly needed educational opportunities to African American youngsters. Little in their training or previous experience prepared the White sisters for the challenges they faced living in a Black community in the segregated Deep South. Few of the students they taught were Catholic; many were extremely poor. The climate, the food and the culture were new and very different from what they were accustomed to. At first, their students seemed to them to speak a foreign language.

During the decades the FSPAs taught at Holy Child Jesus School, they witnessed dramatic changes in the surrounding community. When King led the March Against Fear into Canton in June 1966, the sisters welcomed him to Holy Child Jesus Mission. Inspired by the civil rights movement, African American residents of Canton and Madison County demanded basic human and civil rights: to register and vote without threats or harassment; to be served at restaurants and hotels on the same basis as Whites; to be hired as police officers, bank tellers, cashiers at supermarkets, and salespeople in retail stores. They were largely effective in achieving these goals, although prejudice and racism persisted.

The FSPAs who taught at Holy Child Jesus School can take great satisfaction in the accomplishments of their former students. Brown-Wright was elected Madison County's election commissioner in 1968, the first African American woman in the state to hold this office. Starling-Ratliff followed Sister Thea to Viterbo College, where she studied voice and education, and went on to become a beloved music teacher and school principal in Wisconsin. Pembleton won a scholarship to the University of Notre Dame, earned a PhD in organizational leadership, and is now a professor in the global business leadership department at St. John's University and St. Benedict's College in Minnesota. Walter Saddler became a television broadcaster and news anchor at Jackson-area television stations.

Of course, Sister Thea stands out among the many successful Holy Child Jesus alumni. The list of her achievements is lengthy: the first African American FSPA, a pioneer in the field of intercultural relations, the first Black woman to address the US bishops at their semiannual conference, an organizer of Black Catholic sisters, a gifted singer and song leader, a champion of

113. Terricha Bradley-Phillips, "Catholic School to Shut Doors," *Jackson Clarion-Ledger*, April 19, 2012.

Black pride, a scholar, a courageous fighter against cancer, and an inspirational speaker. Dr. Kim R. Harris, assistant professor in the theological studies department at Loyola Marymount University, has studied Sister Thea's critical role as an advocate and activist for liturgical justice. According to Harris, Sister Thea's advocacy for incorporating Black sacred songs in Catholic liturgies went beyond the need for cultural preservation and stimulating racial pride. Sister Thea saw these songs as a "valuable resource both for catechesis and for knowing those to be catechized." As Harris explained, Sister Thea recognized that Black sacred song "helped to both form the Black Catholic community as well as to inform those who sought to be in relation with them": "For Sister Thea the conscious inclusion of this music when communities gathered for prayer, and particularly for Eucharistic celebrations, was a matter of justice."[114] Her vision of cultural inclusion went beyond "Black Catholics delivering their cultural treasures to enliven worship." She envisioned a future with "Catholics of different races choosing to worship together in ways that welcomed the gifts of all." As Sister Thea famously told the bishops, "Sometime I do things your way; sometimes you do things mine."[115] Ideally, this sharing should extend beyond the liturgy to characterize all social relations and programming of the faith community.

Servant of God

Sister Thea lost her struggle with cancer on March 30, 1990. Hundreds of mourners crowded into St. Mary's Church in Jackson on April 4 for the service celebrating Sister Thea's life. She was buried in Memphis, Tennessee, next to her parents. In the years since her death, the importance of Sister Thea's message has become increasingly recognized. In a 2014 issue of *America*, the Jesuit weekly magazine, Christopher Pramuk stated, "Arguably, no person in recent memory did more to resist and transform the sad legacy of segregation and racism in the Catholic Church than Sister Thea Bowman."[116] Speaking out against racism is easy; finding effective ways of combating racial prejudice is much more difficult. Sister Thea found an answer in multiculturalism, an approach that requires people to respect and honor cultural practices of different groups as well as their own.

Meeting in Baltimore on May 15, 2018, the US Catholic bishops proclaimed Sister Thea a Servant of God, the first step toward possible canonization. On November 14, 2018, they unanimously voted to advance her cause

---

114. Kim R. Harris, "Sister Thea Bowman: Liturgical Justice through Black Sacred Song," *US Catholic Historian* 35, no. 1 (Winter 2017): 118.

115. Thea Bowman, quoted in Harris, "Sister Thea Bowman," 123.

116. Christopher Pramuk, "The Witness of Sister Thea Bowman," *America*, June 24, 2014, https://www.americamagazine.org/faith/2014/06/24/witness-sister-thea-bowman.

Thea Bowman, Servant of God. Portrait courtesy of the National Black Catholic Conference.

for sainthood. Four days later, Bishop Joseph Kopacz, bishop of Jackson, Mississippi, formally opened the investigation of her holiness. Members of a special commission have been charged with documenting Sister Thea's life and good works. One of the requirements for canonization is documented miracles attributed to the intercession of the candidate for sainthood.[117] Sister Mary Ann Gschwind, FSPA, archivist for the order and a member of the commission investigating her cause, joked in an interview, "Getting the bishops to sing 'We Shall Overcome' should be counted as Thea's first miracle."[118]

---

117. Dan Stockman, "Sr. Thea Bowman Takes Step Further Toward Canonization with Bishops' Vote," *Global Sisters Report*, November 14, 2018, https://www.globalsisters report.org/news/spirituality-equality/sr-thea-bowman-takes-step-further-toward-canon-ization-bishops-vote-55620.

118. Mary Ann Gschwind, in an interview with the author, May 1, 2019.

Chapter 5

Father Alan McCoy:
Warrior for Justice

A ctivists for social justice accomplish their objectives in various ways. Charismatic leaders directing noisy protest marches, making fiery speeches, and engaging in civil disobedience capture media attention. Other dedicated individuals outside the public spotlight, working quietly behind the scenes, sometimes have a greater long-term impact. This is true of the career of Father Alan McCoy, OFM. During the 1960s and 1970s, he, more than any other person, was responsible for aligning the St. Barbara Franciscan Province in solidarity with Cesar Chavez and the farm worker movement. As president of the Conference of Major Superiors of Men (CMSM) from 1976 to 1982, Father Alan persuaded male religious orders in the United States to adopt a more militant approach in combating the causes of inequality and oppression, both in the United States and internationally. Those who worked with him praised his ability to inspire Catholic clergy to act for social justice without antagonizing those who disagreed with him. Because he maintained a low profile and did not seek public recognition or write for publication, his name is little known today except among his fellow Franciscans.

Early Years

Alan Edward McCoy was born in Spokane, Washington, on October 7, 1913. After spending eight years in Spokane parochial schools, he enrolled in high school at Old Mission Santa Barbara seminary. In 1932, he entered the Franciscan order and continued his studies in theology and philosophy. One influential teacher was Father Raphael Von Der Haar, OFM, who guided seminarians in studying Catholic social teachings, including the papal encyclicals *Rerum Novarum* (1891) and *Quadragesimo Anno* (1931). This education took place during the Depression, when issues of poverty, unemployment, unionism, and distributive justice were most urgent.

Father Alan was ordained in 1938. The following year, his superiors selected him to study canon law at San Antonio College in Rome, a sign of their high expectations for the scholarly young friar. The outbreak of World

Father Alan McCoy. Photo courtesy of Saint Barbara Franciscan Province archives.

War II canceled his plan to sail to Italy. Instead, he enrolled at the Catholic University of America, where he earned his doctorate in canon law in 1944.

While attending Catholic University, Father Alan attended a retreat preached by Father John Hugo, a controversial priest of the Diocese of Pittsburgh. Father Hugo presented a radical critique of bourgeois Catholicism. As part of his social criticism, he advocated a simple lifestyle and encouraged activism on behalf of the poor and oppressed. Father Hugo was among a handful of American priests who defended Catholic conscientious objectors, an enormously unpopular stand to take during the patriotic fervor of World War II.[1] Dorothy Day, cofounder of the Catholic Worker movement and a friend of Father Alan's, was one of many retreatants profoundly influenced by Father Hugo's preaching. Father Hugo did not convert Day; she was committed to social justice activism and pacifism long before she encountered him. His lasting contribution to her work was his theological framework, based largely on a radical interpretation of the New Testament, which justified these pursuits.[2] It is quite likely that Father Hugo's retreat had a similar effect on young Father Alan.

---

1. See John Hugo, "Catholics Can Be Conscientious Objectors," *Catholic Worker* (May 1943).
2. See Benjamin T. Peters, *Called to Be Saints: John Hugo, the Catholic Worker and a Theology of Radical Christianity* (Milwaukee, WI: Marquette University Press, 2016), 15–28.

Accounts differ regarding the origin of Father Alan's fierce commitment to social justice. In a video interview recorded late in his life, he mentioned a memorable incident that had occurred during the xenophobic hysteria of World War I. Anti-German zealots tried to remove the German American pastor of the Franciscan parish to which the McCoy family belonged. Father Alan admired his father for defending the pastor and preventing his ouster. "That was a great experience for me," Father Alan reminisced, "to get rid of any prejudice against the Germans."[3] In an interview, Father Joseph Chinnici, OFM, recounted another pivotal experience that took place in Arizona while Father Alan waited to begin his studies at Catholic University: "He went to the local community swimming pool [in Tucson] and, as he was swimming, realized that all the African American children lined up outside the chain link fence were not allowed to swim in the same pool with the Whites." According to Father Chinnici, "This living picture of prejudice moved Alan a great deal."[4]

From 1944 to 1949, Father Alan taught canon law and moral theology at Old Mission Santa Barbara. He then moved to St. Elizabeth's parish in Oakland, California, where he filled various administrative positions for the St. Barbara Franciscan Province. Father Alan was assigned to Stockton, California, in 1955 and served in dual roles—pastor of St. Mary's parish and canon lawyer for Bishop Hugh A. Donohoe.[5]

Pastor of St. Mary's, Stockton

St. Mary's was an inner-city church located near the skid row district. It was a post well suited to Father Alan's growing commitment to social justice. While pastor in Stockton, he launched several projects to aid the poor—a dining hall in an abandoned tavern across the street from the rectory, a credit union, a depot for used clothing, a medical clinic, and housing for migrant workers. Many of Stockton's poor were *braceros*, migrant workers brought to the United States under a government program that allowed farm owners to import agricultural laborers from Mexico at harvest time. Years later, he described how San Joaquin County received thirty to forty thousand braceros each year: "Many of them were being sloughed off on the skid row because their usefulness was no longer evident. So we had a great problem with alcoholism, prostitution, dope traffic."[6] A 1975 report credited Father Alan with

---

3. Franciscan Friars—Province of St. Barbara, "Digital Memory Project," August 12, 2020, YouTube video, 21:20, https://youtu.be/eEChGK2wsKQ.

4. Joseph Chinnici, in an interview with the author, July 7, 2020.

5. Father Alan McCoy was elected president of the Canon Law Society of America in 1966.

6. Alan McCoy, oral history interview by Pat Hoffman, Farm Worker Movement Documentation Project, UC San Diego Libraries (hereafter cited as FWMDP), mp3 file, 45:20,

initiating social services that "anticipated the directions of Vatican II."[7] He also advocated for racial equality, leading a 1965 Stockton march in support of the Selma, Alabama, voting rights campaign led by Martin Luther King Jr. At a Mass of reparation following the march, he uttered words that later seemed prophetic: "It may be easy to point out the evil in another part of our country, but it is more difficult to look into our own city."[8]

The Pastoral Year

From 1957 to 1967, Father Alan mentored a hundred or more young priests in a program known as the Pastoral Year. Nearly all of the newly ordained friars of the St. Barbara Franciscan Province went to Stockton, where Father Alan supervised the final phase of their formation after they spent twelve years studying theology and philosophy in cloistered seminary settings. The program was designed to give the young priests practical, hands-on training before placement in their first full-time ministerial assignments. Father Max Hottle, OFM, reminisced in an interview, "Alan McCoy and other progressive-type people realized our formation—our theological training—was outdated or outmoded and we needed a lot more practical experience. . . . The program helped us to somehow meet reality and [taught us] how to use the theoretical stuff we'd been given for eight years."[9]

St. Mary's was a low-income parish with a large Hispanic population. It was "a far cry from seminary life in Santa Barbara, with its mountains, beaches, and middle-class resort atmosphere," observed former Franciscan Mark Day, who arrived in 1965.[10] Father Alan's concern for the poor in the parish was evident in the charitable projects he created. He gained a reputation as an advocate of justice for farm workers while serving as a board member and vice president of the Bishops' Committee for the Spanish Speaking, a body created in 1945. The committee was credited with increasing "the interaction of Catholic laity and clergy interested in the Spanish-speaking people."[11] His

---

https://libraries.ucsd.edu/farmworkermovement/media/oral_history/music/new/Alan-McCoy.mp3.

7. "Putting the Picture Together 20 Years Later—1955–1975," Stockton Box, Saint Barbara Province Archives, Old Mission Santa Barbara, California, hereafter cited as St. Barbara Province Archives. The same report also criticized Father Alan for "being absent from the parish for long periods."

8. Alan McCoy, cited in "Selma March," *The Monitor*, March 18, 1965, Stockton Box, St. Barbara Province Archives.

9. Max Hottle, in an interview with the author, July 9, 2020.

10. Mark Day, *Forty Acres: Cesar Chavez and the Farm Workers* (New York: Praeger, 1971), 15.

11. Leo Grebler, Joan W. Moore, and Ralph Guzman, *The Mexican American People: The Nation's Second Largest Minority* (New York: Free Press, 1970), 462. For more on the

opposition to the exploitation of Mexican seasonal workers brought in part to San Joaquin County by the bracero program won him the enmity of large growers in the region.

During the Pastoral Year program, the new priests rotated through placements in the city and beyond. Some got acquainted with Stockton by taking a census of parish residents. In teams of two, they went from house to house enumerating Catholic residents. Father Hottle recounted the experience of "two lucky guys" from his cohort who called on the house of prostitution across the street from St. Mary's rectory: "They went up the steps, knocked on the door, and this nice lady, the madam, gave them a list of all the girls, indicating which ones were Catholic."[12] Father Hottle got to know the African American residents he ministered to in Parchester Village, a housing development in Richmond. Other friars served as chaplains at the city jail or made hospital calls. Everyone took turns answering the rectory door, receiving people seeking assistance, and answering the phone. On weekends, each of the new priests said Mass in one of the towns outside of Stockton.

Two or three times each week, Father Alan met with the young friars to help them process what they were experiencing in their assignments. Father Ignatius DeGroot, OFM, remembered walking with his mentor in the evenings while both got their daily exercise: "We would ask him questions about how it [our day] went."[13] Father Hottle described Father Alan's method as "very nondirective," recalling that his mentor would ask, "What did you see? What did they say? What do you think it meant? What do you think should be done?" "He did give us input," Father Hottle said, but Father Alan refused to solve their problems for them. One example of this approach was his response to their weekly sermons. Each man in the program dutifully submitted the text of his Sunday sermon for Father Alan's advance approval. Most times, the sermons were returned to their mailboxes without comment. When asked why he did not comment, Father Hottle recalled, Father Alan would say, "I'm not going to tell you what to say. You have to be the one to see the situation, make the judgment, and do what you think is right."[14]

The young priests had numerous opportunities to put his advice into practice. "We had a constant stream of people coming by," Father Hottle recollected: "People needing food. 'Father, I ran out of gas.' 'Father, my family

work of the Bishops' Committee for the Spanish Speaking, see Todd Scribner, "'Mexicans Might Someday Be the Salvation of the Church': The Work of the Bishops' Committee for the Spanish Speaking, 1945–1970," *Southwest Catholic* 27 (2016): 2–16.

12. Hottle, interview.

13. Ignatius DeGroot, in an interview with the author, July 9, 2020.

14. Hottle, interview. These words indicate the influence of the "see, judge, act" Catholic Action methodology popularized by the Belgian Cardinal Joseph Cardijn, founder of the Young Christian Worker movement.

and I just came in from Oklahoma. We have no place to stay.'" The men in the Pastoral Year program had multiple resources to call on to solve the problems they encountered. Father Alan "had established connections with pretty much every social service in the city," Father Hottle observed: "Alan had worked out a system of vouchers with all these different establishments around town. The motels, the markets, the pharmacies, the gas stations." It was up to Pastoral Year participants to listen to the people's stories and decide which services were appropriate. "Challenging. That's a good word for Alan's method with us. He was challenging us," Father Hottle concluded.[15]

In an interview, Father Ray Bucher, OFM, reviewed their daily routine: "We would have classes in the morning and pastoral work in the afternoon, sometimes in the evening, depending on what we were doing. . . . The beautiful thing was, we would come home at night and share our experiences in the kitchen." Each of the friars was responsible for a small part of the parish. "I had a section called the Lafayette neighborhood," Father Bucher recalled. "I really got to know the families. I was like their priest. When there would be problems, they'd call me, and not just spiritual problems. I remember one parent calling me panicked about her child's stolen bike. She was sure I could find out who did it and get it back. And I did. It was a hands-on ministry."[16]

Father Alan invited guest speakers to share their knowledge and expertise with the Pastoral Year friars. Two speakers who impressed the young priests with their dedication to social justice were Fathers Donald McDonnell and Thomas McCullough. Together with two other Spanish-speaking diocesan priests, they made up the Spanish Mission Band, which worked among and advocated for migrant farm workers from 1950 to 1961.[17] San Francisco's Archbishop John J. Mitty released these men from parish duties so they could minister directly to migrant farm workers. Their "day-to-day involvement with Mexican farm laborers created a heightened sensitivity to the larger socioeconomic issues which were seen to underlie their religious condition."[18]

The dedicated young priests soon realized "that providing spiritual care alone was not enough."[19] They began to focus on community organizing. Father McDonnell was responsible for tutoring Chavez about Catholic social justice teachings and introduced him to Fred Ross, who hired Chavez to work

---

15. Hottle, interview.

16. Ray Bucher, in an interview with the author, July 14, 2020.

17. Frank Bardacke, *Trampling Out the Vintage: Cesar Chavez and the Two Souls of the United Farm Workers* (Brooklyn: Verso, 2012), 58–60. Father Alan served as secretary of the Mission Band for several years.

18. Grebler, Moore, and Guzman, *Mexican American People*, 464.

19. Jeffrey M. Burns, "The Mexican Catholic Community in California," in Jay P. Dolan and Gilberto M. Hinojosa, eds., *Mexican Americans and the Catholic Church, 1900–1965* (Notre Dame, IN: University of Notre Dame Press, 1994), 216.

as an organizer. Father McCullough did the same for Dolores Huerta, who later worked with Chavez to found the United Farm Workers (UFW) union. As Spanish Mission Band members became more active in supporting farm worker unionization, they ran into opposition from Catholic growers, who accused the priests of being communist sympathizers. In 1961, the priests incurred the wrath of San Diego's Bishop Charles F. Buddy after they appeared at a meeting in support of striking lettuce workers. Unfortunately, Archbishop Mitty, a staunch defender of the Spanish Mission Band, died that same year, and the members were reassigned by an unsympathetic administrator shortly after.[20] Chavez himself acknowledged the contributions of these activist clergymen, mentioning instances where "priests would speak out loudly and clearly against specific instances of oppression."[21]

Though Father Alan gave his charges considerable latitude to solve problems they encountered, he insisted that they adhere to a simple lifestyle and follow proper clerical procedure. Some of the young men in the program resented the strict rules he laid down. "We were not allowed to go to theaters in town, so of course we found ways to go to the theaters out of town," Father Bucher recalled. "The TV was kept in the closet. We felt as if we were being treated as if we were still clerics in the seminary." One of Father Bucher's ministries that year was being advisor to Catholic students at the University of the Pacific. In April 1966, he encouraged them to turn out in support of striking farm workers who were making a historic pilgrimage from Delano to the state capitol building in Sacramento. Chavez started marching with sixty union members (their number would grow during the march). They covered more than three hundred miles in twenty-five days. Farm worker Roberto Bustos described their objective: "Our mission was to go see the governor (Pat Brown) and complain about the treatment of the strikers by the growers and the police department."[22] Father Alan informed the young friar Father Bucher, "The bishop [Hugh A. Donohoe] doesn't want any of you in the pilgrimage." Father Alan actively supported the farm worker march

---

20. For more on the Spanish Mission Band, see A. V. Krebs, "Don't Waste Any Time in Mourning. Organize," chap. 1 of La Causa: *The Word Was Made Flesh*, n.d., FWMDP, https://libraries.ucsd.edu/farmworkermovement/essays/essays/KREBS%20MANU-SCRIPT%20LA%20CAUSA.pdf; and John Duggan, *John Duggan Autobiography*, n.d., FWMDP, https://libraries.ucsd.edu/farmworkermovement/essays/essays/John%20Duggan%20Autobiography.pdf.

21. Cesar E. Chavez, "The Mexican-American and the Church" (paper, Second Annual Mexican Conference, Sacramento, CA, March 8–10, 1968), FWMDP, https://libraries.ucsd.edu/farmworkermovement/essays/essays/Cesar%20Chavez%20-%20The%20Mexican-American%20and%20the%20Church.pdf.

22. Roberto A. Bustos, "The March to Sacramento," n.d., FWMDP, https://libraries.ucsd.edu/farmworkermovement/wp-content/uploads/2012/05/THE-MARCH-TO-SACRAMENTO.pdf.

by inviting the marchers to stay in St. Mary's parish hall when they passed through Stockton and saying the blessing over their evening meal. However, he did not want Father Bucher, a young priest, getting in trouble by disobeying the bishop. Father Bucher was indignant. "But Father, I talked my students into going at some risk and inconvenience, and now I'm going to back out. It will look cowardly," he remembered objecting. Father Alan advised him to make an appointment to talk with Bishop Donohoe. The young friar met with the bishop, who relented and gave his permission. "As I left, he said, 'If you end up in jail, don't expect me to come bail you out,'" Father Bucher chuckled in an interview. He cited this incident as an example of following Father Alan's advice: "You work it out."[23]

One experience shared by two Spanish-speaking Pastoral Year participants was conducting a *cursillo*, a three-day retreat format first developed in Spain, which spread among Hispanic Catholics in the United States during the late 1950s and early 1960s. The name comes from *cursillos de cristiandad*, meaning "short courses in Christianity." It consists of fifteen talks given by priests and lay people, designed to help lay Catholics become effective leaders in their communities and to develop a more personal relationship to Jesus. Father Alan is credited with introducing the cursillo to California in 1961. Father Hottle described a cursillo that he and Father Finian McGinn, OFM, conducted for seventy-two Spanish-speaking women. They started hearing the women's confessions on Friday evening, a process that continued until two in the morning. The weekend retreat left the two priests completely exhausted, although the women participants seemed "absolutely fine."[24]

The placement that probably had the greatest impact on the young friars was visiting labor camps on islands in the San Joaquin River delta, one of the state's most fertile agricultural regions. Owners of large farms there grew potatoes, tomatoes, asparagus, and other crops. They employed crews of workers, many of them Mexican migrants. The neophyte priests held catechism classes and said Mass for the workers on weekends. According to Jeffrey Burns, "In 1962 more than 100 bracero camps were being visited by the fifth-year Franciscans."[25] Father DeGroot described the living conditions on the islands: "In the labor camps there was mainly guys. There were some families and some

23. Bucher, interview. Later, Bishop Hugh A. Donohoe celebrated Mass at St. Mary's Church for the farm workers and their supporters who were marching to the capitol. "2,500 Gather to Encourage Farm Workers Pilgrimage," *Stockton Record*, April 4, 1966, Stockton Box, St. Barbara Province Archives.

24. Hottle, interview. Cesar Chavez was an enthusiastic *cursillo* alumnus. He encouraged other graduates "to put their cursillo into practice by inviting them to union meetings." Keith Warner, "The Farm Workers and the Franciscans: Reverse Evangelization as Social Prompt for Conversion," *Spiritus* 9 no. 1 (Spring 2009): 74.

25. Burns, "Mexican Catholic Community," 229.

kids. They lived in shacks." The single men ate their meals together and slept in a common dormitory. Many of these workers stayed on the farms year-round, he said, except when "they went back to Mexico for Christmas and New Year to see their families." For most Pastoral Year participants, this was their first exposure to the deplorable living conditions endured by agricultural workers. For Father DeGroot, however, this was nothing new. He identified with the migrants because he had emigrated with his parents and siblings from the Netherlands to the United States. He grew up on the family farm, so he understood the demands of agricultural labor and valued the work the migrants did. His father sometimes hired Mexican workers to help on their farm. At mealtimes, the migrants sat at the table with the DeGroot family. Father DeGroot remembered his father saying, "They work with us, they eat with us."[26]

Equally important in influencing the outlook of the young priests were the documents issued by the Second Vatican Council (1962–65), which reshaped Catholic thinking on the relationship between the Church and society. Mark Day credited the Council's *Constitution on the Church in the Modern World* (*Gaudium et Spes*) with helping to break down the false dichotomies between the Church and the world. He quoted its opening passage as being essential to this revised outlook: "The cares and concerns, the joys and sorrows of all men and women are the joys and concerns of the church as the People of God."[27] Mark Day and other Catholic activists relied on this and other Council teachings to legitimize their participation in movements for social justice.

Provincial Minister

Father Alan was elected provincial minister of the St. Barbara Franciscan Province in April 1967, a time of reform among Catholic religious orders around the globe. From May to July of that year, Franciscan general minister Father Constantine Koser, OFM, presided over an extraordinary general chapter (a gathering for discernment and election) that met in Assisi, Italy. He announced the chapter's objective as reclaiming two basic characteristics of early Franciscans: "fidelity to the Gospel both in spirit and letter and a preference for looser organizational structures."[28] Reverberations from that gathering echoed throughout the Franciscan world.

---

26. DeGroot, interview.

27. Second Vatican Council, *Constitution on the Church in the Modern World* (*Gaudium et Spes*), n. 1, quoted in Mark R. Day, "1967–1970, My Time with the UFW," FWMDP, https://libraries.ucsd.edu/farmworkermovement/essays/essays/043%20Day_Mark.pdf.

28. Joseph M. White, *"Peace and Good in America": A History of the Holy Name Province Order of Friars Minor, 1950s to the Present* (New York: Holy Name Province, 2004), 371.

One year later, Father Alan presided at a historic chapter of the St. Barbara Franciscan Province that came to be known as the Malibu renewal chapter. At this conclave, the friar delegates considered ways in which they might implement the sweeping reforms initiated by the Second Vatican Council. Father Alan hoped to realign the province's mission to better serve the poor and oppressed, and he sought ways to return to the simple lifestyle advocated by St. Francis. According to Father Chinnici, this chapter was the most contentious in provincial history: "You had the social justice contingent associated with Alan, and you had the more conservative people that weren't quite willing to move that far." Discussion grew heated as Father Alan, backed by young friars he had mentored, locked horns with established friars in larger friaries and inherited ministries. Debate was so intense that "they had to take time off . . . because everybody was at each other's throat over the direction of the province."[29]

In an interview, Father Chinnici identified three practical questions under consideration during that chapter:

- Were the friars to be dominantly involved in parish work, and where should those parishes be located?
- Were the friars to be involved in high school work in the five high schools operated by the province at the time?
- What about the retreat centers they ran, that by this time had been serving the Catholic middle class?[30]

A brief story in the *San Francisco Examiner*, dated May 16, 1968, announced key decisions made during the chapter, but it made no mention of the heated debates that produced them. In answer to the first question, it reported, "The Franciscans are moving out of the parishes and into the slums." The article continued, "A large portion of its 490 members in seven western states will be reassigned to poverty areas, migrant worker projects, and even to college campus peace movements." The response to the second question was as follows: "The Franciscans will vacate St Mary's High school in Stockton next month, and at least one more school later."[31] (Eventually, the province abandoned all of the high schools it previously had served.) The article did not mention the third question, however, because the chapter did

---

29. Chinnici, interview. This conflict was not unique to the Saint Barbara Province. Joseph M. White reported a similar divide along generational lines in the Holy Name Province. with younger friars arguing for "greater individual freedom and responsibility to choose their own apostolates." White, *Peace and Good*, 374.

30. White, *Peace and Good*, 374.

31. "Catholic Workers in Slums," *San Francisco Examiner*, May 16, 1968, https://www.newspapers.com/clip/25600184/the-san-francisco-examiner.

not resolve it. According to Father Chinnici, the issue of the friars' presence in the retreat centers festered for years afterwards.[32]

Ministering to Farm Workers

By the mid-1960s, the farm worker movement was gaining momentum. Chavez emerged as its leading spokesman and, after years of frustration and disappointment, began having success in building a disciplined force to challenge the growers' power. After the 1968 Malibu chapter, friars walked away from assignments in more affluent communities to follow more closely the path laid out for them eight centuries earlier by St. Francis of Assisi. The order assumed responsibility for Mexican American parishes in Fresno, San Jose, Union City, and Delano. Father Alan handpicked the friars to serve in these parishes. When they entered full-time ministry, some of the young friars mentored by Father Alan sought positions working with farm laborers. When their pro-union activities were criticized by bishops or lay Catholics opposed to farm worker unionization, he tried to shield his protégés from reprisals while counseling them to avoid unnecessarily antagonizing the hierarchy.

Inspired by Father Alan's guidance, the example of the Spanish Mission Band, and their own experiences in the labor camps, several Pastoral Year alumni participated in the farm worker movement of the late 1960s and 1970s.[33] The first of the young Franciscans to minister to agricultural laborers was Father Eddie Fronske, OFM. As a seminary student, he had made a special effort to learn Spanish, thinking it would be useful in future assignments. Daily he walked the mission grounds with a fellow seminarian from Mexico. "He'd speak English and I'd speak Spanish," Father Fronske reported in an interview. "I really wanted to learn it, and [I] learned it quite well." Following Father Fronske's ordination, when his classmates went to Stockton for the Pastoral Year, Father Alan had other plans for him. The St. Barbara Franciscan Province had recently assumed responsibility for staffing the largely Mexican American congregation at Our Lady of Guadalupe parish in Delano. Its elderly Spanish pastor, Father Francis X. Alabart, was assigned to another parish, so Father Alan sent young Spanish-speaking friars to Our Lady of Guadalupe. He selected Fathers Fronske and Alcuin Peck, OFM. Delano had two Catholic parishes, divided by ethnicity and support for the farm worker union. The east side of town was home to the Anglo population, and the west

---

32. Chinnici, interview.

33. During the 1940s and 1950s, Father Arthur "Arturo" Librantz, OFM, traveled to bracero camps pulling a portable chapel on a trailer, which he used to offer Masses and hear confessions of migrant workers. His was a sacramental ministry that did not involve labor activism. According to Brother Keith Warner, Father Librantz "did not favor union actions against growers." Warner, "Farm Workers and Franciscans," 71.

side was populated by Mexican Americans, Filipinos, and Blacks. "Our parish
was the strike parish, and the other one was the growers' parish," Father
Fronske recalled. "I wasn't that much in the struggle," he explained years
later. "I was getting to know our people who were in the struggle."[34]

Filipino farm workers had launched a strike against Delano-area grape
growers in September 1965, demanding higher wages for their labor. Mexican
American workers, led by Chavez, joined the strike one week later. With his
emphasis on nonviolence, Chavez drew support from labor and religious leaders, but the growers refused to negotiate. In 1965, Chavez called for a
national consumer boycott of table grapes to put additional pressure on growers to settle. By 1968, ten grape growers had signed the first union contracts
with the UFW, but the strike and boycott continued until 1970, when twenty-
six more growers signed.

Chavez was one of Father Fronske's parishioners. "I got to know Cesar
really well and really loved him," Father Fronske declared in an interview. "He
was brilliant. He was kind. He was nonviolent." When Chavez fasted, Father
Fronske took Communion to him, the only food the farm worker leader consumed. When tensions between the farm workers allied with Chavez and their
opponents became especially inflamed, Franciscans helped to cool tempers.
One day in 1970, Father Fronske was called by striking farm workers picketing
in Wasco, a California town not far from Delano. "We're not going to be able
to keep being nonviolent anymore," the caller told him. "It's getting too hard.
Can you say Mass in the park so we cannot resort to violence?" According to
Father Fronske, that morning people "from all over the United States" had
come to reinforce the strikers. Among these supporters were "priests and religious . . . all different denominations of Christians and Jews." The growers
made a serious mistake, he explained, when they "went down the road and
sprayed the people who were on both sides of the road—nuns, priests, rabbis—
with this pesticide."[35] The strike supporters who were soaked with poisonous
chemicals were furious, and some wanted to retaliate. Father Fronske went to
Wasco and offered Mass. Afterward, the strikers thanked him for helping them
avoid responding violently in the face of extreme provocation.

After teaching high school in Oakland for three years, Father DeGroot
joined Father Fronske in Delano in 1970 as pastor of Our Lady of Guadalupe
parish. He too sided with the farm workers, although he considered his role
as being more a peacemaker than a partisan. "There was a ministerial association in the town, and I, as pastor, was part of it," he remembered in an interview. "We would go walk on the picket lines so that there would be no violence, because a group of growers had invited the Teamsters Union to take

34. Eddie Fronske, in an interview with the author, July 14, 2020.
35. Fronske, interview.

over. . . . They came in cars to do violence, to scare people."[36] Father DeGroot and Father Fronske "had to juggle their desire to affirm the farm workers' struggle for justice with the pastoral needs for reconciliation within a fractured parish."[37] Like other Franciscans defending the farm worker movement, the two friars encountered criticism from Catholics opposed to the union, but they remained loyal to the strikers. In 1965, Father Alabart, the parish's elderly priest, had allowed the union to use the parish hall for the meeting that authorized the strike against grape growers, but in the face of intense pressure from growers, he changed his position. According to Burns, Father Alabart "spoke out against the [farm worker] movement and urged the strikers to return to work."[38] The two newly assigned Franciscans reversed this stance and reopened the parish hall to union meetings, prompting growers to cut their financial support for Our Lady of Guadalupe parish. A group of dissident parishioners circulated a petition imploring the bishop to bring back Father Alabart. One of the petitioners complained, "We are urged at church to support Cesar Chavez and the union. We want a priest who will attend to the needs of the parishioners and not just work in politics."[39]

Father Fronske recounted an incident with one disgruntled member of the parish, who called the rectory saying he was coming to take back the bench he had donated to the church. Father Peck, who was then the pastor, told him, "That's fine. You can come on over. We'll have a man here from the press and a photographer. He'll take your picture and you can give an explanation [for] why you're taking a bench out of a church." The complaining caller never showed up to reclaim his gift to the church.[40] Despite the defection of some unhappy parish members, Father DeGroot acknowledged, "I was conscious that I had the strong backing of our provincial"—Father Alan.[41]

Fathers DeGroot and Fronske joined with other Franciscans ministering to Mexican Americans in an informal group known as the Valley Friars. They came together periodically for social analysis and support. They reflected on new concepts flowing from the Second Vatican Council and discussed how these could be applied to their ministries.[42]

The Franciscan friar most deeply involved with the farm workers' cause was Mark Day. In February 1967, as he neared completion of his Pastoral Year program, he visited the Delano headquarters of the National Farm Work-

36. DeGroot, interview.
37. Warner, "Farm Workers and Franciscans," 76.
38. Burns, "Mexican Catholic Community," 232.
39. Quoted in "Delano Petitions Seek Return of Catholic Priest," *Fresno Bee*, May 11, 1968, Alan McCoy file, St. Barbara Province Archives.
40. Fronske, interview.
41. DeGroot, interview.
42. Warner, "Farm Workers and Franciscans," 74.

ers Association, the organization that evolved into the UFW. There he met union leaders Chavez and Huerta. They pleaded with him, he recalled: "Oh my God, please come here. The priests are terrible. The pastor [of the farm worker parish] rails against the people for putting pennies in the collection box, and that's all they have."[43] Although most of the farm workers were Catholic, and Chavez himself was a devout Catholic, he wondered why the California Migrant Ministry (CMM), sponsored by Protestant churches, was the religious organization most active in assisting his efforts to organize agricultural laborers.

In a 1968 essay, Chavez scolded the Catholic Church for its inaction: "Why do the Protestants come out here and help the people, demanding nothing . . . while our own parish priests stay in their churches?"[44] Father Alan was determined to correct this disconcerting situation. He was aware of CMM's efforts and was in regular contact with its director, Reverend Chris Hartmire. In 1967, Reverend Hartmire reported, "They [the strikers] are estranged from the institutional Catholic Church and in need of pastoral care, relevant worship and mission education. The CMM and others have been pressing various Catholic groups to reach out to the strikers and provide such services. We are close to a breakthrough with the Franciscans."[45]

Mark Day promised Chavez and Huerta that he would request an assignment in the Fresno diocese, where the farm workers' Delano headquarters was located. When he returned to Stockton, Day met with Father Alan and told him, "Alan, they really want me to go down there [to Delano] and work." Day felt fortunate to have a mentor like Father Alan and to be a Franciscan at a time when the order "was trying to return to its roots as a brotherhood committed to the poor."[46] Two months after their conversation, when Father Alan took over as provincial minister of the St. Barbara Franciscan Province, he was in a much better position to help Day realize his dream of assisting the farm workers.

In September 1967, Father Alan sent Mark Day to Delano as an assistant at Our Lady of Guadalupe parish. On weekends Day helped Fathers Peck and Fronske, hearing confessions and saying Sunday Mass. "During the week I worked full-time" with the farm workers, he stated. Day was known as the chaplain of the farm worker union. His duties included the usual priestly functions. "I listened to their problems, married their sons and daughters, baptized their babies, and buried their dead," he wrote. He began his ministry to union members by celebrating Mass wearing "a bright red robe emblazoned with

---

43. Mark Day, in an interview with the author, December 14, 2019.
44. Chavez, "Mexican-Americans and the Church."
45. Chris Hartmire, "Report to the Commission on the California Migrant Ministry," September 29–30, 1967, Alan McCoy file, St. Barbara Province Archives.
46. Day, "My Time with UFW." Mark Day later left the priesthood.

Mark Day saying Mass at end of Cesar Chavez's fast, Delano, California March 10, 1968. Father Dave Duran, OFM, on right. Father Eddie Fronske, OFM, and Father Tom Messner, OFM, on left. Photo by George Ballis. Reprinted with permission.

the black eagle [the UFW symbol]."[47] But he also carried out many nontraditional tasks, such as rising at 5:00 a.m. to accompany strikers on picket lines, traveling to distant cities to organize support for the boycott of nonunion grapes, and editing the farm worker newspaper, *El malcriado*.[48]

Mark Day had been in Delano no more than a few weeks when Bishop Aloysius Willinger of the Fresno diocese complained to Father Alan about a young friar stirring up trouble. Father Alan advised Day to make a strategic retreat; he should leave Delano and lie low for a while. The Franciscan provincial knew that Bishop Willinger was due to retire and that a new bishop might be more receptive to Day's efforts. Day withdrew to Fresno, where he found a job as a laborer on a date and raisin farm. "I wanted to get some idea of what it was like to do farm work," he explained in an interview. Toiling in the broiling sun, he lost twenty-five pounds.[49] A few months later, Bishop Timothy Manning took over as leader of the diocese. Father Alan was hopeful that

47. Description of Day's vestments from Miriam Pawel, *The Crusades of Cesar Chavez: A Biography* (New York: Bloomsbury Press, 2014), 146.

48. Day, *Forty Acres*, 20.

49. Day, *Forty Acres*, 20.

Bishop Manning would be more sympathetic to the farm worker cause. "I have known Bishop Manning for many years and respect him very much," Father Alan wrote to CMM's Reverend Hartmire.[50]

Mark Day returned to Delano, but before long the new bishop also wanted him gone from Delano. Day requested a meeting with Bishop Manning. When he told Chavez of his impending consultation with the new bishop and his anticipated second expulsion, the irate labor leader declared, "It's not going to happen." As expected, when Day conferred with Bishop Manning, the bishop bristled when the young priest questioned his authority. As Day exited the bishop's office, he passed a group of farm workers entering the building, all of them women dispatched by Chavez to confront the bishop. One of them was Helen Chavez, Cesar's wife. The women staged a sit-in in Bishop Manning's chamber, refusing to leave until he met with them. In the meantime, the chancery was barraged by phone calls from the *San Francisco Chronicle*, the *Los Angeles Times*, the *New York Times*, and the Associated Press, asking whether it was true that Bishop Manning had expelled Day from Delano. Cesar Chavez had tipped off reporters about what was happening.[51]

Eventually, the bishop met with the women. They told him they needed a priest who believed in their cause and who could minister to their needs as striking farm workers. They needed a priest like Mark Day because he understood their needs.[52] They asked, "Why does he [Father Mark] have to leave?" Bishop Manning replied, "Because I am the bishop, and God speaks through me." Rachel Orendain, one of the farm workers, spoke up: "I'm just a poor farmer, but God speaks through me too." Fearful of negative press exposure, Bishop Manning signed a statement rescinding his order to remove the Franciscan agitator.[53]

Decades later, LeRoy Chatfield, a key Chavez lieutenant, recounted,

> Cesar Chavez was so fed up with the refusal of the California Bishops to defend the rights of farm workers to organize their own union—rights authorized, promoted and sanctioned by the official teaching of the Roman Catholic Church—he decided to use the case of Father Mark Day as an opportunity to "take a shot across their bow" and give the Bishops a real-life example and fair warning about what they should expect to come their way in the near future. . . . Chavez's message was received by the California Bishops, so much so, that within a six month period there was a sea-change of attitude and respect by the Bishops about the rights of farm workers to organize their own union.[54]

---

50. McCoy, to Chris Hartmire, October 30, 1967, United Farm Worker file, St. Barbara Province Archives.

51. Day, interview.

52. LeRoy Chatfield, email message to the author, September 9, 2020.

53. Day, interview.

54. Chatfield, email.

Father Louie Vitale, OFM, who became provincial minister of the St. Barbara Franciscan Province three years after Father Alan left that post, listed other ways his friend and mentor assisted Chavez and the farm worker union:

He [Alan McCoy] would arrange to have Cesar Chavez come and talk [to the friars]. I remember having him at a board meeting. He [Chavez] was very pleased to have access to leadership at that level. Cesar was a very strong, active Catholic and that tends to win people over. . . . The friars were very impressed by him because he was a daily communicant. . . . He would come to some of our meetings and would show a film or whatever he had, and talk about the situation of the farm workers and whatever they were doing.[55]

Huerta credited Father Alan with bringing Franciscans into the farm worker movement: "I don't think there's any other way that one can learn unless you're walking in the other person's shoes. Father Alan was willing to do that, to literally walk in the shoes of the farm workers. . . . So when we got in the middle of this big strike and everything, they [the Franciscans] were there to support us. And it was also very important because at that time we didn't have the bishops supporting us."[56]

Franciscan Support for the Farm Worker Movement

During the winter and spring of 1967–68, the UFW engaged in the prolonged and bitter strike against California grape growers. On occasion, striking farm workers retaliated against strike breakers with vandalism and physical attacks. On February 19, 1968, Chavez announced he was beginning a fast in penance for the violence committed by striking farm workers. Mark Day offered to celebrate a public Mass every night during the fast, which Cesar could attend. At first, the Masses were held indoors; but as the crowds increased in size, they took place outdoors, in front of the adobe building where Chavez rested. Day searched the Bible for passages referring to penance and sacrifice. Special guests were invited to speak.[57] This daily event mobilized farm workers and captured national media attention. As many as five hundred union members camped in tents on the grounds of Forty Acres, the union headquarters, and participated in the evening Masses. They joined in singing "De Colores," the Mexican folk song popularized by the cursillo movement and associated with the union. Chavez would rise from his cot and walk outside to take the Communion host and drink from the chalice. LeRoy

55. Louie Vitale, interview, n.d., Conference of Major Superiors of Men Records (henceforth CMSM Records), AMSM 23463000, University of Notre Dame Archives.
56. Dolores Huerta, quoted in Warner, "Farm Workers and Franciscans," 73.
57. Pawel, *Crusades of Cesar Chavez*, 161–62.

Chatfield, a former Christian Brother, credited these Masses with capturing the meaning of the fast: "If we had not had mass, out at the Forty Acres, much of the meaning of the fast would have been lost."[58]

On March 11, 1968, the final day of the fast, a dozen priests, including Mark Day and Father Vitale, concelebrated a public Mass before a crowd estimated to be between six and ten thousand people. Chavez sat with his mother, his wife, and Senator Robert Kennedy on an improvised stage on the back of a flatbed truck. Biographer Miriam Pawel wrote, "Chris Hartmire handed Chavez the bread to break his fast. Then Chavez reached out to share the bread with Kennedy."[59] The fast was a success because it generated national publicity about the strike, increased Chavez's support among Catholics, and applied more pressure on the growers to settle with the union.[60]

Chavez engaged in a second fast in August 1970, prior to a strike against lettuce and vegetable growers in the Salinas Valley. Tensions were inflamed because three dozen growers had signed "sweetheart contracts" with the Teamsters union to avoid negotiating with the United Farm Worker Organizing Committee (UFWOC). Chavez claimed that his union represented nearly all of the five thousand workers covered by these contracts and that the Teamsters had no right to represent them. This time his penitential ordeal lasted only six days. "The fast was a flop," Chavez later told a writer.[61] It accomplished nothing. Afterward, the farm worker leader sought a safe and secluded place where he could rest and recuperate. He contacted Father Alan, who spoke with Father Gilbert Zlater, OFM, guardian of the St. Francis retreat center in San Juan Bautista. Father Zlater offered to shelter Chavez and his family at Casa San Jose, a small house on the center's property. Chavez stayed there for the next month, directing union staffers, in person and by phone, during ongoing negotiations with the growers. Brother Angelo Cardinalli, OFM, the center's cook, answered the door many times to find process servers looking for Chavez, but the brother refused to disclose his location. By the time Chavez left Casa San Jose, the retreat's divan was piled high with unserved subpoenas.[62]

At a rally in Salinas on August 22, three thousand farm workers cheered as leaders of twenty-seven ranch committees announced their intention to strike against the growers. The following day, "as many as 3,000 active picketers . . . faced off against a few hundred scabs." The three-and-a-half-week

58. Fred Ross Sr., "Interview with LeRoy Chatfield and Mark Day, Part 1," FWMDP, mp3 file, 1:11:43, https://libraries.ucsd.edu/farmworkermovement/media/oral_history/RossSr/fast-15%20Leroy%20A%20and%20B%20Edit.mp3.

59. Pawel, *Crusades of Cesar Chavez*, 168.

60. Bardacke, *Trampling Out the Vintage*, 293–97.

61. Bardacke, *Trampling Out the Vintage*, 366.

62. Angelo Cardinalli, in an interview with the author, December 16, 2019.

strike reduced the lettuce harvest by nearly two-thirds. Production of other fruits and vegetables fell off dramatically. While on strike, the idle workers received weekly union benefits of twenty-five dollars per striker, fifteen dollars per spouse, and five dollars per child. According to author Frank Bardacke, "The money for the benefits came from various large donations, including an interest-free loan of $125,000 from the Franciscan Fathers of California."[63] One by one, most major growers and several smaller ones abandoned Teamster contracts and signed with the UFWOC. Although not all growers came on board, this strike led to a major UFW victory.

The Franciscans' conspicuous support for the farm worker strike hurt the St. Barbara Franciscan Province financially. In prior decades, retreat houses operated by the province "had received substantial financial and material support from growers." Many of those making retreats at the Franciscan facilities came from parishes closely linked to agricultural interests. Catholic growers were outraged when they saw friars actively supporting the union and especially when they learned that Chavez had stayed at one of the retreat houses operated by the province. Brother Keith Warner, OFM, reported, "They [the growers] withdrew their [financial] support and persuaded others to stop attending events." This retaliation brought two of the retreat centers "to the brink of financial collapse in the late 1970s," although they later recovered.[64] Despite these losses, Mark Day wrote, "the fathers took everything in good spirits and looked forward to the time when they could again offer their hospitality to Cesar and his family."[65]

The friars of St. Barbara Franciscan Province assisted the UFW in other ways. In September 1968, Chavez checked into a hospital in San Jose to be treated for a serious back ailment. Upon discharge, he needed a safe place to recuperate. According to Pawel, he "moved to a small room at St. Anthony's seminary in Santa Barbara." After soaking in a hot pool his health improved dramatically.[66] On several occasions the UFW board of directors met at Franciscan properties. On July 1, 1968, Chatfield sent Father Alan a check for thirty dollars, thanking him for the union's use of Mission San Antonio. Father Alan returned the check, writing, "We feel that this is something that we, ourselves, should take care of."[67] In his memoir, titled *Forty Acres*, Mark Day disclosed that in July 1970 the friars at Mission Santa Barbara donated an elaborate printing press to the union.[68]

---

63. Bardacke, *Trampling Out the Vintage*, 371–72.
64. Warner, "Farm Workers and Franciscans," 80.
65. Day, *Forty Acres*, 201.
66. Pawel, *Crusades of Cesar Chavez*, 175.
67. McCoy, to LeRoy Chatfield, August 5, 1968, Alan McCoy file, St. Barbara Province Archives.
68. Day, *Forty Acres*, 57.

Brother Ed Dunn

A latecomer to the farm worker movement was Brother Ed Dunn, OFM. When Father Fronske first encountered him at the Mexican American Cultural Center, Brother Ed belonged to the Augustinian order. "We would go on these long walks, just talk and talk," Father Fronske recalled. "He [Brother Ed] said, 'I don't want to be Augustinian. I don't want to teach all my life. I want to get more involved with people.'"[69] In 1975, Brother Ed joined the Franciscans and soon began working as an organizer with the UFW. In the spring and summer of 1976, Brother Ed assisted the UFW in gathering signatures on petitions to place Proposition 14 on California's November ballot. The previous year Governor Jerry Brown's landmark legislation, the Agricultural Labor Relations Act had passed but funding remained a problem. Proposition 14 sought to guarantee funding for the state's Agriculture Labor Relations Board, which was created to supervise elections for agricultural union representation.[70] In the midst of this campaign, Brother Ed approached Father Oliver Lynch, OFM, pastor of St. Elizabeth's parish in Oakland, with a last-minute request. Brother Ed was bringing a group of farm workers to the city to make presentations about Proposition 14 at churches and community centers. "Would it be possible for 70 farm workers to sleep in the [parish] hall?" Brother Ed asked. When Father Lynch agreed, Brother Ed added, "They'll be coming within an hour." The pastor replied, "No problem." Father Lynch found seventy mattresses, "and the gymnasium was turned into a farm worker encampment for the weekend."[71]

As news of the farm worker movement spread across the United States, other Franciscans joined. Sister Patricia Ann Drydyk, OSF, [see below chapter 6] left her teaching post in Iowa to work at the Franciscan Communications Center in Los Angeles. One of her first projects was making a filmstrip about Cesar Chavez and the farm worker union. Sister Drydyk was impressed by Chavez's dedication and sincerity. She soon went to work full-time on behalf of the farm worker movement, traveling the country to inform sisters about issues affecting agricultural labor and convincing several other sisters to join her working for the UFW. Eventually, Sister Drydyk became a boycott organizer for the National Farm Worker Ministry (NFWM). During the 1980s she

---

69. Fronske, interview.
70. The Agricultural Labor Relations Act passed by the California legislature in 1975 gave farm workers the right to organize unions like industrial workers.
71. Ed Dunn and Oliver Lynch, quoted in Warner, "Farm Workers and Franciscans," 79. For more about Father Oliver Lynch and St. Elizabeth's parish, see David J. Endres, "Working for Justice: Community Activism at St. Elizabeth, Oakland, California, 1961–81," in *Many Tongues, One Faith: A History of Franciscan Parish Life in the United States* (Oceanside, CA: Academy of American Franciscan History, 2018), 148–59.

and Brother Ed worked together on a campaign to limit pesticide use in the
fields. They publicized the grim news about cancer clusters discovered in farm
worker communities, especially among children whose mothers worked in the
fields while pregnant. They educated the public about the carcinogenic effects
of pesticides applied to the grape crops and tried to ban spraying insecticides
while farm workers were laboring.

Reflecting on his experience with the farm workers, Brother Ed said, "It
pushed me as a Friar to think about what solidarity [with the poor] means."
He was forced to ask himself, "What are my vows about?" He insisted that
the farm workers had evangelized him: "A lot of my understanding of Franciscan spirituality has come through the UFW."[72] Brother Keith, in his essay
titled "The Farm Workers and the Franciscans," concluded that the movement
"challenged the Franciscans to re-think the socio-political dimension of their
religious vocations."[73] For Brother Ed and many other Franciscans, he said,
"the farm worker movement was an inspiration and a source of hope."[74]

Direct Aid Versus Dealing with the Causes of Injustice: From Charity to Justice

Father Alan's association with Chavez and the farm workers profoundly
reordered his thinking on the best methods for combating social problems. In
an interview with author Pat Hoffman, he explained how Chavez convinced
him to approach social problems from a more radical perspective. He described
how his early efforts to deal with the problems of migrant agricultural laborers
employed several forms of direct aid: "We started a dining room for the poor,
and a clinic. We had more doctors than we could use. We bought housing for
the transients. We got into a clothing depot, a food depot also for families."
Eventually, he realized that this form of assistance did not address the workers'
fundamental problems. They still were poorly paid for their backbreaking labor
and were excluded under the National Labor Relations Act, which guaranteed
basic rights for workers in other industries. Chavez reportedly told Father Alan,
"That's not the answer. You've got to be concerned with the cause for this
poverty, this degradation, this suffering." Moving in this new direction was
not easy. Father Alan mentioned to Hoffman the resistance he encountered
when he began making workers aware of their rights: "You'd be amazed at the
support you lose for direct aid, because your direct aid is coming from people
who want things to remain as they are."[75] He credited Chavez with helping

---

72. Ed Dunn, quoted in Warner, "Farm Workers and Franciscans," 84.
73. Warner, "Farm Workers and Franciscans," 81.
74. Warner, "Farm Workers and Franciscans," 84.
75. McCoy, interview by Hoffman.

religious people like himself to understand "that you can't be simplistic in your approach. You've got to go on and try to take care of the cause of the poverty." Providing food, shelter, clothing, and medical care would not solve the problems of poor people. Father Alan insisted that one must "also take a good look at the structures of society, of government, the international corporation. All of these things are affecting our economy and the well-being of our country."[76]

Father Alan on Franciscan Values

On October 4, 1981, the eight-hundredth anniversary of the birth of St. Francis of Assisi, Father Alan addressed an audience at the Episcopal Cathedral of St. John the Divine in New York City. His words that evening were perhaps the clearest articulation of his views on how Christians in the modern world can follow the way of St. Francis.

Father Alan called on those who would emulate St. Francis to "stand with their brothers and sisters of all colors, races, creeds" and to see Jesus "in the eyes of the oppressed, the suffering, the hungry." Providing food, clothing, and medical care for the needy, as he had done as pastor in Stockton, "is praiseworthy and surely to be imitated, but it is not the answer," he insisted. Christians need to do more. The radical message Father Alan preached required that "we must acknowledge that the condition of the oppressed and starving of the world is the result of our own life style, our multinational corporations and our government policy."[77]

Just as St. Francis delivered his plea for peace and justice to the leaders of Church and state of his era, modern followers of Francis need to confront policy makers and "speak out clearly against the forces that threaten the welfare of our people today." Prominent among these threats are "the suicidal arms race, [and] the manufacture and deployment of nuclear arms." Those who stand for justice must "be ready to face abuse and to be made fun of," just as Francis did. To ensure that political leaders take their demands seriously, the "Church's immediate concern must be a profound conversion of the middle class," Father Alan preached. Comfortable Americans "must see the reality of those who are suffering today"—the hundreds of millions living in desperate poverty, the tens of thousands starving each day. Father Alan insisted that we must "search for the causes of poverty." Just as Francis "discerned and interpreted the signs of the times" in medieval Italy, the friar said, "our task is to do no less so that eyes are opened, hearts moved and political will redirected."[78]

---

76. McCoy, interview by Hoffman.
77. Alan McCoy, "The Heritage of Francis of Assisi," n.d., Alan McCoy file, St. Barbara Province Archives.
78. McCoy, "Heritage of Francis," St. Barbara Province Archives.

An Anti-War Provincial

Father Alan's tenure as the St. Barbara provincial minister coincided with escalating protests against the Vietnam War. Oakland, where he resided, was a hotbed of anti-war activism. Although not a leading figure in the anti-war movement, he was respected by clergy who opposed the war. He himself spoke out against the war and supported young men who objected to military service based on their religious convictions. His correspondence files contain appeals, statements, reports, announcements, and agendas from a wide range of pacifist and anti-war organizations, including the World Without War Council, Clergy and Laymen Concerned, East Bay Draft Counseling, the Catholic Peace Fellowship, the GI-Civilian Alliance for Peace, and Fellowship of Reconciliation. In May 1968, Father Alan attended a day-long, invitation-only planning meeting of "70 of the most active Clergy (together with some laymen)" sponsored by Northern California Clergy and Laymen at Howard Presbyterian church in San Francisco. He was both a presenter and a responder on panels that day.[79] Also included in his files are copies of numerous letters to military and government officials such as the US Secretary of Defense, the commandant of the Marine Corps, California Senator Thomas Kuchel, and Idaho's Selective Service System director, all supporting the conscientious objector claims of young servicemen and draft registrants.

President of CMSM

In June 1976, at the conclusion of his second term as provincial of the St. Barbara Franciscan Province, Father Alan was elected president of Conference of Major Superiors of Men (CMSM), an organization composed of the leaders of more than two hundred Catholic religious communities of priests and brothers. Established in 1956, CMSM speaks on behalf of its members on matters of common concern and serves as a resource for the leadership of constituent orders.[80] During his nine years as provincial minister, Father Alan represented the St. Barbara Franciscans at CMSM meetings, serving two terms as a member of its board of directors and then serving as its vice president from 1971 to 1973. For the organization's first two decades, its presidents served on a part-time basis and were primarily concerned with strengthening internal administration of member religious bodies. Because Father Alan was a well-known proponent of peace and justice causes, his election was seen as a reflection of the members' desire to increase their involvement in these

---

79. "Meeting of Clergy and Laymen," agenda, 18 May 1968, Alan McCoy file, St. Barbara Province Archives.

80. For more information on CMSM, see its website: https://cmsm.org/.

issues. As the organization's first full-time president, he also was the first not acting simultaneously as head of his religious community. Thus, he was able to devote more time and energy to issues of concern to the membership than did his predecessors, who juggled CMSM duties with responsibilities to their orders. During his three terms as president (1976–82), Father Alan left an indelible stamp on the mission and structure of CMSM. He continued his commitment to domestic social justice causes; but under his leadership, the organization became increasingly involved in international peace and justice issues as well, especially in Central and South America.

When Father Alan became its president, CMSM had no department or staff person responsible for social justice issues. Father Joseph Nangle, OFM, a former Franciscan missionary then working in the international peace and justice office of the then National Conference of Catholic Bishops, noted this lack.[81] He told Father Alan, "When an issue comes up and some of us want to get the major superiors on board with it, no one answers the phone there in terms of justice and peace. I think the Conference [that is, CMSM] needs something like that."[82] Father Alan, who enjoyed a reputation as "Mr. Peace and Justice," readily agreed that CMSM needed a social justice dimension. At the group's 1979 assembly in Kansas City, he proposed creating a peace and justice office, but the membership voted down his plan. After the vote, Father Nangle, an observer at the meeting, approached Father Alan to commiserate on the defeat of the measure. He found that Father Alan was not upset. "We will create a position as special assistant to the president for peace and justice," Father Alan told Father Nangle.[83] A skilled administrator, Father Alan knew there were multiple ways to achieve his desired objectives.

Because the leaders of the US bishops' conference preferred to avoid public involvement in controversial political issues, they often asked CMSM to investigate sensitive situations. According to Father Vitale, the bishops would say, "You people can do things we can't do." They believed that leaders of religious communities had more freedom to tackle contentious issues and could more easily accept the prophetic role required in these situations. Father Vitale said, "The bishops were just afraid to do it. . . . People like Tom Quigley [the Latin America expert at the bishops' conference] quickly learned that when they needed to get a ranking representative of the U.S. Church [to take an unpopular stand], the one person they could get was Alan."[84]

---

81. See chap. 8 for an account of Father Joseph Nangle, OFM, and his work for social justice.

82. Joseph Nangle, in an interview with the author, July 9, 2020.

83. Alan McCoy, quoted in Joseph Nangle, interview, 19 July 1993, CMSM Records, AMSM 234501, University of Notre Dame Archives. In 1982, Nangle began working for CMSM on a part-time basis and later as its full-time justice and peace coordinator.

84. Vitale, interview, CMSM Records.

Father Alan departed on his first international mission in June 1977, when he visited Cuba for ten days as part of an ecumenical delegation of seven American religious leaders. At that time, President Jimmy Carter hoped to normalize relations with the Fidel Castro regime. Because this issue was too controversial to support a conventional government mission, Carter asked a group of clergy to fly to Havana, meet with Castro and other Cuban leaders, and report back to him. Father Alan found conditions in Cuba very different from the picture painted by US media. He noted "restrictions on the public role of the Churches, but also the freedom that was granted for the practice of religion." He found that Cuban Catholics desired better relations with the United States. On its return, the group submitted a report to Carter unanimously recommending that the US embargo of Cuba be lifted. Carter, however, was unable to overcome stiff congressional opposition, and US sanctions remained in place.[85]

In January 1978, Father Alan was dispatched by the US bishops' conference as part of a three-person delegation to Bolivia. The Bolivian dictator, General Hugo Banzer, had fired and jailed striking indigenous tin miners. Fifty women whose husbands were part of the work stoppage staged a public hunger strike that quickly gained wide popular support. According to Father Nangle, "That began a general protest in the region—in La Paz, in the Altiplano—and then more widely in the country. Little by little, in a few days actually, it became an international incident."[86] Four of the women went to La Paz, one of Bolivia's two capital cities, where they continued their fast. International agencies noticed their protest. When members of the US delegation met with them, the women were weak after nineteen days without food. Negotiations with the government ensued. Remarkably, this trip resulted in a salutary outcome. General Banzer relented, the prisoners were released, and the striking miners were hired back at their old jobs.[87]

At the August 1978 CMSM assembly in Cleveland, Ohio, the membership recognized an urgent need to become more involved in global social justice issues. Father Alan described it as "a watershed moment."[88] Two years later, at the 1980 assembly, attendees were polled to identify top priorities for their communities. Asked to rank thirty-one objectives formulated during the meeting, three of the top five choices were causes such as working for the poor, minorities, and human rights. Ranking seventh

---

85. Alan McCoy, interview, 28 February 1993, CMSM Records, AMSM 2345101, University of Notre Dame Archives.

86. Nangle, interview.

87. Nangle, interview. See also Wilson T. Boots, "Miracle in Bolivia: Four Women Confront a Nation," *Christianity and Crisis*, May 1, 1978.

88. McCoy, interview, CMSM Records.

was a call to "expand the role of women and their ministries in the church."[89]

This change in mission to actively dealing with social justice issues also became a source of internal strain. A few contemplative orders preferred a more introspective approach and quietly withdrew from CMSM.[90] Other contemplative orders endorsed this new thrust, although they could not participate directly due to the reclusive nature of their charisms. Another source of concern within CMSM was aired in a four-page letter Father Alan received in 1980 from Father Charles V. Finnegan, OFM, provincial minister of the Franciscan Holy Name Province. Father Finnegan stated that, though he did not doubt the importance of justice and peace issues, "I believe that there are other issues of *equal importance* that we could profitably deal with." The issues he had in mind were "pastoral questions," specifically the lack of a national pastoral plan. This was important, he insisted, because "so many religious men are engaged in the pastoral ministry." Father Finnegan presented a detailed brief supporting his position and listing other "serious pastoral concerns" that needed to be addressed.[91] Father Alan acknowledged some of these concerns as legitimate, but he did not allow objections to deflect him from pursuing the path he had laid out at the beginning of his administration. It should be noted, however, that his single-minded focus on social justice often curtailed consideration of other valid concerns.

Father Alan's success in convincing CMSM members to take a more progressive stance on controversial social issues can be attributed to his distinctive approach, which combined a commitment to social justice with an equally strong emphasis on the importance of prayer. Father Vitale, who observed his brother Franciscan in action as both provincial leader and head of CMSM, explained, "Alan has a two-pole approach to things. One is his social activism. The other is that he is this extremely prayerful person. He was very concerned, almost from the beginning, to draw the contemplatives in [to cooperate on CMSM initiatives]. . . . He claimed he went to them and said, 'We need a prayer that active people can use.' . . . So they came up with the prayer of centering."[92] Friends who traveled with Father Alan "watched him faithfully pray his Divine Office, silently moving his lips on planes, buses, and cars."[93]

---

89. Rick Casey, "Justice Issues Primary, Religious Say," *National Catholic Reporter*, August 29, 1980.

90. McCoy, interview, CMSM Records.

91. Charles V. Finnegan, to McCoy, 7 February 1980, CMSM Records, CMSM 1/23, part 1, University of Notre Dame Archives.

92. Vitale, interview, CMSM Records.

93. John Michael Talbot, "The Passing of Father Alan McCoy," Facebook, October 16, 2009, https://www.facebook.com/notes/john-michael-talbot/the-passing-of-fr-alan-mccoy-ofm/154683178850/.

Father Alan employed his highly developed interpersonal skills to keep CMSM from splitting into competing factions. He consistently communicated a deep respect for all of his fellow religious leaders. When they disagreed with his policies, he often pointed out that they did so for "very good reasons." Despite encountering determined opposition, he never attacked his opponents, insisting they were "fine men," acting from the best of motives.[94]

Sister Joan Chittister, OSB, characterized Father Alan as a leader "with a gentle but very clear touch." In an interview she said she believed he was able to accomplish great things because "he was a master of bringing people together. He was a listener in the first place. He was a committed listener and an honest listener. . . . He could facilitate difficult conversations with the greatest of ease. He didn't bring with him into any conversation a feeling of contention. He was looking for a way through."[95] Indeed, Father Alan used an abbreviated formula—"going inward, going outward and going forward"— to summarize his approach. Peace activist Ken Butigan explained what he meant: "Activism must begin with interior prayer and contemplation which allows one to make contact with the spirit of a God who longs for right relationship, healing, dignity and peace and justice for all. This spirit empowers one to see the world in its brokenness and to take action for its healing. This must become an enduring process in which one goes forward with others to create what Jesus called the Reign of God."[96]

A Voice for Justice in International Affairs

During his six years as president of CMSM, Father Alan was a frequent international traveler, making numerous trips to Central and South America. Many of these missions, especially those to Central America, focused on human rights. In November 1978, he was part of a four-person ecumenical fact-finding mission to Nicaragua. The country was being torn apart by a war between the revolutionary Sandinista movement and the dictatorship of General Anastasio Somoza, which received substantial military assistance from the United States government. What Father Alan learned there reinforced his belief that the corrupt Somoza government must be replaced by one that better served the nation's impoverished population. His group reported that General Somoza and the National Guard he commanded were "the chief obstacles to peace" in Nicaragua. They declared, "Only rapid and decisive actions have any chance of realizing any hope for a nonviolent solu-

---

94. McCoy, interview, CMSM Records.
95. Joan Chittister, in an interview with the author, August 31, 2020.
96. Ken Butigan, *Pilgrimage Through a Burning World: Spiritual Practice and Nonviolent Protest at the Nevada Test Site* (Albany, NY: State University of New York Press, 2003), 87.

tion."[97] Father Alan shared his views on Nicaragua in frequent communications with US government officials. In 1977 he sent a telegram to President Jimmy Carter demanding that the United States "SUSPEND ALL ECONOMIC MILITARY AID TO THE DESPOTIC NICARAGUAN GOVERNMENT."[98] He aided the insurgent Sandinista movement by raising money to establish medical clinics and purchase food to feed hungry people in areas they controlled. In July 1979, Father Alan sent a letter to CMSM members urging them to contribute to the Nicaragua Relief Fund administered by Catholic Relief Services (CRS). "Much of the economy is at a virtual stand-still," he wrote. "The rich have stockpiled such food as could be bought, and the poor are daily more dependent on whatever help groups like Catholic Relief Services and CONFER can provide."[99] In March 1980, Edwin Broderick, head of CRS, thanked Father Alan for helping to raise $44,200 for the fund.[100]

Without doubt, his most dangerous and tragic international mission was a 1980 trip to El Salvador as part of a six-person interfaith team to celebrate the reopening of Archbishop St. Oscar Romero's radio station. A bombing had knocked the station off the air a month earlier, but now it was restored, broadcasting Romero's homilies to most of Central America.[101] The station was an important part of Romero's mission, criticizing the governing military junta for human rights abuses and for failing to promote the welfare of the common people. On Saturday, March 22, the US delegation met with the archbishop. The next day, Sunday, Father Alan concelebrated Mass with Romero. The day after that, the archbishop was shot and killed while saying Mass at a hospital chapel. His assassin was never apprehended.[102] That night, a bomb exploded at the residence where Father Alan was staying, but he was not harmed. Four people Father Alan met on that visit were later murdered.

---

97. American Friends Service Committee, News Release, November 8, 1978, CMSM Records, CMSM 1/20 part 2, University of Notre Dame Archives.

98. McCoy, to Jimmy Carter, 22 May 1977, CMSM Records, CMSM 1/20 part 2, University of Notre Dame Archives.

99. McCoy, to Confreres, 25 July 1979, CMSM Records, CMSM 1/23 part 1, University of Notre Dame Archives.

100. Edwin Broderick, to McCoy, 5 March 1980, CMSM Records, CMSM 1/23 part 1, University of Notre Dame Archives.

101. Father Alan was a vocal critic of US military aid to El Salvador. That is probably one reason why he was selected to be part of this delegation. On February 19, 1980, he sent a telegram to President Jimmy Carter, stating, "I WISH TO URGE YOU STRONGLY TO AVOID SENDING FURTHER MILITARY AID TO EL SALVADOR." McCoy, to Carter, CMSM Records, CMSM 1/23 part 1, University of Notre Dame Archives.

102. See James R. Brockman, *Romero: A Life* (Maryknoll, NY: Orbis Books, 1989), 240–48. For further information on the search for Romero's killer see Matt Eisenbrandt, *Assassination of a Saint: The Plot to Murder Oscar Romero and The Quest to Bring His Killers to Justice* (Oakland: University of California Press, 2017).

"There is no question," he told reporters when he returned to the United States, "that the assassination was committed by the right." Members of the delegation agreed that "Romero's last Sunday homily probably instigated the assassination." In that homily, the archbishop had "urged soldiers to disobey orders to kill in deference to a higher law."[103] In an indignant telegram to El Salvador's ambassador to the United States, Father Alan wrote, "Steps should be taken immediately for responsible leaders to work for a just and lasting solution of the problems in El Salvador."[104]

Father Alan continued to be an outspoken critic of El Salvador's regime and an opponent of providing additional US military assistance to its government. On March 27, he told reporters that "giving military aid to the [Salvadoran] ruling junta would be indecent."[105] In June, he wrote to US Secretary of State Edmund Muskie, reiterating his opposition to the US government's "policy of standing behind a Junta that is increasingly controlled by far-right military forces that justify all repression in the name of anti-communism. The United States should allow the Salvadoran people to decide their own destiny."[106]

The December 2, 1980, kidnapping and brutal murder of four American women missionaries by members of El Salvador's National Guard triggered a wave of protests in the United States. On December 4, Father Alan wired Muskie deploring the murders and urging an end to military aid for El Salvador. He sent a similar telegram to President-Elect Ronald Reagan.[107] On December 17, Father Alan was one of seventy-one American religious leaders who signed a public statement on human rights addressed to Reagan. Kenneth A. Briggs reported in the *New York Times*, "The leaders told Mr. Reagan there was increasing and alarming evidence that military Governments are viewing your election as a green light for suppression of legitimate dissent and for widespread arrest and imprisonment, torture and murder." They urged him to "denounce the use of torture and political oppression."[108] On January 11, 1981, one week before Reagan's inauguration, Father Alan participated in an ecumenical liturgy on the Washington Ellipse in remembrance of the North American missionaries murdered in El Salvador. Later that day, he spoke at a

103. "Millions Mourn Slain Romero," *National Catholic Reporter*, April 4, 1980.

104. McCoy, to Robert E. White, Ambassador of El Salvador, 26 March 1980, CMSM Records, CMSM 1/23 part 1, University of Notre Dame Archives.

105. "El Salvador: Carter Backs Aid Romero Fought," *National Catholic Reporter*, April 4, 1980.

106. McCoy, to Edmund Muskie, 17 June 1980, CMSM Records, CMSM 1/23 part 1. University of Notre Dame Archives.

107. McCoy, to Muskie, 4 December 1980; McCoy, to Ronald Reagan, 4 December 1980, CMSM Records, CMSM 1/23, pt. 2, University of Notre Dame Archives.

108. "Clerics Bid Reagan Speak Out on Rights," *New York Times*, December 18, 1980.

rally demanding an end to all US economic and military aid to the government of El Salvador.[109]

Toward the end of February 1982, Father Alan received an invitation from Representative Ronald Dellums to speak as a witness before a congressional committee holding hearings on US arms sales and transfers. Dellums explained that the hearings were part of a "collective effort to develop a coherent and cohesive rethinking of policy assumptions and spending priorities" regarding "what should be our proper and moral national security role."[110] This was an opportunity Father Alan could not pass up. He asked Father Nangle, who had been a missionary in Bolivia and Peru for fifteen years, to prepare his testimony.

Making one of his most powerful public statements, Father Alan began his testimony with a brief review of the US role as "arms merchant to the world." "We are peace-lovers and peace-makers in what we say; war promoters in what we do," he began. He then pointed to the consequences of making arms sales to less developed nations. The purchase of military equipment, he said, resulted in "the exacerbation of dangerous social injustice, whereby monies better spent for people's needs are diverted to weaponry." A relevant example was the nation of El Salvador, which was receiving millions of dollars of US military assistance to combat a popular uprising. "We would be better advised to . . . use our influence to bring the warring factions to the negotiating table," he recommended. He also criticized the growing weapons industry in nations like India, Brazil, and Argentina. This industry, he said, results in the diversion of "wealth from people-oriented programs to an industry which does not in the end help anyone on the domestic front." Father Alan challenged members of Congress: "Have we so lost our ingenuity and creativity as a nation that we can no longer find peaceful and profitable goals to turn to from our war-making economy and industry?" He proposed that Congress pass legislation to phase out commercial arms sales; retain its veto power over large arms sales; and open arms sale transactions to public scrutiny. Father Alan concluded his testimony with a simple recommendation: the US government should "link conventional arms sales and arms transfers to the growing demand for nuclear disarmament and dedicate ourselves to eradicating the real causes of war—oppression and poverty at home and around the world."[111]

109. "El Salvador: Light Amid the Darkness," program, 11 January 1981, CMSM 1/23 part 3, University of Notre Dame Archives.

110. Ronald Dellums, to McCoy, 26 February 1982, CMSM Records, CMSM 1/25, University of Notre Dame Archives.

111. "Testimony of Alan McCoy, OFM, for the Conference of Major Superiors of Men, USA, Before the Armed Services Committee of the House of Representatives on United States Arms Sales and Arms Transfers," 1 April 1982, CMSM Records, CMSM 1/25, University of Notre Dame Archives.

Father Alan's growing involvement in international peace and justice issues did not mean that he abandoned his interest in domestic causes. He maintained a cordial long-distance relationship with Chavez and accepted invitations to appear at UFW conventions when he was able. In December 1978, Father Alan wrote to US Labor Secretary Ray Marshall, thanking him for a Comprehensive Employment Training Act grant to support the Farm Worker Service Center in Delano, a project sponsored by the UFW. Two months later, Chavez alerted Father Alan about an upcoming meeting between Carter and the president of Mexico. Chavez feared that a renewal of the bracero program, opposed by his union, might be discussed on this occasion.[112] Father Alan promptly dispatched a telegram to the White House urging Carter not to reinstate the bracero agreement.[113]

Frequent Flyer

During his terms as president of CMSM, Father Alan maintained a schedule that would have taxed a much younger man. His itinerary involved nearly constant travel, both in the United States and internationally. His schedule for the last thirteen months of his presidency (August 1981 to August 1982) reveals a man continually on the move to fulfill commitments to multiple constituencies. He traveled to Illinois, Louisiana, and Massachusetts for regional CMSM meetings. A joint board meeting of CMSM with the Leadership Conference of Women Religious (LCWR) and an institute for major superiors took him to Old Mission Santa Barbara twice. Meetings of Franciscan organizations including the St. Anthony Foundation, the Franciscan Communication Center, the Franciscan Council, the English Speaking Conference of OFM, the Nevada Desert Experience (NDE), and the St. Barbara Franciscan Province required more travel. Father Alan also was in demand as a retreat master for male and female religious. In 1981–82 he conducted nine retreats, several lasting four or five days.[114] In addition, he lectured at numerous workshops and institutes across the United States. His varied titles included "Future of Priesthood," "Spirituality for Today," "Leadership in Religious Communities," and "The Church in the Decade Ahead." His final year culminated in the annual CMSM national assembly in San Francisco.

In addition to his domestic travel, Father Alan made five international trips over these final thirteen months. In August, he journeyed to Guatemala

---

112. Chavez, to McCoy, 5 February 1979, CMSM Records, CMSM 1/22 part 1, University of Notre Dame Archives.

113. McCoy, to Carter, 8 February 1979, CMSM Records, CMSM 1/22 part 1, University of Notre Dame Archives.

114. After stepping down as CMSM president, giving retreats and days of recollection for priests and sisters became one of Father Alan's primary vocations.

and Honduras to confer on the condition of Salvadoran refugees. In November, he met with religious leaders in Nicaragua and Colombia and attended a meeting of Latin American theologians in Lima, Peru. At the end of November, he flew to Rome for a conference on relations among bishops and religious. April brought another Latin American trip with stops in Nicaragua, Colombia, Chile, and Paraguay. He spent the month of May in South Africa, where he attended the general assembly of Major Superiors of Clerical Orders.

Collaboration with Women Religious

Father Alan's time as CMSM president was notable for the extent of collaboration between CMSM and LCWR. Both organizations had similar missions. Establishing closer bonds seemed to Father Alan to be a logical step. For a few years, this partnership produced an unprecedented degree of cooperation. In July 1977, Father Alan informed CMSM membership that a proposal to hold assemblies of both organizations in the same city at the same time had been "favorably received by the members in regional meetings."[115] The first joint assembly was held in Cleveland in August 1978. Its theme, "Convergence," suggested recognition of the need for closer cooperation between men and women religious and a willingness to work together on issues of common concern. Sister Joan, then president of the LCWR, recalled in an interview that Father Alan "was very vocal about wanting the two conferences to come together." When the groups convened, they scheduled "a number of days or hours together and a number of days or hours alone." According to Sister Joan, "It was in those common sessions that we found a real unity of vision about where religious life had to go. And where it had to go, in most of our minds, was to the streets."[116]

Cooperation between the two organizations extended beyond joint meetings. Father Alan joined leaders of LCWR at international meetings and took common stands with them on public issues. In 1977, Father Alan and Sister Joan traveled to Medellín, Colombia, where they were guest observers at a meeting of the Inter-American Bishops Conference. Sister Joan remembered, "I don't think we stopped [talking] for five minutes" on their flight to Colombia. They discussed "how to bring the light of the world, of the globe, especially of the United States, to the situation [in Latin America] that the United States itself was fueling."[117] In November 1980, Father Alan and Sister Clare Fitzgerald, SSND, who was by then president of LCWR, sent a three-page letter documenting human rights abuses in El Salvador to the Inter-American

---

115. McCoy, to "Dear Brothers," 18 July 1977, CMSM Records, CMSM 1/21 part 2, University of Notre Dame Archives.

116. Chittister, interview.

117. Chittister, interview.

Commission on Human Rights.[118] In March 1981, Father Alan signed a statement on El Salvador together with the presidents of the National Conference of Catholic Bishops and LCWR.[119] The following January, he and Sister Bette Moslander, CSJ, another LCWR president, released a statement asking the US government "to give political asylum to the refugees from Haiti and allow those from El Salvador to remain on extended visas."[120]

A second joint assembly took place in San Francisco in August 1982, this time with an unhappy outcome. Its theme was "To Build a Bridge." A major event was a liturgy for delegates and guests concelebrated by five bishops and Archbishop Pio Laghi, the apostolic delegate to the United States. On August 17, shortly before the liturgy was to begin, Archbishop Laghi learned that five women religious were going to act as eucharistic ministers, bringing decanters of consecrated wine to the congregation. "This can't be," the archbishop reportedly said. The sisters who had been asked to deliver the wine were informed of the archbishop's edict while the Mass was in progress.[121] "They [the organizers, on behalf of Archbishop Laghi] said, 'No women may step on this floor. No woman may come past this point,'" Sister Joan Chittister recounted. "We were furious. . . . It just blew everything apart."[122] No subsequent joint meetings of the men and women religious took place.

At the conclusion of Father Alan's six years as president of CMSM, the organization issued a press release lauding his accomplishments. It read, in part, "Father Alan has left an indelible imprint on the conference by his concern for the poor and disadvantaged and his total dedication to the cause of human rights for all people everywhere. . . . He has shifted the consciousness of the conference to one of global awareness and quickened the spirit of mission among members."[123]

On the final day of the 1982 CMSM assembly, Father Ronald Carignan, OMI, the organization's new president, presented Father Alan with the Pro Ecclesia et Pontifice award, better known as the Papal Cross, in recognition of his distinguished service to the Roman Catholic Church.[124]

---

118. McCoy and Clare Fitzgerald, to the Inter-American Commission on Human Rights of the Organization of American States, 27 November 1980, CMSM Records, CMSM 1/24, University of Notre Dame Archives.

119. McCoy to James A. Hickey, 6 March 1981, CMSM Records, CMSM 1/23 part 2, University of Notre Dame Archives.

120. CMSM press release, 25 January 1982, CMSM Records, CMSM 1/25, University of Notre Dame Archives.

121. Mark R. Day, "No Women as Ministers as Religious Leaders Meet," *National Catholic Reporter*, August 18, 1982.

122. Chittister, interview.

123. "CMSM President Awarded Papal Cross," CMSM Press Release, 20 August 1982, CMSM Records, CMSM 1/25, University of Notre Dame Archives.

124. "President Awarded Papal Cross," CMSM Records.

Later Life

Following his departure from CMSM, Father Alan returned to California, where he briefly served as executive director of the English Speaking Conference of the Order of Friars Minor. From 1983 to 1986 he was a member of a commission, headed by Archbishop John R. Quinn of San Francisco. Pope St. John Paul II had charged Archbishop Quinn to "bring the bishops of the country and the religious into a closer relationship and to examine the causes for the decline in vocations."[125] Father Alan also taught a continuing education course for friars and priests at Old Mission Santa Barbara. In 1983, he was appointed guardian at Old Mission Santa Barbara, and beginning in 1985, he became guardian at St. Joseph's friary in Los Angeles. He gave frequent retreats for priests and sisters over the next decade, until he retired to the St. John of God care facility. Father Alan died in 2009 at the age of ninety-six, "after a long battle with strokes and a fall that eventually took his life."[126]

His friend, John Michael Talbot, paid a final tribute to Father Alan: "He was a leader in the Order of Friars Minor and the Franciscan family, and a great servant and visionary of the Church, and a champion of the poorest of the poor throughout Central America and whenever terrible poverty and abuse of basic human rights were found. . . . He was a visionary, but practical enough to get things done in the Church. . . . There are many we meet in life who we call saintly. But I believe that Fr. Alan was a saint."[127]

Father Alan's Legacy

Father Alan was a vowed Franciscan for more than seventy-five years. During that time, he was a canon lawyer, a pastor, a mentor to young friars, an advocate for farm workers, a leader of the St. Barbara Franciscan Province, a spokesperson for religious men in the United States and internationally, a popular retreat master, and above all a true son of St. Francis. Some of his brother Franciscans thought he was too tough; others thought he was too liberal. None of them doubted his dedication to the cause of peace and justice.

Father Alan inspired newly ordained Franciscans to fight on behalf of the poor and oppressed. He traveled the globe to bear witness for justice. He redirected the resources of the Franciscan province into ministries with Mexican Americans and Native Americans. He was a friend to Cesar Chavez,

---

125. "Archbishop John R. Quinn: A 'Clear, Powerful Voice,'" *Catholic San Francisco*, July 11, 2017, https://catholic-sf.org/news/archbishop-john-r-quinn-a-clear-powerful-voice.

126. Talbot, "Passing of Father Alan."

127. Talbot, "Passing of Father Alan."

Dorothy Day, and St. Oscar Romero. He learned from Latin American theologians that the Church should exercise a preferential option for the poor,
but he never lost sight of the need to convert middle-class Americans to the
cause of justice.

Father Alan had a very strong sense of right and wrong. He believed that
anyone who is not working for justice is not living the Gospel. He also
believed that, as a Franciscan, he should adopt a simple lifestyle as St. Francis
did. He embraced a prayerful attitude and refused to be discouraged by setbacks and reversals.

In the words of Father Bucher, one of the young friars Father Alan mentored in Stockton, "He really was a warrior for justice."[128]

---

128. Bucher, interview.

Chapter 6

Sister Patricia Drydyk: Organizing for the Farm Worker Cause

Aband of religious activists paced back and forth in front of a Jewel super-market in Chicago at the end of June 1975. They carried signs urging shoppers to boycott nonunion lettuce in support of striking members of the United Farm Workers (UFW). They were demonstrating in response to an appeal by Cesar Chavez, the union's founder and president, to pressure let-tuce growers to negotiate with the farm workers' union. After picketing for an hour or so, four of the demonstrators—two Catholic sisters, a Catholic priest, and a Protestant minister—entered the market and made their way to the pro-duce section. There they prayed over the iceberg lettuce and sang "They Will Know We Are Christians by Our Love." Sister Patricia Ann Drydyk, OSF, opened her Bible and began reading from the Gospel of St. Matthew, chapter 25: "Lord, when did we see you hungry?" When the protestors refused to dis-perse, the store manager called the police. "We were arrested, charged with dis-turbing the peace, jailed and, after eight hours, released on bail," Sister Pat later recounted.[1] In a letter to sisters of her community, she justified her arrest: "Some may find this kind of action hard to understand. I can only say that I believe at times we have to give up some of our own freedoms, to risk arrest and incarceration in order to emphasize the dignity and rights that belong to all human beings, including farm workers."[2] Six months later, a judge dismissed all charges against Sister Pat and her fellow activists.

Sister Pat had come a long way from the shy elementary school teacher who had entered the Wisconsin-based Sisters of St. Francis of Assisi fifteen years earlier. She became a nun during the turbulent 1960s, when women religious began pursuing careers outside semicloistered convents and joined movements for racial equality, economic justice, peace, and nuclear disarma-

---

1. Pat Drydyk, "The Price of Lettuce and Justice," *Modern Ministries*, September 1981, 16.
2. Patricia Ann Drydyk, to "Dear Sisters," 15 September 1975, Box 8, New Assisi Archives, Sisters of St. Francis of Assisi, St. Francis, WI, hereafter cited as New Assisi Archives.

Sister Pat Drydyk, third from left, arrested in Chicago supermarket, 1975. Photo courtesy of Sisters of St. Francis of Assisi archives.

ment. For twenty years following her Chicago arrest, Sister Pat continued to advocate for American farm workers. She was a pioneer in exploring new vocations for Catholic sisters, while valuing her bonds with her Franciscan community. Overcoming youthful reticence, she emerged as an outspoken defender of the rights of America's poorly paid agricultural laborers, as well as a champion for better working and living conditions for them and their families. Sister Pat was the first Catholic sister hired by the National Farm Worker Ministry (NFWM), at that time a mostly Protestant organization, and she rose through its ranks to become its executive director. A tireless organizer, she lived on a subsistence salary, traveled the country to build a network of religious support groups, and recruited other sisters to the farm workers' movement. In the face of seemingly insurmountable odds, she maintained an optimistic outlook rooted in her deep Christian faith.

Early Years

Patricia Ann Drydyk was born in 1937 and, until she was four years old, lived with her parents on her grandparents' truck farm on the outskirts of Milwaukee, Wisconsin. The family eventually sold the farm to make way for the construction of General Mitchell Airport. Pat then moved with her parents to Cedarburg, a small town north of Milwaukee, where they rented a second-floor apartment. Her father labored in an aluminum foundry. "We never had a lot of money," Pat recalled, "but what we had was always sufficient."[3]

After completing eight years at the local public school, she enrolled at St. Mary's Academy, an all-girls boarding and day school on the south side of Milwaukee. St. Mary's was opened in 1904 by the Sisters of St. Francis of Assisi (often referred to as the Lake Franciscans, because of their mother-house's proximity to Lake Michigan). The order was founded by a band of seven women who emigrated from Bavaria to Milwaukee in 1849. In the 1870s they began accepting teaching assignments in rural schools. Educating the children of German immigrants became their primary mission. In the first decades of the twentieth century, the Sisters of St. Francis opened fifty-seven elementary schools, more than half of them in Wisconsin.[4] Following the Second Vatican Council, they branched out to many other ministries.[5]

The English teachers at St. Mary's Academy placed a particular emphasis on journalism, which attracted Pat's interest. She edited the school newspaper and was a member of the yearbook staff. When high school graduation neared, Pat contemplated entering her teachers' religious community; however, her mother, who was not Catholic, objected strongly. Instead, Pat attended St. Mary of the Woods College, outside Terre Haute, Indiana, as a scholarship student. She considered studying journalism but chose a more traditional path by deciding to major in elementary education.[6]

After graduating, Pat taught second grade at Sacred Heart School in Milwaukee for one year. Then in 1960, she defied her mother by entering the Sisters of St. Francis of Assisi. As a postulant and novice, she returned to teach at Sacred Heart. After earning a master's degree in English from Marquette University, she went to Sterling, Colorado, to teach English and journalism at St. Anthony High School. A year later, she transferred to Garrigan High School in Algona, Iowa, where she taught for five more years.[7]

During this time, three of Sister Pat's cousins, two of them diocesan priests, were working at Milwaukee inner-city parishes. This was a period of civil rights turmoil. Beginning in August 1967, Father James Groppi led members of the NAACP Youth Council in two hundred days of open housing marches against often violent opposition. "I'd come back at Christmas time

---

3. Drydyk, interview by Margaret Rose, 3 December 1984, Women Unionists of the United Farm Workers of America Oral History Program," Box 8, New Assisi Archives.

4. Mary Eunice Hanousek, *A New Assisi: The First Hundred Years of the Sisters of St. Francis of Assisi* (Milwaukee, MN: Bruce Publishing Company, 1948), 122.

5. Sisters of St. Francis of Assisi, "History," https://www.lakeosfs.org/who-we-are/history/.

6. Drydyk, interview by Rose, New Assisi Archives.

7. Sister Pat's mother, Harriet, remained opposed to her daughter's religious vocation. Relations between them were strained for the rest of her life. According to Sister Pat, her mother had "opposed most of the things that I have done." Drydyk, interview by Rose, 7, New Assisi Archives.

. . . [and] hear them talking about their involvements," Sister Pat told an interviewer in 1984. Their activism inspired her.[8]

Early in her religious career, Sister Pat demonstrated the probing intellect she later applied to her work for social justice. In 1971, the Franciscan sisters were considering what structural changes to adopt as a result of the reforms of religious life initiated by the Second Vatican Council. Sister Pat urged members of her community to bear in mind four fundamental questions raised by theologian and educator Gabriel Moran: "Who am I? Whom do I love? What do I want to do? How can we work together?"[9]

While Sister Pat was still at Garrigan High School, a vacationing teacher who had taken a job at the Franciscan Communications Center in Los Angeles told her, "We really need people with teaching backgrounds" in communications. Sister Pat was ready to move on, so she seized this opportunity to pursue the journalism career she had contemplated as a college student. She relocated to California in 1971 and began making educational films and filmstrips for Franciscan Communications to be used in parochial schools. "It was a very, very broadening experience for me," she confided to an interviewer. "I worked with very creative people who saw the Church as a Vatican II experience and tried to communicate that idea of an activist church to educators."[10] Later in her career, Sister Pat explained that she had not abandoned teaching: "I am still educating," she maintained, "but my understanding of education has evolved."[11]

Introduction to the Farm Worker Movement

An assignment to produce a seven-minute filmstrip on community building led to a life-changing encounter. To depict a current example, Sister Pat focused on the struggle of the UFW to forge a union of agricultural laborers. She interviewed "farm workers and union staff up and down the California coast." These interviews were Sister Pat's "personal introduction to the union and the sad living conditions of farm workers, mostly migrants." However,

---

8. Drydyk, interview by Rose, 19–20, New Assisi Archives. For more on Father James Groppi and the Milwaukee open housing campaign, see Patrick D. Jones, *The Selma of the North: Civil Rights Insurgency in Milwaukee* (Cambridge, MA: Harvard University Press, 2009).

9. "Sister Asks Vital Questions About Structure; Invites Searching Discussion and Mutual Trust," *Vision*, October 1971, Box 8, New Assisi Archives.

10. Drydyk, interview by Rose, 16, New Assisi Archives. For more on the Franciscan Communication Center, see Raymond Haberski Jr., *Voice of Empathy: A History of Franciscan Media in the United States* (Oceanside, CA: Academy of American Franciscan History, 2018), 177–85.

11. Drydyk, quoted in "Educational Ministry Evolves from Poetry to Picket Line for Sr. Patricia Drydyk," *Vision*, November 1975, Box 8, New Assisi Archives.

one key figure eluded her—Cesar Chavez, the charismatic leader of the UFW. "Chavez was so busy organizing strikes and picket lines," Sister Pat recalled. "He wasn't too interested in speaking to some little nun." Finally, after six months of persistent effort on her part, he sat for an hour-long interview. At the end of their conversation, Sister Pat discovered to her chagrin that she had forgotten to switch on her tape recorder. She later recalled that Chavez smiled and said, "Well Sister, we'll just have to do it over during lunch." Years afterwards, Sister Pat reminisced, "That small act of kindness and understanding organized me."[12] She claimed Chavez as a mentor and role model. "He taught us to use the power we have in behalf of those who are powerless," she declared.[13] Using power on behalf of the powerless is an apt description of Sister Pat's career as an organizer in the farm worker movement over the next two decades.

Sister Pat visited migrant worker camps to see for herself the conditions that Chavez described. There she saw "young children working in the fields, workers hoeing with short-handled hoes so bosses could see and yell at anyone who stood up for a short break, babies sitting in the hot sun at the side of the field while their mothers worked."[14] She asked herself, "You now know about farm workers' lives and their suffering. What are you going to do, Pat Drydyk?" It wasn't long, she said, before "I got myself down to the local boycott office in Los Angeles and talked with LeRoy Chatfield [a UFW organizer]. I offered my services to type or file or do whatever." She recalled that Chatfield told her, "What we really need, Sister, are people in front of supermarkets that carry non-union lettuce." Sister Pat was incredulous: "You mean picketing?" She took a deep breath and said she would report in front of the Safeway store at Third and Vermont Streets on Saturday morning. "That was my first experience of actually getting out on the picket line and trying to convince people not to go into the stores," she said.[15] During the winter and spring of 1973, Pat was a regular on the picket line. "It was every Saturday from 10:00 in the morning until 6:00 at night, talking to folks, a great variety of folks," she recalled. For Sister Pat, picketing was a transformative experience: "[People] would wonder why you were, as a church person, doing something as political as this. . . . It was my small contribution at the time. It was big for me because I had never done it before. . . . It was the beginning of . . . being asked to do more and more for the farm workers and really give of myself in that direction. It was good for me."[16]

---

12. Drydyk, "Price of Lettuce," 15.
13. Drydyk, quoted in Margaret Peter, "Was It Worth It, Sister?," unpublished manuscript, 1993, 47–48, Box 8, New Assisi Archives.
14. Peter, "Was It Worth It?," 48.
15. Drydyk, interview by Rose, 21, New Assisi Archives.
16. Drydyk, "Price of Lettuce," 16.

Another source contributing to Sister Pat's growing identification with the farm workers was the emergence of liberation theology. During her time in California, she began reading books by Paulo Freire (*Pedagogy of the Oppressed*) and Gustavo Gutierrez (*A Theology of Liberation*), who insisted that a close reading of the Gospels confirms Christian believers' role as advocates on behalf of the world's poor. Gutierrez insisted that Christians must stand in solidarity with the poor and take action against the causes of poverty. These works offered theological justification for Sister Pat's decision to devote her energies to the farm workers' movement.[17] She spent the next twenty-two years as an advocate for economic justice in solidarity with migrant farm workers.

Working Full-Time for the Farm Worker Cause

Sister Pat returned to Milwaukee later in 1973. The Sisters of St. Francis of Assisi had joined forces with the Capuchin friars, the School Sisters of St. Francis, and priests and sisters of the Society of the Divine Savior (Salvatorians) to jointly operate the Justice and Peace Center, which had been founded by the Capuchins two years earlier. Its purpose was "to educate the members of our communities and involve them in social justice activities, peace activities." Sister Pat and Sister Tess Browne, OSF, represented their congregation on the center's staff. Sister Tess, a native of Trinidad, had been teaching biology and French at St. Mary's Academy when Sister Pat, then working in California, persuaded her to build local support for the UFW grape boycott. Speaking for the Justice and Peace Center, the pair crisscrossed the country, traveling to houses of their order, making presentations on the farm workers' movement, and discussing ways the sisters could support their program.[18] Sister Pat explained their reason for focusing on the farm worker cause: "We used this as the concrete example of how to attack a problem by listening to farm workers who were changing their situation and doing what they were asking us to do through boycotts and so on."[19] Sister Tess called this a time of learning for both of them:

> Pat was really touched, I think, by what she had seen in California and what the farm workers were going through. I think we both were learning a lot about nonviolence and nonviolent principles with Cesar [Chavez] and Dolores [Huerta]. We took strongly from Dr. King and the civil rights movement and also from the work of Gandhi and St. Fran-

---

17. John Dear, "Gustavo Gutierrez and the Preferential Option for the Poor," *National Catholic Reporter*, November 8, 2011.

18. Tess Browne, in an interview with the author, September 23, 2019.

19. Drydyk, interview by Rose, 19, New Assisi Archives.

cis. . . . The biggest thing probably was what she learned from the farm workers themselves. Their perseverance and their willingness to struggle for a better life for the next generations. That really got to her as well as seeing the conditions under which they were working. Back then, the minimum wage was really abysmal. They were still using the short-handled hoe in California. Things like that, cruel conditions, and lack of amenities, how women were treated. I think all of that influenced her.[20]

Sister Pat sealed her allegiance to the farm worker movement when she attended the 1974 convention of the National Assembly of Women Religious (NAWR), an organization of Catholic sisters dedicated to promoting social justice. Due to illness, Dorothy Day, cofounder of the Catholic Worker movement, was unable to deliver the keynote address. To replace her, Day suggested, "I think you should get Cesar Chavez." Chavez came and spelled out how the sisters could assist the farm worker movement. According to Sister Pat, he said, "What we need from you sisters is a sister working full-time getting other sisters involved with the UFW and the boycott and the picket lines." Later that day, Sister Pat met with "some of the UFW boycott people who were based in the boycott office in St. Louis and other sisters." After praying about Chavez's proposal, Sister Pat volunteered for the job. "If it was all right with my community and if the NAWR agreed to fund it," she recalled, "I would be willing to begin that kind of work."[21]

The NAWR created a program called Solidarity—Sisters and Farm Workers Together and contributed $1,200 to get it underway. Additional funding came from the Claretian order, the Capuchins, and Dominicans. Sister Mary Catherine Rabbitt, SL, chairperson of the NAWR board, outlined five responsibilities of the position for which Sister Pat applied:

1. To mobilize sisters to live out the Gospel values they espouse through active participation in the struggle of the farm workers
2. To enable sisters to communicate this struggle to people they encounter in their present ministries
3. To support sisters currently involved in a farm worker ministry
4. To establish communication links with farm worker organizations
5. To establish communication links with farm worker support groups[22]

---

20. Browne, interview. Sister Tess Browne later became the full-time boycott director covering the state of Wisconsin and served on the NFWM board as well as working as a farm worker organizer and lobbyist in Texas. In 1991 she affiliated with the Daughters of Charity of Nazareth.

21. Drydyk, interview by Rose, 22–23, New Assisi Archives.

22. Report to National Assembly of Women Religious Board, Box 5, folder 17, National Assembly of Women Religious (NAWR) Archives, University of Notre Dame, Notre Dame, IN, hereafter cited as NAWR Archives.

In a letter to members of her congregation, Sister Pat spelled out her reasons for accepting this position: "This work is an extension and intensification of our community commitment to educate for justice. It is a call to move closer to our goal of becoming women of reconciliation in the world that knows so much division. It is a call to community generosity, asking us to believe with Francis that even though we may have needs ourselves, in giving we will receive. It is a call to risk."[23] After much discussion, the Sisters of St. Francis of Assisi decided that Pat should follow this nontraditional calling. Olgha Sandman, a member of the NFWM board, reflected on the qualities Sister Pat brought to this new position: "She was smart. She read a lot. She was very composed. She wasn't going to fly into desperation or spend time arguing with somebody. She was very methodical and very serious about what she was talking about. She was gentle but very firm on what she believed."[24]

After attending a training session and traveling to California to gather first-hand information about the farm workers' movement, Sister Pat began working in the St. Louis area. There she "met with community provincials and social action coordinators, alerted sisters to the needs of farm workers, conducted workshops and helped sisters develop local strategies including task forces to strengthen support in schools and religious communities."[25] She contacted nearly all sixty religious orders present in the St. Louis archdiocese. During her three-month assignment, she lived with five different communities. "I was on the move a lot," she related, "but it was really a chance to have people know me as a person and not just as a spokeswoman for an issue."[26] After leaving St. Louis, Sister Pat, representing the NAWR, addressed a rally of ten thousand farm workers and their supporters in Modesto, California. Chavez had orchestrated the gathering to challenge the Gallo wineries to allow their workers to vote on union representation. To speak in front of such a large crowd, Sister Pat had to overcome her innate shyness. "I brought them greetings from all the church people in St. Louis and told the farm workers, 'They aren't all marching with you here today, but they were certainly praying with you,'" she said.[27] Sister Tess, Sister Pat's fellow activist, observed, "While she herself was giving voice to the farm workers, she was finding her own voice, her own strength in being a public figure."[28]

For the next two years, Sister Pat pioneered a new role for Franciscan sisters. She became an itinerant organizer, traveling to major cities, "staying

23. Drydyk, to "Dear Sisters," 1 November 1974, Box 8, New Assisi Archives.
24. Olgha Sandman, in an interview with the author, September 13, 2019.
25. "'Watch Gallo Sales,' Says Non-Promoter for UFWA," *St. Louis Review*, March 7, 1975, Box 8, New Assisi Archives.
26. Patricia Drydyk, quoted in NAWR, "Cesar's Call," March 1975, Box 8, New Assisi Archives.
27. Drydyk, interview by Rose, 43, New Assisi Archives.
28. Browne, interview.

three to five months at a time and working with the UFW boycott office people."[29] She urged her fellow sisters "to join the picket lines in front of their local [grocery] stores, encouraging them to use the farm worker boycotts as concrete ways of carrying out the social teachings of the church."[30]

Sister Pat's efforts on behalf of the farm workers took her back to California in October 1975 to be part of a task force of thirty religious women and men who observed elections being held to decide whether the UFW or the Teamsters union would represent grape workers.[31] She returned again in the spring and summer of 1976 to help persuade voters to pass Proposition 14, a UFW-sponsored statewide ballot initiative that would have guaranteed funding for the California Agricultural Labor Relations Act signed by Governor Edmund G. "Jerry" Brown in 1975. The Sisters of St. Francis of Assisi made a corporate commitment to this campaign. Three other members of the community—Sisters Tess, Betty Wolcott, OSF, and Margaret Kruse, OSF—joined Sister Pat in California that summer. Sister Pat claimed she worked harder on this drive than on anything she had ever done before. Her responsibilities included finding housing for three hundred campaign volunteers and gathering signatures needed to place the initiative on the November ballot. "I would go and talk to groups and encourage them to sign the initiative [petitions] and also get other people to support it," she recollected. In response, California growers launched a well-funded countercampaign to attack provisions of the proposed legislation as violations of private property rights. On Election Day, Proposition 14 was soundly defeated, with only 37 percent of voters favoring the measure. Sister Pat maintained this loss was "my first real experience of what farm workers go through." She remembered one UFW member saying to her afterwards, "Well, you know that's okay, Sister. It happens to us all the time. We just pick ourselves up and keep on going."[32]

Sister Pat arrived in Cleveland, Ohio, in January 1976, the fourth stop on her rounds of religious communities on behalf of the UFW. A reporter described a work routine that included meetings with UFW staff, conducting door-to-door visits, passing out informational leaflets, setting up contacts with religious communities, and picketing for the UFW on Fridays. Her goal was building awareness of "the UFW, its history, its leader (Cesar Chavez), its battles, and why a boycott of lettuce, grapes and now raisins is necessary."[33]

---

29. Drydyk, interview by Rose, 23, New Assisi Archives.

30. Drydyk, "Price of Lettuce," 16.

31. "Nun Reports Union Election Abuses," *Michigan Catholic*, October 8, 1975, Box 8, New Assisi Archives.

32. Drydyk, interview by Rose, 26, New Assisi Archives.

33. "Nun 'Joins' UFW Local Staff," *Cleveland Universe-Bulletin*, March 12, 1976, Box 8, New Assisi Archives.

In March 1977, Sister Pat sent the NAWR board a report detailing her work over the previous three months. She listed sixty-eight separate meetings in twenty-nine cities in Michigan, Ohio, Missouri, Oklahoma, Texas, West Virginia, Louisiana, Arkansas, Tennessee, and California. The people she spoke with included communities of sisters, high school students, local farm worker support organizations, sisters volunteering with the UFW, church groups, television talk show hosts, and guests at a fundraising event—a schedule that would exhaust the most dedicated political campaigner.[34] On her travels, she emulated the mendicant lifestyle of the first Franciscans. Sister Pat noted, "To keep expenses down I begged my way from convent to convent staying three to four weeks as the guest of many different religious communities. Never was I refused."[35]

In addition to building support for the UFW, Sister Pat recruited sisters to work in California for the UFW. One of these volunteers was Sister Margaret Kruse, an Iowa farm girl who became a Sister of St. Francis of Assisi. In 1975, she and Sister Jean Molesky, OSF, went to La Paz, the UFW headquarters in the mountain town of Keene, California, where they ran a daycare program for the children of union staff. The following year, both sisters moved to Delano, California, where the UFW had created a center for the children of agricultural workers. Sister Margaret recalled, "We opened the daycare at 5:00 or 5:30 in the morning and went to 6:00 or 6:30 in the evening" to accommodate the laborers' work schedules. "We had fifty to one hundred kids, maybe even more, every day." On Saturdays, the daycare volunteers drove to Los Angeles, where they picketed grocery stores as Sister Pat had done. Sister Margaret described those demonstrations: "We would go on a Saturday morning to either a grocery store or somewhere the organizers had set up for the boycott. We would march back and forth with signs saying to boycott lettuce or boycott grapes and other things that were being boycotted at the time. We would do that all day and then get back in the car and travel back to Delano or La Paz. . . . On a good day the signs would get people's attention not to buy grapes or the lettuce."[36]

Chavez's strong religious faith enhanced Sister Pat's efforts to enlist Catholic sisters in the farm workers' cause. Over objections of some of his staff, Chavez insisted that UFW members carry an image of Our Lady of Guadalupe at the front of their marches.[37] Their rallies often ended with a Mass celebrated by a priest sympathetic to the union. In November 1973, the National Conference of Catholic Bishops endorsed the UFW and its boycott

---

34. Report to NAWR Board, March 1977, Box 7, folder 02, NAWR Archives.
35. Drydyk, to "Dear Sisters," 15 September 1975, New Assisi Archives.
36. Margaret Kruse, in an interview with the author, July 9, 2019.
37. Chavez insisted that incorporating religious symbolism "was a way of making the association attractive to the mostly Catholic farm workers. It also would generate moral and financial support." Frank Bardacke, *Trampling Out the Vintage*, 214.

of table grapes, a measure the bishops reaffirmed in 1975.[38] Chavez's widely publicized private audience with Pope St. Paul VI in 1974 also boosted the organizer's credibility with American Catholics. The pope warmly welcomed Chavez as "a faithful son of the Catholic Church" and offered his support of the UFW's political activism on behalf of farm workers.[39]

On the National Farm Worker Ministry Staff

In 1976, when funding from the NAWR ran out, Sister Pat joined the staff of NFWM, a coalition of church groups, most of them Protestant, that built support for the farm worker movement among religious bodies.[40] NFWM traced its origin to the California Migrant Ministry (CMM), which had been founded in 1920 by the United Church of Christ to provide "direct aid to migrant workers in a variety of forms including food, clothing, day-care for children, health literacy education, sports activities, and acting as a liaison between schools and parents or advocates for acquiring water access for farm worker housing." During the 1940s, leaders of the CMM began advocating for the rights of agricultural workers, backing legislation to include them in Social Security coverage and to expand public services to farm workers and their families.[41] In the 1950s, they did grassroots organizing in farm worker communities. Then in the 1960s, under the leadership of Reverend Hartmire, the CMM began placing "more emphasis on assisting people in their attempts at self-determination." Reverend Hartmire concluded that the most effective way Christians could meet the needs of oppressed farm workers was by actively cooperating with them to build the UFW into a force strong enough to protect their rights and to improve their working and living conditions.[42]

Sister Pat explained the nature of her work with the NFWM in a 1981 article: "I do not, as most people would suppose, work in rural areas providing food, clothing, and other services to destitute farm workers. I may not see farm workers for weeks or months at a time. But I definitely do work *with* farm workers. I am a staff member of the National Farm Worker Ministry, an

---

38. The bishops' endorsement was largely due to the persistent lobbying of Monsignor George Higgins. See Marco G. Prouty, *Cesar Chavez, the Catholic Bishops, and the Farmworkers' Struggle for Social Justice* (Tucson: University of Arizona Press, 2006).

39. Adam Varoqua, "History Rediscovered: The Holy Alliance of the Catholic Church, Seton Hall University, and Iconic Labor Rights Activist Cesar Chavez," *Latino Institute News*, March 21, 2019, https://www.shu.edu/latino-institute/news/charter-day-exhibit-displays-seton-hall-mark-on-labor.cfm.

40. National Farm Worker Ministry, "Our History," http://nfwm.org/about/our-history/.

41. For the history of the CMM, see Alan J. Watt, *Farm Workers and the Churches* (College Station: Texas A&M University Press, 2010).

42. Wayne C. Hartmire, "What Form: Servanthood Among Seasonal Farm Workers?," n.d., 5, http://www.unionoftheirdreams.com/PDF/Hartmire_report.pdf.

ecumenical organization made up of 36 church groups. We are clergy, lay people, and sisters working together with farm workers who want to change their working and living conditions."[43]

Sister Pat next moved to Lansing, Michigan, where she organized a statewide group of farm worker supporters "similar to the NFWM in terms of its goals and thrust." The Michigan Farm Worker Ministry Coalition (MFWMC) began with ten member church groups. Sister Pat's first challenge was bringing "church groups to an understanding that charity was simply not enough. Food baskets, turkeys, toys were not the answers to the farm workers' problems. They'd have those problems next year. Something had to be done to change the system." Before long, Sister Pat was coordinating a consumer boycott of nonunion lettuce to support striking UFW members. In addition to educating religious groups and union members about the boycott, she often led picketing outside supermarkets selling nonunion lettuce. Sister Pat shared a small house in a Hispanic neighborhood and lived on a subsistence stipend that covered room and board plus five dollars a week for personal expenses. She learned how to shop for clothing in secondhand stores. When she left Michigan in 1979, another nun, Sister Theresa Grekowicz, IHM, took over her position with the MFWMC. "I always find sisters to replace me when I leave a place," Sister Pat told an interviewer.[44]

Sister Pat's next destination was Miami, Florida, where she directed a statewide lettuce boycott. She and her five-person staff shared a rambling old house with faulty plumbing, which they occupied rent-free in return for doing maintenance. *Miami Herald* reporter Mike Winerip described Sister Pat as a "mobilizing dynamo" who "persuaded the Miami Archdiocese Priests' Senate to endorse the farm-worker boycott of Red Coach lettuce. She convinced the YWCA [Young Women's Christian Association] to do the same." In Miami and other cities, Sister Pat employed a technique known as "human billboarding" to publicize the farm workers' cause. Winerip captured her energetic method: "When you drive home from work along S. Dixie Highway, you may see her holding a large UFW boycott sign. She's the one smiling and waving and having a grand old time. [She said,] 'I like it. It's my favorite sport in the union. People are driving home tired after a day at the office and all of a sudden they see you waving and smiling and they're smiling too. It's a good-spirited feeling.'" An iconic photo of Sister Pat holding a large UFW sign during a roadside billboarding session illustrated the article. It was reprinted many times in accounts of her pro-union activism.[45]

---

43. Drydyk, "Price of Lettuce," 15.
44. Drydyk, interview by Rose, 27–29, New Assisi Archives.
45. Mike Winerip, "Nun Takes Boycotting Religiously," *Miami Herald*, June 13, 1980, Box 8, New Assisi Archives.

The UFW boycott in Florida received a major boost when Chavez visited the state for a six-day tour in December 1979. Chavez told a reporter his general approach would be to contact the consumer and "ask her not to buy the product—lettuce—and stores will be asked not to sell it." The principal target of the lettuce boycott was the Publix supermarket chain. Florida had an extensive network of UFW supporters, more than any other state except California, which made a statewide effort possible. Farm worker support groups were active in Miami, Orlando, Jacksonville, Tampa, St. Petersburg, Tallahassee, Gainesville, Daytona Beach, West Palm Beach, and Fort Lauderdale. The boycott campaign was a sophisticated effort that employed multiple methods including picketing, billboarding, letter writing, and marching. The NFWM staff prepared detailed instructions for small groups of customers who met with store managers to express their displeasure at the sale of nonunion lettuce, for individuals writing letters and phoning Publix management, and for protestors to know how to conduct themselves on picket lines. In November 1980, Sister Pat helped organize a march of five hundred followers on the largest Publix market in Tampa.[46]

Sister Pat moved to Arizona in 1981. There, for the first time, she dealt directly with farm workers, assisting them as they formed union-organizing committees for laborers in the onion and melon fields around Phoenix. She found this a challenging task, in part, because she spoke very little Spanish. Sister Pat explained how she reached out to the workers: "I drove out to their houses in the communities in which they lived. I sat down and talked with them. Some farm worker families were long-time supporters of the UFW. From the beginning, they were the ones that would lead me to other farm workers. Then together we'd organize from house to house and they would organize other workers in the fields."[47]

One of her proudest accomplishments in Arizona was pulling together the state's first farm workers' convention. "It was very, very good," she recalled, "to see farm workers stand up with those microphones, some for the first time in their lives, presenting resolutions." One emotional issue raised at the convention was the use of the twelve-inch hoe, *el cortito*. Field laborers especially hated this implement because it forced them to bend over to cultivate crops, contributing to prevalent back pain. Growers required them to use this tool, but the workers wanted to use a standard-length hoe so they could stand upright as they worked. Soon after Sister Pat left Arizona, the state legislature enacted a ban on the twelve-inch hoe.[48]

---

46. "Procedure for Delegation to Publix," National Farm Worker Ministry Records, Box 49, folder 1, National Farm Worker Ministry Records, Walter P. Reuther Library, Wayne State University, hereafter cited as NFWMR.

47. Drydyk, interview by Rose, 33, New Assisi Archives.

48. Drydyk, interview by Rose, 33, New Assisi Archives.

In January 1983, Sister Pat became associate director of NFWM; her Florida colleague Reverend Fred Eyster, a Congregational minister, moved into the director's position. Sister Pat and Reverend Eyster agreed: "With this strengthened ecumenical leadership, we have a real opportunity to broaden the involvement of the religious communities in the farm workers' struggle for justice."[49] They split their responsibilities geographically—with Reverend Eyster covering the western states, while Pat dealt with states east of the Mississippi River from an office in Detroit.[50] "The titles are still executive director and associate," Sister Pat said in 1984, "but our working relationship is one of dividing up the responsibilities and consulting each other on major decisions."[51] One year later, the NFWM board acknowledged that "codirector" titles better defined the working relationship between Sister Pat and Reverend Eyster. Prior to Sister Pat's appointment, all of NFWM's top leaders had been Protestant and male. She was largely responsible for recruiting Catholic sisters into the farm worker movement. By 1979, the NFWM staff consisted of fourteen Protestants and fifteen Catholics.[52] When Reverend Eyster resigned as director in December 1985 due to poor health, Sister Pat succeeded him as executive director.

On July 27, 1984, Sister Pat enjoyed a rare opportunity to speak to the hierarchy of the Catholic Church when she testified before the National Conference of Catholic Bishops, which was preparing a pastoral letter on the US economy. She began by describing the mission of NFWM as "being present with and supporting farm workers as they organize to overcome their powerlessness and achieve a measure of justice, equality and freedom." To accomplish this objective, she stressed the importance of learning by listening to the farm workers, and she urged the bishops to do the same. She explained how her organization embraced voluntary poverty, supporting twenty-one staff members and their families on an annual budget of $200,000. She also emphasized the value of ecumenical cooperation: "United around the farm workers issue, we discover how much we have in common and we learn to be more inclusive in our language and attitudes." In closing, Sister Pat urged the bishops "to examine the structures within the Catholic Church" in order to strengthen its impact "on behalf of farm workers and others at the bottom of the economic ladder" and to continue "to speak out boldly on behalf of workers' rights."[53]

49. Quoted in "NFWM Board Appoints New Director & Associate," *National Farm Worker Ministry Newsletter* 11, no. 3 (December 1982): 1, NFWMR.

50. Drydyk, interview by Rose, 37, New Assisi Archives.

51. Drydyk, quoted in *National Farm Worker Ministry Newsletter* 14, no. 2 (Summer 1985), NFWMR.

52. *National Farm Worker Ministry Newsletter* 8, no. 1 (March 1979), NFWMR.

53. Drydyk, "Testimony for Roman Catholic Bishops' Pastoral Letter on the U.S. Economy," 27 July 1984, Box 8, New Assisi Archives.

New Year's Day 1985 found Sister Pat in a philosophical mood. In a holiday letter to friends, she reflected on her ten years spent organizing with the farm workers: "Every once in a while it hits me . . . being part of a movement like this means you help make a lot of history. . . . Very few of the daily activities create a great sense of accomplishment, but taken collectively—with all the people and all their efforts over the years—I look at it in amazement and think, 'Oh my God, we really have come a way!'"[54]

The Farm Labor Organizing Committee (FLOC)

The cause that absorbed much of Sister Pat's energies during her second decade with NFWM was FLOC, a midwestern union of agricultural workers in the tomato and cucumber fields of Ohio and Michigan.[55] Baldemar Velasquez, a Texas-born organizer, had followed the midwestern migrant stream with his family as a child. He began working in the fields at the age of six. "I could pick sixty or seventy baskets [of tomatoes] a day," he declared. "As I grew older, I could pick 200 baskets during the peak season, that's ten or twelve hours straight, without any breaks. The highest wage we ever got was twenty-two cents [per basket]." Velasquez founded FLOC in 1967. He learned from Chavez's example, and like Chavez, he believed in nonviolent protest. Agriculture in the Midwest differed from that of California, which was dominated by large growers and corporate concerns. In Ohio, the farms that hired migrants were "family owned, often as small as fifty or sixty acres." As Velasquez began organizing Ohio tomato pickers, he realized that the power to improve working conditions did not rest in the hands of the growers. He needed to focus on corporate food processors like Heinz, Hunt's, Libby's, and Campbell's, all of which bought vegetables grown by the small farmers. In 1978, Velasquez called a strike by two thousand workers on farms that sold their produce to the Campbell Soup Company, the largest processor in the region.[56]

NFWM forged an alliance with FLOC during Pat's years as associate director. NFWM's relations with the UFW had cooled, due in part to Chavez's increasingly authoritarian leadership.[57] NFWM embraced FLOC as a new voice in the struggle for farm workers' rights. While Reverend Eyster continued working with the UFW, Sister Pat was responsible for coordinating NFWM's efforts on behalf of FLOC. She approached FLOC's leadership and asked, "What can we do as church people to get church people involved in

---

54. Drydyk, to "Dear ____," 1 January 1985, Box 8, New Assisi Archives.
55. National Farm Worker Ministry, "Farm Labor Organizing Committee," http://nfwm.org/farm-workers/farmworker-partners/floc-campaign/.
56. Bob Sanders, "Boycott Campbell's: Ohio Farmworkers Take It to the Top," *Dollars & Sense*, December 1983, 16.
57. Olgha Sandman, in an interview with the author, September 15, 2019.

your program and your boycotts? What kind of support do you want and need?" Because FLOC was a small union with limited resources, it readily accepted this open-ended offer. This began a long and fruitful relationship.[58]

Workers represented by FLOC were on strike against tomato growers in Ohio and cucumber growers in Michigan. Among their demands were "a guaranteed minimum wage, a halt to pesticide spraying while workers were in the field, installation of outdoor plumbing in the one-room shacks they lived in, and work-site toilets with running water." Borrowing the strategy used effectively by the UFW against California grape and lettuce growers, FLOC launched a boycott of Campbell's, which bought tons of tomatoes for its famous soup and its Prego-brand spaghetti sauce, as well as cucumbers for its Vlasic pickle brand. The company's management claimed the boycott was unfair because the growers, not the company, hired and housed the striking workers. Campbell's executives argued they were not responsible for mistreatment of farm workers. FLOC leadership rejected this reasoning. They defended their boycott, pointing out that Campbell's set the terms and prices paid for tomatoes and cucumbers; these terms and prices then determined how much the farmers could pay their laborers. Thus, they insisted, Campbell's was largely responsible for the low wages, inadequate housing, and miserable working conditions on the farms.[59]

By 1980, NFWM had formed support groups for FLOC around the country. These volunteers approached church groups, unions, and other civic organizations, urging them to join the Campbell's boycott. NFWM also targeted Campbell's Labels for Education program, which rewarded participating schools with donations of athletic gear and audiovisual equipment in exchange for labels collected from Campbell's brands. In 1981, the Catholic Diocese of Cleveland announced it would stop purchasing Campbell's products. The following year, the Catholic Rural Life Commission endorsed the boycott.[60]

Although Campbell's corporate profits remained robust, FLOC's campaign was having an impact. In 1983, the *Wall Street Journal* reported: "The long-simmering fight [between FLOC and Campbell's] is coming to a boil. To promote their boycott, the farm workers have begun a media campaign against the Company. . . . At stake for Campbell is the Company's squeaky-clean public image, cultivated through its 'soup-is-good-food' commercials and its corporate

---

58. Drydyk, interview by Rose, 35, New Assisi Archives.
59. Sanders, "Boycott Campbell's," 17. Secondary boycotts such as the Farm Labor Organizing Committee's (FLOC) anti-Campbell campaign were not allowed under the National Labor Relations Act (NLRA) governing union-management relations, but because agricultural workers were excluded from coverage by the NLRA, their unions could legally employ this tactic.
60. "Support Grows for FLOC," *National Farm Worker Ministry Newsletter* 12, no. 2 (June 1981), PAGE, NFWMR.

giving record. Officials consider that all-American reputation a priceless asset."[61] Velasquez conceded that Campbell's corporate reputation was a target. In 1984, he told the *New York Times*, "They pour millions of dollars [into] promoting a certain image. I know the boycott has affected that image."[62] Company officials acknowledged that the strikers represented by FLOC had raised some valid issues. Jerimiah F. O'Brien, Campbell's director of community relations, admitted, "There is no question that FLOC and others have made us aware of what was going on." He pointed to recent company investments of more than $100,000 to upgrade worker housing and start daycare centers for workers' children.[63] However, Velasquez was not willing to absolve Campbell's management. He noted that they still dictated what crops were grown, how they were sprayed and harvested, and how much they sold for.[64]

FLOC organizers and their supporters came up with some innovative methods to publicize the boycott. The union was present at the 1984 Democratic National Convention in San Francisco when Reverend Jesse Jackson, one of the presidential candidates, addressed the delegates. NFWM staff had approached Reverend Jackson, who agreed to put a line in his speech about the Ohio farm workers. A month before the convention, NFWM staff members sent a mailing to all delegates asking whether they would be willing to help the farm workers. At the convention, sympathetic delegates carried boycott signs into the arena on the night of Reverend Jackson's address. Reverend Jackson implored his audience to make room in the party for "farm workers from Ohio who are fighting the Campbell Soup Company with a boycott to achieve legitimate workers' rights."[65] At this point, hundreds of FLOC supporters rose from their seats holding up signs saying, "Boycott Campbell's Cream of Exploitation Soup." The most conspicuous demonstrator that evening was NFWM staffer Sharon Streater, who danced in the aisles dressed in a seven-foot-tall Campbell's Cream of Exploitation Soup costume.[66] FLOC and NFWM staffers celebrated and thanked Reverend Jackson for "bringing the farm workers over a million dollars of free advertising on TV."[67]

---

61. Paul A. Engelmayer, "Campbell Soup Image on Line in Union Fight," *Wall Street Journal*, July 21, 1983, 29.

62. Baldemar Velasquez, quoted in "Boycott Aims at Campbell," *New York Times*, September 9, 1984, 13.

63. Jerimiah F. O'Brien, quoted in "Boycott Aims at Campbell," *New York Times*.

64. "Boycott Aims at Campbell," *New York Times*.

65. Jesse Jackson, "1984 Democratic National Convention Speech," July 18, 1984, American Rhetoric, https://www.americanrhetoric.com/speeches/jessejackson1984dnc.htm.

66. "Rev. Sharon Streater," *75 Years: National Farm Worker Ministry*, 29–30, n.d., United Farm Worker Collection, Box 23, folder 23–5, NFWMR; "Campbell Boycott Shines at Demo Convention," *National Farm Worker Ministry Newsletter* 13, no. 3 (September 1984): 6, NFWMR.

67. Drydyk, interview by Rose, 39, New Assisi Archives.

The following month, NFWM staff generated additional support for the Campbell's boycott by escorting fifty religious and civic leaders on a tour of tomato and cucumber fields in Ohio and Michigan. These observers saw "inadequate toilet facilities, crowded living conditions, children in the fields and children lacking fresh drinking water, electricity and window screens." The tour group also heard workers tell of wages that fell below the federal minimum and their fear of retaliation if they complained about their wages. Reverend Daniel Garcia of the United Methodist Church criticized the share-cropping system that treated workers as independent contractors, which forced them to pay their own Social Security and income tax withholding. Frances Moore Lappe, author of *Diet for a Small Planet*, denounced the court decision that ratified the growers' assertion that the farm workers were independent contractors. She said that it "wipes out whatever progress farm workers have achieved in securing human rights."[68]

Another tactic employed by NFWM was protesting at the Campbell Soup Company's annual shareholder meetings. Six FLOC supporters spoke to endorse two pro-union resolutions at the 1983 meeting. One resolution proposed that the company should publish a report on issues raised during the union-organizing struggle; the other called on Campbell's to appoint representatives of farm workers, growers, and consumers to its corporate board. Neither measure passed.[69] On November 16, 1984, sisters from four religious communities introduced a resolution calling on the company "to bargain collectively with the growers, the farm workers and FLOC." "We had over 18 speakers—farm workers and church people and labor people—all speaking on behalf or in support of farm workers," Sister Pat reported of that 1984 shareholders meeting, outside which seventy farm workers and three hundred supporters demonstrated in favor of the resolution.[70] Fifty FLOC members and friends rallied for corporate responsibility at the 1985 annual meeting of Campbell's.[71] In an interview, Sister Dorothy Diederichs, IHM, shared her vivid memories of the action staged by FLOC members as Sister Pat was presenting her resolution to the shareholders: "They sat on the end seat of each row on either side of the auditorium. At a certain point, when Pat was reading the resolution, they were to stand up—they were all dressed in their Sunday best—and open their shirts." Messages supporting the union were silk-screened on their T-shirts. Sister Dorothy recalled: "They stood up, faced the center of the auditorium . . . and

68. Frances Moore Lappe, quoted in "Leaders Tour Michigan, Ohio Fields," *National Farm Worker Ministry Newsletter* 13, no. 3 (September 1984): 6, NFWMR.
69. *National Farm Worker Ministry Newsletter* 12, no. 4 (December 1983): NFWMR.
70. Drydyk, interview by Rose, 40, New Assisi Archives.
71. "FLOC Appeals to Shareholders for Corporate Responsibility," *National Farm Worker Ministry Newsletter* 14, no. 3 (Fall 1985): NFWMR.

just stood there while she read this particular section of the resolution. The people sitting there, the shareholders, didn't know what was going on. Here were these all dressed-up farm workers standing at attention, saying nothing. It was shocking. It was absolutely shocking. I will never forget that sight."[72]

The event that generated the most publicity for the strike and boycott took place in the summer of 1983: a thirty-two-day, 560-mile march of striking farm workers from FLOC headquarters in Toledo, Ohio, to Campbell's corporate headquarters in Camden, New Jersey. A reporter from the *Wall Street Journal* described the progress of the march during an early stage: "As Mr. Velasquez leads his caravan two-abreast through Lorraine, [Ohio], about 20 miles west of Cleveland, the marchers are greeted by honks, waves and shouts of support from passing motorists. Occasionally, residents offer small donations and water and fruit to help marchers cope with the heat."[73] After the march concluded, FLOC vice president Fernando Cuevas expressed his gratitude for "the tremendous support that greeted us in every town . . . people opening up their homes to us, church folks feeding us, unions buying us new shoes when the first ones wore out."[74]

A demonstration of such scope and duration could not have happened without a huge amount of advance planning and logistical support. This was Sister Pat's responsibility. Her team of NFWM staffers worked furiously behind the scenes arranging schedules, obtaining permits, securing housing along the route, feeding marchers, coordinating volunteers, issuing press releases, and much more. In an appeal to NFWM supporters, she listed several ways that they could help: joining the first day of the march in Toledo or its final day in Philadelphia, human billboarding to publicize the Campbell's boycott, encouraging churches and unions to endorse the march, sponsoring a marching farm worker with a contribution, or volunteering with the advance team to prepare march logistics.

As the marchers neared Philadelphia, Cesar Chavez joined the procession, lending his prestige to their cause. Sister Pat had primary responsibility for organizing the last stages of the march into Philadelphia and across the Ben Franklin Bridge to Camden. She scheduled radio and television interviews, prepared press releases, and made arrangements for the rally at Philadelphia's Liberty Square, a religious service in Camden's Catholic cathedral, and the final rally outside Campbell's headquarters building.

While Sister Pat was taking care of logistical details, FLOC leader Velasquez was marching with his fellow farm workers. "Sister Pat and I were

---

72. Dorothy Diederichs, in an interview with the author, May 5, 2020.

73. Engelmayer, "Soup Image on Line," 29.

74. Fernando Cuevas, quoted in "March for Justice Continues," *National Farm Worker Ministry Newsletter* 12, no. 3 (September 1983): 6, NFWMR.

going back and forth [over mobile phone] on issues every day while I was marching," he recalled. She "was in the middle of coordinating" logistics with other teams along the route. "I knew I could get ahold of her just about any time day or night," he said. Perhaps her most valuable contribution was her optimism. "She was always upbeat," Velasquez observed. "I could always rely on her to be a spark and get people moving again and create the necessary enthusiasm to make things feel successful."[75]

On Sunday, August 7, the farm workers and their supporters assembled outside Philadelphia's Independence Hall, where Chavez and Velasquez addressed the throng. Later they led five hundred people across the Delaware River into Camden, where the day's events concluded with a community Mass at the Immaculate Conception Cathedral. Inside the cathedral, fifteen Catholic priests bent down to wash the feet of weary marchers, a replication of Jesus' washing the feet of his disciples on Holy Thursday. It was the most affecting moment during the month-long protest. That night, farm workers and their friends maintained a vigil outside Campbell's corporate headquarters.

Although the march, boycott, and other protests did not immediately bring Campbell's to the bargaining table, Ray Santiago, FLOC's secretary/treasurer, voiced confidence that the union would prevail: "Something is going to break within the next couple of years—sooner if the boycott takes hold. There was a time when Campbell's didn't heed the farm workers. Now a time is coming when they will have to deal with us—when they will see it is in their best interest to do so."[76] Extensive outreach by Sister Pat and NFWM staff garnered hundreds of endorsements for FLOC's strike and its boycott of Campbell's products. Endorsers included labor unions such as the Indiana and Ohio AFL-CIOs and the United Auto Workers, as well as religious bodies like the Archdioceses of Cincinnati and Detroit, the Diocese of Columbus, plus the Catholic Conference of Ohio, the Disciples of Christ, the United Methodist Church, and the United Church of Christ.[77]

In January 1985, Campbell's finally bowed to pressure and entered into negotiations with FLOC. These talks resulted in an agreement with two innovative provisions: (1) formation of an independent labor relations commission to mediate between all parties to find solutions to difficult issues and (2) the creation of a growers' association to represent the interests of the farmers who supplied vegetables to Campbell's. Negotiations continued until February 1986, when FLOC signed contracts with Ohio tomato growers and Michigan

75. Baldemar Velasquez, in an interview with the author, November 15, 2019.
76. Ray Santiago, quoted in Sanders, "Boycott Campbell's," 18.
77. W. K. Barger and Ernesto M. Reza, *The Farm Labor Movement in the Midwest* (Austin: University of Texas Press, 1993), 77–80.

pickle growers. Among the benefits farm workers gained from these contracts were an increase in their base wage to $4.50 per hour, improved housing, and major medical and hospitalization insurance.[78] In addition, the commission set up study committees "to investigate the use of pesticides, and the conditions of housing, childcare, and health care on migrant farms."[79]

Answering Criticism from a Sister Franciscan

One assignment that Sister Pat never anticipated when she began working for NFWM was responding to anti-union attacks disseminated by a fellow Franciscan. Sister Thomas Moore Bertels, a professor of history at Silver Lake College in Manitowoc, Wisconsin, belonged to the Franciscan Sisters of Christian Charity. In 1976, she wrote an article in *Farm Journal* criticizing consumer boycotts staged by the UFW and "the city-minded ecclesiastics and academics" who supported them.[80] In 1980, she continued her critique of farm worker unions, this time attacking FLOC's boycott of Campbell's Soup in a seventeen-page pamphlet that was later reproduced and circulated by the company.[81] Sister Thomas Moore claimed that the farm workers "were not underpaid," that FLOC leader Velasquez aspired to be a "messiah" seeking Hispanic American political power, and that the boycott of Campbell's products was based on a "fraudulent rationale."[82]

Sister Pat felt compelled to respond. In 1982, she, Sister Tess, and Sister Betty coauthored a fifteen-page booklet published by NFWM, *Why We Support the FLOC Boycott*, a point-by-point rebuttal of Sister Thomas Moore's arguments. They wrote, "Sister Bertels' rhetoric is unsubstantiated by facts . . . and marked by shrillness and innuendo. She resorts to name calling and attacking the motives and integrity of people she does not know. This adds nothing to the debate and to the resolution of the issues." They questioned the accuracy of her research and faulted her for relying on information provided by "those with a vested interest in the status quo" and ignoring research that contradicted her conclusions. They cited endorsements of FLOC made by the National Catholic Rural Life Committee and the US

---

78. Ruth Padawer, "Campbell's Boycott Brings Home Settlement," *Multinational Monitor*, March 15, 1986, 13.

79. Jim Sielicki, "FLOC Ends Campbell's Boycott," UPI Archives, https://www.upi.com/Archives/1986/02/21/FLOC-ends-Campbells-boycott/6375509346000/.

80. Thomas More Bertels, "Why Chavez Falls Back on Boycotts," *Farm Journal*, April 1976.

81. Thomas More Bertels, "To the Sisters of My Community, the Franciscan Sisters of Christian Charity, on the Matter of the Boycott of the Campbell Soup Company," Institute for Responsible Research and Reporting, n.d., New Assisi Archives.

82. Thomas More Bertels, "Soup Labels Stir Controversy," *Herald-Times Reporter* (Manitowoc–Two Rivers, WI), October 5, 1980, 4, New Assisi Archives.

bishops' Campaign for Human Development.[83] In their conclusion they quoted the encyclical *Laborem Exercens* by Pope St. John Paul II, which endorsed the right of farm workers to share in "decisions concerning their services."[84]

Sister Pat Continues to Work for Economic Justice

Conservative Catholics might have wondered what motivated a nun to picket and march on behalf of striking farm workers, but for Sister Pat, working for the UFW and FLOC was an extension of her religious vocation. In 1984, she reflected: "My involvement in the union has helped me integrate what we call spirituality, the relationship with God and with my brothers and sisters. I see them as one. There is no way I can, having gone through the experiences of seeing farm workers' needs and seeing what ways they want me to work with them, saying no to that and be saying yes to God at the same time. There's just no way. . . . You pray always when you're giving yourself with your brothers and sisters."[85]

In March of 1988, Sister Pat was back in California working out of the NFWM office in Delano. She was awakened from her sleep in the middle of the night by a call from local police saying that someone had broken into the office and set a fire in the central room. "I found that the building was seriously damaged, and that almost all of our files were either burned or seriously mutilated by smoke and water," she reported. But Sister Pat was determined not to let this incident interfere with her efforts to obtain justice for farm workers: "We intend to redouble our efforts to do our job."[86]

The Wrath of Grapes Boycott

The use of pesticides on crops, especially grapes, and the incidence of cancer among farm worker families was an increasingly important issue during Sister Pat's second decade with NFWM. In May 1986 Chavez announced a nationwide boycott of table grapes, which he named the Wrath of Grapes Boycott. The key demand of this campaign was that five cancer-causing pesticides used in grape production must be banned. Sister Pat believed that

---

83. Patricia Drydyk, Tess Browne, and Betty Wolcott, *Why We Support the FLOC Boycott*, August 1982, Box 49, folder 12, NFWMR.

84. John Paul II, *Laborem Exercens*, n. 21, quoted in Drydyk, Browne, and Wolcott, *Why We Support FLOC*.

85. Drydyk, interview by Rose, 50–51, New Assisi Archives.

86. Drydyk, to "Dear Sisters," 25 March 1988, Box 8, New Assisi Archives. Fearing for their safety, the NFWM board closed the Delano office and opened a new headquarters in Detroit.

Sister Pat Drydyk with Rev. William Sloane Coffin and Cesar Chavez, New York, 1985. Photo courtesy of New Assisi Archives.

NFWM could play an important role in educating the public about the carcinogenic properties of agricultural chemicals. She announced that the NFWM board had decided "to focus our work on a ministry to pesticide victims." In the small rural community of McFarland, California, she said, "eleven children have gotten cancer there during the past two years. Six of them have died. Teachers are warning the children not to drink from the water fountains—the drinking water is contaminated by pesticides." Sister Pat announced plans to conduct seminars about the health hazards of pesticide spraying and to publicize the problem among church people around the country.[87] "Hardly a month goes by, now," she wrote to her fellow Franciscans in 1988, "that a new case [of cancer] is not reported. And with every new case, comes a family devastated through huge medical expenses, emotional trauma, and, in many cases, the grief of a child's death." She cited the experience of the Rodriguez family, who "lost their 5 year old son. Both parents worked in the local grape fields—the mother, Elia, until she was eight months pregnant." For Sister Pat, collective action was a necessary response to such a tragedy: "We are active in developing outreach to media organizations, so that more

---

87. Drydyk, to "Dear Sisters," 16 June 1986, Box 8, New Assisi Archives.

people can know of this tragic situation which farm worker families are subject to in this region."[88]

The spring 1987 NFWM newsletter reported on efforts by church groups in Delano and McFarland to increase awareness of pesticide-related illnesses among farm workers and to pressure state agencies to investigate these ailments. It also announced two NFWM-sponsored community seminars on pesticide poisoning.[89] Brother Ed Dunn, OFM, of the St. Barbara Franciscan Province assisted Sister Pat in this effort.

In 1989, Sister Pat reported the discovery of another cancer cluster in the farming community of Earlimart, California. She informed members of her religious community about four-year-old Natalie Ramirez, who had one malignant tumor removed from one kidney at age eleven months and had a second tumor removed from her other kidney three months later. Her father, Gonzalo, had worked as a pesticide sprayer, and her mother, Ramona, had worked in the fields through her eighth month of pregnancy. By publicizing cases like Natalie's, Sister Pat hoped to pressure grape growers to discontinue use of cancer-causing pesticides.[90] Soon after this revelation, she issued an appeal to NFWM affiliates to join another boycott of table grapes with the objectives of banning "the five most dangerous pesticides used in growing grapes" and initiating a testing program for pesticide residues on grapes sold in stores.[91]

Difficult Times

In the late 1980s and early 1990s, as news about the farm workers' movement largely disappeared from national media, Sister Pat's duties as executive director became more challenging. Internal dissension wracked the UFW, and Chavez's death in April 1993 signaled the end of an era.[92] Funding for NFWM dried up, and staffing was cut back; Sister Pat was forced to do more with less. In 1985, she wrote to friends that a budget crunch "creates an exciting and challenging life for me."[93] NFWM's Michigan affiliate announced that it

---

88. Drydyk, to "Dear Sisters," 25 March 1988, New Assisi Archives.

89. "Ministry Among Pesticide Victims Continues," *National Farm Worker Ministry Newsletter* 16, no. 2 (Spring 1987): 3, Box 3, folder 23, United Farm Workers Collection, Walter P. Reuther Library, Wayne State University.

90. "A Letter from the Church of California," December 1989, Box 8, New Assisi Archives.

91. NFWM, "Straight Talk on the Fresh Grape Boycott," n.d., UCLA Library Special Collections, Charles E. Young Research Library.

92. For dissension within the UFW, see Miriam Pawel, *The Union of their Dreams: Power, Hope, and Struggle in Cesar Chavez's Farm Worker Movement* (New York: Bloomsbury Press, 2009).

93. Drydyk, to "Dear _____," 1985, New Assisi Archives.

was closing its office for financial reasons. The *NFWM Newsletter* went from appearing four times yearly to issuing once a year. Despite these setbacks, Sister Pat remained committed to the farm worker cause.[94] In April 1994, she coordinated the participation of religious leaders in a Sacramento rally at the conclusion of a memorial march for Chavez. It was her last public involvement in a major farm worker event.

Sister Pat was diagnosed with ovarian cancer in 1987. Following traditional treatment and her adoption of a macrobiotic diet, the disease went into remission. According to Sister Tess, Sister Pat "stayed in Chicago and continued working; she thought maybe she could lick it. Then in early '95 it came back with a vengeance."[95] Sister Pat took a leave of absence from NFWM to focus her energies on combating the disease with the same determination she used in fighting for the rights of farm workers. But the cancer spread. Her friend and companion, Sister Stella DeVenuta, OSF, witnessed the rapid progress of the disease. After a week's absence, Sister Stella returned to the apartment the pair shared and was shocked to see how much Sister Pat's health had worsened in seven days: "She couldn't go up and down the stairs."[96] When Sister Stella could no longer care for Sister Pat, she was transferred to St. Joseph's Hospice. Sandman, former chair of NFWM board, drove from Chicago to reach Sister Pat's bedside the day before she died. A small group of Sister Pat's close friends gathered around her sickbed and staged a spontaneous farewell. In an interview, Sandman remembered saying,

> "Why don't we have a demonstration for Pat?" We grabbed these big sheets of paper and markers and wrote her name on each: "Viva Pat," "You will get well," "We love you, Pat," "God loves you, Pat," in big letters. We stood at the foot of the bed holding these signs. We began singing for her. She opened her eyes and saw the signs, and she raised her right hand in a fist like we do in demonstrations. She put her hand down and closed her eyes. We were crying buckets of tears. That was our goodbye to her.[97]

Sister Pat lost her battle with cancer on September 13, 1995. Hours after her death, Baldemar Velasquez arrived at the hospice with the news that FLOC had signed another contract with growers. As word of her passing spread, tributes to Sister Pat flooded the Franciscan motherhouse. Demetria Martinez wrote in the *National Catholic Reporter*, "Whether praying over non-union lettuce in a grocery store or preaching the power of the boycott,

---

94. *National Farm Worker Ministry Newsletter* 20, no. 1 (Winter 1993): NFWMR.
95. Tess Browne, in an interview with the author, April 13, 2020.
96. Stella DeVenuta, in an interview with the author, October 1, 2019.
97. Sandman, interview, September 13, 2019.

Drydyk helped ignite a new vision of farm worker ministry rooted in change and not just charity."[98] She quoted Mary Ann Haren, Pat's former administrative assistant, who said it was impossible to turn Sister Pat down when she called about a meeting or a rally: "She was a real model for the rest of us."[99] Sister Betty, who worked with Sister Pat in NFWM, reflected, "Faithfulness is the word I associate with Pat; faithfulness over the long haul, both in the cause of justice, in victories and setbacks, and faithfulness as a friend."[100] Sister Tess shared a memory of her good friend sitting with Friere's *Pedagogy of the Oppressed* in one hand and a beer in the other: "She was a true Milwaukeean."[101]

Celebrating Sister Pat's Life

Sister Stella, Sister Pat's companion in her last months, together with Sisters Tess and Adele Thibaudeau, OSF, helped organize the ceremony celebrating Sister Pat's life. It was far cry from a traditional Catholic funeral. Sister Stella recalled:

> We had her body present in what is now the Troubadour Room [at the Sisters of Saint Francis of Assisi motherhouse]. I decorated the environment near her casket with the farm worker flag and cloth from Guatemala, and fruits and vegetables all down the steps. It was stunning. The whole chapel did the Farm Workers' clap [clapping in unison that begins slowly and rises to a powerful crescendo]. It became thunder. Across the aisle, as her body was brought out, the farm workers' flags were [extended] crisscrossed over the aisle. It was a tunnel of farm worker flags over her as her casket was rolled out under them. It was stunning. It was holy. It was spectacular.[102]

When her death was imminent, Sister Pat had dictated her wishes for her funeral service and its participants. It was a final statement of her values and was probably the most multicultural liturgy ever staged by the Sisters of St. Francis of Assisi. Sister Pat asked to recognize the Native American people who had occupied the site of the Franciscan convent before European settlers claimed the land. The funeral rite thus began with Native American drumming and a prayer for Sister Pat's journey offered by Lawrence Henry of the Ojibwa nation. It closed with the traditional smudging of the body by Sherri Roberts

---

98. Demetria Martinez, "Drydyk's Life a Paradigm for Justice," *National Catholic Reporter*, October 6, 1995, 12

99. Mary Ann Haren, quoted in Martinez, "Drydyk's Life a Paradigm," 12.

100. Betty Wolcott, quoted in Martinez, "Drydyk's Life a Paradigm," 12.

101. Betty Wolcott, quoted in *We of Nojoshing*, October 1995, New Assisi Archives.

102. DeVenuta, interview.

of the Oneida people. The pallbearers included family members (a niece and a cousin), representatives of FLOC and the UFW, and two Franciscan sisters. Other participants included relatives, Catholic sisters from five other communities, four Protestant ministers, and fellow activists in the farm worker movement. Mourners sang "De Colores," the Mexican folk song associated with the UFW. Sisters Tess and Adele performed a liturgical dance titled "The Spirit of Life." For the concluding hymn, the congregation acknowledged Sister Pat's Franciscan commitment as they sang the "Canticle of the Sun," composed eight hundred years earlier by St. Francis of Assisi.[103]

Sister Maureen Leach, OSF, offered this recollection at Sister Pat's funeral:

> I can still hear her laugh. Sometimes it was at obstacles that seemed so insurmountable that she would laugh first and then plow ahead. Others would have given up. When faced with people who did not appreciate her tireless efforts for justice, she would shrug her shoulders and go on. She always worked for unity in the movement. She was willing to bend her agenda if it was for the good of the farm workers. She was a fiery woman. She never hesitated to call agribusiness to accountability for their unjust practices. She wasn't one to seek personal glory. When she came to visit Texas, she was just as willing to set up chairs or run copies as to handle a press conference. On the picket line, her energy was contagious. You could not be near her without feeling it. The board meetings were events to be anticipated with eagerness. Pat, with others, set an agenda that always included looking at reality, theological reflections, and action. They stretched me, challenged me, and deepened my ability to connect faith and action. Even after a day with a packed agenda, Pat would take time for a late night talk about life. Her work stretched across decades, spanned distances of this country from west to east and south to north, and crossed endless social and political barriers. Thank you Pat, for giving your life for the farm workers.[104]

Sister Pat's Legacy

In 1995, to mark its seventy-fifth anniversary, NFWM prepared a commemorative booklet containing reminiscences about individuals who had served the organization over the years. Several of Sister Pat's colleagues included tributes to their recently deceased executive director. Sister Dorothy, former director of the MFWMC, wrote, "Pat had incarnated the farm worker struggle in her whole person. . . . In the name of all the churches and religious groups represented by NFWM, Pat as director had to keep a delicate balance

---

103. "Funeral program for Sister Pat Drydyk," Box 8, New Assisi Archives.
104. Margaret Leach, handwritten notes, 17 September 1995, Box 8, New Assisi Archives.

between the constant and urgent demands from UFW and FLOC." Sister Betty, who had worked for NFWM in California from 1976 to 1978 and later became its associate director under Pat, emphasized her friend's optimism: "Pat was nearly always hopeful," she wrote, "even after that fire [the arson that damaged their Delano office] she said, 'This act of violence against us shows we are having an effect.'" Roger Yockey, a union organizer in Washington and a Secular Franciscan, noted that Sister Pat had played an important role in helping farm workers in that state gain a union contract with the Chateau Ste. Michelle winery: "Sister Pat spoke loud, long, and clear as an advocate for the workers, not only before national, state, and local church groups, but at corporate headquarters." The reminiscences included a heartfelt poem about Sister Pat by Reverend Bill Noel, a Northern California supporter of the UFW, which read in part:

> The earth,
> on our brows and on our boots,
> in our eyes and in our mouths,
> Called her,
> And she became our sister.
> Under the feet of Jesus,
> in our Lord's place,
> Stood his sister,
> full of heart and muscle.[105]

Years later, Sister Margaret, whom Sister Pat had recruited to the farm worker movement, offered this evaluation of her good friend: "Pat really lived what she believed. She was true to her heart and very passionate with her direction that she felt she was being called to. She was very inspirational in the sense that she was for issues of justice, and because of that, she attracted a lot of different groups of people to follow and work with the United Farm Workers union. I think she was just a person who was true to her heart, true to who she was."[106]

Baldemar Velasquez praised Sister Pat's generosity: "Sister Pat was never pretentious. You never got the sense that anything she did was about herself. That total unselfishness, the Christian concept of thinking of others first, Sister Pat lived that."[107]

After her death, an unnamed writer paid a final tribute to Sister Pat in the NFWM newsletter:

---

105. *National Farm Worker Ministry 75th Anniversary Booklet*, 27, 49, 65, 31, Box 23, folder 23–5, United Farm Worker Collection, Walter P. Reuther Library, Wayne State University.

106. Margaret Kruse, in an interview with the author, October 1, 2019.

107. Velasquez, interview.

Sister Pat Drydyk doing human billboarding, Miami, 1980. Miami Herald photo by Joe Rimkus Jr. Photo courtesy of New Assisi Archives.

Pat dared to confront growers, corporate executives, and celebrities alike if it meant gaining some ground for the farm workers' cause. She dared to challenge church folks to "practice what they preached." She knew it could be done—she was *doing* it. . . . Pat gave no quarter to those who would abstract away the fact that sacrifices are required if the oppressed are ever to see justice. . . . Many of us once donated a piece of our lives to the farm workers' movement. Rare beings like Pat Drydyk came and stayed, embracing the farm workers' struggle as their own.[108]

The Sisters of St. Francis of Assisi honored Sister Pat's commitment to the farm workers cause in May 2019, when they dedicated their new motherhouse. Overlooking its main hall is an extensive mural depicting the history of the order from its founding in 1849. One section contains a portrayal of Sister Pat billboarding on behalf of the UFW lettuce boycott. Her fighting spirit lives on.

---

108. "Looking Back, Forging Ahead," *NFWM Newsletter* 22, no. 1 (Spring 1996): 1, Box 8, New Assisi Archives.

Chapter 7

Father Joseph Nangle: Missionary to the United States

More than two hundred Catholics assembled outside the United States Capitol on July 18, 2019, to protest the detention and mistreatment of immigrant families on the US border with Mexico. Speakers denounced policies of the Trump administration and demanded humane treatment of refugees. Many of these activists then entered the Russell Senate Office Building carrying photos of children who had died in the custody of US Immigration and Customs Enforcement (ICE). After praying the Rosary, five demonstrators lay down on the marble floor, forming a cross. When the group refused to leave, US Capitol Police arrested seventy-one people for holding an unlawful demonstration.[1]

Father Joseph Nangle, OFM, then an eighty-seven-year-old former missionary to Latin America, was marched out of the building, his hands bound in front of him with plastic zip ties. Speaking in English and Spanish before his arrest, Father Joe had addressed his remarks to the migrants held by ICE: "First, a plea for pardon of you our sisters and brothers. We love you and welcome you to the United States. You have a right to be here. We will continue to struggle toward that day when you will hear the words of God through the Prophet Isiah: 'Comfort, comfort my people, your trial is at an end . . . I have heard the cry of my people.'"[2]

Father Joe singled out President Donald Trump for criticism. He accused the chief executive of "dragging us back to those evil times, with a combination of irrational fears, hatred of people not like him, and sheer cruelty."[3] He later told an interviewer, "The collaboration and support of the Trump horror

---

1. Rose Marie Berger, "A Cross of Human Bodies," *Sojourners*, July 25, 2019, https://sojo.net/articles/cross-human-bodies.
2. Joseph Nangle, quoted in Berger, "Cross of Human Bodies."
3. Joseph Nangle, quoted in Wojtek Wacowski, "Resisting Is Part of Faith," *Front Page Live*, July 19, 2019, https://www.frontpagelive.com/2019/07/19/resisting-is-part-of-faith-70-arrested-in-senate-rotunda-while-demanding-an-end-to-detention-of-immigrant-children/.

Father Joe Nangle arrested in Senate Office Building, Washington, July 18, 2019.

by our Christian and or Catholic brothers and sisters is a tragedy, a scandal and something incredible."[4]

This was not Father Joe's first arrest. The Franciscan social justice advocate estimated he has been jailed at least ten times for his beliefs, including a 1987 protest of Ronald Reagan's Central American policies and a 2006 demonstration against the war in Iraq.[5]

Early Years in Latin America

Father Joe was not always a militant activist for peace and human rights. He grew up an only child in a conventional, middle-class, Irish Catholic home in suburban Lexington, Massachusetts, outside Boston. He was an avid athlete, playing baseball and hockey, and became a lifelong fan of the Boston Red Sox. At seventeen, he enrolled at St. Bonaventure College (now University), where his great-uncle, Father Gabriel Nangle, OFM, had been a vice president. Another uncle was a diocesan priest in New York City. Therefore, it "wasn't unusual for me, a nice Catholic boy, to be thinking about the priest-

---

4. "Br. Joseph Nangle: 'Catholics' Collaboration with Trump Is Scandalous,'" OFM JPIC, July 23, 2019, https://www.ofmjpic.org/en/br-joseph-nangle-catholics-collaboration-with-trump-is-scandalous/.

5. Joseph Nangle, in an interview with the author, October 31, 2019.

hood," he recalled years later. After two years of college, he entered the Franciscan order. He credits Father Reginald Redlon, OFM, then a young priest and later president of St. Bonaventure, with sparking "in me the notion that I could become a friar."[6]

During his seminary years, Father Joe said, he "felt a stirring within" himself to become a missionary.[7] A year and a half after his 1958 ordination, he went as a missionary to Latin America. "I was a very, very healthy 27-year old," he wrote in 2004, "and I think the Provincial jumped at the opportunity for me to go to Bolivia, which was our toughest mission." Ministering in the mountainous country was a formidable challenge. Friars who returned from Bolivia spoke of "long treks over rugged terrain, outdoor living, dangerous river crossings [and] precarious mountain roads." It was "the right stuff to spark the imagination of a twenty-something newly ordained Franciscan," he explained.[8]

The friars ministered to Bolivian people who were nominally Catholic, but whose faith was not deeply rooted. Father Joe remembered his first Christmas in the country. He celebrated Masses in three different locales and said he "had one person go to Holy Communion. One." Initially, the language was an obstacle. Father Joe had arrived in Bolivia with "barely a smattering" of Spanish. Thanks to intensive tutoring by Colombian religious sisters, he developed a facility in Spanish, but he never mastered the languages spoken by indigenous people. It was a difficult assignment for the young Franciscan. "I came to know how much loneliness I could stand as I worked, often by myself, among people who were vastly different in terms of education and life experience," he wrote.[9]

After he spent four years living in very primitive conditions, his New York superiors transferred Father Joe to a much different situation in Lima, Peru. At the age of thirty-one, he became the founding pastor of Santísimo Nombre (Most Holy Name) parish in a newly built upper-middle-class neighborhood of Peru's capital city. Many of his parishioners were professionals, successful businesspeople, and well-connected government officials who welcomed the gregarious, energetic young friar and his fellow Franciscans as their parish priests. During his first years in Lima, Father Joe did not question the status quo. He described his approach as being a "nice guy," one "who would influence people with his outgoing personality, together with genuine personal concern and attention." The new pastor quickly became a popular figure among his parishioners, but as he later observed, his approach was "lacking in any social analysis or the challenges of the church's social teachings."[10]

---

6. Nangle, interview, October 31, 2019.
7. Joseph Nangle, *Birth of a Church* (Maryknoll, NY: Orbis Books, 2004), 4.
8. Nangle, *Birth of a Church*, 4.
9. Nangle, *Birth of a Church*, 4.
10. Nangle, *Birth of a Church*, 9.

Gradually, Father Joe became more aware of the wide divide between the three social classes in his parish: well-to-do homeowners, their live-in servants, and the unskilled, uneducated laborers who protected mini-mansions under construction. He visited humble homes of the poor people living in the parish. "I came to love them, and I wanted to serve them in any way I could. I would have to have had a heart of stone not to do so," he professed.[11]

In *Birth of a Church*, his 2004 account of his years as pastor of Santísimo Nombre, Father Joe described a particularly difficult incident that changed his perspective. One Saturday afternoon, he was summoned to the scene of a fatal hit-and-run accident on a nearby highway. The victim, Jose Valencia, was a nine-year-old student at the parish school. The boy had been returning from begging scraps of food from affluent families to provide an evening meal for his parents and siblings. Father Joe spent two days trying, with Jose's parents, to persuade uncaring officials to release their son's body. The driver who struck their son refused to pay for Jose's funeral. Four days after the accident, Father Joe helped the Valencias inter their son's lifeless body in a temporary niche in the poor people's section of the local cemetery. Jose's death painfully illustrated the social realities of "inequitable economic opportunities, lack of education, subhuman housing, hunger, joblessness, racism, classism, sexism" pervasive in Peru and other third-world nations. "My preaching thereafter was never the same again," Father Joe noted.[12]

Impact of Liberation Theology

During the post–Vatican II years, the Catholic Church in Latin America underwent a remarkable transformation due to the reforms instituted by the Council and the emergence of liberation theology. Bishops, missionary priests, and native clergy began to argue that the Church should stop siding with the wealthy classes and align itself with poor and oppressed people. Father Gustavo Gutierrez, the Peruvian priest, theologian, and author of the influential text *A Theology of Liberation*, initiated this new theological approach. He maintained that the Church must employ "a preferential option for the poor" and work to overturn social institutions responsible for perpetuating Latin America's widespread poverty. Inspired by this radical ideology, activist Catholic clergy began supporting reforms within the Church and in civil society.

In August 1968, the bishops of South America, Central America, and the Caribbean met in Medellín, Colombia, to apply the insights and teachings of the Second Vatican Council to their part of the world. The bishops resolved, "The Church . . . will lend its support to the downtrodden of every social class

---

11. Nangle, *Birth of a Church*, 148–49.
12. Nangle, *Birth of a Church*, xix–xxvi.

so they might come to know their rights and how to make use of them."[13] This resolution gained wide acceptance in Peru because of the extreme disparity between a very wealthy elite and impoverished masses. Gutierrez won the support of Cardinal Juan Landazuri, OFM, the archbishop of Lima, who placed liberationists in key positions throughout the archdiocese.

Liberation theology proponents sought out priests like Father Joe. "They thought I had some possibilities," he reminisced years later. The young American friar was a willing convert. "I fell into it quite easily," he recollected. "I remember saying to somebody, 'We have to put those old theology books aside.'" Father Joe and the other Franciscans at Santísimo Nombre realized that traditional charitable works such as feeding the hungry and providing health care for the sick were not enough. They began implementing insights gleaned from these new teachings in all activities at their parish. Charity must be coupled with justice, they insisted. In addition to treating the symptoms of poverty, Christians must ask why poverty exists and then attack its causes. Father Joe recognized that "both charity and justice are necessary."[14]

Father Joe described the shift at Santísimo Nombre as a movement "from a parish ministry that consoled, domesticated and centered on the individual to one that disturbed, challenged and concentrated on the common good."[15] One change he instituted was a revised admission policy for the parish school. Instead of enrolling only students whose parents could afford the tuition, the school began admitting children of domestic workers and caretakers on the same basis as children from more affluent families. Higher tuitions paid by well-to-do parents covered the costs of educating additional children from poor families. Within a year, pupils from the lower classes made up nearly 30 percent of the student body.[16] The school also began offering evening classes for domestic workers employed by wealthy parishioners.

During the eleven years Father Joe served at Santísimo Nombre, the parish auditorium doubled as its Sunday worship space. On weekdays and evenings, the building was used by the day and night schools. This setup was consistent with documents produced by the Medellín episcopal conference, which said churches should be modest and functional, "without show or ostentation."[17] When the archbishop tried to convince Father Joe to build a larger church, he resisted, saying, "The Medellín vision of a preferential option for the poor surely called into question spending money on ostentatious churches."[18]

---

13. Second Episcopal Conference of Latin America, quoted in Nangle, *Birth of a Church*, 58.

14. Nangle, *Birth of a Church*, 152.

15. Nangle, *Birth of a Church*, 148.

16. Nangle, *Birth of a Church*, 81.

17. Quoted in Nangle, *Birth of a Church*, 134.

18. Nangle, *Birth of a Church*, 135.

Another consequence of following the principles of liberation theology was a significant alteration in the priests' personal lifestyle. Although all Franciscans take a vow of poverty, Father Joe began questioning his own standard of living. When he had first come to Lima, he adopted the North American clerical custom of taking a day off once a week. These days usually included, he said, "a round of golf, dinner at an upscale restaurant and perhaps a movie in the company of other U.S. priests." However, he and his colleagues soon realized that these activities "reeked of privilege." They decided to forego these pleasures.[19]

Challenging the lifestyles of affluent parishioners disturbed and divided the Santísimo Nombre congregation. "They didn't like to hear that message," Father Joe wrote. His call for "an option on behalf of the poor, together with the lifestyle changes involved in that option, touched very sensitive nerves with our middle class parishioners."[20] Some of them left Santísimo Nombre for other parishes. This dissension was a source of pain for Father Joe, who worried, "How can a Franciscan cause such situations in his pastoral work?"[21]

Missionary to the United States

Father Joe's Franciscan superiors called him back from Peru in 1975. He wrote that this was when he began a "mission to my own wealthy and privileged United States society."[22] On earlier trips to the United States for provincial chapter meetings, he had been "making noise about what we needed to do in Latin America. We were very unprepared, all of us going to Latin America." He was enticed to return to the United States by the promise of a newly created position directing "a mission oversight office, which would screen, prepare and to some extent monitor our province's overseas personnel." However, on his arrival, he learned that one group of missioners whom he was supposed to supervise had voted against his assuming these duties.[23] His reason for leaving Latin America suddenly vanished. "The rug was pulled out from under me," he recalled. Father Joe swallowed his disappointment and moved on. "I picked up the pieces of my life, and pretty quickly went on to other ministries in the United States," he said. However, his experiences in Bolivia and Peru remained foremost in his mind and "marked every aspect of the work that followed."[24]

Father Joe moved back to the United States with the deep conviction that "the church at every level of her life and in every one of her members is there

19. Nangle, *Birth of a Church*, 84.
20. Nangle, *Birth of a Church*, 88.
21. Nangle, email message to the author, May 23, 2020.
22. Nangle, *Birth of a Church*, 142.
23. Nangle, *Birth of a Church*, 150.
24. Nangle, *Birth of a Church*, 150–51.

on behalf of and in service to God's Reign of universal dignity and justice." By this he meant that the Church's ministers must "denounce clearly what stands in [the] way" of its realization. He soon discovered "that too often our U.S. churches err by neglecting or ignoring this prophetic mandate." He resolved to do everything in his power to make "all our Christian institutions and the people who belong to them as prophetic as they are pastoral."[25]

In essence, Father Joe continued doing missionary work, but now he sought to convert Americans to the liberating vision of the Church that he had absorbed during his years in Peru. Ever since, he has demonstrated an adroit balance between pastoral and prophetic pursuits in his ministry. Father Joe's experience is not unique. In her comprehensive study titled *The Missionary Movement in American Catholic History*, Sister Angelyn Dries, OSF, noted, "Returned missionaries . . . questioned the values promoted by the American way of life. . . . They had discovered that a comfortable life for U.S. citizens often came at the cost of the lives of poor persons they knew."[26]

Freed by his provincial superior to pursue any work he desired, Father Joe chose to live in Washington, DC. "People in Peru said to me, 'If you're going to work in the United States, you need to go to Washington because that's the heart of the empire, and that's where you will be heard and where you can make your most valuable contribution,'" he explained in an interview. He listed three key objectives for his US labors. First, he wanted to live in a poor area and adopt a simple lifestyle commensurate with the way he had lived in Latin America. Second, he needed to continue in pastoral ministry, "to be in a parish, doing parish work." Third, he said, "I wanted to work for some organization that had a national projection."[27]

His first job on returning to the United States was a staff position with the US Catholic Mission Association, an organization promoting awareness of overseas missions among US Catholics. Father Joe did some writing and spoke to Catholic groups for the association. "It was a good way for me to get familiar with the church in the US," he reflected.[28] He also began ministering at St. Luke's church in suburban McLean, Virginia. Marie Dennis, then a member of the parish social justice committee, recalled that committee members convinced the parish board to hire a social justice minister, and Father Joe responded to their ad. "It was a very interesting encounter because we had been reading Gustavo Gutierrez's writing on liberation theology," Marie recollected in an interview. Father Joe "was absolutely on fire with his

25. Nangle, *Birth of a Church*, xxvi.

26. Angelyn Dries, *The Missionary Movement in American Catholic History* (Maryknoll, NY: Orbis Books, 1998), 241.

27. Nangle, interview, October 31, 2019.

28. Joseph Nangle, in an interview with the author, April 4, 2020.

experience in Lima." Right away, she realized that he could help parish members "understand what life looked like from more marginal places in the world like Peru." She praised his "ability to say and preach and write about extremely challenging social justice causes, yet he is able to do it without offending people."[29] That appointment began a collaboration between Father Joe and Dennis that has thrived for more than four decades. Father Joe eventually left St. Luke's due in part to his disagreement with the decision to construct an elaborate new church edifice. He told his friend and later colleague, Dolores Leckey, the first director of the Secretariat for the Laity of the USCCB, "I cannot work with those people when there is so much suffering and they have the money and could be helping."[30]

Around this time, Father Joe also started collaborating with the PAX community, a nongeographic organization of progressive Catholics. PAX began as a federation of about one hundred likeminded families who took the teachings of the Second Vatican Council to heart. They met at St. Luke's parish, Father Joe described, but "had their own 9 o'clock Mass for which they prepared the liturgy, they prepared the homily." He was one of a rotating pool of priests who presided at their eucharistic celebrations. Lay people took full responsibility for organizing these services. "I was thrilled to see it," Father Joe said. "They reminded me so much of the base Christian communities in Latin America."[31] His involvement with the PAX community and a similar group, the Nova community, has continued for more than forty-five years.

A major issue that Father Joe addressed while at the US Catholic Mission Association were abuses committed by government intelligence agencies, especially the CIA, when dealing with American missionaries overseas. A 1975 investigation by a US Senate select committee headed by Senator Frank Church revealed that these organizations, during the Cold War, regularly prevailed upon American missioners to gather intelligence for the United States. Father Joe had become aware of this practice during his years in Bolivia and Peru. In addition to criticizing the government, he faulted the missioners who aided American intelligence agents. He condemned this practice as a betrayal of the people the missioners were supposed to be serving, and he decried cooperating American clergy for their naiveté. In fairness to the missionaries, it is important to remember these actions took place at the height of the Cold War, in which anticommunism was the greatest virtue advocated by church and state. Father Joe clearly saw the inadequacies of this position.

---

29. Marie Dennis, in an interview with the author, December 19, 2019.
30. Dolores Leckey, in an interview with the author, January 14, 2020.
31. Nangle, interview, April 4, 2020.

The Conference of Bishops

Father Joe left the US Catholic Mission Association in 1977 and went to work for the then National Conference of Catholic Bishops, where he was chief of staff in the Department of Social Development and World Peace. He was hired by Father Bryan Hehir, an expert on foreign relations and a priest of the Boston archdiocese. In an interview years later, Father Hehir related that he had hired Father Joe because of his "deep experience in Latin America" and because of his "interest in the public life of the Church." Another asset Father Hehir valued was Father Joe's connection with a "whole network of contacts throughout the religious community, particularly with people who were interested in international affairs and US foreign policy."[32]

Much of Father Joe's work for the Conference was administrative in nature. Because Father Hehir had teaching duties at Harvard University and speaking obligations that frequently took him out of town, he depended on Father Joe "to see that things kept flowing from me to my colleagues. . . . He would help to organize the workflow from me to them and them to me."[33] Father Joe recalled, "My duties were trying to keep abreast of every area of the staff's work, which basically covered worldwide geographical and issue areas, and was a Catholic voice in the U.S. national policy area."[34] Gradually, he began working on substantive foreign policy issues as well.

During the 1960s and 1970s, American missionaries serving overseas "became more involved in terms of the impact of US policies on the countries where they were," Father Hehir recalled. "The missionaries used to write to the Bishops' Conference asking us to testify before the Congress to try and influence US policy."[35] Because of his experience in Latin America, Father Joe was able to bring a third-world perspective to international issues.

One issue he researched for the Conference was the campaign against the promotion of baby formula in third-world nations. The Swiss-based Nestlé corporation, best known as a maker of chocolate products, was the target of an international boycott to halt its promotion of infant formula instead of breastfeeding among mothers in less developed nations. Boycott organizers asked the Conference to join other US religious bodies in endorsing their efforts. They argued that using the formula presented a health risk for infants because the mothers often were unable to read product warning labels, could not afford to purchase enough formula, and frequently mixed formula powder with contaminated water, causing diarrhea in their infants. Once mothers

---

32. Bryan Hehir, in an interview with the author, April 25, 2020.
33. Hehir, interview.
34. Joseph Nangle, personal communication to the author, January 7, 2020.
35. Hehir, interview.

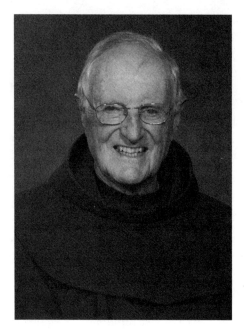

Father Joe Nangle, 2017. Photo courtesy Holy Name Franciscan Province.

stopped breastfeeding their milk stopped flowing, so they had no alternative but to continue using the formula. This problem was something Father Joe had encountered during his time in Peru: "As a pastor in Lima, I saw this happening to the poor women." For people living in slum areas, "the water [quality] was terrible. They couldn't sterilize anything." As a result, "we were getting these little children in our parish clinic. They were dehydrated; they were dying."[36] Father Joe prepared information about this issue to support the Nestlé boycott and presented it to the bishops. He was bitterly disappointed when they declined to take any action.

A second issue Father Joe studied for the Conference was the impact of US arms sales to developing nations. Staff people at the Conference had prepared a letter, to be circulated with the bishops' approval, discussing the moral implications of overseas arms sales. Chief among these was diverting government funds in third-world nations from badly needed social welfare measures. This was another problem where Father Joe's firsthand experience was applicable. While he was pastor in Lima, the Peruvian armed forces purchased twelve French Mirage jet fighter planes at a total cost of $144 million. "Peru had no need for supersonic jet fighters," he exclaimed years later. "I

---

36. Joseph Nangle, in an interview with the author, May 8, 2020.

thought, How many hospitals could they build? How many nurses and doctors could they train? How many children could be saved if the money had gone where it should go?"[37] Once again, however, the bishops took no action on this question.

In 1978, Father Joe represented the US bishops on a trip to Nicaragua to ascertain the views of that country's bishops regarding the Sandinista revolutionary movement, then gathering strength. The rebels were attempting to overthrow the corrupt military dictatorship headed by General Anastasio Somoza. On Father Joe's return to the United States, he reported that the Nicaraguan bishops estimated fifty thousand lives would be saved if the US government ceased its military assistance to the Somoza regime. The Conference forwarded this information to the White House; but sadly, the Carter administration did not act on this advice, and thousands of people died in the ensuing revolution.[38] This was the first of Father Joe's frequent trips to Latin America as a representative of the US Catholic Church.

Encountering the Homeless in Boston

In 1980, Father Joe left his post with the Conference and moved to Boston to care for his elderly mother. He lived with a group of Franciscans in East Boston and worked at St. Anthony's Shrine on Arch Street, in the heart of the business district. There he became aware of the growing population of homeless people who congregated near the shrine. Early each morning, the shelters where the homeless spent the nights discharged them "back on the street until five o'clock, when the men and women could go back to the shelters." Father Joe saw that these individuals would benefit from a noontime meal, so he created a breadline at the shrine. "We made the sandwiches inside the church, then we would take them out on the street, even in the wintertime," he said. "We'd have coffee for them—nice hot coffee—and sandwiches, as many as they wanted." Although Father Joe had seen widespread poverty in Bolivia and Peru, his interactions with homeless people on the streets of Boston opened his eyes to the impact of poverty in the affluent United States. He concluded that being poor in the United States was "in many ways worse than poverty in the Third World, because poor people in the US are right next to, immersed in our affluent world. . . . When they saw these well-to-do people, I often thought they probably felt put down and hurt by them."[39]

While living in Boston, Father Joe also conducted a series of social justice-themed retreats for diocesan priests. Father Alan McCoy, OFM, former

37. Nangle, interview, May 8, 2020.
38. Nangle, interview, April 4, 2020.
39. Joseph Nangle, in an interview with the author, April 9, 2020.

provincial minister of the St. Barbara Franciscan Province, had originally agreed to preach these retreats "with the specific objective of getting the priests onto social justice, the spirituality of social justice."[40] However, Father McCoy was unexpectedly elected to a second term as president of the Conference of Major Superiors of Men (CMSM), the organization representing congregations of Catholic priests and brothers. He needed to find a replacement and persuaded Father Joe to substitute for him. Twice a month for two years, Father Joe preached retreats in dioceses across the United States. (For more about Father McCoy's social justice work, see chapter five.)

Social Justice Work for CMSM

Father McCoy was a leading advocate of increased clerical involvement in social justice issues. As provincial of the St. Barbara Franciscan Province, he facilitated the involvement of California friars with Cesar Chavez and the farm workers movement.[41] Father Joe regarded Father McCoy as "a towering example of Franciscan involvement in areas of justice, peace, and integrity of creation. I counted him among my principal mentors."[42] At CMSM's 1979 assembly, Father McCoy proposed creating a justice and peace office within CMSM. When delegates voted his proposal down, Father McCoy did not become discouraged; he simply said, "We'll go ahead and do it anyway. We'll have a special assistant to the president for justice and peace." When this position became vacant in 1982, Father McCoy offered the job on a part-time basis to Father Joe, who eagerly accepted. He remained in Boston and made trips "every couple of weeks" to Washington, where the CMSM office was located. When his mother died in 1984, Father Joe relocated to Washington to work full-time for CMSM. "I always thought this was one of the best jobs anyone could have," he remarked in a 1993 interview. CMSM "had the capacity to be extremely prophetic in the church and society in the U.S. . . . . The Bishops really sat on a lot of things. I felt the CMSM and LCWR [Leadership Conference of Women Religious] would have much more freedom in this area."[43]

One of Father Joe's first assignments as CMSM's special assistant for peace and justice was to revisit the question of US arms sales to developing nations. US Representative Ronald Dellums, a member of the House Armed Services Committee investigating this topic, invited Father McCoy to testify. The press of other duties limited his time to prepare for the hearing, so he turned to Father Joe to ghostwrite his testimony. When Father McCoy

40. Nangle, interview, October 31, 2019.

41. Joseph Nangle, personal communication to the author, December 21, 2019.

42. Joseph Nangle, interview, 19 July 1993, Conference of Major Superiors of Men Records (hereafter CMSM Records), AMSM 234501, University of Notre Dame Archives.

43. Nangle, interview, CMSM Records.

addressed committee members on April 1, 1982, he opened with an anecdote about the impact of arms sales on an impoverished third-world nation—an anecdote related to him by an unnamed American missionary in Peru, who happened to be Father Joe. Father McCoy declared that American "sales of military equipment means the exacerbation of dangerous social injustices, whereby monies better spent for people's needs are diverted to weaponry." He went on to cite the millions of dollars of American military assistance provided to El Salvador as a major cause of the escalation of an internal conflict rather than "bring[ing] the warring factions to the negotiating table." He concluded with an appeal to the US government to limit arms sales and "dedicate ourselves to eradicating the real causes of war—oppression and poverty at home and around the world."[44] Father McCoy voiced this plea, but his words came directly from Father Joe. In a 1993 interview, Father McCoy praised the testimony prepared by Father Joe: "He did a magnificent job. I was a little embarrassed. It wasn't mine, it was his."[45]

During the 1970s, much of Central America, especially Nicaragua, El Salvador and Guatemala, was torn apart by armed struggles between insurgent revolutionary movements and authoritarian governments. Reflecting the influence of liberation theology and its "preferential option for the poor," the Catholic Church played an important role in these conflicts. This was especially true in El Salvador, where religious leaders actively challenged the status quo, "denouncing injustice and defending human rights." St. Oscar Romero, who became archbishop of San Salvador in 1977, was "a leading voice for the protection of human rights and for the transformation of the nation."[46] His 1980 assassination came as a direct result of his outspoken criticism of the ruling political regime.

Dealing with the consequences of these conflicts was a major focus of Father Joe's work at CMSM. "There was a great demand for action [on Central America] from the Conference, almost from my first month on the job," he asserted in a 1993 interview. He saw this assignment as a "natural fit" with his prior experience, he said, "because I had come out of Latin America and spoke Spanish and was very interested in that area."[47] Continuing his role as a liaison with the Catholic Church in Central America, Father Joe made sev-

---

44. "Testimony of Alan McCoy, OFM, for the Conference of Major Superiors of Men, USA, before the Armed Services Committee of the House of Representatives on United States Arms Sales and Arms Transfers," 1 April 1982, CMSM Records (CMSM) 1/25, University of Notre Dame Archives.

45. Alan McCoy, interview, 28 February 1993, CMSM Records, AMSM 23451, University of Notre Dame Archives.

46. Michael E. Lee, *Revolutionary Saint: The Theological Legacy of Oscar Romero* (Maryknoll, NY: Orbis Books, 2018), 86–87.

47. Nangle, interview, CMSM Records.

eral fact-finding trips on behalf of CMSM to nations in turmoil. In 1984, Father Joe traveled to Nicaragua with Father Philip Land, SJ, when rumors circulating in Washington suggested that the Reagan administration was planning to send US troops to overthrow the recently installed revolutionary Sandinista government. The priests spent ten days as part of an ecumenical group that went "to see what was going to happen," and then they returned and presented their findings in Washington. "I saw a military base near the Nicaraguan border that was loading up with American troops to go there," Father Joe reported.[48] The US bishops were meeting in Washington when the priests returned. Fathers Joe and Land briefed the bishops on the situation in Nicaragua and then joined with several bishops in a vigil outside the White House to protest possible US intervention. The outcry by American anti-war groups may have forced the Reagan administration to cancel the planned invasion. "Was that a victory?" Father Joe asked. "I don't know. He [Reagan] never did send the troops there."[49]

In 1987, Father Joe flew to Honduras to escort a group of peasants who had fled from El Salvador and were returning to their homeland after ten years in exile. He and other international observers acted as witnesses, in hopes that their presence would protect the refugees from reprisals. "There were five thousand of them," Father Joe recounted in an interview. "I was one among many whom they asked to go down and accompany them on their trip back to El Salvador from Honduras. It could have been very dangerous, but they got back safely." Asked to recall his peak experience of his years at CMSM, he cited this journey: "To watch those people go back home—children who had never ridden on a bus before, had never seen El Salvador, and the older people pointing out the mountains in the distance. They would point. 'That's your home. You're going home.' The wonderful excitement of those people."[50]

On a third trip, he accompanied another group of exiles going back to El Salvador. These, he said, were "men who had been very prominent in politics in El Salvador . . . [before] the army took over and there was a repression of anyone who associated with the left." Father Joe went as a representative of the US Catholic Church. He made a fourth trip with self-exiled Guatemalan political dissidents, who were going "to test the waters to see if they might come back [to Guatemala] and continue their work in their own country."[51]

---

48. Nangle, interview, October 31, 2019. US armed forces did not invade Nicaragua, but the Reagan administration provided arms and training for the counterrevolutionary "Contras" who waged war against the leftist Sandinista government. See Theofilo Cabestrero, *Blood of the Innocent: Victims of the Contras' War in Nicaragua* (Maryknoll, NY: Orbis Books, 1985).

49. Nangle, interview, October 31, 2019.

50. Nangle, interview, October 31, 2019.

51. Nangle, interview, April 4, 2020.

Included among this group was indigenous human rights activist Rigoberta Menchu, who later became a Nobel Peace laureate.

A related issue that absorbed Father Joe's attention while at CMSM was support for the Sanctuary Movement. Refugees from the conflicts in Central America were fleeing to the United States seeking asylum to escape political persecution. Many crossed the border without required documentation. US religious and humanitarian organizations assisted the refugees regardless of their legal status. This network became known as the Sanctuary Movement.[52]

In 1984, Father Joe proposed that CMSM pass a resolution affirming the movement. Because sanctuary activists sheltered illegal migrants to help them avoid deportation, the activists also were in violation of US law. "Many [people] thought an establishment group like CMSM would never take a position like this," Father Joe noted in an interview. "It was quite a political exercise because some of the superiors were timid about doing anything too public and too radical." Father Joe lobbied superiors behind the scenes to muster support for the resolution. One member congregation was the Weston Priory of Benedictine monks in Vermont. The monks seldom came to CMSM assemblies because of their cloistered status. Father Joe described his efforts to gain their endorsement: "I went up to Vermont and sat down with the monks. I told them what we were trying to do. I said, 'If you would come to the assembly and publicize that you are in favor of this resolution, we could get it passed, because you have a lot of influence as cloistered monks.' They agreed and they did [pass the resolution]."[53] Father Joe was "enormously pleased" with the vote. He saw it as "a stunning kind of breakthrough. . . . People really took notice. [Here was] a group in the church that was taking positions no one else was taking."[54]

Although public statements by CMSM were important, Father Joe stressed that the work done at the regional meetings of the justice and peace office was more critical. It was at this level that the conversion process took place. At these gatherings, rank-and-file members of religious orders wrestled with the question, How do we see the Gospel applying to public issues? Father Joe insisted that CMSM's regional structure was an ideal vehicle to promote this kind of spirituality.[55]

Father Joe's opposition to US foreign policy in Central America led to his first arrest for civil disobedience on Ash Wednesday, March 4, 1987.

---

52. See Renny Golden and Michael McConnell, *Sanctuary: The New Underground Railroad* (Maryknoll, NY: Orbis Books, 1986).

53. Nangle, interview, April 4, 2020.

54. Nangle, interview, CMSM Records. Although Nangle's assessment might be correct for a national body, local church groups had previously come out in support of sanctuary.

55. Nangle, interview, CMSM Records.

Lenten Witness for Peace and Justice in Central America, a coalition of nine-teen Protestant and Catholic groups, sponsored a demonstration in Washing-ton, DC. Two hundred demonstrators denounced the Reagan administra-tion's support for the Contras, the counterrevolutionary force seeking to overthrow the Nicaraguan government. "They violate fundamental rights to self-determination, liberty and justice," the group declared in a prepared state-ment.[56] Father Joe was one of five religious leaders jailed for taking part in this protest. "It was a very, very good arrest at the steps of the Capitol on Ash Wednesday," Father Joe reminisced in an interview. "The symbolism was ter-rific. We stood there or sat there in ashes and sackcloth." When asked to justify his civil disobedience, he answered, "It is a further demand and statement of the importance of these issues that you were willing to break the law to say, 'Look at this problem, for God's sake.'"[57]

Seven weeks later, on April 27, Father Joe was arrested a second time. On this occasion, he was one of 557 protestors detained at the conclusion of a three-day protest against the policies of the Reagan administration outside the CIA headquarters in Virginia. Others jailed at the same time included anti-war activists Daniel Ellsberg and Father Philip Berrigan. A reporter from the *New York Times* quoted Father Joe's observation: "It's kind of a 60's crowd. That's not bad. They stopped the Vietnam War that way."[58] Asked how his brother Franciscans reacted to news of his arrests, he replied, "I heard nothing either pro or con. They were silent."[59]

The Assisi Community

During his tenure at CMSM, Father Joe collaborated with three other Catholic activists to create the simple living arrangement he had desired since his return to the United States. In 1986, he and three close friends founded the Assisi Community: Marie Dennis, Sister Rita Studer, SSND, and Jim McIntosh. Dennis was a single mother and peace activist who later became copresident of Pax Christi International. Sister Rita Studer was a former mis-sionary to Guatemala, and McIntosh ran a shelter for homeless men and later became a Franciscan friar.

-----

56. Lenten Witness for Peace and Justice in Central America, quoted in Marjorie Hyer, "U.S. Policy on Contras Protested," *Washington Post*, March 5, 1987, https://www. washingtonpost.com/archive/local/1987/03/05/us-policy-on-contras-protested/ 80c47c1a-6d99–48da-97c3-f72737480ec8/.

57. Nangle, interview, October 31, 2019.

58. Joseph Nangle, quoted in Bernard Weinraub, "Hundreds Arrested at C.I.A. in Protest on Foreign Policy," *New York Times*, April 28, 1987, https://www.nytimes.com/ 1987/04/28/us/hundreds-arrested-at-cia-in-protest-on-foreign-policy.html.

59. Nangle, interview, December 4, 2020.

During the previous year, the four had participated in a group that met twice a month to discuss their experiences with community living. Members shared their views on what had worked and what had failed. The four founders decided to establish an intentional community: "people living together, sharing their lives with one another and supporting each other in their various works." Father Joe received permission from his provincial superior to live in this non-traditional arrangement. The group rented a row house in what was then a run-down Black neighborhood in Washington, DC, and established a routine they have continued for more than thirty-five years. Residents pursue outside careers during the day. They maintain separate purses, but they contribute to a household fund that covers common expenses such as food, rent, and utilities. Each morning, they gather for prayer, and in the evening, they share a common meal. They also cooperate with meal preparation and household chores. Every Monday evening, members meet to discuss world events, issues in their lives, and routine housekeeping concerns. They make all decisions by consensus.[60]

A homeless family from El Salvador became the first guests in the house. Over the years, community members have come and gone. Four of Dennis's children moved in. "We've probably had eighty to ninety members, mostly Catholics and most of them lay people," Father Joe reported.[61] When they needed more space, they purchased a second home nearby. Occasionally, members join public protests together. One such occasion was a twenty-four-hour vigil outside the White House in the spring of 1996. Community members supported Dianna Ortiz, an Ursuline sister who had been kidnapped and tortured by government security forces while a missionary in Guatemala.

Writing in 1999, Father Joe described his life in the Assisi Community as "fun . . . real, varied, faith-filled, changeable, and always challenging." Members chose a location in a largely African American, inner-city neighborhood "to share the city's uncertainties, fears, and noise, as well as the neighborliness, occasional heroism, and respect that most people exhibit here."[62] The Assisi Community continues as a viable intentional living arrangement.

Working with the Sojourners Community

When Father Joe's term with CMSM ended in 1990, Jim Wallis, founder of the Sojourners community, hired him to be the organization's outreach

---

60. Jim McIntosh, "Assisi Community Celebrates 25 Years," Franciscan Friars: Holy Name Province, December 17, 2011, https://hnp.org/assisi-community-celebrates-25-years/.

61. Breaking in the Habit, "A Friar Life: Father Joe Nangle," YouTube video, 12:47, https://www.youtube.com/watch?v=T2C8GTlzZ3A.

62. Joseph Nangle, "The Daily Grace of Give and Take," *Sojourners* 28, no. 2 (March 1999): 40.

director. Sojourners is a social justice organization established in 1971 by a group of progressive evangelical Protestants now based in Washington, DC. Best known for publishing *Sojourners* magazine, this ecumenical organization also "formed a worshipping community, got involved in neighborhood issues, organized national events on behalf of peace and justice."[63] Father Joe's first major assignment for Sojourners was planning a Capitol Hill press conference for religious leaders who opposed the first Iraq War. He acted as master of ceremonies for the event, calling on the various speakers to state their reasons for opposing the US invasion of Iraq.[64]

Much of his job involved traveling with Wallis and arranging his speaking engagements. Another task was assisting with Let Justice Roll, a kind of touring progressive revival meeting featuring music and preaching focused on social justice issues. Over time, his responsibilities expanded into a senior advisory position.

Father Joe began writing for *Sojourners* magazine in 1991. His first article was a review of Catholic social teachings. Another writer originally had this assignment, but the submission was unsatisfactory. Father Joe read the draft and told the editor, "We shouldn't publish it. It's not accurate; it's not good. I'll do it. I'll write the thing."[65] After that, he became a regular contributor to the magazine, writing on Latin America and a wide range of other topics. In his second article, he denounced the US invasion of Iraq in Operation Desert Storm. "We continue to believe," he wrote, "that Desert Storm, by its own inherent evil, has become Desert Shame. George Bush's war had no chance to accomplish anything good. The end never justifies the means."[66]

The *Sojourners* article of which he is proudest is a cover story profiling Father Pedro Arrupe, SJ, the recently deceased superior general of the Society of Jesus (Jesuits). Initially, Father Joe resisted when Wallis tried to give him the assignment. "I'm a Franciscan," he protested. "You should get a Jesuit to do it."[67] However, after consulting with Jesuit colleagues, he went ahead with the project. Father Joe found much to admire in Father Arrupe's career. The Jesuit leader began as a missionary to Japan. On August 6, 1945, he was in Hiroshima, not far from the blast site when the first atomic bomb exploded. Father Joe pointed out that Father Arrupe's experiences caring for the bomb's victims convinced him "that the pursuit of justice was central to the life of Jesus" and "that justice meant structural change in every aspect of human

63. Sojourners, "Our History," https://sojo.net/about/about-sojourners.

64. Nangle, interview, April 4, 2020.

65. Nangle, interview, April 4, 2020. See "New Grace in the Church," *Sojourners* 20, no. 4 (March 1991): 6–7.

66. Joseph Nangle, "An American Disgrace," *Sojourners* 20, no. 5 (June 1991),: https://sojo.net/magazine/june-1991/american-disgrace.

67. Nangle, interview, April 4, 2020.

life." Father Arrupe went on to institute a series of reforms in the Jesuit order based on "a commitment to promote justice and to enter into solidarity with the voiceless and the powerless."[68]

While praising the good work of the Jesuits and other Catholic clerics, Father Joe never hesitated to criticize the Church when he disagreed with its policies. In 1994, he penned an angry article titled "Pastoring Those Excluded by the Pope." The document that provoked this response was the encyclical *Ordinatio Sacerdotalis*, by Pope St. John Paul II, which concluded that the Church has no authority to ordain women. Father Joe expressed his profound disagreement with this position. "Never have I written on a more difficult subject," he began. Then he asked, "How are we ever to get on as a church when more than half of our body is cut off from consideration of their fitness for priestly ministry? Are we facing a schism in the American Catholic Church, wherein sincere and devout women claim a call to ordination? Where is the Holy Spirit in this? What will be the price our church will have to pay in losing the enormous and unique gifts that women bring to the ministry?"[69]

During his four years on the Sojourners' staff, Father Joe filled another role not included in his formal job description. "As an organization we never had a position of pastor," said Jim Rice, then editor of *Sojourners* magazine, "but Joe was our pastor during those years. He provided an important pastoral presence to an organization where you need that kind of presence." Father Joe baptized both of Rice's children and counseled him through a difficult personal crisis. He also presided at the wedding of writer Danny Collum and his wife. In an interview, Rice identified the personal quality that made Father Joe effective in the pastoral role: "It is his ability to listen. He always made me feel like I was a special person. He was very present to me. Someone I looked up to. Kind of a mentor. I just felt it was a tangible expression of love for the people around him."[70]

After leaving Sojourners in 1994, Father Joe continued writing a column for the magazine titled "Life in Community." In it he explored "the different dimensions of community life—lay communities, religious communities, virtual communities"; the column appeared monthly for five more years. One of his last columns described the funeral of Father James Healy, CSSp, who died from AIDS (by his own admission, due to "poor choices" he had made). "I talked about the many communities this priest had been part of," Father Joe recounted in an interview. "He had been an amazing guy. . . . The funeral

68. Joseph Nangle, "Pedro Arrupe," *Sojourners* 20, no. 10 (December 1991), https://sojo.net/magazine/december-1991/pedro-arrupe.

69. Joseph Nangle, "Pastoring Those Excluded by the Pope," *Sojourners* 23, no. 7 (August 1994): 35.

70. Jim Rice, in an interview with the author, March 5, 2020.

was amazing. There were all of these people whose lives he had touched. It was a three-hour funeral because everybody wanted to talk about him. The bottom line I wrote was, 'Who's going to throw the first stone? His many sins are forgiven because he had loved much.'"[71]

Franciscan Mission Service

Father Joe spent the next twelve years as director of the Franciscan Mission Service (FMS), an organization founded in 1985 by Father Anselm Moons, OFM, a Dutch Franciscan, and Father Finian Kerwin, OFM, a former Holy Name provincial. They created FMS to educate the American public about the missionary world. "They began by doing conferences and retreats and writing," Father Joe related in an interview. However, he explained, "after a few years, [Father Moons] thought the best way to concientize the Catholic population of the US is to send people to these places as missionaries. That was the beginning of the overseas dimension of the FMS." "The people went overseas for three years in those days," he continued. "We supported them. We trained them. We brought them back when they were finished. We said, 'Now you're back home, your final dimension of this service is FMS service to the US. Bring back your experiences to the Catholic population, but also to the country.'"[72] After developing a cardiac condition, Father Moons left the United States to return to his native Holland in 1993. Father Joe heard that FMS was experiencing difficulties and, in 1994, was hired as its executive director.

Father Joe discovered serious financial problems at FMS. "We were always behind financially," he recalled: "There was a time around 1996. We had about five hundred dollars in the bank and twenty people overseas. I realized we could not bring them home if something collapsed." Father Joe consulted a financial planner and put together a plan to restore FMS to solvency. "We got into the Propagation of the Faith [lecture] circuit," he recounted. During these engagements, he would "tell the stories of these lay missioners. They were sending back interesting stories. On weekends, I would travel to parishes all over the East. I was young then. I'd just turned sixty around that time. I still had a lot of energy."[73]

Another problem at FMS was its lack of an established base of operations: "We were sort of like vagabonds. We didn't have a base. We were renting. . . . I thought, We've got to get some kind of a house, a center." Father Joe heard of a large house being vacated by the Glenmary Home Missionaries. "It was

---

71. Nangle, interview, April 4, 2020. See Joseph Nangle, "His Life Dilemma," *Sojourners* 26, no. 2 (March/April, 1997): 38.

72. Nangle, interview, April 4, 2020.

73. Nangle, interview, April 4, 2020.

a great house, [with] something like twenty bedrooms," he recalled. The Glenmarys were willing to sell the property for $300,000, but they "wanted cash, a clean sale, no outstanding debt." Father Joe approached a group of Croatian Franciscans for whom he had once given a retreat. "They were going out of business, but they had money. So I called them up." He secured a donation of $150,000. The other half of the purchase price came in the form of smaller loans from several US Franciscan provinces. "We paid that back in five years," he proudly declared.[74]

FMS honored Father Joe for his twelve years of service by naming him the recipient of the organization's 2006 Anselm Moons Award. The press release announcing this honor read, "He integrated Catholic social teaching, a radical Franciscan Commitment to the Gospel, a preferential concern for the poor and a sense of humor into the formation of more than 80 lay women and men who answered the call to the international mission."[75]

Father Joe continued his writing career during his time with FMS. In 2004, Orbis Books published his *Birth of a Church*, an account of his eleven years as pastor of Santísimo Nombre parish in Lima. He traced the origin of the book to a 1976 conversation with Philip Scharper, a cofounder of Orbis Books. "You have a book inside you," Scharper told him. When Father Joe delivered his first manuscript, Scharper informed him the book was not yet ready. "Joe, it's too green. It's too much Latin America. It's not going to be understood by an American audience," he advised. "Put it in the bottom drawer and let it go for a few years and then listen to what people are saying about your stories and then pick it up again."[76] Some years later, Father Joe submitted a revised manuscript, which was accepted.

Not long after *Birth of a Church* appeared, a friend suggested, "Well you've written about the outward journey. Why don't you write about your inward journey?" That led to Father Joe's second book, *Engaged Spirituality: Faith Life in the Heart of the Empire*, published in 2008.[77] In his preface, he wrote that this work was largely a reaction to the "individualistic, highly psychologized . . . approach to spiritual matters" that he found in American culture.[78] His intent, he said, was to replace this "me-centered" spirituality with

---

74. Nangle, interview, April 4, 2020.

75. "Joseph Nangle Recognized for Mission Service Commitment," Franciscan Friars: Holy Name Province, October 25, 2006, https://hnp.org/joseph-nangle-recognized-for-mission-service-commitment/.

76. Nangle, interview, October 31, 2019.

77. Nangle, interview, October 31, 2019.

78. Joseph Nangle, *Engaged Spirituality: Faith Life in the Heart of the Empire* (Maryknoll, NY: Orbis Books, 2008), xv.

one that is "other oriented." *Engaged Spirituality* reflects his belief that spirituality "is mostly about the other—the Other who is God and the other who is sister and brother."[79] Father Joe placed blame for this "me-centered" spirituality on an incomplete reading of the Scriptures. Too many preachers and teachers, he claimed, ignore the "social, structural, and political realities" of life in the First World."[80] To correct this, Father Joe advocated "a political reading" of the Scriptures. This means discerning "the way biblical texts focus on, illuminate, and question the structures of societies and their impact on the lives of human beings."[81]

Later in *Engaged Spirituality*, Father Joe introduced the concepts of "social sin" and "social grace." He defined social sin as "all those things in a society or culture that cut off human beings from a full life—things like malnutrition, illiteracy, unemployment, racism, classism, sexism, and so on."[82] Social grace is the obverse of social sin as seen in "those organizations and communities, structures and mechanisms which promote the humanization of those vulnerable and suffering."[83] According to Professor Thomas M. Kelly, the crux of Father Joe's argument is "that there is no such thing as spirituality apart from the interpersonal, the social and the political."[84]

Our Lady Queen of Peace

Beginning in 1990, Father Joe has celebrated weekend Masses and administered the sacraments at Our Lady Queen of Peace parish in Arlington, Virginia. This parish has an unusual history reaching back to 1945. According to Father Joe, "fourteen [Catholic] African American families found they were not welcome in the white churches in that area. They had to sit in the back and go to Communion last. . . . They asked Bishop Peter Ireton of Richmond, Virginia, for their own parish." The bishop agreed, but said, "You'll have to do it on your own." The families collected enough money to purchase a piece of property and began building a church, the same structure they still use. "They brought in a group of missionary priests, the Holy Spirit Fathers, as their pastors." Over time, White Catholics started attending Mass at Our Lady Queen of Peace. "The White people began to realize" that African Americans "have a style that's quite wonderful," Father Joe remarked. Then, during the 1980s, Hispanic Catholics began showing up. By 1990, Father Joe recounted,

79. Nangle, *Engaged Spirituality*, xvi.
80. Nangle, *Engaged Spirituality*, 19.
81. Nangle, *Engaged Spirituality*, 21.
82. Nangle, *Engaged Spirituality*, 56.
83. Thomas M. Kelly, "Review of *Engaged Spirituality*," *Spiritus* 9, no. 1 (Spring 2009): 102.
84. Kelly, "Review of *Engaged Spirituality*," 103.

"they needed a Spanish-speaking priest. The pastor, Father Jim Healy, called me and asked if I would help out for a couple of weeks while they got someone permanently": "That was 30 years ago, and here I am 30 years later. . . . I had a sense of what they [the immigrants] were coming from and I had a sense of what they were going through here in the States."[85] Since leaving FMS, Father Joe has continued working at Our Lady Queen of Peace as pastoral associate.

According to Father Joe, Our Lady Queen of Peace parish can serve as a model for other Catholic parishes in the United States: "The community is just amazing, the dynamic between the people themselves and us who are their pastors. It's just a great place. I'm thrilled to be there." He believes its emphasis on social justice is something other parishes should emulate. Supporting this claim, Father Joe points out, is "the scripture [verse], Matthew 25, 'I was hungry and you gave me to eat,' . . . the theme or the slogan the parish always cites as its visionary statement."[86] Members of Our Lady Queen of Peace parish are diverse, both ethnically and economically. "You can be sitting next to a woman who cleans your house," said parishioner Dolores Leckey in an interview. "Who you are in your work life doesn't really matter. We have had ambassadors there who have heard about it and then the people who do day labor."[87]

Addressing Clergy Sexual Abuse

Father Joe has never hesitated to speak from the pulpit on controversial issues within the Catholic Church. Myrtle Hendricks Corrales, a retired educator who first met Father Joe in 1975, praised his advocacy for victims of clergy sexual abuse: "He was the first priest in this diocese who had a Mass to ask forgiveness and healing of people who had been abused by the clergy. . . . [He spoke out] recognizing the awfulness of what had been going on with the abuse of these children by the clergy."[88] She recalls that he said, "I ask forgiveness for my brother priests who have acted in a way they shouldn't have."[89]

Father Joe revealed how his understanding of the clergy abuse scandal deepened after an encounter with members of Voice of the Faithful, an organization of lay Catholics formed in 2002, many of them victims of abuse, who advocate greater transparency and accountability in the Church:

> They had a meeting one time in a public library in McLean [Virginia]. They invited priests. The pastor [of Our Lady Queen of Peace, Father Leonard Tuozzolo, CSSp] and I went. I said, "Why are you meeting in

---

85. Nangle, interview, April 4, 2020.
86. Nangle, interview, April 4, 2020.
87. Leckey, interview.
88. Myrtle Hendricks Corrales, in an interview with the author, January 3, 2020.
89. Joseph Nangle, quoted in Corrales, interview.

a library?" They said, "We don't think we'd be welcome in a Catholic church." I said, "Well, you'd be welcome at our place," and the pastor said, "Absolutely." That led to engaging with these people who were calling for accountability from the hierarchy. We were hearing all the stories about the victims. It was a natural that we would have a Mass of healing and repentance for the sins of our clergy against needy and dependent people. . . . They said to me, "You may have some problems from the hierarchy." I said, "Let them come on. I don't care." We never heard anything from the diocese. In fact, I think the bishop after that had his own Mass of healing.[90]

The Mass of repentance was not a one-time gesture. Father Joe said he continues to ask for forgiveness for his fellow priests and bishops whenever he says Mass: "Every time in the Mass at the *lavabo* (washing of the hands), usually during the Mass the priest goes somewhere and does something nobody really sees with a bowl of water. I bring it up onto the altar right after the offering of the gifts. With the microphone on, I ask forgiveness for my sins and for the sins of my fellow priests and our bishops for violating the trust which vulnerable children and adults have in us."[91]

In 2010, he wrote about the clergy sex abuse scandal in *Sojourners*: "People have been hurt, damaged, and disillusioned and I believe that only serious corrective measures, together with public repentance—especially by Catholic ministers—over a long period of time, will excise this malignancy. . . . I fear that as yet many among us, including and perhaps especially our leadership, fail to comprehend how bad this situation has become."[92]

Prophetic and Pastoral

On February 6, 2008, in Washington, Father Joe was among a group of thirty Catholic protestors who marched from St. Matthew's Cathedral to smear ashes on sidewalks in front of the White House. They called it a symbol of repentance for US involvement in the Gulf War and the torture of Guantanamo detainees. "Our only hope is that you are a forgiving God and this sign of repentance will stay your hand over an evil empire," Father Joe pronounced as he participated in the ashes ceremony.[93]

90. Nangle, interview, April 4, 2020.
91. Nangle, interview, April 4, 2020.
92. Joseph Nangle, "Why I Remain a Priest," *Sojourners*, July 2010, 10, https://sojo.net/articles/why-i-remain-catholic-priest-despite-scandal.
93. Joseph Nangle, quoted in Erin Kutz, "Washington Catholic Groups Observe Ash Wednesday with White House Protest," Boston University Washington News Service, February 6, 2008, https://www.bu.edu/washington/2008/02/06/washington-catholic-groups-observe-ash-wednesday-with-white-house-protest/.

Father Joe does not limit his criticism to one political party. He has called out Democrats as well as Republicans. At the time of Barack Obama's 2009 inauguration, Father Joe questioned whether the new president would continue the imperialistic policies of past administrations: "I cannot help but wonder if your campaign promises of change . . . will extend to the contradiction between our stated democratic system and this overlay of global overreach."[94] In 2013, Father Joe was among a group of religious leaders who questioned the morality of President Obama's use of remote-controlled drones in the "war against terror." Father Joe spoke in a short video deploring casualties inflicted by these weapons: "How can we hold our heads high when remote controlled killer aircraft like drones are raining death and destruction on populations half a world away from our borders, on women, men and children who pose no threat to our safety and well-being?"[95]

Another of Father Joe's distinctive traits is his consistent preference for a simple lifestyle. His longtime friend, Myrtle Corrales, was with Father Joe one day in the church sacristy as he changed out of his vestments. In an interview, she recalled that she saw that "his undershirt probably had twenty holes in it. . . . I said, 'Joe, do you think that shirt might be ready to fall apart?' He said, 'It keeps me warm, serves its purpose.' End of conversation." On another occasion, Father Joe's friends wanted to give him a guitar for a birthday gift to replace one that had been lost or misplaced. "It can't be new," someone aware of his desire to live frugally said, according to Corrales. "He'll take it, but it can't be a new guitar. It's got to be used and it can't be real nice."[96]

Father Joe has a wide circle of friends. Among them is Representative Jim McGovern of Massachusetts, one of the most liberal members of Congress, a critic of the war in Iraq, and an outspoken opponent of human rights abuses in Myanmar, Darfur (in Sudan), and elsewhere. They met because of their shared interest in Latin America and became fast friends—"two Boston Irish Catholics discussing politics and moral values over glasses of beer," Corrales said in another interview.[97] McGovern was the keynote speaker at the party celebrating Father Joe's eighty-fifth birthday in 2017. The occasion was a fundraiser for Pax Christi International. About 160 people attended; the evening raised $40,000.[98]

94. "Joseph Nangle on Ending U.S. Imperialism," *Tikkun* 24, no. 1 (January 2009), https://read.dukeupress.edu/tikkun/article-abstract/24/1/73/99858/Joseph-Nangle-on-Ending-U-s-Imperialism.
95. Joseph Nangle, quoted in Robert Greenwald, "This Easter, Religious Leaders Join Forces to Denounce U.S. Drone Policy," *Huffington Post*, March 27, 2013, https://www.huffingtonpost.com/robert-greenwald/this-easter-religious-lea_b_2964895.html.
96. Corrales, interview.
97. Myrtle Hendricks Corrales, in an interview with the author, January 4, 2020.
98. Jocelyn Thomas, "Joe Nangle Honored at Pax Christi Event," *Friar News*, December 6, 2017, https://hnp.org/joe-nangle-honored-pax-christi-event/.

Commitment to the Franciscan fraternity is also central to Father Joe's life. Marie Dennis, his close friend and associate of forty-five years, observed, "He's lived the vows he made to the Franciscan order with absolute integrity." Thus, he was greatly distressed to be alienated from his fellow friars for several years. "After he came back from Latin America, he was pretty much on the edges of Holy Name Province, [he was] kind of tagged as a radical," Dennis reported in an interview. "A lot of people did not understand his experience, what it was like living where he did and engaging with the extraordinary insights of liberation theology."[99] Father Joe acknowledged that he felt estranged from other members of the Holy Name Province for many years: "When I began to get a sense of liberation theology and began to talk about it, particularly when I came back to the States, there was a long time, maybe thirty-five or forty years, I felt like I was in the shadows. I was listened to, but very unpopular. . . . I know I was kind of a thorn in everybody's side. I felt to be on the fringe of province life."[100]

He identified a specific a turning point that occurred in about 2010:

> I gave a homily at our [Franciscan] house of studies. I talked about Mike [Father Mychal] Judge, who died on 9/11. There was a book written about him around that time. The inference in the book was that there was something more than friendship there [in his relationship with another man]. So I talked about it. I said, "We can't judge Mike Judge. He's gone to heaven. But if this is true, if he had an improper relationship as is intimated in the book, that was wrong. That is not what we're sup-posed to be about. We have a vow of chastity." I felt it very important to make that point with these young men. After that Mass, an older friar came to me and said, "I used to hate you for all the things that you were about. I think you should be in leadership now for this province to thank you for what you just said."[101]

Since that event, Father Joe's brother friars have expressed greater appre-ciation of his contributions to the order. One sign of his reintegration with Holy Name Province was his election to two terms on the provincial council. Another indication came in May 2019, when St. Bonaventure University, his alma mater, presented him with an honorary degree.

Asked to describe Father Joe's distinctive approach to his priestly mission, friends and colleagues consistently responded with two adjectives not often paired—"prophetic" and "pastoral." In this context, they use "prophetic" to

---

99. Dennis, interview.

100. Nangle, interview, April 4, 2020.

101. Nangle, interview, April 4, 2020. Father Mychal Judge, OFM, was a chaplain with the New York Fire Department who died on September 11, 2001, while responding to the attack on the World Trade Center. He was among the first casualties.

mean characteristic of a messenger from God who denounces the rich and powerful for their sinful ways. The Old Testament prophet Amos comes to mind. Father Joe's outspoken censure of contemporary politicians whose policies favor the wealthy and who employ rhetoric that disparages immigrants echoes the forceful condemnation of corrupt rulers recorded in the book of Amos (5:12):

> I know how many are your crimes,
> how grievous your sins:
> Oppressing the just, accepting bribes,
> turning away the needy at the gate.

But Father Joe is also a pastor, a shepherd who cares for all members of his flock. While working for the US bishops, CMSM, and FMS, he also sought positions with local parishes. He has treated these weekend duties as seriously as his responsibilities to the organizations that employed him during the week. He is able to carry out these sometimes conflicting roles successfully because of his unique ability to speak forthrightly on controversial social issues without offending those who hold opposing views. Dennis, who probably knows Father Joe better than any other person, declared, "He has absolutely no concern about speaking out on any social or ecological issue from the pulpit or in a conversation. That's just a part of who he is. He's learned how to do that without alienating people, because he does not attack the individual. He always draws people to understand what justice might look like and how they can support it."[102]

Leckey, Father Joe's good friend since they worked together at the National Conference of Catholic Bishops, identified another reason for his success in relating to people with differing backgrounds and political viewpoints: "He has the ability to concentrate on the other. He sort of steps out of himself in some way or other and concentrates on you. He is happy. He strikes you as a happy person, so you want to spend some time with him. . . . He knows who he is and he's comfortable with who he is. He has a genuine humility, the kind that really deals with the truth. That is catching to people. They trust him. I trust him."[103]

In a meditation on the meaning of Advent, Father Joe wrote the following passage that sums up his approach to contemporary social problems:

How are we to celebrate the once and future promise that sustains our own existence? Is it not that we must become an "Advent presence" for these thousands of at-risk sisters and brothers? Are we not called to let

---

102. Dennis, interview.
103. Leckey, interview.

them know that there are people like us in the United States who rever-
ence each one of them as family? Is it not our duty as comfortable citizens
of this nation to act on the ancient biblical command: "You shall not
molest or oppress an alien, for you once were aliens yourselves. . . ?"
(Exodus 22:20). Are we not impelled to BE HOPE for the aliens of
today?[104]

---

104. Joe Nangle, "Faith Calls Us to Be Neighbors," Franciscan Mission Service,
https://franciscanmissionservice.org/2017/12/faith-calls-us-neighbors-advent-promise-
no-resonance/.

Chapter 8

Father Louie Vitale: Antinuclear Activist and Friend of the Homeless

Although eight hundred years separate their lives, several parallels exist between the lives of Franciscan Friar Louie Vitale, OFM, and Francesco di Bernardone, better known as St. Francis of Assisi. Both men were born to wealthy families. Francis was the privileged son of a prosperous cloth merchant in medieval Italy; Louie's father owned a successful seafood processing business in Southern California. Biographers portray young Francis as a popular figure among his affluent contemporaries in Assisi. Franciscan historian Michael Robson, OFM Conv, wrote that Francis "was intent on games and songs and [that] day and night he roamed about Assisi with his companions. He was a spendthrift, and all that he earned went into eating and carousing with his friends."[1] Young Louie liked fast cars—he drove a Jaguar for a while—frequented jazz clubs, and confessed to "developing a wild streak with partying companions."[2]

Both Francis and Louie sought to emulate military figures of their eras. Francis dreamed of becoming a famous knight like Walter of Brienne, a leader of martial exploits in southern Italy. Among Louie's youthful heroes were Generals Douglas MacArthur and George Patton, who led American troops to victory in World War II. In 1202, Francis experienced warfare when he joined forces from Assisi in a war against its rival, the neighboring city of Perugia. He saw his "companions and friends butchered in a bloody and savage battle," and he was captured and held in prison "under miserable and trying conditions" for eighteen months before being ransomed by his family.[3] Louie was a Reserve Officer's Training Corps (ROTC) cadet while a student at

---

1. Michael Robson, *St. Francis of Assisi: The Legend and the Life* (London: Geoffrey Chapman, 1997), 12.

2. Louie Vitale, *Love Is What Matters: Writings on Peace and Nonviolence* (Las Vegas, NV: Pace e Bene Press, 2015), 11.

3. Augustine Thompson, *Francis of Assisi: A New Biography* (Ithaca, NY: Cornell University Press, 2012), 10.

Loyola University in Los Angeles (now Loyola Marymount). Upon graduation, shortly after the end of the Korean War, he entered the US Air Force as
a lieutenant. Louie served during the Cold War, when the United States and
the Soviet Union were at odds, each threatening to annihilate the other with
nuclear weapons. He was an intercept officer, riding behind the pilot in the
cockpit of jet aircraft (poor eyesight prevented him from being a pilot). His
responsibilities included communications and navigation.

One Sunday morning, Louie's fighter plane was scrambled to pursue a
Soviet aircraft tracked on radar heading over the North Pole toward the
United States. As the target came within range, Louie prepared to shoot down
the enemy bomber. "I had a missile locked . . . and it was counting down to
launch," he recounted. Then, at the last moment, he saw civilian passengers
aboard the plane and realized the target was an American airliner. His pilot
dropped the nose of their jet, unlocking the missile, narrowly averting a
national tragedy.[4] For years after this incident, Louie suffered nightmares,
which he self-diagnosed as a symptom of post-traumatic stress disorder. In
much the same fashion, Francis suffered persistent aftereffects from his own
military adventures and imprisonment.

Francis's father, Pietro Bernardone, was distressed when he learned that
his son intended to give away his possessions and devote his life to serving
the poor. Thomas of Celano, author of the first biography of St. Francis,
recounted the legendary incident when Francis's father hauled his defiant son
before the bishop of Assisi. Pietro Bernardone demanded that Francis account
for the money he had taken and given to the poor. Francis responded by strip-
ping off his clothing, which he returned to his father, thereby symbolically
embracing a life of voluntary poverty.[5]

Despite his own hedonistic lifestyle, Louie felt a recurrent calling to religious life. During his junior year at Loyola, he had approached a Jesuit campus
chaplain, who advised him to finish college and complete his obligation to
the US Air Force before making a decision about the priesthood.[6] Toward
the end of his tour of duty, Louie went on retreat at the Trappist monastery
of Gethsemani in Kentucky. Once again, he thought about the priesthood,
he reported, "but I was scared to death."[7] Louie's father was not happy to
hear that his son desired to enter the Franciscan seminary: "My father thought
maybe it was because I had gotten too much oxygen in those high flying
planes. He thought I should go to Italy and find a nice seniorina [*sic*] to marry

---

4. Max McGee, "Evangelization of Peace: The Radical Life of Father Louis Vitale,"
Nations, December 4, 2019, https://nationsmedia.org/father-louis-vitale/.

5. Thomas of Celano, *Saint Francis of Assisi* (Franciscan Herald Press: Chicago,
1988), 17.

6. Vitale, *Love Is What Matters*, 12.

7. Vitale, *Love Is What Matters*, 12.

. . . settle down and forget all that crazy stuff."[8] When Louie called long-distance to tell the elder Vitale that he would not be taking part in the family business, his father was distraught. Louie remembered, "My dad got all upset and said that everything he had worked for would go away, and that I would be letting him down."[9]

Friar Louie

Louie completed his seminary training and was ordained in 1962. For a time, he taught Franciscan seminarians at San Luis Rey College. He then enrolled in graduate school at UCLA, pursuing a PhD in sociology. This was the era of great popular movements pushing for social change—civil rights, anti-war, farm workers—and Louie embraced all of them with gusto. While taking summer classes in Chicago, he shook hands with Martin Luther King Jr. "I had a great admiration for him," Father Louie recalled half a century later.[10] According to his great-nephew, Max McGee, "the impressionable young priest drew lifelong admiration from his early encounter with King."[11] During the Vietnam War, Father Louie counseled draft resisters and participated in nonviolent demonstrations to halt the fighting. He also marched with farm workers and their leader, Cesar Chavez, "in a new kind of pilgrimage through California's Central Valley to the state capitol in Sacramento," in solidarity with striking grape pickers.[12]

In 1968, having completed his doctoral studies at UCLA, Father Louie relocated to Las Vegas, Nevada.[13] Bishop Joseph Green, newly appointed as prelate of the Reno diocese, sought to implement the reforms of the Second Vatican Council. With an eye to developing programs to aid the poor, he invited the thirty-six-year-old Franciscan to study social needs in Las Vegas, the largest population center of his diocese. Father Louie resided at St. James Catholic Mission in the city's Westside neighborhood, with Father Ben Franzinelli, a diocesan priest, and a group of seminarians. Six women religious from three different communities also staffed the mission. Westside Las Vegas was an African American community. Sister Mary Litell, OSF, a partner in Father Louie's social activism, said in an interview that she found the sur-

---

8. "Street Sheet Interviews Father Louis Vitale," *Street Sheet Online*, September 1, 2005, https://streetsheetsf.wordpress.com/2005/09/01/street-sheet-interviews-father-louis-vitale/.

9. Vitale, *Love Is What Matters*, 12.

10. Louis Vitale, quoted in McGee, "Evangelization of Peace."

11. McGee, "Evangelization of Peace."

12. Vitale, *Love Is What Matters*, 14.

13. Ken Butigan suggested that Father Louie was "essentially exiled to Las Vegas" by Cardinal James McIntyre, who disagreed with Father Louie's anti-war activism. Ken Butigan, in an interview with author, January 15, 2020.

roundings "pretty depressing. Just blocks of development. Not good housing or anything. Some projects, then large empty blocks, just desert with trash thrown in. It was a ghetto. That's where you lived if you were Black."[14] Westside residents half-jokingly called their city "the Alabama of the West." Father Louie was shocked by the segregation he found in Las Vegas. "It felt like being in the heart of the South. . . . It was very, very impoverished. The streets were just dirt," he told author Annelise Orleck.[15]

Father Louie never was a disinterested academic researcher. For him, studying social problems was a prelude to action. Not long after arriving in Las Vegas, he began working with an organization of mothers on welfare. Sister Mary heard about a gathering of mothers at the neighborhood school. She and Reverend Jerry Furr, an activist Methodist clergyman, attended the meeting. Sister Mary was surprised to find that the mothers never mentioned problems with the school. "They didn't talk about the school at all," she said. "They talked about their kids being hungry."[16] Some of the women were employed, but they did not earn enough to feed their children. Others struggled to raise their children on minimal welfare benefits.

When Father Louie heard about their fledgling organization, he offered the church as a gathering place. According to Orleck, "From 1968 on, the Clark County Welfare Rights Organization met at St. James Church every two weeks, more often when crises occurred."[17] At first, Louie hung back, listening to the mothers. "They would talk about the difficulties of getting their children off to school and finding clothes. . . . they said that the two most difficult days of a welfare mother's life were Christmas and the first day of school," he recounted.[18] The women educated Father Louie about the inadequacies of public assistance. He heard them talk about their infuriating experiences with the welfare system. "We all felt that the welfare department was just mean and vicious," said Ruby Duncan, the principal organizer of the welfare rights group.[19]

Frustrated by their inability to persuade Nevada's governor and state legislature to increase welfare benefits, the mothers resolved to air their complaints before a wider audience. They decided to shut down the casinos on the famous Las Vegas Strip, a move that Father Louie endorsed. Casino owners were reputed to be a rough bunch, and the protestors feared what might happen. "We were not too far from the Mafia days," Father Louie

---

14. Mary Litell, in an interview with the author, November 17, 2019.
15. Louie Vitale, quoted in Annelise Orleck, *Storming Caesars Palace: How Black Mothers Fought Their Own War on Poverty* (Boston: Beacon Press, 2005), 105.
16. Litell, interview.
17. Vitale, quoted in Orleck, *Storming Caesars Palace*, 106.
18. Orleck, *Storming Caesars Palace*, 106.
19. Ruby Duncan, quoted in Orleck, *Storming Caesars Palace*, 104.

recounted. "Many people in Las Vegas were afraid that forcing a shut-down of casino gambling, even briefly, might spark a violent response."[20] To draw attention to their cause and discourage potential attacks, the organization recruited out-of-state welfare reform advocates and celebrities, including Hollywood star Jane Fonda and civil rights leader Ralph David Abernathy, to join their demonstration. On March 6, 1971, protestors invaded Caesars Palace, disrupting gambling operations for a short time without encountering any serious opposition.

The following week, marchers targeted Las Vegas's Sands Casino. On their arrival they found the doors locked. Instead of sitting down in the casino as planned, about "one hundred men, women and children sat down across the Strip's six lanes of traffic, singing civil rights anthems."[21] Shutting down the Strip was "a masterstroke in many ways," Father Louie remembered: "The city was supposed to be an escape for people. They didn't want to come all the way here and be reminded of all the problems of the '60s and '70s." Eighty-six demonstrators were arrested that day, among them Father Louie. It was his first arrest. Beforehand, he had come up with a plan to bail everyone out of jail. "We might get arrested," he recalled telling a fellow friar. "If we do, come down to the jail with bail money. But, whatever you do, don't bail me out and leave all the mothers in there." Father Louie feared that the bishop would run him out of town when he learned of his arrest: "I thought surely I would get fired." But this did not happen. He and the organization of mothers continued fighting for increased benefits.[22] His work for welfare reform gave Father Louie a practical education in movement dynamics. "To make a movement work you have to have a really broad base," he observed to Orleck. The movement the women created provided a model of how one can build a successful community-based organization without losing its grassroots identity.[23]

Working for Peace and Disarmament

In June 1979, Father John Vaughn, OFM, head of the St. Barbara Franciscan Province, became minister general of the Order of Friars Minor, the leader of all Franciscan friars scattered around the globe. Father Louie was vice-provincial by that time, and he succeeded Father Vaughn as provincial minister. Two years later, Father Vaughn sent a letter to Franciscan provinces worldwide, encouraging them to undertake creative projects during the coming year in celebration of the eight-hundredth anniversary of the birth of

20. Vitale, quoted in Orleck, *Storming Caesars Palace*, 152.
21. Orleck, *Storming Caesars Palace*, 159.
22. Vitale, quoted in Orleck, *Storming Caesars Palace*, 160–61.
23. Vitale, quoted in Orleck, *Storming Caesars Palace*, 294.

their founder, St. Francis of Assisi. His letter launched Father Louie's career
as an antinuclear activist. According to Ken Butigan, Father Louie "thought
that a project highlighting Franciscan peacemaking would be appropriate,
especially at a time when the Reagan administration had vowed to modernize
the U.S. military." Reagan's efforts offended Father Louie's pacifist sensibil-
ities. Not only would they increase the danger of nuclear war, they also would
"lavish economic resources on weapons systems at a time when social programs would be slashed across the U.S."[24]

Religiously motivated protest against war and the weapons of war in the
United States was nothing new; it dated back to the Revolutionary and Civil
Wars. In earlier conflicts, however, most protestors had come from the historic
"peace churches"—Quakers, Mennonites, Church of the Brethren. Prior to
the Vietnam War, Catholic pacifists were rare. Of the few Catholic conscientious objectors, a number came from the Catholic Worker movement.
Dorothy Day and Peter Maurin, founders of the movement, preached a radical
interpretation of the Gospels, which included refusal to participate in warfare.
They supported the small band of Catholic conscientious objectors who resisted the World War II draft, a position at odds with the just-war theory
advanced by most Church theologians of that era.[25]

During the Cold War, the Catholic Worker movement was among the
pacifist organizations criticizing American preparations for nuclear war. Day
and her followers were prominent among the small network of US peace
activists who challenged the accepted wisdom of stockpiling nuclear weapons
to deter the military threat posed by the Soviet Union. In 1954, the US Civil
Defense Administration instituted an exercise called Operation Alert, an
annual drill that took place on the same day in scores of major American cities.
Citizens in the "target areas" were ordered to take cover for fifteen minutes
during a simulated air raid. For New Yorkers, failure to seek shelter during
the exercise was an offense punishable by a fine of up to five hundred dollars
and a year in jail.[26] Day and A. J. Muste of the War Resisters League staged
the first protest against Operation Alert in 1955. When New York City residents were supposed to seek shelter during the drill, Day, Muste, and twenty-
six followers stayed above ground in Manhattan's City Hall Park and were
hauled to jail by police. Similarly small groups were arrested in each of the

24. Ken Butigan, *Pilgrimage Through a Burning World: Spiritual Practice and Nonviolent Protest at the Nevada Test Site* (Albany, NY: State University of New York Press,
2003), 45.

25. Of 11,887 conscientious objectors during World War II, only 135 (0.01%) were
Catholic. Patricia McNeal, "Catholic Conscientious Objection During World War II,"
Catholic Historical Review 61, no. 2 (April 1975): 222–42.

26. PBS, "Race for the Superbomb: Operation Alert," http://www.pbs.org/wgbh/
amex/bomb/peopleevents/pandeAMEX64.html.

next four annual drills. The 1960 protest, however, was a much different story, with more than one thousand people turning out, many of them mothers pushing small children in strollers. A spokeswoman argued that the only purpose of the civil defense exercise was "to frighten children and fool the public into thinking that there is protection against the H-bomb." The next year more than 2,500 participated. Federal officials permanently canceled the drill prior to the 1962 exercise.[27]

Worldwide protests against the testing of atomic bombs spread, due in large part to mounting public concern about cancer-causing radioactive fallout. In the United States, a highly effective campaign was coordinated by the National Committee for a Sane Nuclear Policy (SANE). Heightened tensions between the United States and the Soviet Union following the Cuban Missile Crisis also helped to bring major powers to the negotiating table. This resulted in the 1963 Partial Test Ban Treaty signed by the Soviet Union, the United Kingdom, and the United States (later joined by France and China). The treaty halted testing on land, in the atmosphere, and underwater. Underground tests were not included in the ban because they were not seen as contributing to fallout. Organized opposition to nuclear weapons and their testing markedly declined after the treaty.

Two young Catholic Workers, Tom Cornell and Chris Kearns, staged the first protest against the US military role in Vietnam when they picketed outside the home of South Vietnam's representative to the United Nations in July 1963.[28] As US involvement in the Vietnam War escalated following the 1964 Gulf of Tonkin Resolution, so did anti-war protests, with Catholic activists taking a prominent role. Catholic Worker David Miller was the first man convicted under a new law making it a felony to destroy draft cards. In the late 1960s, Fathers Philip and Daniel Berrigan were notable among the radical anti-war protestors who raided draft offices in Baltimore and Catonsville, Maryland. Their actions and highly publicized trials inspired other peace advocates to replicate their controversial tactics. As many as 250 similar protests occurred between 1967 and 1971.[29]

Small-scale demonstrations against nuclear testing had taken place at the remote Nevada desert site where the United States began testing nuclear

---

27. Quoted in Dee Garrison, "'Our Skirts Gave Them Courage': The Civil Defense Protest Movement in New York City, 1955–1961," in Joanne Myerowitz, ed., *Not June Cleaver: Women and Gender in Post-War America, 1945–1960* (Philadelphia: Temple University Press, 1994), 201–26.

28. Anne Klejment and Nancy L. Roberts, "The Catholic Worker and the Vietnam War," in Anne Klejment and Nancy L. Roberts, eds., *American Catholic Pacifism: The Influence of Dorothy Day and the Catholic Worker Movement* (Westport, CT: Praeger, 1996), 157.

29. Sharon Erickson Nepstad, *Religion and War Resistance in the Plowshares Movement* (New York: Cambridge University Press, 2008), 45–49.

devices in 1951. On August 6, 1957—called Hiroshima Day, the anniversary of the atomic bombing of Hiroshima—a group of eleven protestors, organized by Quaker activist Larry Scott, had been arrested after entering the test site in a nonviolent protest against continued nuclear testing.[30] Twenty years later, Sister Rosemary Lynch, OSF, on the staff of the Las Vegas Franciscan Center, was alarmed by the news that an "enhanced radiation" neutron bomb had been developed at the test site. She organized a protest at its gates on Hiroshima Day 1977. Michael Affleck described how "nineteen people [including Japanese atomic bomb survivors] met at the main gate of the Nevada Test Site (NTS) before dawn to hold a prayer vigil and conduct a teach-in about Hiroshima."[31] In subsequent years, Sister Rosemary and friends returned to the test site on important anniversaries. They "would wander off together or alone or into the desert" and "find a place to sit and pray for hours," she reminisced.[32]

A year before the planning for the Franciscan-initiated Nevada protests began, more radical Catholic activists, several of them veterans of the Vietnam-era draft board raids, launched the Plowshares movement, which sought to symbolically disarm nuclear weapons using household hammers. On September 9, 1980, eight antinuclear protestors, the Berrigan brothers among them, entered the General Electric plant in King of Prussia, Pennsylvania, where workers assembled guided missiles carrying multiple nuclear warheads. The protestors hammered on the missile reentry vehicles and poured blood over security documents. Three months later, a second action took place at the General Dynamics Electric Boat shipyard in Connecticut. The Plowshares movement carried out dozens of similar actions at nuclear installations in the United States and at least six other nations through 2003.[33]

During the post-Vietnam era, support for curtailing the international arms race grew, both in the United States and in many other countries. American peace activists built a strong popular movement under the Nuclear Freeze banner. Unlike previous antinuclear campaigns calling for a ban on all nuclear weapons, the Nuclear Freeze movement adopted a more limited objective: freezing the testing, development, and deployment of nuclear weapons at their

30. Larry Scott continued protesting with the Nevada Desert Experience. He died in an auto crash while returning to his home in 1986 following that year's Hiroshima Day demonstration. See Vinton Deming, "Among Friends: He Listened and Then He Walked," *Friends Journal* 32, no. 15 (October 15, 1986): 3.

31. Michael Affleck, *The History and Strategy*, quoted in Butigan, *Pilgrimage Through Burning World*, 48.

32. Rosemary Lynch, quoted in Butigan, *Pilgrimage Through Burning World*, 48.

33. Nepstad, *Religion and War Resistance*, 31–33. Other actions have happened as recently as 2018. See Yonat Shimron, "Dorothy Day's Granddaughter Sentenced to Prison for Nuclear Base Break-In," *National Catholic Reporter*, November 16, 2020, https://www.ncronline.org/social-tags/plowshares-movement.

current levels. Eventually, the movement gained the support of almost all US peace groups as well as mainstream religious, professional, and labor organizations. Support swelled rapidly, culminating in a June 12, 1982, rally that drew nearly one million people to New York's Central Park. Similar Nuclear Freeze movements sprang up in Great Britain, West Germany, the Netherlands, Norway, Denmark, Japan, Australia, New Zealand, and nations of the Soviet bloc.[34] In Great Britain, a group of women calling themselves Women for Life on Earth established a peace camp outside a Royal Air Force base at Gresham Common that generated international publicity. Their objective was to force the removal of ninety-eight nuclear-equipped US cruise missiles. In December 1982, thirty thousand women formed a ring around the base. In April of the following year, their numbers swelled to seventy thousand.[35]

Not long after Father Vaughn's 1981 letter, Affleck, an anti-war activist and recent graduate of the Franciscan School of Theology, approached Father Louie with a proposal to organize a program he called Instruments of Peace. According to Anne Symens-Bucher, his idea was "to travel around and meet with the Franciscan sisters and the friars of the Santa Barbara province with an education program for nuclear disarmament." Symens-Bucher, a Third Order Franciscan with five friars on her family tree, participated in these early meetings. She recalled that Father Louie was "delighted with Affleck's proposal" but insisted that one of the events must take place at the NTS for nuclear weapons. A preliminary planning group consisting of Franciscan friars and sisters, Symens-Bucher, and her then boyfriend, Duncan MacCurdy, met in a small reflection center in East Oakland, California. One issue they discussed was the likely consequences of civil disobedience. "We thought it was very possible we would have the book thrown at us [for trespassing on government property] and get some serious [jail] time," Symens-Bucher remembered in an interview.[36]

While working in Las Vegas with the Westside mothers on public assistance, Father Louie had learned about the US Department of Energy's testing of atomic weapons at its 1,360 square mile facility in the Nevada desert. He became curious about activities at the test site after a conversation with the editor of *Commonweal*, a liberal Catholic magazine. The editor remarked, "Even if they stopped the bloodshed in Indochina, there are still tens of thousands of nuclear weapons aimed at the world's children."[37] Father Louie soon found out that the US military had exploded hundreds of atomic weapons at

---

34. Lawrence S. Wittner, "The Nuclear Freeze and Its Impact," Arms Control Association, December 2010, https://www.armscontrol.org/act/2010_12/LookingBack.

35. Greenham Common Women's Peace Camp, "Greenham Common Women's Peace Camp, 1981–2000," http://www.greenhamwpc.org.uk.

36. Anne Symens-Bucher, in an interview with the author, November 24, 2019.

37. Quoted in Butigan, *Pilgrimage Through Burning World*, 46.

this secure desert site, some that involved US troops deployed within miles of the blasts. Of the 1,021 nuclear explosions at the Nevada site, 100 were atmospheric, and 921 were beneath the Earth's surface.[38] Prior to the 1963 treaty, Las Vegas hotel guests could view flashes and mushroom clouds from the explosions sixty-five miles away. In later years, residents continued to feel aftershocks from the frequent underground testing.

Affleck believed that "every single military and nuclear facility should have a Christian witness outside it." Father Louie hoped that "drawing the nation's attention to the fact that the government continued to explode nuclear bombs at least once every three weeks in the Nevada desert . . . would make an important contribution to peace."[39] He enthusiastically endorsed Affleck's organizing project and drew on the provincial treasury for an initial grant of $8,000.[40]

Planning for what would be called the Year of St. Francis began in autumn 1981 at the Las Vegas Franciscan Center. A team that included Affleck, Father Louie, and Sister Rosemary chose Lenten Desert Experience (LDE) as the name for forty days of prayer and fasting planned for the test site beginning on Ash Wednesday 1982. Unlike other antinuclear groups, the Franciscans took a conciliatory stance toward authorities and personnel at the Nevada site. The protestors were interested in change, not confrontation, so they emphasized grievances with government policies and did not disparage those working at the site. Sister Rosemary arranged a meeting with General Mahlon Gates, director of the facility, to brief him on their plans. The general turned out to be surprisingly accommodating and promised to supply water and portable toilets for those demonstrating. At the conclusion of their meeting, the general and Sister Rosemary prayed together.[41]

Organizers of the LDE revealed their plans with a demonstration on the steps of the Las Vegas federal building. The date was January 27, 1982, the thirty-first anniversary of the first atomic explosion at the NTS. Sister Rosemary announced the goal of the forty-day series of protests. "We are calling for an end to nuclear testing everywhere," she said. "There's an array of experience out at the test site which could be used for something more constructive."[42]

Early on the cold morning of February 24, 1982, carpools delivered fifty demonstrators to the NTS. They "formed a ragged circle at the edge of Camp Desert Rock," where soldiers had camped during atmospheric tests in the

---

38. Atomic Heritage Foundation, "Nevada Test Site," https://www.atomicheritage. org/location/nevada-test-site.

39. Butigan, *Pilgrimage Through Burning World*, 46.

40. Butigan, *Pilgrimage Through Burning World*, 46.

41. Butigan, *Pilgrimage Through Burning World*, 49.

42. Rosemary Lynch, quoted in "Demonstrators Mark Nuclear Anniversary," *Las Vegas Review-Journal*, January 28, 1982.

1950s. After a service at which Father Louie and an Episcopal priest distributed ashes to the group, they carried signs to the side of the road and waved to the employees arriving at the grounds.[43]

Affleck later reflected, "We began to understand that if testing was going to end, it would end on the day that the workers joined our side." Their first encounter with local law enforcement, in the person of Lieutenant Sheriff Jim Merlino, proved to be surprisingly congenial. "He was actually interested in helping us get our point across," Affleck recalled. This initial contact set the tone for the following months and years of protests. "Slowly, things began to move in the direction of building a movement where we could no longer call anyone else an enemy."[44]

On most days, only a handful of activists drove from Las Vegas to the main gate of the test site, where they waved signs and banners to greet the thousands of workers arriving for the day shift. A gathering for prayer, song, and silence followed. Sometimes a formal religious service took place. Then, singly or in groups, people wandered into the nearby desert for prayer or silent contemplation. By 10:30 a.m., everyone would return to Las Vegas. On April 9, 1982, which was Good Friday, 150 people took part in a two-mile procession from the freeway exit to the test site. They carried a quarter-mile length of rope decorated with black ribbons symbolizing the hundreds of explosions conducted at the facility. At Camp Desert Rock, they erected a nine-foot-tall cross, which was blessed by Father Louie. Nineteen people, including Father Louie, Daniel Ellsberg, and Symens-Bucher, were arrested when they crossed onto government land in a premeditated act of civil disobedience. After his arrest, Father Louie remarked, "For 15 years I wanted to see this happen. . . . The heart of the beast is nuclear war and that huge whale of a test site out there is the belly of the beast. The next step is banning nuclear war." When those arrested refused to pay the hundred-dollar bond, they were jailed for five days and then released after the district attorney dropped all charges against them.[45]

The Instruments of Peace project was slated to conclude after the Easter Sunday service in the desert, but Father Louie was eager "to keep the momentum at the test site going." Affleck returned to New York, so Father Louie expanded Symens-Bucher's role with the St. Barbara Franciscan Province to have her "take over the Instruments of Peace program, mainly to focus on the Nevada Test Site."[46] She helped organize the second LDE in 1983, a scaled-down version of the previous year's protest, with events happening only

43. Butigan, *Pilgrimage Through Burning World*, 51.
44. Michael Affleck, quoted in Butigan, *Pilgrimage Through Burning World*, 55–56.
45. Louis Vitale, quoted in Butigan, *Pilgrimage Through Burning World*, 62–67.
46. Symens-Bucher, interview.

during the last two weeks of the Lenten season. In 1984, a larger LDE lasted from April 1 to April 30. Organizers considered it a partial success because no nuclear tests occurred during the month of their protest, although testing resumed three days after the vigil participants departed.

Members of the planning group agreed that they needed to convert the Lenten demonstration into a year-round campaign to stop nuclear weapons testing. They adopted Nevada Desert Experience (NDE) as the name for the permanent organization. Father Richard Rohr, OFM, a well-known author on spirituality and peacemaking, delivered the keynote address at the first gathering of the permanent NDE in October 1984. The schedule of events at the test site expanded to include August commemorations of the atomic bombings at Hiroshima and Nagasaki.

The protests also grew beyond their Catholic origins. "We would bring in different groups for weekends, including the Unitarians, the Quakers, the Episcopalians. It really was ecumenical from the start," said Symens-Bucher in an interview. "We would also have a seder at the test site. We had sunrise ceremonies with the Shoshone, whose land was stolen to create the Nevada test site."[47] An array of prominent figures—including Dom Helder Camara, the activist Brazilian archbishop; Dutch theologian Father Henry Nouwen; Rabbi Arthur Waskow, an advocate of nonviolent action for peace and civil rights; UFW leader Dolores Huerta; and Arun Gandhi, grandson of Mahatma Gandhi—participated in the NDE demonstrations.

Because his responsibilities as provincial of the St. Barbara Franciscan Province kept Father Louie in Oakland, California, much of the time, he was not directly involved in planning or organizing NDE events. His role was to be the organization's inspirational leader. "He would come down for the events," Symens-Bucher said. "He was our spokesperson. He would rally people, encourage people, and inspire people."[48] Without fail, he would join those being arrested at the test site. On some occasions, he would be arrested, released, and arrested again several times in one day.

After 1984, other peace and antinuclear organizations began demonstrating at the NTS using tactics pioneered by NDE. One large event took place on February 5, 1987, when two thousand protestors participated in a demonstration jointly sponsored by the Nuclear Freeze movement, American Peace Test (APT), and Greenpeace, the environmental advocacy group. Among the 438 people arrested that day were astronomer Carl Sagan and actors Martin Sheen, Kris Kristofferson, and Robert Blake.[49] Around this time, the district

---

47. Symens-Bucher, interview.

48. Symens-Bucher, interview.

49. Robert Lindsey, "438 Protestors Are Arrested at Nevada Nuclear Test Site," *New York Times*, February 6, 1987.

Father Louie Vitale at Nevada Test Site. Photo courtesy Saint Barbara Franciscan Province archives.

attorney for Nye County, Nevada, announced he would no longer prosecute people arrested in these demonstrations due to the expense of processing so many cases.[50] On March 12, 1988, twelve hundred people were arrested at the site, with one hundred more jailed on each of the following eight days. An estimated five thousand people participated in this ten-day action, which was organized by APT.[51]

On May 5, 1987, Pax Christi USA, the US affiliate of the worldwide Catholic peace organization Pax Christi International, staged a demonstration in which Bishops Thomas Gumbleton of Detroit and Charles Buswell of Pueblo, Colorado, were among ninety-eight people arrested. Their arrests coincided with the fourth anniversary of the US Catholic bishops' pastoral letter on war and peace. In this lengthy document, titled *The Challenge of Peace*, the bishops addressed the nuclear arms race and disarmament: "We support immediate, bilateral verifiable agreements to halt the testing, production and deployment of new nuclear weapons systems."[52]

---

50. "Prosecution of Nuclear Protesters Halted," *Los Angeles Times*, May 5, 1987.

51. James Coates, "Protest Brings Back the 60s," *Chicago Tribune*, March 20, 1988.

52. National Conference of Catholic Bishops, *The Challenge of Peace: God's Promise and Our Response*, May 3, 1983, https://www.usccb.org/upload/challenge-peace-gods-promise-our-response-1983.pdf.

Bishop Gumbleton went beyond this rather cautious position, declaring, "It is time to resist our participation in government policies in conflict with the gospel."[53]

The last US nuclear test of any kind took place on September 21, 1992. Nine days later, President George H. W. Bush signed legislation imposing a nine-month moratorium on nuclear testing. One year earlier, Soviet leader Mikhail Gorbachev had unilaterally called a halt to all testing by his nation. Republican and Democratic congressional leadership supported a similar ban. Leaders of NDE claimed credit for generating pressure on members of Congress to pass the test ban bill.

On September 24, 1996, leaders of all five nuclear powers signed the Comprehensive Test Ban Treaty, negotiated by the United Nations. Although the US Senate failed to ratify the treaty, no nuclear weapons have been exploded by any of the major powers in the subsequent years.[54] Opponents of nuclear testing celebrated the treaty. Their joy was tempered, however, by the knowledge that the development of new weapons continued despite the ban on testing; that other nations were racing to build their own nuclear bombs; and that the major powers still maintained huge stockpiles of nuclear weapons capable of destroying civilization many times over.

Nearly forty years after its first demonstration, NDE continues to work for peace and disarmament. According to Julia Occhiogrosso, a founder of the Las Vegas Catholic Worker community, "At a certain point after the moratorium, there was some debate about whether they should fold altogether or keep it going."[55] Motivating people to come out for the demonstrations was difficult, but a small group decided to keep the project going, albeit on a much-reduced scale. Each April NDE sponsors the Sacred Peace Walk, a six-day, sixty-mile pilgrimage, much like the one first staged in 1984, from Las Vegas to the test site. Over the years, new elements have appeared. Today's marchers demand that the land currently occupied by the government be returned to its original occupants, the Western Shoshone people, and that the proposed expansion of radioactive waste storage at the site be halted. Native American religious elements are now incorporated in the annual observances.

---

53. Thomas Gumbleton, quoted in Christian Smith, ed., *Disruptive Religion: The Force of Faith in Social Movement Activism* (New York: Routledge, 1996), 216. While Father Louie Vitale was pleased to see *The Challenge of Peace*, the bishops' pastoral letter on peace, he thought it did not go far enough. Two issues were the bishops' failure to condemn the use of nuclear weapons under any circumstances and their leaving room for applying the just-war theory. Anne Symens-Bucher, email message to the author, December 17, 2020.

54. Since that date, India, Pakistan, and North Korea have exploded nuclear weapons.

55. Julia Occhiogrosso, in an interview with the author, January 21, 2020.

NDE also participates in the movement to halt US drone warfare that is coordinated from Creech Air Force Base outside Las Vegas.[56]

Over the years, the presence of Father Louie has remained a vital element of events organized by NDE. Jane Hughes Gignoux, who was arrested at the 1987 NDE, identified Father Louie as "the spirit behind the protest and vigil movement," even though "he prefers to remain in the background and allow others to coordinate the complicated preparations." This "light-hearted, loving, compassionate" man comforted others and helped them feel safe, she told Butigan. Following Gignoux's arrest at the site, she said, "his gentle, radiating energy acted as a soothing ointment to my open wounds."[57] Symens-Bucher, part of NDE since its inception, commented in an interview: Father "Louie was the charismatic, spiritual and Franciscan leader of the movement. He was always a voice for nonviolence, especially after seeing how some radical elements in the anti-Vietnam movement turned away from the principles of nonviolence."[58]

Butigan, author of *Pilgrimage through a Burning Desert*, the definitive study of NDE, examined the reasons for its effectiveness. In a blog post, he claimed that much of its success can be attributed to a strategy that differed from other antinuclear organizations, one based on "relentless persistence, ongoing presence, action and occupation." "This continuity established a growing legitimacy and visibility, which attracted people to this largely invisible site at a time when the emerging anti-nuclear weapons movement . . . was looking for tangible and concrete focus. Once people woke up to the fact that the government was still exploding nuclear weapons in the western part of the United States—and had not stopped in 1962 when the tests went below ground—people wanted to get involved, and a growing number of them thought about going out to the desert for themselves."[59]

Perhaps the most important factor contributing to NDE's success was the peaceful atmosphere created by "striking a balance between resistance and openness in their relationship with test site personnel and the local sheriffs." This combination of "noncooperation with violence *and* steadfast regard for the person as a human being," greatly "reduced the likelihood of violent interactions with employees and law enforcement." The relatively peaceful atmosphere "emboldened a growing number of people to risk arrest and face the consequences."[60]

56. See the website of the Nevada Desert Experience at http://nevadadesertexperience.org/.

57. Jane Hughes Gignoux, quoted in Butigan, *Pilgrimage Through Burning World*, 99, 111.

58. Symens-Bucher, interview.

59. Ken Butigan, "Lessons in the Desert," *Waging Nonviolence*, January 20, 2020, https://wagingnonviolence.org/2012/04/lessons-in-the-desert/.

60. Butigan, "Lessons in the Desert."

Founding Pace e Bene Nonviolence Service

In March 1989, when participation in NDE protests peaked, Father Louie called together several key leaders—Sister Rosemary, Julia Occhiogrosso, Father Alain Richard, OFM, and Peter Ediger—to discuss a new venture. This meeting grew out of a perceived need to educate activists about nonviolence. "We really needed to go deeper in understanding what we were doing when we said we were doing nonviolent actions," recalled Occhiogrosso in an interview.[61] The pilgrims who participated in NDE shared a desire to halt the testing of nuclear weapons and prevent the catastrophic disaster of nuclear warfare. They also were committed to employing nonviolent methods to achieve these goals. However, their previous experience with nonviolence was often limited and superficial. Participating in protests at the test site strengthened their commitment to nonviolence and stimulated their desire to learn more. In his own interview, Butigan described conversations between NDE staff and the people arrested protesting at the gates of the NTS: "They'd be driving people to the airport after getting out of jail from the test site, and they started having these big conversations about the culture of violence and the need for nonviolence."[62]

"We would meet monthly or every six weeks, and we would have a topic that we would reflect on," Occhiogrosso stated.[63] These gatherings of antinuclear activists evolved into an informal think tank known as the Pace e Bene Nonviolence Service, *pace e bene* being the traditional Franciscan greeting translated as "peace and all good." According to Butigan, this new organization "was meant to complement the activism of the NDE by reflecting deeply on the foundations of the culture of violence and ways to foster a more nonviolent culture of peace." The organizers saw their work as helping "our society see more clearly the power of nonviolence and ways to integrate it into our lives and world."[64] Group members began reaching out to other nonviolent activists to learn from their experiences. "People from Pace e Bene would go around and interview different groups who were involved in communities of nonviolence or justice work, getting their ideas about what their experience with violence was and what was their experience with nonviolence," Butigan explained.[65] One conclusion on which all group members agreed was the need to develop a curriculum for training others in nonviolence.

---

61. Occhiogrosso, interview.
62. Butigan, interview.
63. Occhiogrosso, interview.
64. Ken Butigan, email message to the author, December 16, 2020.
65. Butigan, interview.

The St. Barbara Franciscan Province provided financial support for Pace e Bene. Butigan came to work as its executive director in 1990. He described his unconventional job interview with Father Louie: "We met in a park in Washington, DC, and spent a couple of hours talking about nonviolence. Then, a couple of days later, I got a call that said, 'We want to hire you for Pace e Bene.'" That began a relationship with Father Louie that has endured for more than thirty years. Butigan learned to appreciate Father Louie's unique operating style. "He's got vision. He is very charismatic," Butigan explained. "Louie will suggest a course of action, and people will say, 'That's a good idea. Let's go ahead and create a strategy and tactics.'" Father Louie is "the one who's a catalyst, but he's not an organizer," Butigan observed in an interview. "He's not going to be the one ordering the buses."[66]

From the core group's discussions emerged a consensus that systematic training in the theory and practice of nonviolence was both desirable and necessary if they were to continue working to realize the broader goals of NDE. Because of its close Franciscan connection, Pace e Bene became a special project of the St. Barbara Franciscan Province. The first concrete Pace e Bene product was a curriculum on nonviolence: *From Violence to Wholeness*.[67] Occhiogrosso described the inductive approach this course employed: "A lot of the curriculum involved having people talk to each other about their own experiences and getting insight into how they actually had knowledge about how to do things nonviolently and what nonviolence was." Over the years, the curriculum has been revised and refined several times to address people at different levels of awareness and with different needs. One revision expanded the religious content to be more reflective of non-Christian faiths. A more recent emphasis, Occhiogrosso explained, is "mainstreaming nonviolence"—so the curriculum no longer aims primarily at the activist community but is now "more accessible to people from all walks of life" and relevant in people's daily lives.[68]

The training in nonviolence offered by Pace e Bene filled a great need. As the demand for its services grew, so did the need for additional staff. Laura Slattery, a West Point graduate and former army officer, worked for Pace e Bene for seven years as its international liaison and LGBTQ+ outreach coordinator. She conducted training sessions in far-flung destinations like East Timor, Papua New Guinea, Colombia, Uruguay, and Australia. Slattery estimates that tens of thousands of people have experienced training with this curriculum.[69] Pace e Bene also publishes books on nonviolence, including

---

66. Butigan, interview.
67. Ken Butigan with Patricia Bruno, *From Violence to Wholeness* (Las Vegas, NV: Pace e Bene Press, 1996).
68. Occhiogrosso, interview.
69. Laura Slattery, in an interview with the author, November 25, 2019.

Father Louie's *Love Is What Matters: Writings on Peace and Nonviolence.* Its online bookstore offers dozens of other titles for sale as well as CDs and DVDs on nonviolence.

A recent Pace e Bene project is Campaign Nonviolence, which consists of three related initiatives: Nonviolent Cities Project, Nonviolence Training Hub, and National Week of Action. The Nonviolent Cities Project engages with key activists across the United States to create more just and nonviolent cities. More than fifty cities participate. The Nonviolence Training Hub is "a partnership of 50 nonviolence training organizations and individuals offering educational programming for nonviolent transformation in our lives and in our world." The National Week of Action takes place every September, when Pace e Bene supporters "mobilize across the country and around the world for a culture of peace, economic equality, racial justice and environmental healing."[70]

As with other ventures he has started, Father Louie has been content to leave the day-to-day operation of Pace e Bene in the hands of trusted colleagues. "He would always be there for the larger retreats and things like that," said Slattery, "but on a day-to-day basis, he wasn't active in that way."[71] In recent years, Father Louie's participation in Pace e Bene has been limited due to his advanced age. However, he still appears on its webpage as an "action advocate."

For four decades, Pace e Bene has been leading nonviolence trainings, publishing books on nonviolence, and taking action for nonviolent social change. Its website proudly proclaims, "In the spirit of St. Francis, Gandhi, Dorothy Day and Dr. Martin Luther King Jr., we have persistently invited people everywhere to walk the path of nonviolence."[72] Its continued vitality stands as a lasting tribute to the inspirational leadership of Father Louie.

Sanctuary

As provincial, Father Louie also gave his support to the Sanctuary Movement, a network of faith-based organizations that provided aid and shelter for refugees from civil conflicts in Central America, especially El Salvador and Guatemala. Their actions defied policies of the Reagan administration, policies that denied official refugee status to those who illegally crossed into the United States. Thomas Ambrogi, a Catholic human rights activist, was raising money to support the movement, but his efforts lacked 501(c)(3) status, a

---

70. Pace e Bene, "Join Campaign Nonviolence," https://paceebene.org/campaign-nonviolence.
71. Slattery, interview.
72. Pace e Bene, "Join Campaign Nonviolence."

designation granted by the Internal Revenue Service to charitable, religious, and educational nonprofits. He approached Father Louie to see if he could channel these funds through the St. Barbara Franciscan Province, a move that would make all donations he collected tax-deductible. Father Louie did not think twice. "Of course! We can do that," he said, according to Butigan, who explained: "This was a very big deal because the Sanctuary Movement was committing civil disobedience. They were illegally housing refugees." Father Louie was not worried. "He's not a company man. He just leads with his heart," Butigan explained.[73]

Advocate for the Homeless

Father Louie left Las Vegas and came to San Francisco in 1992 as a temporary replacement for the pastor of St. Boniface parish. What originally was supposed to be a two-month assignment stretched out to a thirteen-year stay. St. Boniface is located in San Francisco's downtown Tenderloin district, an area known for its concentration of poor people, drug abusers, and prostitutes—and especially in recent years, a large population of homeless individuals. Father Louie's initial concern as pastor was a major, seismic retrofit to make the church, school, and friary buildings earthquake-proof. The retrofit had been mandated by the City for buildings throughout San Francisco following the devastating Loma Prieta earthquake of 1989. However, Father Louie's attention soon focused on the plight of the homeless people he saw sleeping on the streets.

During his tenure as provincial minister (1979–88), one of his duties had been overseeing St. Anthony's Dining Room, a program to feed the Tenderloin poor, established in 1950 by Father Alfred Boeddeker, OFM. Father Louie discovered that Father Boeddeker "had accumulated some funds . . . because he was very good at getting funds and he was not real quick at spending them." Father Louie made sure that some of the money held in reserve was spent on housing for the homeless.[74] By the time he returned to San Francisco in 1992, the number of unhoused people had grown exponentially. Shelters provided places to sleep through the night, but they required overnight occupants to leave during the day. This policy created problems for those with no place else to go, especially during the winter months. In 2014, Slattery

---

73. Butigan, interview.

74. "Street Sheet Interviews Vitale." St. Anthony's Foundation has since expanded its services to reach San Francisco's unhoused population. Today, in addition to its dining room, which serves nearly one million hot meals each year, it distributes clothing, operates a medical clinic, provides addiction recovery services, opens a digital technology lab for guests to use, and offers seasonal overnight shelter. See the foundation's website at https://www.stanthonysf.org.

reviewed the numbers: "The last homeless count said there are at least 6,500 homeless in San Francisco and 1,200 shelter beds. You can do the math. There are 2,500 [people] on the streets at any given time. . . . We are responding to people's needs for a safe, warm place for them to go during the day."[75]

In his straightforward fashion, Father Louie proposed a simple solution: allowing the homeless to stay inside St. Boniface during the day. In a video interview, he explained how he decided to open the church doors to the homeless:

> When I came into the pastor's office [at St. Boniface], looking through the files I found a policy. The policy was that you welcomed the [homeless] people to come [into the church], but they had to be sitting up and attending to the services. . . . I remember how I used to travel through Denver going to the committee meetings for the [Catholic] Campaign for Human Development. I had a layover in the middle of the night. I found a chapel there and went in. By gosh, they had the same exact policy that said that people were welcome to be there, but please don't lie down in the pews. It was about two in the morning, nobody else in there. I looked around. Finally, I had a little meeting with Jesus about that. "Jesus, do you mind if I lie down on this bench and get a little sleep?" Jesus gave me permission. Said it was okay. Then, when I came here and saw this policy I said, "Jesus gave me permission to sleep in his church. How can I deny it to others who really belong in this parish here?" So we did.[76]

In 2004, Father Louie teamed with community activist Shelly Roder to create the Gubbio Project, named after the medieval Italian town where, according to legend, St. Francis persuaded frightened townspeople to befriend a hungry wolf who had been preying on their flocks and terrorizing the community. The program's three goals are as follows:

- To provide a clean, beautiful, quiet, and safe space for people to rest during the day
- To cultivate a sense of community among the homeless and a sense of understanding and shared responsibility in the broader community
- To attend to the physical, social, psychological and spiritual well-being of homeless guests who share the Gubbio space

The project served an average of 225 homeless guests each weekday. Trained volunteers welcome them. The Gubbio Project website explains, "No

---

75. Laura Slattery, quoted in Meredith May, "Nonprofit's Leader Helps St. Boniface Give Sanctuary to the Homeless," *SFGate*, December 28, 2014, https://www.sfgate.com/bayarea/article/Nonprofit-s-leader-helps-St-Boniface-give-5982422.php.

76. Gubbioproject, "Father Louie Talks about the Founding of Gubbio," YouTube video, 2:29, https://youtu.be/7Ah6WmYe0Ng.

questions are asked when our guests walk into the churches; in an effort to remove all barriers to entry, there are no sign-in sheets or intake forms. No one is ever turned away; all are welcomed, respected and treated with dignity." Those resting on the pews occupy the rear two-thirds of the sanctuary, whereas those attending the mid-day Mass use the front third. In addition to offering a safe place to rest, the project provides other needed services including distributing blankets, socks, and personal hygiene kits; making referrals to outside agencies; and providing foot care, chaplaincy services, and massages free of charge.[77]

The homeless are not the only ones affected by the Gubbio Project. The volunteers and parishioners at St. Boniface also realize great personal satisfaction from their affiliation. Tina Esquer, a hospitality minister at the Gubbio Project, reflected its philosophy: "The homeless are our brothers and sisters, those less fortunate among us who need our help. It's an honor to assist them."[78] Slattery, who worked for the project for eight years, observed in an interview, "People are moved to tears at the Mass happening in the front and the hundred people sleeping on the pews. I myself get choked up walking in because of the beauty of the Gospel being lived."[79]

Father Louie's activism for the homeless extended beyond establishing charitable services for the poor and unhoused. He often said, "We can't just feed people. We've got to change the system."[80] Early on, he joined forces with Sister Bernie Galvin, CDP, founder of Religious Witness for Homeless People. Together, they led protests against the draconian policies for dealing with the homeless introduced by San Francisco's Mayor Frank Jordan. The mayor's Matrix program was a law enforcement approach to the problem of homelessness. Butigan remembered, "Homeless people were being arrested for sleeping in public parks, doorways; people were arrested for eating in public; people were arrested for giving food to the homeless, for delivering food to people in public."[81] These policies resulted in 135,000 police citations and arrests.[82] Butigan described some of the actions in which he and Father

77. The Gubbio Project, "About Gubbio," https://www.thegubbioproject.org/about-gubbio.

78. Tina Esquer, quoted in Jim Graves, "The Gubbio Project Serves San Francisco's Least Fortunate," *National Catholic Register*, September 7, 2013, https://www.ncregister.com/daily-news/the-gubbio-project-serves-san-franciscos-least-fortunate.

79. Slattery, interview. The Sacred Sleep program of the Gubbio Project was suspended in 2019 due to the COVID-19 pandemic. It is uncertain when or if it will be reopened.

80. "Street Sheet Interviews Vitale."

81. Butigan, interview.

82. Matt Hayashi, "Everyday Activist: Sister Bernie Galvin," *BeyondChron: The Voice of the Rest*, January 24, 2005, http://beyondchron.org/everyday-activist-sister-bernie-galvin/.

Louie took part: "We slept out with the homeless. We created this banquet outside city hall, the most forbidden place where homeless people were being arrested at the drop of a hat. That led to changes because we had really great media attention. Those particular statutes or ordinances were ended in part because we did these actions. . . . We tried to get the Presidio that was closing, the army base, to turn some housing over the homeless people. We weren't successful in that."[83]

Richard C. Paddock, who profiled Father Louie in the *Los Angeles Times* in 2009, described a walk the two of them took through the Tenderloin: "Homeless men and women call out, 'Father Louie.' A man in a scruffy camouflage jacket stops him and shakes his hand. A middle-aged woman, a little unsteady on her feet . . . gives Vitale a big hug."[84]

Fighting for Peace

Entering his eighth decade, Father Louie continued his peace activism, protesting against war, torture, and weapons of war. When US forces invaded Iraq in March 2003, he "got very involved" with Direct Action to Stop the War, a Bay Area organization that mobilized thousands of residents to disrupt business in San Francisco's financial district. "I probably got arrested a dozen times in those first two weeks," he told a reporter.[85] Father Louie also embarked on a forty-six-day fast to end the war.

After retiring as pastor of St. Boniface, Father Louie found more freedom to follow his activist bent. In 2006, he took his crusade to end the Iraq War to Washington, DC. On July 28, officers arrested Father Louie and four other demonstrators outside the White House while President George W. Bush and British Prime Minister Tony Blair met inside. Several hundred demonstrators organized by CodePink, a feminist anti-war group, maintained a vigil in nearby Lafayette Park.[86] "Our vigil was symbolic," Father Louie told reporter Agostino Bono. "We told Bush and Blair to stay in the White House until they came up with a plan to get our troops out."[87]

On November 19, 2006, military police arrested Father Louie and his friend, Father Steve Kelly, SJ, as they knelt in prayer at the front gate of Fort

83. Butigan, interview.

84. Richard C. Paddock, "His Spirit Won't Be Confined," *Los Angeles Times*, April 9, 2009, https://www.latimes.com/archives/la-xpm-2009-apr-09-me-protest-priest9-story.html.

85. "Street Sheet Interviews Vitale." For more on Direct Action to Stop the War, see "Direct Action to Stop the War," *Skyehome*, blog, http://skyeome.net/wordpress/?p=68.

86. Agostino Bono, "Franciscan Priest Arrested During White House Vigil Against Iraq War," *Catholic Voice*, August 7, 2006, http://www.catholicvoiceoakland.org/2006/06-08-07/inthisissue2.htm.

87. Bono, "Franciscan Priest Arrested."

Huachuca in Arizona. Authorities charged them with trespassing and refusing to obey police orders. The two activist priests had come to the army base to protest the use of torture during the interrogation of prisoners at Abu Ghraib prison in Iraq and at the prison in Guantanamo Bay, Cuba. Human rights advocates charged the United States with torture following revelations of "enhanced interrogation" methods such as waterboarding, sleep deprivation, sexual humiliation, and other extreme measures approved by the Bush administration following the 2001 attack on the World Trade Center. Father Louie and Father Kelly selected Fort Huachuca because it is home to the US Army's Intelligence Center, which trains military personnel in interrogation methods and prepares manuals describing how to employ these techniques. The two priests charged that using these methods violated the United Nations Convention Against Torture. The priests attempted to deliver a letter condemning the "illegality and immorality of torture" to the post commander, Major General Barbara Frost.[88] "The training of torturers must immediately stop. Nothing justifies the inhumane treatment of our fellow brothers and sisters," they declared.[89] When their case came to trial, the presiding judge sent both men to jail for five months. On the night before his sentencing, Father Louie received a phone call from retired Major General Antonio Taguba, the officer who wrote the army's report on the Abu Ghraib prison scandal. The major general endorsed Father Louie's stand: "History will honor your actions."[90]

Drone warfare was the reason for an April 2009 demonstration at Creech Air Force Base in Nevada, which resulted in the arrest of fourteen people including Father Louie, Father Kelly, Sister Megan Rice, SHCJ, Father John Dear, SJ, and Father Jerry Zawada, OFM. At their trial, held in Las Vegas twenty months later, all were found guilty of misdemeanor trespass. Sister Megan spoke for the group when she decried remote drone attacks on targets in Afghanistan and Pakistan directed by US Air Force personnel stationed in Nevada. She denounced "the evil of killing and destroying people in lands 8,000 miles away using bombs targeted by Air Force technicians who control computer-programmed joysticks." Another defendant, Dennis DuVall, pointed out, "Drones don't prevent or eliminate terrorism, but incite more hatred, revenge and retaliation against American military." Judge William Jansen found all defendants guilty but released everyone after giving them

---

88. Bill Quigley, "Incident at Fort Huachuca, the Army's Torture Training Center," *Counterpunch*, April 4, 2007, https://www.counterpunch.org/2007/04/04/incident-at-fort-huachuca-the-army-s-torture-training-center/.

89. Louis Vitale, "History Will Honor Your Actions," *Sojourners* 37, no. 7 (July 2008): 34.

90. Vitale, "History Will Honor," 34.

credit for time served. "Go in peace" were his parting words to the so-called Creech 14.[91]

Demonstrators from CodePink and NDE returned to the base on July 13, 2009. On this occasion Father Louie denounced the military use of drones, saying, "These are war crimes being committed from our own back-yards. . . . It's unbelievable that from thousands of miles away, we're dropping bombs on people's houses." The demonstrators also urged Congress to stop spending tax dollars on drones but instead to use the funds for humanitarian aid and diplomacy.[92]

Authorities arrested Father Louie again on August 23, 2009, when he and Sister Megan tried to enter Vandenberg Air Force Base in California. This time they were protesting the test launch of an unarmed Minuteman III mis-sile capable of delivering a nuclear warhead. "It is our hope, prayer, our ardent effort to prevent the use of nuclear weapons," he said following his arrest. "The missile tests are evidence of our willingness [as a country] to commit mass murder." The judge hearing their case was not persuaded and slapped Father Louie with a five-hundred-dollar fine. Father Louie told the judge, "I am committed to doing anything I can" to prevent the use of nuclear weapons.[93] Another member of the anti-war group that organized the demon-stration explained that its members had no objection to peaceful uses of mis-siles such as launching communications satellites. "Our mission as an organ-ization is the end of the nuclear weapons threat," he said.[94]

Father Louie's longest prison sentences have come from his involvement in the yearly demonstrations organized by former Maryknoll priest Roy Bour-geois at Fort Benning, Georgia. The target of these protests is the School of the Americas (SOA), a program established by the US Army to train Latin American military personnel in counterinsurgency warfare.[95] Researcher Vicki Immerman revealed that officers who graduated from this program were responsible for the brutal repression of popular movements for needed social

91. Megan Rice and Dennis DuVall, quoted in Dave Toplikar, "'Creech 14' Found Guilty of Trespassing, Judge Says 'Go in Peace,'" *Las Vegas Sun*, January 27, 2011, https://lasvegassun.com/news/2011/jan/27/creech-14-found-guilty-trespassing-judge-says-go-p/. Father Louie was not present for the trial. He was serving a six-month sentence in federal prison for protesting at the School of the Americas in Fort Benning, GA.

92. Louis Vitale, quoted in CodePink, "Peace Activists to Rally Monday Outside Creech Air Force Base: Will Call For End to US Drone Attacks in Afghanistan, Pakistan," Common Dreams, July 13, 2009, https://www.commondreams.org/newswire/2009/07/10/peace-activists-rally-monday-outside-creech-air-force-base-will-call-end-us.

93. Louis Vitale, quoted in Paddock, "Spirit Won't Be Confined."

94. Nicholas Walter, "Two Arrested at Base Protest," *Santa Maria Sun*, August 25, 2009, http://www.santamariasun.com/news/2856/two-arrested-at-base-protest/.

95. The School of America (SOA) is sometimes called the "School of Assassins." It has since been renamed the Western Hemisphere Institute for Security Cooperation.

change.[96] The first protest took place in 1990 on the one-year anniversary of the murders in El Salvador of six Jesuit priests, their cook, and her daughter by SOA graduates. Bourgeois and two associates entered the base, planted a cross to commemorate the victims, and splashed blood on the building where the training took place. The trio were arrested, tried, and sentenced to terms in federal prison. Bourgeois received a sixteen-month sentence; his coconspirators got six months each. That same year, Bourgeois founded SOA Watch, an organization dedicated to shutting down the military training program. In subsequent years, nonviolent demonstrations sponsored by SOA Watch at Fort Benning became major events.[97]

While Bourgeois was in prison, Imerman, an army veteran, took over the SOA Watch office and began researching the school's alumni. She uncovered numerous instances of Latin American officers returning to their home nations and leading or participating in atrocities against civilians who challenged dictatorial rule and agitated for social justice. She publicized evidence she discovered of gruesome crimes committed by SOA alumni.[98]

By 1997, the annual November SOA protest was drawing more participants, due largely to increased backing from faith-based communities. More than six hundred people crossed into the base that year, indicating their willingness to go to jail for the cause. One hundred thirty Catholic bishops signed a petition stating that the SOA must be closed. The following year, the number of demonstrators tripled, with 2,319 crossing the line. In 1999, that number rose again, this time to 3,500. By 2005, an estimated 20,000 people joined the protest.[99]

No one who knew Father Louie was surprised to learn that he gravitated to the SOA protests. His first arrest at Fort Benning took place in November 2001, when he and thirty-six others participated in a mock funeral procession mourning victims murdered by SOA graduates. Their crime was stepping across the boundary onto the military base, where demonstrations were forbidden. In both 2009 and 2010, he was jailed for walking onto the base as part of the annual SOA Watch event. On all three occasions, Father Louie was found guilty of trespass and served time in prison. The sentence for his first offense, in 2001, was three months. Following his 2009 arrest, he stated,

---

96. Linda Cooper and James Hodge, "SOA Watch Marks 25th Year of Speaking Out Against 'School of Assassins,'" *National Catholic Reporter*, November 18, 2014. https://www.ncronline.org/news/accountability/soa-watch-marks-25th-year-speaking-out-against-school-assassins.

97. For an in-depth account of the SOA and related protests, see James Hodge and Linda Cooper, *Disturbing the Peace: The Story of Father Roy Bourgeois and the Movement to Close the School of the Americas* (Maryknoll, NY: Orbis Books, 2004).

98. Hodge and Cooper, *Disturbing the Peace*, 142–44.

99. Cooper and Hodge, "SOA Watch Marks 25th Year."

"The evil is still there. It's the right thing to do."[100] That time, he received a six-month sentence, most of which he served at Lompoc Federal Prison in California. He wrote from his cell, "If I start to feel sorry for myself, I think of the suffering experienced in the horrific situations around the world. How can I really complain? . . . When I think about these situations, I am able to cope with my own deprivations."[101] Father Louie returned to Fort Benning in November 2010 and was one of twenty-nine people arrested during the annual protest.[102] He was sentenced to a second six-month prison stay at the age of seventy-eight.

The friars of the St. Barbara Franciscan Province have not always agreed with Father Louie's frequent arrests. Some have felt the level of his activism was excessive. According to Symens-Bucher, however, even the ones who have disagreed with him respect his integrity and understand that his values are Franciscan and Gospel-based.[103]

Father Louie in Retirement

In recent years, Father Louie has resided at the Mercy Care Center in Oakland, close to Canticle Farm, the urban intentional community and education center created by Symens-Bucher and her husband, Terry. Anne Symens-Bucher observed in an interview, "I think it was very difficult for Louie when he was sent to Mercy Center and was limited in what he could do. He bears it with a lot of grace and humility. . . . But no matter where Louie lives, he is a true Franciscan in terms of his vision, his leadership, his heart, and his commitment to peace, justice, and deep ecology. . . . His commitment in those three tenets of Franciscan spirituality—justice for the poor, peace for the world, and protection for our Earth—has been profound, deep, unwavering, and impactful."[104]

Few people who have encountered Father Louie have been unmoved by the experience. Slattery, who has worked with both Pace e Bene and the Gubbio Project, reflected on the ways in which Father Louie has affected her life: "His impact on me is mostly his vision. The way he sees things. One of

---

100. Louis Vitale, quoted in Lily Gordon and Alan Riquelmy, "Four Arrested at SOA Protest," *Common Dreams*, November 23, 2009, https://www.commondreams.org/news/2009/11/23/four-arrested-soa-watch-protest.

101. John Dear, "Fr. Louie's Letters from Prison," *National Catholic Reporter*, June 15, 2010, https://www.ncronline.org/blogs/road-peace/fr-louies-letters-prison.

102. Front Lines of Revolutionary Struggle, "Ft. Benning, Georgia: 29 People Arrested Outside US Military's Counter-Insurgency School for Latin America," December 4, 2010, https://revolutionaryfrontlines.wordpress.com/2010/12/04/ft-benning-georgia-26-arrested-outside-the-us-militarys-school-of-assassins-for-latin-america/.

103. Symens-Bucher, email.

104. Symens-Bucher, interview.

my first memories is being in his Liberating Nonviolence class and him talking about doing a thought experiment and saying, What would it be like if we had sent ships filled with food to Iraq instead of the bombs? How would that have made the relationship between the United States and Iraq different? It was such a simple thought experiment, but I was kind of blown away. [I thought,] Oh, we can do things differently than the way they are being done."[105]

In an interview, Occhiogrosso, who moved to Las Vegas to be part of NDE, recounted an illustrative instance of civil disobedience she shared with Father Louie:

> They [authorities] were bulldozing this encampment for the homeless [in Las Vegas]. We served [meals] out of the back of a truck in this open area by the railroad tracks. The homeless had set up mattresses in a little dormitory style. Everything was orderly. We saw these bulldozers and thought they were going to bulldoze the area. Kind of impromptu, Louie and myself and another woman sat down in front of the bulldozers. There was a Bible on the heap of belongings and we grabbed the Bible, turned to Matthew 25, and started reading as the police were coming to arrest us.[106]

Butigan, who worked closely with Father Louie for more than three decades, reflected, "Louie's strength is his heart and his absolute commitment to a better world. He is not the person who is going to get on the phone and call 50 organizers. He's got vision. He is very charismatic in the sense that people will say, 'That's a good idea. Let's actually go ahead and create a strategy and tactics and all that.'"[107]

Sister Mary Litell, his longtime associate, insisted that Father Louie possesses a unique gift, "the ability to think along six tracks at the same time," a trait she attributes to his Italian heritage. Because of this gift, she says, "he can be involved in, and a major influence in, six different projects at the same time, and getting everybody else involved in all of them." In addition, she praised his "ability to always see a larger context—to see everything in context—and to recognize the inadequacies of the context."[108]

Sister Bernie Galvin, a leading advocate for the homeless, praised Father Louie for his "nonviolent civil disobedience on issues, such as protesting the war in Iraq, support for hotel workers fighting for a fair contract, and the

---

105. Slattery, interview.
106. Occhiogrosso, interview. In Matthew 25 (verse 40), Jesus describes the Judgment of Nations, which concludes, "Whatever you did for one of these least brothers of mine, you did for me."
107. Butigan, interview.
108. Litell, interview.

struggle for just and compassionate public policies that impact the lives of our homeless sisters and brothers."[109]

Salt Lake City Archbishop John Wester, who got to know Father Louie during his tenure as auxiliary bishop of San Francisco, has not always agreed with his actions, but he said of his friend, "He is a very holy man and a very good priest. He is following in the footsteps of Saint Francis."[110]

Father Louie's Legacy

Father Louie's frequent arrests—demonstrating for peace, against torture, on behalf of the homeless and mothers on welfare, for bans on nuclear testing and weaponized drones—have garnered numerous headlines and made him one of the most recognized peace activists of his generation. He does not keep count of his arrests, but he guesses they may total four hundred or more. However, his record as a visionary may ultimately prove to be a more important contribution to nonviolent social change.

The three organizations he is largely responsible for creating are monuments that will endure after Father Louie is called to his heavenly reward. He was the prime mover behind NDE, the organization that mobilized Catholics and people of other faith traditions to respond to the ongoing threat of nuclear testing at the NTS. The protests in the desert, beginning in 1982 and rapidly growing through the rest of the decade, were part of an international movement that helped to generate the political pressure that brought about the 1996 Comprehensive Nuclear Test Ban Treaty. Although the US Senate failed to ratify the treaty, the United States has observed a moratorium on testing and has not detonated a nuclear weapon since 1992.

A valuable offshoot of the NDE is the Pace e Bene Nonviolence Service, which provides training and resources to groups seeking a deeper understanding of the philosophy of nonviolence and its application to a variety of difficult situations. Trainers from Pace e Bene have worked with people around the globe seeking to use nonviolent tactics to promote needed social change. Materials created by Pace e Bene serve as guides for others who cannot attend these training sessions. Though Father Louie has not been involved in the day-to-day operation of Pace e Bene, his vision helped to bring it to reality.

A third undertaking dear to Father Louie's heart, one that is unique in the nation, is the Gubbio Project. Father Louie wondered why homeless individuals should remain sleeping on the streets while his church in San Francisco was largely empty during the day. Emulating St. Francis, who dismounted from his horse and embraced the leper he encountered along the road, Father

109. Bernie Galvin, email message to the author, February 10, 2020.
110. John Wester, quoted in Paddock, "Spirit Won't Be Confined."

Father Louie Vitale at his desk, Mercy Center, Oakland, California, 2017. Peter Jordan photo courtesy St. Barbara Franciscan Province archives.

Louie has embraced the unfortunate souls who populate the streets of our large cities. The Gubbio Project insists that its guests be treated with dignity and respect; it shows more privileged volunteers how they can heed Jesus's admonition to feed the hungry, give drink to the thirsty, shelter the stranger, clothe the naked, and care for the ill (see Matt. 25:35–36).

In recent years, Father Louie's pace has slowed. Following his doctor's orders, he no longer does long-term fasts. From his retirement apartment, he can look back on a career in which he influenced thousands to follow the path of nonviolence while seeking peace and social justice. Father Louie leaves a legacy of service and advocacy in the eight-hundred-year-old Franciscan tradition.

Conclusion: Many Paths to Justice

Franciscan efforts to achieve social justice and peace since the end of World War II have taken many forms. Some have emerged from mission parishes established to evangelize minority communities. Others have combined traditional charitable outreach to the poor with advocacy for social change. Franciscans have collaborated with members of other faiths in ecumenical ventures as well as establishing uniquely Franciscan agencies. Some Franciscan justice seekers have employed public protest and civil disobedience as their favored method of communication. Others have lobbied religious and secular institutions to adopt policies and practices that promote justice. Increasingly, Franciscans have worked as individual change agents outside established religious communities.

Just as St. Francis's preaching produced controversy in his day, so too have the strivings of modern Franciscans working for peace and justice often generated debate and criticism. Their most notable contributions have been evident in the areas of racial justice, economic justice, nuclear disarmament, and foreign policy.

Racial Justice

In the years following World War II, American religious communities experienced a surge in vocations, which enabled them to enter new fields. The friars of Assumption Province and the Franciscan Sisters of Perpetual Adoration (FSPA) established missions in Mississippi towns, where they sought to win African American souls for Christ. Neither the friars nor the sisters were prepared to confront the entrenched racism they encountered in the Deep South—the rigid segregation of Blacks and Whites, the limited education available to African American children, the brutal poverty endured by displaced sharecroppers. As Catholics and as Yankees, these Franciscan missionaries were viewed with suspicion by local residents. They walked a fine line to avoid antagonizing local segregationists who monopolized political power, controlled the economy, and supervised law enforcement.

Despite the obvious need to confront pressing issues of racial inequality, in their early years the Franciscan friars and sisters concentrated on evangelization, works of charity, and social and recreational programs. Education was especially important, both as a means to win converts and as an essential tool for gaining civil rights. As Mother Albertine Semsch, then head of the

FSPA, wrote in 1948, the sisters aimed to help their students take their rightful place "as true loyal citizens of this country" and to "break down the bigotry which is rampant in the South."[1] Franciscan missioners adopted a long-range strategy, based on their understanding that well-educated graduates of their schools would be better equipped to claim the rights guaranteed them by the US Constitution.

For their first decade and a half in Mississippi, the Franciscans remained on the sidelines of the struggle for African American civil rights. They witnessed the acquittal of Emmett Till's killers, the rise of the White Citizens' Council following the Supreme Court's *Brown v. Board of Education* decision, the arrests of Freedom Riders, and attacks on Black citizens trying to register to vote. Although sympathetic to African American aspirations for equality, they refrained from openly confronting common racist practices. Nevertheless, they resisted segregation in other less obvious ways.

In Greenwood, the Pax Christi Franciscans, an institute of White and Black women, worked side by side in the heart of the Black community. After completing her formation as a Sister of Perpetual Adoration, Sister Thea Bowman returned to Canton, Mississippi, to join the faculty of her alma mater, Holy Child Jesus School. In addition to living as an equal with the White sisters, she imbued her students with an appreciation of African American music and literature. After a stint teaching at Viterbo College in Wisconsin, Sister Thea came back to Mississippi and created the Office of Intercultural Understanding in the Diocese of Jackson. She went on to become a leading national spokesperson for the inclusion of African Americans and people of other races as valued members of the Catholic Church in the United States.

During the mid-1960s, the friars and sisters of both the St. Francis and Holy Child Jesus missions openly demonstrated their support for African American civil rights. In May 1965, the Sisters of Perpetual Adoration marched with the Black parishioners of Holy Child Jesus Mission to Canton's White Catholic church to protest the city's refusal to grant a building permit for the construction of a new church for Blacks. The following summer, the sisters welcomed civil rights demonstrators to the Holy Child Jesus campus and provided first aid to those injured in a tear gas attack by state and local police. In 1967, Father Nathaniel Machesky assumed a leading role in the Greenwood Movement, a well-organized campaign to win respect and employment opportunities for the African American citizens of Greenwood, Mississippi. Friars, Pax Christi members, and Sisters of St. Joseph participated

---

1. "An Account Gleaned from Mother Assistant's Diary and from Her Talks to Various Groups," *Sisters' Newsletter*, June 1948, Franciscan Sisters of Perpetual Adoration Archives, La Crosse, WI.

in an eighteen-month boycott of White merchants. They weathered abusive racist propaganda, economic reprisals, verbal and physical threats, and a law-suit, all to win important concessions from Greenwood's government and local businesses. Today, Franciscan friars at St. Francis of Assisi parish continue to assist and advocate for the poor in Greenwood.

Sister Antona Ebo was thrust into the national spotlight when she traveled to Selma, Alabama, to demonstrate her support for African American voting rights. Reporters and photographers focused their attention on the diminutive Black sister, and she did not disappoint. Her forthright statement that Black citizens in the South were entitled to the same right to vote that she exercised in St. Louis succinctly expressed the need for the Voting Rights Act that became law a few months later in 1965. She continued speaking out against racial injustice in American society and the Catholic Church over the next fifty years, inspiring generations of young activists.

The fight for civil rights was waged in the North as well as the South. Brother Booker Ashe launched his career as an advocate for racial justice in cities and small towns of Wisconsin. He communicated to White audiences the grievances that fueled the civil rights movement and outlined a Christian approach to racial reconciliation. After becoming director of the House of Peace in Milwaukee, Wisconsin, he created programs that combined Capuchin charitable services for impoverished inner-city residents with racial pride and cultural uplift. Like Franciscans working in the South, he also stressed the importance of education as an essential means for African American advance-ment. Throughout his career Brother Booker joined with other African Amer-ican Catholic priests, sisters, and brothers, to combat the racism they encoun-tered within the Church.

Economic Justice

Franciscan friars and sisters also made notable contributions to Mexican American farm workers' movement for economic justice during the 1960s and 1970s. As provincial minister of the St. Barbara Franciscan Province, Father Alan McCoy was instrumental in committing Franciscan resources to assist the organizing efforts of Cesar Chavez and the United Farm Workers (UFW). At the historic 1968 provincial chapter, he championed the proposal that shifted friars from teaching assignments in middle-class high schools to pastoral work in Mexican American parishes. The young Franciscans he assigned to these parishes embraced the farm workers' cause as part of their ministry. The province aided the United Farm Workers's organizing campaigns. The UFW held board meetings in provincial facilities. Father Alan authorized an interest-free loan to the union, which it used to pay benefits to striking members. The province donated a printing press to the UFW and sheltered Chavez during a difficult time in one organizing campaign, a move that angered Catholic grow-ers who had financially supported Franciscan institutions.

Franciscan sisters also joined the farm worker movement. Sister Patricia Ann Drydyk is a sterling example of a woman religious deeply committed to economic justice. Over a twenty-year career, she occupied a variety of impor-tant roles. She began by producing educational media at the Franciscan Com-munications Center. Next, she promoted the farm workers' cause in religious communities across the United States. After joining the staff of the National Farm Worker Ministry (NFWM), she worked with people from many denom-inations to build support for union-organizing campaigns, boycotts of nonunion produce, and campaigns to ban the use of harmful pesticides on agricultural crops. A tireless organizer, Sister Pat forged a path for other women religious working for justice in nontraditional roles.

Peace and Disarmament

Father Louie Vitale of the St. Barbara Franciscan Province is a leading example of a Franciscan dedicated to the cause of world peace and disarma-ment. To celebrate the eight-hundredth anniversary of St. Francis's birth, he brought together Franciscan friars, sisters, and lay people to oppose the under-ground testing of nuclear weapons in the Nevada desert. The original protest evolved into the Nevada Desert Experience (NDE), a national ecumenical organization that staged annual Lenten demonstrations at the Nevada Test Site (NTS) involving thousands of individuals. NDE was committed to non-violence throughout these protests and won the respect of employees of the government testing facility by focusing criticism on the political leaders who set national policies—refusing to demonize the workers employed at the test site or the officers who arrested the protestors. As part of the worldwide move-ment to ban nuclear weapons, they celebrated when leaders of the major world powers signed the Comprehensive Test Ban Treaty in 1996. An ongoing spin-off from NDE is the Pace e Bene Nonviolence Service, begun by Franciscan friars of California in 1989, to provide education and training in nonviolence, publish resources on nonviolence, and organize actions for nonviolent change.

Franciscans in the United States have also have been leaders seeking to shape national policies on peace and economic justice. During the late 1970s and 1980s, their primary focus was the conflicts in Central America, especially Nicaragua and El Salvador. Father Louie Vitale three times served prison sen-tences after being arrested for protesting outside the School of the Americas, where the US military trained Latin American officers in techniques to repress social dissent. Father Alan McCoy, as president of the Conference of Major Superiors of Men (CMSM), frequently traveled to these nations as an observer and peacemaker. In 1980, he was present in El Salvador when Archbishop St.

Oscar Romero was assassinated. On his return to the United States, he worked with other religious leaders to publicize widespread human rights abuses in this region and urged the US government to cease providing military assistance to repressive regimes. Father Alan in turn hired Father Joseph Nangle, formerly a missionary to Bolivia and Peru, to be his special assistant for social justice. They worked together to put CMSM on record as supporting the Sanctuary Movement for refugees entering the United States. Father Joe has continued his advocacy for human rights, most recently protesting government treatment of refugees detained on the border with Mexico.

Looking to the Future

Franciscan efforts for peace and justice in the twenty-first century will differ in many respects from many of the good works chronicled in this volume. A primary factor in this change is the declining number of professed religious men and women. Among the Order of Friars Minor, for example, the number of vowed members is currently less than 1,000, down from a peak of 3,253 in the 1960s.[2] For Catholic sisters of all orders, statistics show a similar drop: from 181,421 in 1966 to just 49,883 in 2014. Of those remaining, less than 10 percent are under age sixty.[3] Due to these shrinking numbers, the FSPA were forced to give up Holy Child Jesus School in Canton, Mississippi, and the Sisters of St. Joseph of the Third Order of St. Francis left St. Francis School in Greenwood, Mississippi.

More recently, Franciscan friars from the Assumption Province withdrew from Sacred Heart parish in McAllen, Texas, on the border with Mexico. However, the parish continues as the site of the Humanitarian Respite Center, established with the assistance of Franciscan friars to serve undocumented immigrants, but now without a Franciscan presence. The center opened in June 2014 when the US Border Patrol was overwhelmed by a surge of migrants seeking to "escape extortion and brutality from gangs and drug cartels in Honduras, Guatemala, and El Salvador." Many were released with temporary papers pending a hearing. An article described how, "confused and exhausted, they were left at the bus station to fend for themselves."[4] Sister

---

2. "U.S. Franciscans in Six Provinces Vote to Form One Organization," *National Catholic Reporter*, May 31, 2018, https://www.ncronline.org/news/people/us-franciscans-vote-form-one-new-organization-out-six-provinces.

3. Erick Berrelleza, Mary L. Gautier, and Mark M. Gray, "Population Trends Among Religious Institutes of Women," *CARA Special Report*, Fall 2014, 2–3, https://cara.georgetown.edu/wp-content/uploads/2018/06/Women_Religious_Fall2014_FINAL.pdf.

4. Toni Cashnelli, "Franciscan Respite for Refugees," *St. Anthony Messenger* 124, no. 1 (June 2016): 32–37.

Norma Pimentel, director of Catholic Charities of the Rio Grande Valley, asked Father Tom Luczak, OFM, pastor of Sacred Heart parish, if she could "borrow" the parish hall for a couple of days. Father Luczak readily agreed. He told Sister Norma, "You stay here until it ends." The parish grounds were transformed into a refugee camp by the addition of a mobile shower unit and a large tent filled with cots. The hall was crowded with comfort stations, racks and stacks of clothing, tables laden with baby supplies and hygiene essentials, and dining tables near the kitchen. In its first two years, the center served more than thirty thousand refugees. Although Franciscan friars no longer reside at Sacred Heart parish, the good work of the Humanitarian Respite Center continues at a new location under the management of Catholic Charities.[5]

Because Franciscan communities lack sufficient personnel to staff existing missions, much less mount new initiatives on their own, individual sisters and friars now often cooperate in joint social justice endeavors with people of faith from other denominations. Sister Pat pioneered this path when she joined the staff of NFWM, eventually becoming its executive director. Brother Ed Dunn from the St. Barbara Franciscan Province collaborated with her in this work, as did Sisters Tess Browne and Betty Wolcott.

Since returning to the United States from Latin America forty-five years ago, Father Joe Nangle has worked as an independent agent, mostly with Catholic organizations but also with the ecumenical Sojourners community. Although affiliated with the Holy Name Franciscan Province and operating with approval from its provincial ministers, since 1986 he has resided with lay people and members of various religious orders in an intentional community in Washington, DC. Our Lady Queen of Peace parish, where he serves as pastoral associate, is administered by the Spiritan Fathers, not the Franciscans.

Sister Carmen Barsody, OSF, a member of the Little Falls (Minnesota) Franciscan community, is another example of a professed Franciscan living and working independently of other members of her order. She relocated from a mission in Nicaragua to the Bay Area of California in 1997. Since 2000, she has resided in San Francisco's Tenderloin district, where she and her colleague, Sam Dennison, run Faithful Fools, an agency serving the homeless. Their website declares, "We seek to meet people where they are through the arts, education, advocacy, and accompaniment."[6]

One of Faithful Fools's distinctive programs is the street retreat, which takes people from more affluent communities and introduces them "to what it means to be present in a neighborhood like the Tenderloin." Unlike religious retreats that take place in serene settings, sheltered from the distractions of urban life, these retreats plunge participants into the reality of life on the

5. Cashnelli, "Franciscan Respite for Refugees."
6. Faithful Fools, "Our Mission Statement," https://www.faithfulfools.org/about-us.

Sr. Carmen Barsody, on right, with Kim Diamond in the Tenderloin. Photo courtesy Sister Carmen Barsody.

streets, challenging popular myths about people living in poverty. The goal of the street retreats is as much to develop self-knowledge in the participants as it is to increase their understanding about the problems of the homeless.[7]

Faithful Fools is also an advocacy organization. Carmen, as she prefers to be known, explained, "We work daily with community members, residents, and folks from other organizations to bring about policies and practices that meet the needs of the people we live and work with." Residents and representatives of community organizations often gather at the Faithful Fools offices to talk about what needs to be done. They work "to keep the voice of the community present" and to call for public accountability when decisions affecting the Tenderloin are made by government and private institutions.[8]

"We are not a formal social service agency," Carmen explained in an article, although "we provide services as needs arise." She and Dennison are able to help individuals in need in ways other agencies cannot because, she said, "we can move beyond the boundaries. We aren't confined by the institutional protocols. . . . We can help with a continuity of relationships that a lot of times professional people aren't able to provide." Faithful Fools also serves as a critical link with the world beyond the Tenderloin, providing information and

---

7. Carmen Barsody, in an interview with the author, September 11, 2020.
8. Barsody, interview.

insight on the problems faced by its residents. Carmen wrote, "We are the on-the-ground connection for media, volunteers, friends and colleagues, as each seeks a relevant connection to the larger picture of what is happening and what is needed."[9]

At age fifty-nine, Carmen is the youngest North American member of her community. She is acutely aware of living in a time of transition for religious congregations. She said in an interview, "We need to be faithful to the mission, not the form. Our responsibility is to continue to evolve with the Franciscan charism in the world, but not be confined to the [old] forms."[10]

The Franciscan Action Network (FAN) is one of these evolving forms of social justice activism. Created in 2007, FAN is a collaborative venture "representing all the different branches of the Franciscan family, including leaders from all four orders as well as leaders from the Secular Franciscan Order, Episcopal Franciscans and the Ecumenical Franciscans." Its mission is simply stated as "the propagation of a restorative course of action for our culture through intelligent advocacy . . . rooted in the spiritual strength of an eight hundred year old faith tradition that obligates us."[11] Its membership includes fifty-four Franciscan institutions as well as many individual members. Although a majority of the FAN board of directors are professed Franciscans, most of its professional staff, including the executive director, are lay people.

Without doubt, the issues that provoke future Franciscan social justice activism will change and evolve, as will the forms that activism takes. Environmental activism, inspired by Pope Francis, has become increasingly important and will continue to grow in prominence. Economic inequality, especially the enormous gulf between rich and poor nations, will not recede as a cause for concern. Dedicated Franciscans who envision a world without war will continue to work for peace and international understanding. Whatever the pressing issues confronting humankind, the daughters and sons of St. Francis will be in the forefront of those who work for peace and justice.

---

9. Carmen Barsody, "Here . . . Actively in Place," *Fools E-News*, May 2020, http://www.icontact-archive.com/archive?c=970584&f=43064&s=46952&m=1051482 &t=dc1ed7cc5766f3b70ac62fbf2fc914ea89b59448cf69235631f4f8180637620b.

10. Barsody, interview.

11. Franciscan Action Network, "History of FAN," https://franciscanaction.org/about/history-of-fan.

Acknowledgements

Twenty-five years ago, when I first read *Local People: The Struggle for Civil Rights in Mississippi* by my friend and former neighbor John Dittmer, I was struck by a single sentence. Writing about the Civil Rights Movement in Greenwood, Mississippi, John said, "At first only Father Nathaniel at the Catholic Center made his facility available." Years later, when I began researching Catholic civil rights activists, I called the St. Francis Mission in Greenwood. The person on the other end of the line remarked, "You're calling from Albany, New York? You should talk to Carolyn Harris. She was one of Father Nathaniel's first converts and she lives in Albany."

To my amazement, I discovered that Carolyn lived just three blocks from my home. She was the first in a long succession of individuals who helped to make this book possible. Father Dan Dwyer, O.F.M., a history professor at Siena College, read my article about Father Nathaniel. In 2018, shortly after my retirement, he asked if I would be interested in writing about other Franciscans working for peace and justice in the United States. Professor Jeffrey Burns, director of the Academy of American Franciscan History, offered me the opportunity to embark on this project. I agreed with one condition, that I include Franciscan sisters as well as friars.

For the past two years, this project has been my constant preoccupation. Many people assisted me in this pursuit. First and foremost, I must thank my wife, Suzanne, who has proofread every chapter three or four times. Her constant encouragement and critical insights have sustained me. My neighbor, Sandy Stone, has faithfully transcribed dozens of interviews. Sage advice from Jeff Burns and Father Joe Chinnici has helped me navigate through the many branches of the Franciscan family tree. In my pursuit of published sources, I have been assisted by the staff of the Standish Library at Siena College, especially the indefatigable Catherine Crohan. Gary Thompson, the library's retired director has prepared the index.

A summer research grant from Siena College supported my initial research trip to Mississippi to learn more about Father Nathaniel. Archivists Brother Jude Lustyk, OFM, and Father Bill Stout, OFM, guided my research on the Franciscans of the Assumption Province. Mark Conway graciously gave me research notes and recordings from his senior thesis on Father Nathaniel. Genevieve and Kathleen Feyen enlightened me about Miss Kate Jordan and the Pax Christi Franciscans. Chantal Baten, Sister Barbara Krakora and Sister Helen Skok, shared their memories of teaching at St. Francis School in Greenwood. Sister Debra Weina, SSJ-TOSF, assisted my exploration of the Sisters of St. Joseph archives. Woody and Madge Bishop offered hospitality in their home during my stay in Stevens Point.

Sister Mary Ann Gschwind, archivist for the Franciscan Sisters of Perpetual Adoration, welcomed me to the FSPA archives in La Crosse. There she introduced me to retired sisters who had known and worked with Sister Thea Bowman. Sister Mary Ann also gave me a CD of Sister Thea leading the Holy Child singers, a recording that I treasure. In addition, Professor Kim Harris gave me access to her research on Sister Thea's role as an advocate for liturgical inclusion. Holy Child Jesus alumnae Flonzie Brown-Wright, Nola Jo Starling Ratliff and Deborah Pembleton described for me the influence of Sister Thea. Mary Woodward, archivist for the Catholic Diocese of Jackson, aided my search for information on Sister Thea's career.

John Buchkoski, then a graduate student at the University of Oklahoma, put me on the trail of Sister Patricia Drydyk. The excellent staff of the Walter P. Reuther Library of Labor and Urban Affairs at Wayne State University helped me explore the records of Sister Pat's work with the National Farm Worker Ministry. My sister Liz Golen and her husband, Jerry, welcomed me into their home during my Detroit research trip. Sister Pat's brother, Jay Drydyk, and her cousin, Jerry Ceille, told me about her family. Many of her associates, especially Sister Marie Tess Browne, provided accounts of Sister Pat's work for the farm workers. Sister Celia Struck, OSF, was unfailingly helpful in delving into the records in the New Assisi Archives. I am especially grateful to Baldemar Velasquez, president of the Farm Labor Organizing Committee, for taking time from his busy schedule to share his memories of Sister Pat.

Father Joe Nangle has been consistently responsive to my frequent inquiries and expounded on his work for peace and justice in a series of interviews. Likewise, Father Joe Chinnici graciously answered my many questions and helped me understand the organization and politics of the Saint Barbara Franciscan Province. Father Tom West, OFM, gave me permission to examine records of the province. The staff at the Old Mission Santa Barbara Archives expedited my search for sources on the life of Father Alan McCoy. Joe Smith, an archivist at the University of Notre Dame Archives, directed me to documents and tape recorded interviews in the records of the Leadership Conference of Women Religious and the Conference of Major Superiors of Men. Anne Symens-Bucher was a great help in chronicling the history of the Nevada Desert Experience, as was Ken Butigan. Anne also invited me to Canticle Farm in Oakland where I had the great pleasure of meeting Father Louie Vitale. Alumni of the Stockton Pastoral Year generously discussed their experiences in that program with me. Mark Day was very cooperative in discussing his involvement with the United Farm Workers. Sister Joan Chittister took time off from her own writing to tell me about her experiences with Father Alan McCoy.

Father Perry McDonald made my research on Brother Booker Ashe much easier by sending me a copy of his comprehensive *History of the House of Peace*. Willy Thorn's biography of Brother Booker Ashe, *It's Amazing What the Lord Can Do*, was an essential aid to my research. Junia Yasenov at the St. Joseph Capuchin Province was very helpful in finding photos of Brother Booker. Scott Grimwood, archivist for the Franciscan Sisters of Mary, likewise helped find photos of Sister Antona.

Indispensable in compiling this history of Franciscan activism are the dozens of individuals who consented to my interrogation in person, by email and over the phone. Their names are listed in the following appendix. Their observations and personal insights made this work much richer.

Interviews Conducted

Nola Jo Starling Ratliff
Sister Rita Heires, FSPA
Deborah Jackson Pembleton
Sister Nancy Lafferty, FSPA

Chapter 5
Father Joseph Nangle, OFM
Father Joseph Chinnici, OFM
Father Ray Boucher, OFM
Father Eddie Fronske, OFM
Father Ignatius DeGroot, OFM
Brother Angelo Cardinalli, OFM
Mark Day
Sister Joan Chittister, OSB
Anne and Terry Symens-Bucher

Chapter 6
Sister Tess Browne, SCN
Olgha Sandman
Sister Margaret Kruse, OSF
Sister Dorothy Diederichs, IHM
Baldemar Velasquez
Sister Stella DeVenuta, OSF
Roger Yockey
Jay Drydyk
Jerry Ceille

Chapter 7
Father Joe Nangle, OFM
Father Bryan Heir
Marie Dennis
Dolores Lecky
Myrtle Hendricks Corrales
Jim Rice
Danny Colum

Chapter 8
Sister Mary Littel, OSF
Anne Symens-Bucher
Julia Occhiogrosso
Ken Butigan
Laura Slattery

Conclusion
Sister Carmen Barsody, OSF

Index